Introduction to the Music Industry

"Professor Radbill's unique entrepreneurial approach to understanding the ever-changing world of the music business is a must-read textbook for emerging professionals. With enlightened examples, hands-on research suggestions, and discussion prompts, this textbook will bring a classroom to life. Students will enjoy the engaging stories and will relish the opportunities afforded through this innovative approach!"

—Timothy Channell, Associate Professor and Director
of Music Business, Radford University

"*Introduction to the Music Industry: An Entrepreneurial Approach*, Second Edition is a comprehensive and engaging text ideal for today's entrepreneurial music industry students. The website, supporting materials, and learning activities are suited to all student learning styles; instructors will find it foundational and adaptable."

—Mary Anne Nelson, Music Industry Program
Director, The College of Saint Rose

"For emerging music professionals wanting to set the world on fire, here's your essential entrepreneurial guide to the global music industry. Loaded with inspiring profiles crossing all genres, the book provides readers with the foundation needed to prosper in today's music careers."

—Angela Myles Beeching, author of *Beyond Talent:
Creating a Successful Career in Music*

Introduction to the Music Industry: An Entrepreneurial Approach, Second Edition is an introductory textbook that offers a fresh perspective in one of the fastest-changing businesses in the world today. It engages students with creative problem-solving activities, collaborative projects and case studies as they explore the inner workings of the music business, while encouraging them to think like entrepreneurs on a path toward their own successful careers in the industry.

This new edition includes a revised chapter organization, with chapters streamlined to focus on the topics most important to music business students, while also maintaining its user-friendly chapter approach. Supported by an updated companion website, this book equips music business students and performance majors with the knowledge and tools to adopt and integrate entrepreneurial thinking successfully into practice and shape the future of the industry.

Catherine Fitterman Radbill is an Arts Consultant with more than fifteen years of university teaching experience. She is the founder of the Entrepreneurial Center for Music at the University of Colorado at Boulder, and served as professor and chair of the Steinhardt School Undergraduate Music Business Program at New York University.

Introduction to the Music Industry

An Entrepreneurial Approach

Second Edition

Catherine Fitterman Radbill

Routledge
Taylor & Francis Group

NEW YORK AND LONDON

Second edition published 2017
by Routledge
711 Third Avenue, New York, NY 10017

and by Routledge
2 Park Square, Milton Park, Abingdon, Oxon, OX14 4RN

Routledge is an imprint of the Taylor & Francis Group, an informa business

First edition published 2012 by Taylor & Francis

Library of Congress Cataloging in Publication Data
Names: Fitterman Radbill, Catherine, author.
Title: Introduction to the music industry : an entrepreneurial approach / Catherine Fitterman Radbill.
Description: Second edition. | New York, NY ; Abingdon, Oxon : Routledge, 2017. | "2017
Identifiers: LCCN 2016010201 (print) | LCCN 2016013192 (ebook) | ISBN 9781138924802 (hardback) | ISBN 9781138924819 (paperback) | ISBN 9781315684147 ()
Subjects: LCSH: Music trade. | Music entrepreneurship.
Classification: LCC ML3790 .F596 2017 (print) | LCC ML3790 (ebook) | DDC 780.68—dc23
LC record available at http://lccn.loc.gov/2016010201

ISBN: 978-1-138-92480-2 (hbk)
ISBN: 978-1-138-92481-9 (pbk)
ISBN: 978-1-315-68414-7 (ebk)

Typeset in Stone Serif
by Swales & Willis Ltd, Exeter, Devon, UK

Editor: Genevieve Aoki
Editorial Assistant: Peter Sheehy
Production Manager: Swales & Willis
Marketing Manager: Amy Langlais
Copy Editor: Swales & Willis
Proofreader: Swales & Willis
Cover Design: Mat Willis

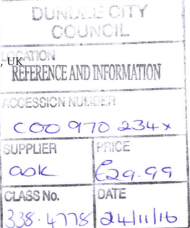

MIX
Paper from responsible sources
FSC www.fsc.org   FSC® C014174

Printed and bound in the United States of America by Sheridan

BRIEF CONTENTS

DETAILED CONTENTS

PREFACE

I'd like to tell you a story. It's a tale based on the hopes, fears, successes, failures, and collective wisdom of the thousands of students and music professionals with whom I've had the distinct honor of working for more than 15 years as a music entrepreneurship evangelist.

I've met you in classrooms, meeting rooms, coffee shops, railroad stations, airports, and online. You are 17, or 30, or 55. You are performers, educators, composers, technicians, administrators, inventors, venue managers, DJs, recording artists, bloggers, music retail store workers, record label owners, publicists, or a hundred other things—all working in the service of this thing we can't live without called music.

When I founded the Entrepreneurship Center for Music at the University of Colorado in 1998, I spoke the musical language of the faculty and students: classical music, jazz, and composition. After moving to New York University in 2002, my vocabulary expanded to include commercial music—pop, rock, hip-hop, country, electronic—and the variety of ways music is used to make money.

No matter where I've met you or how you're currently employed, your stories all revolve around a common underlying question: How can I make a living doing what I love? Or more specifically: How can I work in the music industry in whatever area I'm passionate about right now, and sustain myself economically?

The answer is straightforward: You will need to learn how to think and act like an entrepreneur. Music is a business with its own distinct culture. If you want to find your place in it, you'll need to look under the hood to see how all the moving parts fit together. Learning to think like an entrepreneur as you explore the inner workings of the music industry will catapult you into a mindset that allows you to see opportunities where others see only problems. The world around you will look like one gigantic suggestion box, full of great ideas for you and other entrepreneurial thinkers. You will be able to control your own destiny.

The market conditions are perfect for entrepreneurial activity in the music industry. Many aspects of it are in flux as we adapt to changing consumer habits and new technologies. There is no longer a fixed shape or direction to the landscape. How did we get here? Where are we going? It's messy and chaotic. It's a perfect *entrepreneurial opportunity*.

Creativity, innovation, opportunity, and a "why not…?" attitude are the hallmarks of entrepreneurship. These are the skills and tools you will acquire in the chapters ahead. We'll apply some myth-busting to conventional wisdom and reject a "that's just the way things are done" mentality so you can find your place in the music industry. In each chapter, I will urge you to ask questions, challenge my answers, look under every rock for opportunities, and make meaning in all that you do. I invite both teachers and students to add their own imagination, creativity, wisdom, and energy to this story.

As an entrepreneurial thinker, how will your passion and enthusiasm guide the music industry? What areas of the business will intrigue you? What creative ideas and insight will you bring to solving some of our industry's challenges? The opportunities for you to have a satisfying and sustainable career in the music industry are abundant if you learn how to develop an entrepreneurial mindset.

I want to hear *your* story. Please contact me through the book's website as you journey through the textbook with your class. I look forward to hearing from you.

GOALS OF THIS BOOK

Introduction to the Music Industry: An Entrepreneurial Approach, Second Edition is a textbook that offers a fresh look at one of the fastest-changing businesses in the world today. It is written for both upper-level undergraduate and graduate students who want to learn about the global music industry through an entrepreneurial lens. Emphasizing the importance of entrepreneurial thinking for the music industry, it engages students in learning the fundamentals while discovering ways to shape the industry's future. As entrepreneurial thinkers, students develop a creative mindset that allows them to recognize opportunities where others see only problems.

Introduction to the Music Industry: An Entrepreneurial Approach, Second Edition provides a thorough, comprehensive exploration of today's global music industry. It includes discussions of artistic practice as well as commercial applications, both for-profit and nonprofit. The word choice, tone, stories, case studies, and artist profiles will appeal to students in all musical genres, including classical musicians who intend to be professional performers. Every chapter includes practical strategies and guidance for young people who want to create a sustainable life in music.

It will be beneficial to students who want to be involved in the music industry in some way: as a professional working in support of artists, as an artist trying to launch his or her performing career, or as an active fan.

In its pedagogical approach, this textbook is designed to help create lively classrooms that enhance learning. Every chapter includes questions for the students to "Pause and Reflect," encouragement and suggestions for discovering new opportunities, inspiring stories of actual music entrepreneurs, a "Talk Back: class discussion" section, and key terms for study.

The textbook's website provides multimedia content, study guides, and an instructor's manual with lesson plan suggestions, ideas for collaborative projects, quizzes, and tests.

HOW THIS BOOK IS ORGANIZED

Introduction to the Music Industry: An Entrepreneurial Approach, Second Edition is structured chronologically in four parts:

1. The Creative Economy

2. Opportunities Ahead

3. Music Revenue Streams

4. You as Entrepreneur

In Part 1 we'll focus on the fundamentals of entrepreneurship and entrepreneurial thinking, examine the aesthetic, social, political and ethical value of music, tackle creative problem solving, and learn why music professionals need to think like entrepreneurs.

Part 2 will help students understand branding, marketing, and global rights management in order to practice looking for opportunities where others see only problems.

Part 3 allows students to dig into detail about how a twenty-first-century music professional can earn money in today's industry. The revenue streams that are highlighted include global performing and licensing, music publishing, broadcasting, and digital media and recorded music.

Part 4 is a complete guide to designing and launching a new venture, from finding the right opportunity to making financial projections and finding funds. For US residents there is a section on legal and tax issues for new ventures.

LEARNING TOOLS INSIDE THE BOOK

The music industry seems to change shape almost daily, so I've designed this book to be used alongside an open internet connection. The book's companion website, with links to each chapter, will keep students up to date on changes and developments in the many areas that impact the global music industry, such as digital technology, copyright law, consumer behavior, communications, and music trends. The links also will provide context and background for each chapter, and give a jumping-off point for class discussion.

I've designed each chapter so that students will have different ways to learn the material and prepare for class. Here are some of the chapter tools:

- Chapter openers—each chapter begins with an overview of topics to be presented and key terminology that will be discussed in the chapter.

- Mini-Case Studies—short, candid snapshots of working music entrepreneurs.

- Opportunities Ahead—highlights entrepreneurial possibilities for students to explore.

- Self-reflection—questions and activities for students to reflect upon as they read each chapter.

- Talking Back—multi-faceted issues questions that help students prepare for lively class discussions.

- Tools for the DIWO (Do It With Others) Entrepreneur—special sections throughout the book that give practical advice to students on specific topics.

- Internet Resources—suggested resources that encourage deeper study of the chapter's topic.

- Links in each chapter on the book's companion website to articles and blogs, video material, and study guides.

We learn well through stories, and there are many storylines flowing through the book to help illustrate key points. All of the characters in the stories are real people, but in some cases I've given them new names or a slightly altered circumstance to protect their privacy.

Using case studies is a very effective pedagogical tool for creating interactive classrooms. In addition, the case study method helps students acquire analytical and diagnostic thinking skills, which they will put to use in a free-flowing environment where circumstances are always changing. The classroom becomes the laboratory for comparative reflection on and lively discussion of the students' findings and conclusions. There are long and mini-case studies throughout the book.

ONLINE RESOURCES

www.routledge.com/cw/radbill

The companion website for *Introduction to the Music Industry: An Entrepreneurial Approach*, Second Edition features:

- Flash cards—to help students master the key concepts of each chapter.

- Links to videos, interactive materials, and useful websites.

- RSS Feeds for social media, blogs, and industry news updates.

- PowerPoint presentations that reinforce chapter learning goals.

- Instructor's Manual and test bank.

- Suggested resources for deeper research and study.

INSTRUCTOR'S MATERIALS

The textbook's companion website includes an Instructor's Manual that is not accessible to students. In it, instructors will find a guide to creating a syllabus for the semester and weekly lesson plans. In addition, the manual will include helpful tips on how to:

- incorporate interactive projects and media into traditional lectures;

- prepare for a case study class session;

- create homework assignments and projects for both small and large classes;

- assess students' work;

- help students enjoy the class and become life-long learners.

ACKNOWLEDGMENTS

Thank you to the hundreds of students with whom I have had the pleasure of learning and teaching. Your passion for music has inspired me to find new ways to think about the music industry, resulting in this textbook. Gregory Allis, Pedro Avillez Costa, Katonah Coster, Jillian Ennis, Stacey Ferreria, Shrayans Jha, Chris Lane, Christine Mayer, and Yifan Qin are former students who contributed to researching and writing several sections of the book.

My academic colleagues Jim Anderson, Cathy Benedict, Judith Coe, Lawrence Ferrara, E. Michael Harrington, Larry Miller, Rich Nesin, Peter Spellman, John Steinmetz, Heather Trussell, and Shirley Washington spent many hours reading and editing my drafts, and encouraged me during those dark moments when I was tempted to walk away from this enormous undertaking. Chief among these wonderful colleagues is Angela Myles Beeching, whose supportive phone calls guided me with wisdom and humor.

I owe a debt of gratitude to my editor, Constance Ditzel, and to the anonymous reviewers who read my drafts and gave me valuable insight into how to make this a better book.

Finally, to my family—who I am amazed and delighted to say are still speaking to me after the burdens I placed on them while writing this book—I give my deepest thanks.

PART 1

The Creative Economy

CHAPTER 1

Welcome to the Creative Economy

CHAPTER OVERVIEW

The music industry represents a constant balancing act between art and commerce. In this chapter you will see why humans are "addicted" to music and learn how the creative economy contributes value to communities aesthetically, socially, politically, and ethically. Jeri Lynne Johnson and the Black Pearl Chamber Orchestra are profiled for their success in upending the status quo of racial diversity in classical ensembles. The conductor-composer-opera director Iván Fischer is spotlighted for courageously upending the status quo of politics and the music industry in Hungary.

KEY TERMS

Artist branding	Post-genre musical age
21st century music entrepreneur	El Sistema
Artist-entrepreneur	Big Data
Music business-entrepreneur	Music's tangible and intangible values

ART AS COMMERCE, COMMERCE AS ART

The music you're listening to right now is the music you'll feel connected to for the rest of your life. From an artistic point of view, this is the essence of music. It binds us to a time and a place when we moved from child to adult. From a commercial point of view, exploiting this strong emotional connection to music has enormous potential for connecting brands (products and services) to bands (the artists who wrote and performed that music) in the music marketplace. Today, branding is a key opportunity for both artists and corporations. And it's a perfect example of the tug between art and commerce in the music industry.

It's true that everything begins with a song or composition (the art), but if a songwriter, composer, or performer wants to make a living at her craft, there has to be a sale or measurable use of the music in a product or service (the commerce). To many of us, music seems more like air or water than a commercial product. We can't live without it. Our very identities are closely tied to music. Each of us has special songs, melodies, or concert experiences that define who we are as unique individuals. How can something so vital, so intimate be called a product?

It's worth taking a brief look at why we, as a species, are . . .

ADDICTED TO MUSIC

Music has enchanted humans since we first appeared on the planet. From simple drumbeats and instruments made of wood and bone to stadium shows with multimedia and pyrotechnic displays, humans have always made music. Nearly every cultural community has specific musical traditions that have evolved over time and are proudly passed down to successive generations.

When we hear a song or even a distinctive melodic fragment, it can instantly transform our mood, or bring us back to another time and place in our lives. The reason for this lies in biology, chemistry, and anthropology.

Brain with headphones

PASIEKA/Getty Images

In *This Is Your Brain on Music*, session musician-sound engineer-record producer-neuroscientist Daniel J. Levitin explores the connection between music and the human brain. This fundamental human endeavor called music making has become a multi-billion dollar global industry.

Levitin explains: "music taps into primitive brain structures involved with motivation, reward, and emotion."[1] He identifies complex chemical reactions that take place in regions of the brain when a person listens to music. Some of these reactions involve a neurotransmitter called dopamine, a chemical "messenger" that is similar to adrenaline.[2] "Dopamine affects brain processes that control movement, emotional response, and the ability to experience pleasure and pain. It is also one of the neurotransmitters that plays a major role in addiction."[3]

How does this work? Levitin found a direct correlation between positive mood changes and higher levels of dopamine. He explains that, just as the world around us unfolds in varying rhythms and speeds, our brain finds satisfaction in speeding up or slowing down to match the pace of music we hear. When a song veers away from what our brains predict will come next—a rhythmic pattern or melodic sequence—our emotional response is pleasure and amusement.[4]

One of the most fascinating sections of Levitin's book focuses on why we identify so strongly with the music that we listened to in our teenage and early adult years. Musical tastes revolve around a young person's choice of communities. As we grow up and discover a world of ideas beyond those of our family, we begin to explore different ways of seeing and thinking. Musical discovery is a highly emotional way of connecting with others. As we search for our unique identity, we form groups of friends who have traits that we admire or want to emulate. We bond with our friends through the clothes we wear, the way we spend our free time, and through the musical tastes we share. In other words, music is a powerful and defining aspect of both our individual and group identity.[5]

Levitin states: "Our brains on music are all about connections. Music we love reminds us of other songs we've heard, which then sets up a chain of emotional response to connect us with the past . . . Part of the reason we remember songs from our teenage years is because those years were times of self-discovery, and as a consequence, they were emotionally charged."[6]

If music making and listening involve emotions and are driven by passion and enthusiasms, how can metrics and numerical values be applied to things that cannot be captured by numbers?[7] Once again, we feel that tug between art and commerce.

Before moving into the data-driven aspects of the creative arts later in the book, we first will look at the *aesthetic, social, political and ethical value* of music. This will build a foundation for remembering what drives this marketplace, and that is passion for expressing our lives through music.

DEFINING THE CREATIVE ECONOMY

Today we live in a global economy powered by human creativity.[8] The creative sector—aspects of the global economy powered by things like advertising, art, crafts, design, entertainment software, fashion, film, music, publishing, performing arts, radio and television, and visual arts—helps define our cultural touchstones and the social environment in which we want to live. In this sense, culture refers to the attitudes, values, beliefs, and behaviors shared by members of a group. The culture with which we identify is absorbed when we are quite young, and guides the ways we solve problems and live our daily lives.[9]

What Is Entrepreneurship?

Entrepreneurship is a rather dreary word, yet it describes an activity that is thrilling, terrifying, satisfying, and bristling with freedom. The *spirit* of "entre" is doing, acting, starting. It focuses us on the excitement and immediacy of creating something new.[10]

Entrepreneurship is about upending the status quo. That means turning upside down the traditional ways of doing and seeing things that can get in the way of an open-minded search for opportunity. We need only look at the generations of creative economy workers who have brought us today's thriving entrepreneurial world. Many who came before us broke down the barriers that had rigidly defined art, artist, music, and musician. Today we are no longer constrained by an inflexible vocabulary, a world in black and white. Our dreams can take us anywhere. Entrepreneurs in the creative economy can see opportunity where others see only problems.

Creating something of value from practically nothing is the definition of a creative entrepreneur. Pulling together the right ingredients to start building an altogether amazing product or service demands skill and focus. It amply rewards in excitement and the thrill of the endeavor.[11]

21st Century Music Professionals

Rather than use language that separates the work of performers from those who work in the business side of the creative economy, we will use the term "music professional" throughout the book to refer to a person who is serious about centering his or her life within the field of music. A music professional may be involved in any aspect of music as part of the creative industries: a composer or songwriter, rock band manager, performer in any musical genre, booking agent, venue operator, publicist, concert presenter or promoter, publisher, music supervisor—the list is long and open.

Music professionals are not defined as one thing to the exclusion of the other. Today's young musician may be training to be a performer while concurrently serving as an artist manager. Someone working in a music publishing company may be planning to launch her own band in the next year. Everyone working in the creative industries is deeply involved in creating a healthy music ecosystem that includes all the necessary working parts to bring music to a culture. The traditional boundaries of career and work are blurred, giving people the freedom to explore, experiment, and change direction when opportunity presents itself.

People change over time. We may discover a new path, or an entirely different way of participating in the creative economy throughout our professional lives. We are not forced to stay in one place—now there will be many things that will catch our interest. Over the years, all our choices together will add up to a sustainable and satisfying life as a music professional.

Artist-Entrepreneur

For some, the contemporary term "artist-entrepreneur" confirms a long-feared outcome: our market-driven economy has put an end to protection for artists from the rough and tumble world of commerce. But a closer look and an open mind reveal that most creative economy workers have understood the need to integrate the arts into the everyday aspects of their culture and daily lives.[12]

"I think of artists like scientists," states professional dancer and author Andrew Simonet. "Just like scientists, we begin with a question, something we don't know. We go into our studio or practice room and research that question. Like scientists, at the end of our research, we share the results with the public and with our peers. Some research is theoretical, useful primarily to other researchers. Some is 'applied,' relevant to everyday life. Both are essential. And most artists do some of both, creating experimental work that pushes the form as well as work that is more broadly relevant."[13]

The idea of what it means to be an artist has never been set in stone, but has evolved in many different ways over time. In the Baroque era, master composer J.S. Bach saw himself as a craftsman and servant of the church. Bach applied his creativity to pragmatic assignments like composing music to help a count overcome insomnia. Musicians of this time looked to long relationships with wealthy patrons to help them pay the bills.[14]

The Romantic period, led by poets, painters and musicians like Keats, Wordsworth, Delacroix, Monet, Chopin, and Debussy, imagined the artist as a solitary genius who was held prisoner and tortured by his artistic talent.[15]

In the 20th century some artists began questioning the very definition of art, bringing the audience into the creative process. Marcel Duchamp said "the creative act is not performed by the artist alone; the spectator brings the work in contact with the external world by deciphering and interpreting its inner qualification and thus adds his contribution to the creative act."[16] John Cage, Merce Cunningham, Duchamp, and others used their art to upend the status quo and create real social change.[17]

Today, some productive artist-entrepreneurs can be called social entrepreneurs. These artists participate in the cultural health and structure of their communities. Their artistic discourse includes concepts such as providing value in the new economy of ideas and public life, and social and community design.[18]

Artistic social entrepreneurs strive to remove artificial barriers that can make the arts feel inaccessible and elitist. They work to embrace the diversity of class, race, and gender in their communities and integrate the arts into everyday activities.[19]

Music Business-Entrepreneur

Music business-entrepreneurs may be artists themselves, but primarily are focused on developing very deep knowledge about business structures of the music and creative industries. They help artists develop revenue streams by understanding both the intrinsic value of music and the means of distributing it to the public. Music business-entrepreneurs are confident in their knowledge of performance, marketing and branding, broadcast and digital media, music publishing, copyright, licensing, and recording, and use their expertise to connect music creators with music consumers.

The Post-genre Musical Age

No matter what one's musical background or formal training, it is impossible to remain aloof from the musical soundtrack of everyday life. Today we are surrounded by the sounds of popular music in offices, airplanes, shopping malls, and restaurants. The musical palette of today's composers is infused with the rhythms and sounds of all kinds of music, contributing to the breakdown of once-rigid genre distinctions. Some might even say we are moving toward a post-genre musical age.[20]

"This moment in music is so exciting because the creative avenues an artist can explore are limitless," says singer-songwriter Taylor Swift. "Pop sounds like hip hop; country sounds like rock; rock sounds like soul; and folk sounds like country—and to me, that's incredible progress. I want to make music that reflects all of my influences, and I think that in the coming decades the idea of genres will become less of a career-defining path and more of an organizational tool. In this moment in music, stepping out of your comfort zone is rewarded, and sonic evolution is not only accepted . . . it is celebrated. The only real risk is being too afraid to take a risk at all."[21]

Taylor Swift The 1989 World Tour Live in Manchester
Shirlaine Forest/Getty Images Entertainment

In this book we will explore all musical genres, without prejudice, to find their commonalities and celebrate their differences.

BREAKING DOWN BARRIERS: CLASSICAL MUSIC BECOMES THE NEW POP

In his history of 20th-century classical music, *The Rest Is Noise,* critic Alex Ross predicted that there would be much more blurring of musical genres in the 21st century. "There is no escaping the interconnectedness of musical experience," he writes. "Young composers have grown up with pop music ringing in their ears, and they make use of it or ignore it as the occasion demands."[22]

Ross cites the example of using previously recorded sound in a new work. He found a wide range of genres using this technique, from classical electro-acoustic music (called *musique concrète*) to the Beatles' album *Sgt. Pepper's Lonely Hearts Club Band* to hip-hop sampling. Composers Philip Glass and Steve Reich, champions of minimalism, have in turn influenced contemporary classical American composers like Mason Bates, whose work combines symphonic music with elements taken from jazz and techno.[23]

Even as the vexing challenges of decreasing attendance and funding cuts beset the traditional classical music industry, new forms on the border between classical and popular genres are thriving. Blending in elements of hip-hop, electronic music, and indie rock, the composers, record labels, and concert promoters of the growing "neo-classical" (sometimes called "indie classical") movement are introducing classical music to new listeners. Some classical purists and critics decry the "watering down" of music they disparagingly call "crossover." No matter what it is called, composers today are pushing the boundaries of the usual genre silos.[24] Thanks to the accessibility of millions of recorded music tracks via YouTube, Spotify, and other streaming services, composers can now easily reach across once-rigid genre boundaries to create a fresh 21st century sound.

Genre-Bending Musical Collaborations

Even as classical musicians are experimenting with elements taken from other genres, leading pop and alternative musicians have stepped into the classical world, collaborating on serious new classical works that have won widespread recognition.[25]

"All this is happening spontaneously," says composer and Juilliard instructor Greg Sandow, who teaches a course on "The Future of Classical Music." "When an artist like Nico Muhly works with a Grizzly Bear, it's not so he can get a new audience. He does it because he loves the music."[26]

Examples of these cross-genre works abound. Bryce Dessner, guitarist of the Brooklyn band The National, composed a chamber music album, *Aheym*, in 2013, which was recorded by the Kronos Quartet, and in 2014 released an orchestral collaboration with Radiohead lead guitarist Jonny Greenwood on iconic classical label Deutsche Grammophon. Greenwood had his own previous experience with classical music, having recorded with the Copenhagen Philharmonic.[27]

Canadian-American singer-songwriter Rufus Wainwright has written two complete operas for the Canadian Opera Company. Mandolinist Chris Thile (of Nickel Creek and the Americana band Punch Brothers) has composed works for mandolin and orchestra, and has collaborated with superstar cellist Yo-Yo Ma, bluegrass fiddler Stuart Duncan, and double-bass player Edgar Meyer on the album *The Goat Rodeo Sessions*.[28] Avant-garde jazz-rock band the Bad Plus released a reimagining of Stravinsky's "The Rite of Spring."[29]

Nico Muhly not only composes a great range of classical music, but has written orchestrations for artists as diverse as Grizzly Bear and Bjork. Chilly Gonzales has written a collection of 24 piano *études* and also collaborates with hip-hop artists such as Drake.[30]

Opera singer Renée Fleming released an album in 2010 featuring works by bands like the Mars Volta and Death Cab for Cutie.[31] Superstar pianist and cultural ambassador to China, Lang Lang, joined Metallica at the 2014 Grammys in an exuberant rendition of "One."[32]

The string quartet Brooklyn Rider was described by the *Pittsburgh Post-Gazette* as "four classical musicians performing with the energy of young rock stars jamming on their guitars, a Beethoven-goes-indie foray into making classical music accessible but also celebrating why it was good in the first place."[33] The quartet has toured with the Silk Road Ensemble and has played alongside the banjo virtuoso Béla Fleck.

Are these musicians creating the future of classical music or abandoning it for pop? How many of the millions of 2Cellos fans who have experienced the classically trained, Sony Masterworks-signed cellists Luka Šulić and Stjepan Hauser covering AC/DC on

Kronos Quartet with Bryce Dessner
Hiroyuki Ito/Hulton Archive/Getty Images

YouTube will go on to seek out traditional classical music? The answer probably doesn't matter if the listeners are enjoying the music.[34]

Farewell to Music Genres, Says Spotify

With the advent of streaming music services, curated playlists designed to match a listener's mood or activity offer another way to break down fixed musical genres. Spotify is betting that its curated playlists, which mix and match songs from many genres, will subtly make listeners aware of new music and artists. The company estimates that every day its more than 60 million active listeners discover at least one new artist, which is an incentive to Spotify users to be open to change.[35]

"What we want to do is make Spotify more of a ritual," said Shiva Rajaraman, the company's vice president of product. "You'll begin to use it for a set of habits, and we will start to feed content for every slot in your day."[36]

Luka Sulic, Stjepan Hauser (2Cellos)
David Wolff-Patrick/Redferns/Getty Images

Offering well over 30 million songs, Spotify and other streaming services guide listeners to "discover" music that may be just slightly beyond the narrow band of songs they think they like. In matching listeners' moods and activities with playlists such as Spotify's "Running," designed to detect and complement a user's running pace, streaming services are helping to blur the staid boundaries of music genres.[37]

Pause and Reflect

You may never know what you *aren't* being exposed to because streaming services' massive virtual music library is so extensive. Do you think a technology company's management of your music "discovery" involves a narrowing or an expansion of your musical tastes?

On the Future of Classical Music

On his 2014 "The Ben Folds Orchestra Experience" tour, songwriter and rock pianist Ben Folds performed his hit rock songs and piano concerto with orchestras in Germany, the Netherlands, Ireland, England, Scotland, and the US. Folds shared the following observations about classical music with Ricky O'Bannon, journalist-in-residence with the Baltimore Symphony Orchestra.

> I do think rock musicians are fairly well ahead of classical players in terms of getting to the point musically. There's a huge system to circumvent when you're playing with the symphony orchestra. You can't just say "I'm going to pound my foot on the floor, and we're going to do this slowly in four for two measures and get it right" . . . With a rock band you just yell "Stop! Stop! Let's get that right for a couple of bars!" And I actually think classical musicians could learn to adjust their system a little bit. At the same time, I'm learning an incredible vocabulary of stuff that as a rock musician I never knew existed. I like symphony orchestras. It's like you're unpacking a lot of toys. The combinations are endless. They don't seem endless until you start to get into it, and then you realize that the textures [you can] get are absolutely incredible.[38]

John Steinmetz, composer and UCLA faculty bassoonist, gave a thought-provoking commentary in the September 18, 2014 posting on the blog "On the Future of Classical Music," curated by Greg Sandow. Steinmentz's comments appear in full below, with his permission:[39]

> I think that the field [of classical music] keeps talking about outreach and education because of *some pernicious assumptions*:
>
> - Ignorance is the only factor preventing a stampede on the box office.
> - The only broken part of the business is the non-attenders, so they need to be fixed.
> - Educate them, and they will come.
> - Classical music is just fine as it is.
> - Non-fans will be happier when they change their taste and become fans.

The Chicago Symphony (CSO) is an excellent example. While it has yet to rewrite its actual mission statement, it is clear that its de facto mission has greatly expanded. Obviously that mission includes great music making in a concert hall. But look closely at what it is doing with the Citizen Musician initiative and The Institute, the mission of which is "transforming lives through music," and you see an organization that has re-imagined its purpose and its role in the community. Ricardo Muti, Yo-Yo Ma, and scores of CSO and Chicago Civic Orchestra musicians are not going out to do this extraordinary community work as an apologetic exercise in self-justification. They are doing it to make a difference—not just for the people for whom they play and with whom they work, but also in their own lives.

From that point of view, outreach and citizenship and education programs are indeed a less-than-fully-effective strategy for audience development, and a rather anemic rationale for self-justification. How many tickets or subscriptions are nursing home residents, prisoners, middle-school students, and low-income people ever going to buy, after all? It doesn't really build an audience, and you are counterproductively trying to justify your existence on the basis of secondary activities that are only tangential to your primary purpose.

But what if the game itself has changed but most of us didn't notice?

What if it's no longer about presenting concerts, but it's actually about "transforming lives through music?" What if being connected to current culture means being socially relevant and engaged? What if concerts—while still essential and central—are (just) one of many ways of fulfilling that larger mission?

What if you can't be connected to current culture if all you do is give concerts?

If that's the case, then education and civic engagement activities are *not* secondary functions meant to support a primary concert-presenting function. They are *coequal* with concert performance and have become intrinsic to the mission.

Particularly for younger players, these less formal concerts and activities, which have had a social impact, are deeply energizing. They are already living in the new, socially connected, music-as-transformation paradigm, whether they have articulated it for themselves or not. The energy of those socially engaged, intimate performances and other music activities can be a major factor in the kind of engaged and engaging, powerful concerts that create enthusiastic, break-down-the-doors audiences.

It's a new time. It's a new culture. And I don't think it is possible to do great, fully alive performances without being engaged in making a difference with music outside the concert hall. We have to embrace our full humanity, and to do that, most of us need to get out and connect with people.[40]

Pause and Reflect

Do you think that classical music has the power to "change lives through music?" What could that look like? Where would you begin in creating "engaging, powerful concerts that create enthusiastic, break-down-the-doors audiences?"

The Role of Contemporary Composers in Community Engagement

American composer Dan Visconti believes that music can play a strong role in social change. His compositions draw from many traditions, including jazz, rock, and blues. One of his community projects took place at the Mississippi State Penitentiary, also known as Parchman Farm, where blues giants like Leadbelly and Son House were once incarcerated. Visconti's goal was to draw attention to the crisis in American prisons.[41]

For the project, Visconti partnered with Los Angeles Philharmonic violinist Robert Vijay Gupta, the Kronos Quartet, the Mississippi Prison and the Southern Poverty Law Center. The community event featured old blues singing, a sampling of prison food, and guest speakers who spoke about social conditions and issues like racism and violence in prison. Says Visconti: "When people are given a visceral, emotional experience, they are often moved to action. I want to impart passion and a desire to get involved to people who wouldn't get it by attending a symphony concert and reading program notes in a little booklet. That's just passé at this point."[42]

Composers like Visconti are showing people how to listen to and think differently about the role of music in social engagement. "There's music all around, but we just don't listen for it. That's something where the West is behind—a lot of Eastern cultures and early pre-industrial cultures are often more close to that," he says.[43]

Classical Power at an Indie Rock Festival

Classical music lovers might not think of the South by Southwest (SXSW) music festival in Austin, Texas (US) as a friendly environment for their kind of music. But the festival known for discovering up-and-coming indie rock bands is a champion of the genre-bending music scene.[44]

The 2015 SXSW festival's Composer Showcase featured both the Cordova String Quartet, which performs a traditional string quartet repertoire, and the group Mother Falcon, a group of classically trained musicians who perform an eclectic mix of indie rock, jazz, and hip-hop. In a nod to community engagement, Mother Falcon runs a music lab in Austin that brings together symphonic and rock high school musicians.[45]

Symphonic Dialogues

Composer Tod Machover, the director of the Massachusetts Institute of Technology Media Lab's Opera of the Future Group, has been exploring creative ways to blend classical music with digital technology for many years. Machover invented the Hypercello, a string instrument that uses computers to sense the player's movements and turn them into sound, in 1991, with a debut performance by cellist Yo-Yo Ma. The Hypercello concept later became the basis for the development of the bestselling video game *Guitar Hero*.[46]

More recently, Machover's experiments with music and technology have resulted in collaborative symphony-making in Toronto (Canada), Detroit (US), and Lucerne (Switzerland). His orchestral works are based on the sonic landscape of each city, transformed into highly unusual and evocative sounds and experimental performances. He enlists the participation of local residents in recording city sounds using a smartphone app that he developed. "I made these symphonies to have a dialogue," he said. "These pieces are about what the city means to me and the people who live in it—what it was historically, what it is now, and what it will be in the future."[47]

A Challenge Their Pop Friends Don't Have

A further challenge for classical music in today's world is the persistent lack of ethnic diversity in American orchestras. US Census Bureau statistics show that 13.2 percent of the nation's population identify themselves as black or African-American, and 17.1 percent as Hispanic or Latino. Yet only four percent of American orchestral musicians are African-American and Latino, according to the League of American Orchestras. This imbalance also shows up in the lack of ethnic diversity in orchestra boards and top-level administrators, as well as among conductors and guest soloists.[48]

Efforts are being made to spur diversity in the classical music field. Nearly 20 years ago, Aaron Dworkin founded the Detroit-based Sphinx, a music organization that encourages youth from minority communities to find their way to classical music. Dworkin and Sphinx have helped increase diversity by helping hundreds of young minority musicians from different backgrounds become part of the classical music world.[49]

SPOTLIGHT ON . . . JERI LYNNE JOHNSON AND THE BLACK PEARL CHAMBER ORCHESTRA

Jeri Lynne Johnson, an African-American classical music conductor, refuses to accept the status quo. She is the founder of the award-winning Philadelphia-based Black Pearl Chamber Orchestra. Black Pearl's 40 players hail from top-ranked schools, such as the Juilliard School and the Curtis Institute—and reflect American diversity with players from African-American, White, Latino, Asian, and Middle Eastern backgrounds. The orchestra performs an eclectic and culturally diverse array of programming.[50]

"When you have a sea of white faces on the stage, that sends a message," Johnson says. "Before their audiences hear a note, too many orchestras are saying: 'This is not for you.'" With the Black Pearl Chamber Orchestra, she set out to build an alternative to the insularity of the classical music world.[51]

Johnson's dream was born out of an early career setback. She drew motivation after being rejected for a California orchestra's music director position (she was told "You don't look like what our audience expects our conductor to look like" by the head of the search committee). "Clearly, I couldn't change: I'm a young black woman," she said. "So the more I thought about it, the more I realized that being outside of the system was the only way to effect the real, radical change the system required."[52]

Johnson transformed her anger about the job rejection into a passion to make change in a positive way, launching Black Pearl in 2007. As Black Pearl grew, she found that it was easier for her to create her start-up to align with the new market realities than it was for others to try and change a traditional music organization that was fighting to maintain the status quo. "Every year, orchestras spend thousands of dollars on ambitious marketing surveys. I'm convinced they keep surveying because they don't like the results that come back," she says. Unfortunately, many institutions seem unable to adapt to changing markets and audiences in time to avoid bankruptcy, labor unrest, or season cancelations.[53]

In bringing diversity to both the musicians and the music they play, Black Pearl provides a fun experience for its casually dressed, youthful audiences. Its success proves that upending the status quo has brought about the radical change Johnson was seeking.[54]

Happily Stealing Each Other's Music

Two decades ago, in his early twenties, British composer Thomas Adès became a rising star in the classical composer world. Today he has become a role model and inspirational source of musical ideas for many young American composers.[55]

Adès' strong commitment to both classical tradition and the avant-garde has had a strong impact on composers from many different music backgrounds. "The boys and I have listened to a ton of Adès," says Chris Thile, the frontman for progressive bluegrass band The Punch Brothers. "Particularly in the poly-rhythmic department—that's absolutely affected what Punch Brothers is up to these days."[56]

Adès' 1997 composition "Asyla" offered many other musicians a blueprint for a new way of writing instrumental music that managed to be at once unconventional and accessible. "There was this moment where the third movement of 'Asyla' circulated in the new-music community almost like a hit single," the composer Gabriel Kahane said.[57]

Christopher Cerrone, composer of "Invisible Cities," a finalist for the 2014 Pulitzer Prize in Music, says: "I'm influenced by music by my peers all the time; I try to steal from it as much as possible." Kahane agrees: "The history of all art can also be expressed as a conversation between members of a community who are all stealing from each other." Cerrone and Kahane are part of the six-member American composers' collective, Sleeping Giant.[58]

Douniamag-Paraguay-Music-Trash-Instruments

NOBERTO DUARTE/AFP/Getty Images

Classical Music Thrives in Latin and South America

While North America and Europe fret about the elitist image that clings to classical music, Latin and South America's lower and middle classes are enthusiastically embracing this music. *El Sistema*, a Venezuelan program of musical and social education for children, is widely credited with starting this phenomenon. Founded by José Antonio Abreu in 1975, it is a training system for young musicians that focuses on disadvantaged and impoverished children. Its symphony orchestra regularly tours the world to wide acclaim, and programs modeled after it have been established in other countries, including the US. El Sistema's most famous alumnus is Gustavo Dudamel, who is Music and Artistic Director of the Los Angeles Philharmonic and *Music Director* of the Simón Bolívar Symphony Orchestra of Venezuela. Only recently has a cloud appeared in the El Sistema universe, caused in part by its alleged association with the Venezuelan government's authoritarian regime.[59]

The *Recycled Instrument Orchestra of Cateura* is based in the Bañado Sur community of Paraguay, one of the poorest slums of Latin America. The orchestra is made up of local youth who play on instruments made from repurposed garbage. Favio

Chavez, its director, sees the orchestra as an educational program to help young people escape from desperate social and economic conditions. The orchestra performed at the 2015 South By Southwest Music Festival, along with a documentary about the group titled "Landfill Harmonic."[60]

The youth orchestra *Filarmónica Joven de Colombia* (FJC) is a social project in Bogotá led by the Fundación Nacional Batuta in partnership with the Youth Orchestra of the Americas. Its mission is "to promote culture and support the construction of artistic life in Colombia." After the FJC performed at Bogotá's Mozart Festival in April 2015, critic Mark Pullinger (Bachtrak) wrote: "Its superb string playing was a match for any of the European ensembles I heard during the week . . . with a fine sense of Mozartian style." The Fundación Nacional Batuta was created in 1991 and was modeled on El Sistema.[61]

THE AESTHETIC VALUE OF MUSIC

Sensory values, such as one's taste in music or judgment about an artwork, form the basis of the branch of philosophy known as aesthetics.[62] The blurring of musical genres and the easy availability of nearly every recorded piece of music in the world has given this somewhat sleepy academic field a jolt. In this section we'll examine how the traditional terminology of "high" and "low" culture is affected by the debate about the musical aesthetic of pop music.

Music making has played a key role in the development of human sociability. Most people make music as a normal part of their daily social routine, in the course of activities like celebrating a birthday, religious worship, or playing with a child. The percentage of the population that makes a living from music is relatively tiny. Many musicians today earn far more from playing at weddings than on returns from copyrights, licensing fees, or record sales. While the industry surrounding music-making may be driven by financial considerations, making music itself is simply part of being human.[63]

The conversation around musical aesthetic value relies heavily on standards of evaluation and personal taste. Many would argue that "pop music" and "serious music" are distinctly different types of cultural expression, and so cannot be judged by the same standards of evaluation. Fair enough, you may say, but then how did we arrive at musical value judgments with labels like high (serious music) and low (popular music)?[64]

Clearly, a Beethoven symphony and a jazz improvisation should not be judged by the same criteria. Listeners must use culturally acquired skills and a specific vocabulary in order to have anything but the most superficial and naïve discussion of these two genres' aesthetic values.[65]

Only the most stubborn and elitist of music lovers would suggest that the very term "aesthetic value" may only be applied to a work such as Verdi's *Rigoletto,* which they consider "high culture." This thinking would then classify a pop song such as Garth Brooks' "The Dance" as aesthetically impoverished "low culture."[66]

Paradoxically, there appears to be an entrenched popular suspicion of applying "high culture" concepts such as music theory and analysis to popular music by pop musicians themselves. John Lennon's well-known interview with a London *Times* music critic who mentioned "the Aeolian cadence at the end" of an early Beatles song is a good example:[67]

> Lennon: But the basic appeal of the Beatles was not their intelligence. It was their music. It was only after some guy in the London Times said there were Aeolian cadences[68] in "It Won't Be Long" that the middle classes started listening to it—because somebody put a tag on it.

Critic: *Did* you put Aeolian cadences in "It Won't Be Long?"

Lennon: To this day, I don't have *any* idea what they are. They sound like exotic birds.[69]

Lennon appears to be saying that intelligence and music are in opposition. He suggests that people cannot hear his music for what it is if they intellectualize it through terms like "Aeolian cadences." Ironically, this type of mindset indicates that pop culture, too, has bought into an elitist definition of the divide between high and low.[70]

Pause and Reflect

Do you think it is possible to engage meaningfully with pop music without first acknowledging that it has intrinsic aesthetic value?

Each musical genre requires listeners to hear it using culturally appropriate context and terminology. For example, today's "country music" requires something very different of its listeners than did 1950s honky-tonk. Obviously, pop music's appeal cannot be distilled into just one aesthetic value. How could we then expect a listener to appreciate the aesthetics of a genre for which she has no culturally acquired listening skills?[71]

In another twist in evaluating music's aesthetic value, academics cannot even agree on the definition of "popular music." One possibility is that "popular" means music that is widely enjoyed by many people. Using record sales as a yardstick, Bing Crosby (one billion) is more "popular" than Madonna (300 million) and Cher (100 million) combined. Flipping this logic for argument's sake, it would seem that music that fails to attract an audience is *not* popular. By this criteria, artists like blues singer Skip James or Yoko Ono might fail to count as *popular* music.[72]

A second definition is that "popular" means anything belonging to the "low" end of the high/low divide, regardless of how many people actually enjoy it. This thinking, however, doesn't provide a clear boundary, since what is seen as "low" or "high" tends to change over time. For example, both Louis Armstrong and the Beatles began their musical careers in small clubs in the dodgy sections of town, yet they are now treated with reverence and studied seriously by academics.[73]

For the third criterion, we flip our first: "popular" now includes all music that is *intended* to be widely accepted and possibly even commercially profitable. Thus, we can include almost all music that is tied to commercial culture and mass entertainment, and Yoko Ono and Skip James can return to the "popular" category. But this thinking creates another moving target because, by definition, "popular" music ceases to be pop when only an elite group has access to it. For example, much of the commercially recorded music of the first decades of the 20th century is no longer easily accessible. If the recordings are still under copyright protection and there is no commercial incentive to re-release them, thousands of western swing and polka band recordings cease to be pop music because only a handful of people have access to them. In yet another twist, oral traditions from isolated communities that normally would be considered "popular" no longer would be, as they were never intended to be widely available or commercially profitable.[74]

The fourth definition of "popular" flips the third by labeling "pop" as the cultural works that people actually produce *for themselves*. In other words, the music has to be "by" the average person rather than "for" the average person, which puts it firmly outside the mainstream commercial music industry. Now our folk tradition recordings above have returned to being authentically "pop."[75]

In short, an aesthetic look at pop music is what philosophers call an "open concept." There are no universally accepted criteria for defining "pop," and its definition continues to expand and contract.[76] However, one thing is certain: pop music's aesthetic value is firmly established within the academic world and in the creative economy.

THE SOCIAL VALUE OF MUSIC

It is widely believed that music and arts studies have specific social contributions to make in our communities. We read that the arts helps at-risk youth, providing the critical thinking and communication skills needed in a competitive workforce. We see without a doubt that the arts preserve unique aspects of our culture and heritage. And we believe that artistic endeavors engage citizens in civic discourse and encourage collective problem-solving.[77]

If we place such a high social value on art and music, why is it that the creative economy has relied for decades on *economic* arguments to make the case for government funding and support? In fact, music and art are often required to demonstrate their value by directly competing for limited public funds with service providers in the health, educational, and other life-saving nonprofit sectors.[78]

Big Data

We have entered the era of Big Data, which many in the cultural economy fear has eliminated any chance of persuading the general public that the arts have an inherent social value. Today nearly all human activities are quantifiable and measurable, and the information this generates is easily shareable. Even more disheartening is the realization that all data, no matter how personal, can be a source of (someone's) profit.[79]

The Canadian Community Knowledge Exchange recently held a summit in Toronto for nonprofit organizations from all sectors to debate this motion: "Be it resolved that the only way for arts and culture to be fully valued is to demonstrate their impact with hard facts."[80]

Attendees offered various arguments for and against the motion. Some argued that "hard facts" could not fully account for the transformative and inspirational effects of art. The economists made a case for the hard facts by warning that economic impact numbers used in grant proposals are often inflated. Yet everyone there could agree on one stark realization: "as long as there are politicians who consider public spending to be some kind of 'gravy train,' the arts had better marshal some arguments." In the end, the audience remained split on the issue.[81]

Pause and Reflect

While the story we just read focused on issues facing the nonprofit cultural community, the social value of commercial music cannot be ignored. How do events that make money, such as pop music festivals, benefit a community?

Tangible and Intangible Value

The creative arts have value to their communities in tangible and intangible ways. It may be challenging to put an economic value to benefits that are difficult to see and feel.

In Lebanon, the Zoukak Theatre Company is dedicated to works that engage audiences both socially and politically. The company spreads its social messages on issues such as domestic violence, politics, civil war, and questioning religious censorship in performances around the world. Their plays are performed in Arabic and subtitled in the host country's language.[82]

Musicians serve their communities in many areas of the health and educational system. For example, music therapy is a health profession that uses music within a therapeutic relationship to address the physical, emotional, cognitive, and social needs of individuals.[83] Music thanatologists use music to care for dying patients. They provide music vigils of harp and vocal music with a personal touch, based around diagnosis, vital signs, and responses in the moment.[84]

A recent report by the Community Arts Network (US) lists these intangible but none-the-less valuable benefits of music and arts:

The arts contribute to community vitality. Citizen engagement in the arts creates a strong shared identity and instills pride in a country's cultural heritage.[85]

The arts bring public spaces to life. Artworks and arts activities make public spaces livable, attractive and distinctive.[86]

The arts contribute to wellness and healthy aging. According to a recent US medical study, senior citizens who regularly participate in the arts report lower medication usage, higher mental acuity, better mental health, and higher rates of social engagement.[87]

Making Music Matters

Recent studies led by neuroscientist Nina Kraus of Northwestern University have shed new light on how studying music affects students' brains. It turns out that music classes can have great cognitive benefits—but only if students are actively engaged. "We like to say that 'making music matters,'" said Kraus. "Because it is only through the active generation and manipulation of sound that music can rewire the brain. Our results support the importance of active experience and meaningful engagement with sound to stimulate changes in the brain."[88]

Kraus was approached by Margaret Martin, the founder of the Harmony Project, a community music program in Los Angeles that works with low-income children. The program was seeing an extraordinary level of success: since 2008, 93 percent of high school seniors in their program had gone on to college, even though they were living in neighborhoods with high school dropout rates of 50 percent or more. To help understand why this was happening, the Northwestern team began to study the effects of the Harmony Project on students' cognition, using electrodes to track how children's brains responded.[89]

In two studies, the researchers found that not only did music training have real biological effects on children's brains, but students who were actively engaged in music class gained more cognitive benefits. After two years of music classes, students who actively participated scored measurably higher on speech and reading tests than those who were less involved. "Even in a group of highly motivated students, small variations in music engagement—attendance and class participation—predicted the strength of neural processing after music training," Kraus explained.[90]

What's more, children who actually played instruments in their class showed more improvement in their neural processing than children who only attended a music appreciation class. "It turns out that *playing* a musical instrument is important," Kraus said. Just listening to music isn't enough to cause changes in neural processing. "I like to give the analogy that you're not going to become physically fit just by watching sports."[91]

Music's Contribution to Human Wellbeing

Recent research from the Social Impact of the Arts Project (SIAP) at the University of Pennsylvania suggests that cultural participation is an important component of the broad concept of human wellbeing. The report, "Cultural Ecology, Neighborhood Vitality and Social Wellbeing—A Philadelphia Project," by researchers Mark Stern and Susan Seifert introduces a conceptual framework based on the "capability approach," an approach to measuring wellbeing devised by the economist Amartya Sen and the philosopher Martha Nussbaum.[92] At the center of the capability approach is the idea that "wellbeing derives from a person's ability to make choices that allow them to lead a life that they have reason to value," not just access to material resources. [93] This approach is the theoretical basis for the Human Development Index, a measurement of wellbeing used by the United Nations.[94]

THE POLITICAL VALUE OF MUSIC

Countries vary widely in terms of the level of financial and other support they provide to their creative economies, particularly the arts sector. Both politics and cultural identity play significant roles in influencing how countries demonstrate the importance and value of their citizens' musical and artistic endeavors. Here is a look at the way ten very different nations approach the issue:[95]

Australia. In Australia, government spending on the arts and cultural activities in the 2012–13 period was US$5.22 billion, the equivalent of US$228 per person.[96] The Australian government supports the arts through programs including arts training, music, film festivals, and radio and television. The majority of funding is distributed through each state's arts council.[97]

The UK. The Department for Culture, Media and Sport (DCMS) oversees the arts in the UK. The DCMS distributes grants for the arts through Arts Council England, and National Lottery funds are used to support "good causes" in the arts. Currently, the National Lottery has provided a benefit of US$269 per person in London, in contrast to US$76.64 per person for the rest of England, which has provoked concern over unfair regional distributions. In 2012–13, the DCMS funded 16 major national museums and galleries totaling US$728 million.[98] The Cultural Gifts Scheme allows UK taxpayers to donate important works of art and other heritage objects for the benefit of the nation. In return, donors receive a tax reduction based on a set percentage of the value of the object they are donating. In 2012–13, tax reductions through the program totaled more than US$536,000.[99]

Finland. In Finland, funding for arts and culture is managed by the Ministry of Education, which directly supports individual artists through wide-ranging cultural and professional training programs. In 2011, government expenditure on culture amounted to US$8.42 for each of Finland's 5.3 million citizens, with

US$18.93 million spent on individual artists. Notably, government grants are for a salaried period lasting from six months to five years. Grants with terms up to ten years may be given to highly acclaimed artists.[100]

France. French museums house some of the most renowned and beloved art in the world, and are visited by more than 20 million viewers each year. The budget of the French Ministry of Culture for 2013 was close to US$10 billion, with US$4.73 billion dedicated to the cultural field alone. As high as these figures seem, they actually represent a 2.3 percent drop in art funding from the previous year, a decline which has prompted citizen protests and strikes across the country.[101]

Germany. In 2013, Germany's cultural budget was approximately US$1.63 billion, the eighth consecutive year for cultural budget increases, even as the country's overall federal budget decreased by 3.1 percent. The *Bundeskulturstiftung* is the German federal foundation for the arts. Arts spending is not seen as a subsidy, but as "an essential investment in the future of our society," according to German culture minister Bernd Neumann. Germany has run a federal program for art purchases and the collection of contemporary art by its citizens since the 1970s.[102]

Mexico. Like Britain and other countries, Mexico supports the arts through tax incentives ranging from direct subsidies to tax credits for donations to arts organizations. The Pago en Especie (Payment in Kind) program allows artists to pay federal income taxes with their own artwork. Under the program, the government displays the art in museums and government offices, and loans it out for special exhibitions. To date, there are approximately 700 artists registered on the program, and the Mexican government has acquired 8,000 works of art.[103]

According to John O'Hagan, an economics professor at Trinity College in Dublin, "one of the arguments used most frequently in relation to tax subsidies to the arts relates to national identity." That's certainly true in Mexico, where the association between the arts and nation has a long history. "Murals were how Mexican history was first portrayed to the public," said José Ramón San Cristóbal Larrea, director of Mexico's Cultural Promotion and National Heritage Office. "A country's culture and its understanding of itself evolve through its art. And that's something we are in need of, especially now."[104]

The Netherlands. Since the 1970s, the state has almost wholly shouldered the responsibility of supporting artists and cultural organizations across the Netherlands. Corporate funding for the arts is limited, with no significant tradition of private sponsorship. The Netherlands has almost the highest spending on culture in Europe: US$368 per capita (2010), which comes close to the figures in Norway and is about three times higher than that in Germany.[105] However, in response to the ongoing economic recession in Europe, federal financing for the arts in the Netherlands has dropped by 22 percent, or US$259.1 million, while local, regional, and provincial governments accounted for an additional US$252.6 million decline in subsidies. Approximately 40 of the 120 cultural arts organizations in the country became ineligible for federal grants in 2012, and many were forced to close.[106]

Northern Ireland. The Arts Council of Northern Ireland is the development and funding agency for the arts in Northern Ireland. The Council awarded US$21 million to arts projects in 2013, including theater and literature, for its 1.8 million population. It distributes public money and National Lottery funds to develop art projects and events throughout the country.[107, 108]

Sweden. The Swedish Arts Council implements national cultural policy by allocating more than US$115 million in 1,700 grants each year to performing arts, music, and literature for its nine million people.[109] In 2011, cultural spending accounted for 2.6 percent of Sweden's total central government budget.[110] In addition, the Nordic Culture Fund supports artistic and cultural cooperation between all the Nordic countries.[111]

The US. The US funds the arts at approximately US$0.41 per capita, one of the lowest rates in the developed world. Federal funding to the National Endowment for the Arts (NEA), created by Congress to offer support and funding for art projects, has remained static at US$146 million for the years 2014 and 2015.[112] To put this into context, the US has spent more than 1,600 times that amount bailing out banks and financial institutions, according to Pro Publica.[113] Government expenditure on the arts is negligible when compared to the amount of money spent in other areas of the public sector. For example, the National Science Foundation's annual budget was US$6.9 billion in 2013.[114]

Europe, Where Art Is Life

For artists, institutions and arts administrators in Europe, the recent loss of substantial government support has been an affront to their way of life. In Europe, unlike in the US, the arts have long been viewed as a vital shared heritage that should be supported and preserved, rather than as commodities whose value is dependent on market forces.[115]

"Culture is a basic need," explained Andreas Stadler, director of the Austrian Cultural Forum in New York and president of the New York branch of the European Union National Institutes for Culture. "People should have the right to go to the opera."[116]

As the largest and most stable European economies, France and Germany have so far kept their arts funding relatively unaffected. But in other countries, including Italy, Hungary, the Netherlands, and Britain, cultural budgets have really taken a hit. To remain in the euro zone, Greece, Portugal, Spain and Ireland were all forced to slash their spending on public projects, including culture.[117]

The ongoing financial strains in Europe have led researchers and journalists to speculate on the politics behind government cutbacks in the arts. Some see a political left-wing/right-wing undercurrent to the funding cuts.[118]

Others, such as Andreas Wiesand, Executive Director of the European Institute for Comparative Cultural Research, say there are too many differences among the countries to reduce the argument to a simple left/right discussion. "Budget cuts of right-wing governments like the one currently reigning in Hungary—with their open contempt of progressive views in the arts and intellectual life—should not really be placed on the same shelf as cuts made by technocratic and market-liberal politicians, like the ones forming the government in the United Kingdom . . . One could surely find just as many "left" governments that currently apply austerity measures than those with opposite leanings."[119]

Ultimately, Wiesand says, the level of governmental priority given to culture will depend primarily on the personalities of those in charge of public affairs, and on the value the arts and artists enjoy in a society at large.[120]

Fair Access to the Arts

In the marketplace and among private philanthropists, motivations such as personal goals and advertising exposure drive funding decisions.[121] In the best of all worlds, government investment is neutral and transparent, designed to serve the public interest. Governmental funding should ensure that all citizens receive the benefits of the arts by providing fair access to arts resources, especially among under-served populations. Fostering civic participation, serving as a communications asset in a global society, and enhancing our ability to see things through the eyes of others are all common reasons for governments to support the cultural economy. [122, 123]

Politics Upends the Arts in Australia

In July 2015, a surprise move by Australian Arts Minister George Brandis removed US$79.77 million over four years from the Australia Council's budget to create a new fund, which will be allocated at the discretion of the Arts Minister. This unexpected and largely unwelcome news appeared to be the result of a political tug-of-war between Brandis and the Council over who gets to decide where the money goes. The creation of the new Ministry for the Arts fund in effect delivers a cut of 16 percent for the Australia Council on the 2014 appropriation.[124]

The cornerstone of the Australia Council's operations for four decades has been to invite expert panels of artists and creative professionals to judge the merits of arts funding applications. Brandis' action appears to undo Australia's long-standing cultural policy called "arm's-length funding," meaning that individual politicians or government officials yield the funding decision-making to arts professionals.[125]

Professor Simon Frith, Tovey Professor of Music at the University of Edinburgh, gave a keynote address to the 2013 European Music Council in Glasgow that foreshadowed the recent Australian upheaval: "One crucial aspect of a healthy local music ecology is that new entrants (with new ideas, constructing new audiences) should have the space and time to get established. This is where public funding and resources can be significant. What is unnecessary is for the state to act as a kind of ersatz music business—its role is to *support* entrepreneurs, not to *be* entrepreneurial."[126]

Using a Musical Bully Pulpit to Speak Their Political Minds

"A musician is also a man, but more important than his music is his attitude to life." The great cellist Pablo Casals spoke and lived these words. Casals would not perform in countries that didn't respect democratic principles. In protest against Francisco Franco's fascist regime, he went into exile from his native Spain and refused to perform in public for four years.[127]

More recently, Chinese scrutiny of visiting musicians tightened after singer-songwriter Björk shouted "Tibet! Tibet!" at the end of her song "Declare Independence" during a 2008 performance in Shanghai. Four years later, Beijing police arrived to "interview" Elton John shortly after he announced from the stage that his concert was dedicated "to the spirit and talent of [Chinese activist artist] Ai Weiwei."[128]

Many international artists, politicians, and musicians voiced support for the members of the Russian band Pussy Riot after the band members' 2012 arrest, trial, and imprisonment. Paul McCartney, Bryan Adams, Sting, and Madonna were among those who spoke out.[129]

Recent controversial actions by Vladimir Putin's government in Russia have set off a flurry of protests by music professionals. At the last night of the 2013 BBC Proms, opera singer Joyce DiDonato dedicated a performance of the gay anthem "Somewhere Over the Rainbow" to "voices silenced" over gay rights.[130] She has refused to perform in Russia.

Lisa Batiashvili, a 35-year-old Georgian violinist, speaks openly about the political responsibilities of an artist.[131] When Russian conductor Valery Gergiev invited Batiashvili to perform with the Rotterdam

Philharmonic Orchestra in 2014, her humanitarian convictions were put to the test. Gergiev had publicly supported Russian President Putin's policies in the 2008 conflict with Batiashvili's home country of Georgia. Batiashvili vowed not to perform in Russia to protest the country's annexation of Crimea.[132]

"I didn't want to be part of this whole society of musicians who actually disagree with [Gergiev] totally about his position, about his support of Putin, but don't ever say anything," Batiashvili explained. In the end, she accepted Gergiev's invitation, but, as an act of protest, she commissioned an encore for solo violin from a Georgian composer, titled "Requiem for Ukraine," which she performed after her concerto. Batiashvili feels that, by attending and booking concerts by Russian artists who support Putin's policies, Western audiences and arts presenters bear responsibility in the repercussions of those policies.[133]

Nino Gvetadze, a Georgian pianist who lives in the Netherlands, has also refused to play in Russia. "We all have our agencies and impresarios that advise you to do certain things," she says. "For some people, it's very difficult to turn these engagements down. But it's about how you want to build your career, whether you want to sacrifice your ideals for the sake of a step up on the career ladder."[134]

Some journalists have commented on the fact that they see prominent classical musicians singling out Putin's government for protests while giving implied support to China, the Gulf States, and other regimes which have far more repressive human rights violations.[135]

Lisa Batiashvili
ullstein bild/Getty Images

DiDonato acknowledges the slippery slope of mixing music and political activism. She states: "I am a work in progress. As an artist and as a human being, I have always given myself permission to misstep, to fail, to succeed, to live, to learn . . . staying open to growth has always seemed to me to be the best shot at evolving. Knowing this about myself is precisely why I recognized that my decision to decline the invitation to sing in Moscow was perhaps not the correct one. Or, perhaps it was? That is not for me to determine, and I will never know if it was the 'right' decision. But it is what I felt compelled to do at that time, and so I acted."[136]

"Basically, You're a Billboard for an Oil Company"

Statoil, the huge state-controlled oil company, has been hyper-present in the economic and social life of Norway for more than 40 years. However, the company is experiencing pressure from activists who are concerned about the effects of global warming and climate change. Norway's oil and gas industry accounts for nearly 25 percent of the country's gross domestic product and contributes to greenhouse gas emissions worldwide. Norwegian activists are not only questioning Statoil's environmental impact but are also raising concerns about the company's pervasive presence in their lives.[137]

Statoil's US$12 million annual financing of academic research at the University of Bergen and other schools has been called into question by professors and students. Musicians and artists have voiced displeasure about the company's pervasive sponsorship of Norwegian cultural events and organizations, including cash awards to performers whom Statoil calls "Heroes of Tomorrow." Statoil is a principal sponsor of the Bergen International Festival, a center for the northern European arts scene.[138]

"Basically, you're a billboard for an oil company," states Martin Hagfors, an Oslo musician. "And if you have any sense that we need to change direction, you can't be a billboard for an oil company."[139]

Politics and Censorship

The New York Youth Symphony (NYYS) has sponsored an annual competition for young composers for many years. In 2015, an Estonian-born composer, Jonas Tarm, was awarded a commission from the NYYS and his work, "Marsh u Nebuttya" ("March to Oblivion" in Ukranian) was to be performed by the NYYS at Carnegie Hall. Shortly before the concert, it came to the symphony administrators' attention that the piece included about 45 seconds of the "Horst Wessel" song, the Nazi anthem. When asked to explain why this musical reference was in his work, Tarm declined to elaborate on its meaning, stating that "the music should speak for itself." The piece was canceled for the Carnegie performance.[140]

Critic Zachary Woolfe wrote that the cancelation was "a misguided, mishandled decision and a blot on the reputation of NYYS and its justly praised First Music competition, which has awarded commissions to 139 young composers since its start in 1984." He stated that, rather than condemn Tarm, NYYS should be zealous in protecting young artists and supportive of the ways in which they choose to express themselves.[141]

Woolfe examined the "March to Oblivion" score and stated: "It is simply impossible that someone could hear Tarm's sour take on "Horst Wessel" as a neutral or sympathetic presentation of this material. Obviously the melody may lead listeners to think of the Nazi period—that is its point. It is not the role of an arts institution to spare audiences from history that might upset them. Quite the contrary."[142]

Pause and Reflect

Weigh the pros and cons of governmental support of the arts. Debate the issue from a variety of perspectives, such as preserving cultural identity, the desire of developing nations to modernize, and the positive and negative consequences for countries that have neighbors with well-established and powerful cultural economies.

SPOTLIGHT ON . . . IVÁN FISCHER—TAKING POLITICAL RISKS WITH HIS MUSIC

In Hungary, conductor-composer-opera director Iván Fischer is upending the status quo of politics and the music industry.

Fischer's 30-year-old ensemble, the Budapest Festival Orchestra (BFO), has an international reputation not only for superb music but also for its startlingly innovative approach to staging its concerts. Fischer, the recipient of some of the highest musical honors in the world, has a subversive streak regarding the usual business of concert promotion. He also is unusually vocal about his political views.[143]

Fischer is a committed opponent of the Hungarian right-wing party, Fidesz, which has been creeping toward authoritarianism since 2010. He speaks of his political dissent in his music and in the press. In a 2011 interview with *Frankfurter Allgemeine Zeitung,* he said that Hungary "is now in danger of sinking into a nationalistic dictatorship. The world must not passively stand by if this fragile democracy finally breaks down." His 2013 opera, *The Red Heifer*, is a satirical censure of the governmental tolerance for growing anti-Semitism in Hungary. It was no surprise to him that Hungary's right-wing press gave *The Red Heifer* scathing reviews.[144]

Fischer is not concerned that his politics could negatively impact his career or the existence of the orchestra. "If it ever reached a point where they said, 'We will not support an orchestra which is the flagship of Hungarian culture around the world because their conductor made critical remarks,' then it would become such a level of dictatorship that I wouldn't want to serve it anymore. So I will stay free, and they will decide how tolerant they are."[145]

Fischer is one of several artists who have challenged the Hungarian government under Prime Minister Viktor Orban. Conservative political parties are on the rise across Europe, and members of the global arts world are speaking out in protest. Fischer has been joined in his criticism by fellow Hungarians András Schiff, an internationally renowned pianist, and Robert Alfoldi, a theater director who was derided by rightist politicians for his homosexuality.[146]

Classical concerts in the West tend to be docile and unsurprising. In contrast, the BFO is a collection of entrepreneurial, out-of-the-box thinkers. To break down the barrier between orchestra and audience, the stage at a recent concert had bleachers and

Budapest Festival Orchestra with Ivan Fischer
Hiroyuki Ito/Hulton Archive/Getty Images

beanbag chairs positioned among the players' music stands so that listeners could sit near the musicians. Various stage props may appear onstage to heighten an element of the music. The evening's program is not always announced prior to the concert so that audience members may participate in choosing the music.[147]

The BFO's Midnight Music concerts are aimed at a younger, rowdier crowd. At one recent concert, Fischer asked the Czech chorus performing in Borodin's "Prince Igor" to sit with the audience and sing from their seats. Midnight Music concerts start later and typically end at 1AM, but many concert-goers linger to discuss the show.[148]

BFO has a freelance membership, which is uncommon for a major orchestra. The trade-off for musicians in not having a union-protected, full-time position is more autonomy than their colleagues in other high-level orchestras. For example, the BFO musicians, rather than the music director, are in charge of programming the concert series for children. And Fischer doesn't hesitate to seek his musicians' opinions during orchestra rehearsals.[149]

Over the years of serving as a frequent guest conductor all over the world, Fischer grew discontented with the limited amount of time he had to work with each orchestra. He concluded that the traditional orchestra system was flawed, especially in the US. He felt the unions were too rigid in their rules and that the traditional audition format of playing orchestra excerpts gave very little useful information about how a potential musician would be as member of the orchestra. In his characteristically blunt fashion, he predicts that "all the orchestras will die out in twenty or thirty years [because] they have grown too big," and only exist to satisfy other, non-musical needs, such as the "career mania" of orchestra soloists and conductors.[150]

Fischer saw an opportunity to put his radical entrepreneurial ideas into action when he founded the BPO along with Zoltán Kocsis. "I knew the orchestra had to be smaller in profile—not a dinosaur but a tiger . . . And I imagined a different driving force for the organization. This would be the artistic fulfillment of the musicians. It is their passion that must be satisfied. But for that to work there would have to be a big change in structure . . . No union, no job security. They are free to pursue other work, and they come back refreshed."[151]

Fischer's unconventional programming can also be seen and heard at Berlin's Konzerthaus, where he is Music Director, and in his two-week annual engagement with Amsterdam's Royal Concertgebouw Orchestra. But for the most part, he practices what he calls "negative marketing." "I have no [booking] agency. Nobody can find me. It is liberating."[152]

Pause and Reflect

Fischer takes a calculated risk in speaking his mind about the Hungarian government. What role do you feel global musicians can (or ought to) play in influencing politics?

THE ETHICAL VALUE OF MUSIC

An ever-present ethical dilemma for the music world involves its financial dependence on corporate sponsorship. For decades, classical music has been dependent on the largesse of the banking and financial services sector in Europe and the US. A recent study[153] shows that at least 45 percent of corporate sponsorship for ten of the leading orchestras in Europe and North America comes from banking and financial services companies. The dilemma arises when corporate funders are linked to questionable ethical issues, such as Deutsche Bank's US$202.3 million settlement with the US in 2012 over reckless mortgage lending practices. Such behavior by the sponsors of classical orchestras raises questions about what ethical price classical music is prepared to pay for funding.[154]

Another area for ethical examination is the classical music sponsorship from the much-maligned cigarette industry. JTI, which stands for Japan Tobacco International, is the world's third-largest cigarette company. JTI's website boasts that its partners in the arts include "a number of the most prestigious cultural, artistic and musical institutions and festivals in the world."[155] Recipients of JTI funding include the Salzburg Whitsun Festival, the London Philharmonic, the Ulster Orchestra,[156] the Mariinsky and Bolshoi Theatres in Russia, and Kuala Lumpur's Performing Arts Centre in Malaysia.[157]

Even funding from government coffers can raise ethical issues. For example, the UK government's massive gambling operation, the National Lottery, donates more than US$53 million each week to perfectly acceptable "good causes," such as grants to UK filmmakers and the Royal Shakespeare Company.[158]

But government money comes from taxes on the profits and wages earned in such dubious industries as pornography, junk food, oil, armaments, tobacco, and alcohol.[159] This begs the question: "Does ethically compromised money magically become ethically cleansed once it passes through the hands of the state?"

Opportunities Ahead

From a global viewpoint, what specific opportunities do you envision for yourself, your music, or music in general? Think about this from a social, economic, political, and ethical point of view.

CONCLUSION

Artist-entrepreneurs and music business-entrepreneurs challenge the status quo, the mundane, and the ordinary as they balance their art with commerce. The creative economy contributes in many important ways, elevating communities to higher ideals and strengthening common bonds. The rigid definitions of musical genres are fading as young composers weave together their cultural traditions and the music they hear in the marketplace. Countries have different ways of thinking about and supporting their cultural entrepreneurs. Sources of governmental funding for some arts organizations are at risk due to the prolonged global recession. At the end of the day, we wonder if artists and arts organizations are obligated to speak out about human rights violations and ethically compromised sources of the very funding they need to survive.

 Talking Back: Class Discussion

Many people feel it is impossible to find any large corporations, governments, or even wealthy philanthropists that are not ethically compromised in some way. Do you think that artists and arts organizations are obligated to consider the ethical implications of accepting public and private funding?

NOTES

1 Daniel J. Levitin, *This is Your Brain on Music* (New York: Plume, 2006), 191.
2 Barbara Sorensen, "What Is Dopamine Responsible for?" *LiveStrong*, May 31, 2015, www.livestrong.com/article/208418-what-is-dopamine-responsible-for (accessed May 4, 2016).
3 Ibid.
4 Levitin, *This Is Your Brain*, 191.
5 Ibid, 232.
6 Ibid, 231.
7 Leon Wieseltierjan, "Among the Disrupted," *New York Times*, January 7, 2015.
8 Richard Florida, *The Rise of the Creative Class* (New York: Basic Books, 2004), 4–6.
9 "What Can Be the Potential Socio-economic Impacts of Culture?" *Compendium: Social Policies and Trends in Europe*, http://culturalpolicies.net/web/socio-economic-impact-of-culture.php (accessed May 4, 2016).
10 Simon Cronshaw and Peter Tullin, "Intelligent Naivety," http://slideshare.net/culturelabel/culturelabel-intelligent-naivety (accessed May 4, 2016).

11 Ibid.

12 Tonya Lockyer, "Who's the Artist Now?" *Stance*, February 4, 2015, http://velocitydancecenter.org/stance/whos-the-artist-now (accessed May 4, 2016).

13 Andrew Simonet, *Making Your Life as an Artist* (Manitoba, Canada: Artists U, 2014), www.artistsu.org/making/#.VpUbSKMo5oI (accessed May 4, 2016).

14 Lockyer, "Who's the Artist Now?"

15 Ibid.

16 "Marcel Duchamp: Source Texts and One-Liners," Institute of Artificial Art Amsterdam, http://iaaa.nl/cursusAA&AI/duchamp.html (accessed May 4, 2016).

17 Lockyer, "Who's the Artist Now?"

18 Ibid.

19 Ibid.

20 Ben Ratliff, "Seeking Genuine Discovery on Music Services," *New York Times*, June 28, 2015.

21 Taylor Swift, "For Taylor Swift, the Future of Music Is a Love Story," *Wall Street Journal*, July 7, 2014, http://wsj.com/articles/for-taylor-swift-the-future-of-music-is-a-love-story-1404763219 (accessed May 4, 2016).

22 Ricky O'Bannon, "A Classically-Minded Guide to South By Southwest," *BSO Music*, May 8, 2015, http://bsomusic.org/stories/a-classically-minded-guide-to-south-by-southwest (accessed May 4, 2016).

23 Ibid.

24 Selim Blount, "Just Don't Call It 'Indie Classical,'" *The Guardian*, November 1, 2013, www.theguardian.com/music/musicblog/2013/nov/01/neo-classical-nils-frahm (accessed May 4, 2016).

25 Jim Farber, "Classical Music Explodes, Both in Sales and in Expanding Boundaries," *New York Daily News*, February 21, 2014, www.nydailynews.com/entertainment/music-arts/classical-music-blowing-article-1.1618623 (accessed May 4, 2016).

26 Ibid.

27 Ibid.

28 Tom Huizenga, "Yo-Yo Ma, Edgar Meyer, Chris Thile, Stuart Duncan: Tiny Desk Concert," *NPR*, November 17, 2011, www.npr.org/event/music/142242654/yo-yo-ma-edgar-meyer-chris-thile-and-stuart-duncan-tiny-desk-concert (accessed May 4, 2016).

29 Farber, "Classical Music Explodes."

30 Ibid.

31 Ibid.

32 "Heavy Metal Is Serious Stuff," Lang Lang on Metallica: *GRAMMY.com*, April 14, 2014, www.grammy.com/videos/lang-lang-on-metallica-heavy-metal-is-serious-stuff (accessed May 4, 2016).

33 Megan Doyle, "Tonight: String Quartet Brooklyn Rider Brings New Life to Classical Music," *Pittsburgh Post-Gazette*, July 18, 2013 (accessed May 4, 2016).

34 "Stories: Crossover Classics," *Baltimore Symphony Orchestra*, www.bsomusic.org/stories/crossover-classics (accessed May 4, 2016).

35 Farhad Manjoo, "Spotify Wants Listeners to Break Down Music Barriers," *New York Times*, June 3, 2015.

36 Ibid.

37 Ben Ratliff, "Seeking Genuine Discovery on Music Services," *New York Times*, June 28, 2015.

38 Ricky O'Bannon, "Five Questions with Ben Folds," *Baltimore Symphony Orchestra*, www.bsomusic.org/stories/five-questions-with-ben-folds (accessed May 4, 2016).

39 Greg Sandow, "What We Should Do? On the Future of Classical Music," *Arts Journal*, September 18, 2014, www.artsjournal.com/sandow/2014/09/what-we-should-do.html#comment-70406 (accessed May 24, 2016).

40 Ibid.

41 Karen Eng, "Classic Rock: Dan Visconti, the 21st-Century Composer," *TED Blog*, May 23, 2014, http://blog.ted.com/dan-visconti-and-a-new-breed-of-21st-century-composer (accessed May 24, 2016).

42 Ibid.

43 Ibid.

44 O'Bannon, "A Classically-Minded Guide to South By Southwest."

45 Ibid.

46 Daniel Grushkin, "Music's Mad Scientist," *Departures*, May/June 2015, 157.

47 Ibid.

48 "Black History Month 2015, *WQXR*, www.wqxr.org/#!/story/American-orchestras-grapple-diversity (accessed March 1, 2016).

49 Michael Cooper, "Sphinx, a Diversity Advocate in Classical Music," *New York Times*, March 3, 2015.

50 Larry Platt, "A Conductor of Change: Her Orchestra Is Diverse in Both Look and Sound," *Philadelphia Inquirer*, June 23, 2013.

51 Ibid.

52 Ibid.

53 Ibid.

54 Ibid.

55 William Robin, "They're Always Borrowing His Stuff," *New York Times,* February 8, 2015.

56 Ibid.

57 Ibid.

58 Ibid.

59 Ivan Hewett, "El Sistema: Does Reality Match the Rhetoric?" *The Telegraph* (UK), November 24, 2014, www.telegraph.co.uk/culture/music/classicalmusic/11249849/El-Sistema-does-reality-match-the-rhetoric.html (accessed April 23, 2016); Daniel J. Watson, "Music Meets Chavez Politics, and Critics Frown," *New York Times*, February 17, 2012, www.nytimes.com/2012/02/18/arts/music/venezuelans-criticize-hugo-chavezs-support-of-el-sistema.html (accessed April 23, 2016).

60 "Price of Success: Will the Recycled Orchestra Last?" *CBS 60 Minutes Overtime*, aired November 17, 2013, www.cbsnews.com/news/price-of-success-will-the-recycled-orchestra-last (accessed May 17, 2016).

61 Mark Pullinger, "Transforming Colombia's Youth through Music," *Bachtrack Review*, April 12, 2015, www.bachtrack.com/youth-orchestra-batuta-colombia-bogota-april-2015 (accessed May 12, 2016).

62 "Aesthetics," *Art and Popular Culture*, www.artandpopularculture.com/Aesthetics, (accessed May 13, 2016).

63 Simon Frith, University of Edinburgh, "Keynote Address to the European Music Council Annual Forum in Glasgow on April 19 2013," www.livemusicexchange.org/blog/the-social-value-of-music-in-the-context-of-european-regeneration-policy-simon-frith (accessed April 23, 2016).

64 Theodore Gracyk, *Listening to Popular Music* (Ann Arbor: University of Michigan Press, 2007), 2.

65 Ibid, 3.

66 Ibid.

67 Ibid.

68 In his book *A Hard Day's Write: The Stories Behind Every Beatles Song* (London: Carlton Books, 2012), Steve Turner states: "An 'aeolian cadence' is not a recognized musical description and generations of music critics have puzzled over exactly what [London Times music critic William] Mann was referring to."

69 David Sheff, "Playboy Interview with John Lennon and Yoko Ono," *Playboy*, January 1981, www.beatles interviews.org/dbjypb.int3.html (accessed June 13, 2016).

70 Gracyk, *Listening to Popular Music*, 8.

71 Ibid, 4.

72 Ibid, 7.

73 Ibid.

74 Ibid.

75 Ibid, 8.

76 Ibid.

77 "State Policy Briefs," *National Assembly of United States State Arts Agencies*, 2010, www.nasaa-arts.org/Advocacy/Advocacy-Tools/Why-Government-Support/WhyGovSupport.pdf (accessed May 13, 2016).

78 Ibid.

79 Kate Taylor, "What's the Social Value of the Arts? Big Data Has Some Answers (Even if Artists Don't Want to Hear It)," *Globe and Mail* (Canada), November 21, 2014, www.theglobeandmail.com/arts/music/whats-the-social-value-of-the-arts-big-data-has-some-answers-even-if-artists-dont-want-to-hear-it/article21697303 (accessed April 21, 2016).

80   Ibid.

81   Ibid.

82   "About Us," *Zoukak Theatre Company*, www.zoukak.org/pages/about-us (accessed April 29, 2016).

83   "What Is Music Therapy?" *American Music Therapy Association*, www.musictherapy.org/about/musictherapy/ (accessed May 3, 2016).

84   Jennifer L. Hollis, "Providing the Soundtrack for Life's Last Moments," *New York Times*, August 2, 2015.

85   Mark J. Stern, Susan C. Seifert, and Domenic Vitiello, "Migrants, Communities and Culture," *Creativity and Change*, January 2007, www.trfund.com/wpcontent/uploads/2013/06/Migrant.pdf (accessed May 2, 2016).

86   Ibid.

87   Gene D. Cohen, "The Creativity and Aging Study," *George Washington University*, April 30, 2006, www.cahh.gwu.edu/sites/cahh.gwu.edu/files/downloads/NEA_Study_Final_Report_0.pdf (accessed April 28, 2016).

88   Melissa Locker, "This Is How Music Can Change Your Brain," *TIME*, December 16, 2014, www.time.com/3634995/study-kids-engaged-music-class-for-benefits-northwestern (accessed April 28, 2016).

89   Ibid.

90   Ibid.

91   Ibid.

92   Thomas Wells, "Sen's Capability Approach," *Internet Encyclopedia of Philosophy*, www.iep.utm.edu/sen-cap (accessed May 4, 2016).

93   Katie Ingersoll and John Carnwath, "A New Way to Think about Intrinsic vs. Instrumental Benefits of the Arts," *Create Equity*, March 2015, www.createquity.com/2015/03/a-new-way-to-think-about-intrinsic-vs-instrumental-benefits-of-the-arts/ (accessed March 19, 2016).

94   Ibid.

95   Jodie Gummow, "Culturally Impoverished: US NEA Spends 1/40th of What Germany Doles Out for Arts Per Capita," *AlterNet*, February 5, 2014, www.alternet.org/culture/culturally-impoverished-us-nea-spends-140th-what-germany-doles-out-arts-capita (accessed May 4, 2016).

96   "4172.0 – Arts and Culture in Australia: A Statistical Overview, 2014," *Australian Bureau of Statistics*, www.abs.gov.au/ausstats/abs@.nsf/Lookup/4172.0main+features82014 (accessed May 4, 2016).

97   "What We Do," *Australia Council*, www.australiacouncil.gov.au/v (accessed May 3, 2016).

98   David Powell, "Hard Evidence: Does London Get Too Much Arts Funding?" *The Conversation*, February 5, 2014, www.theconversation.com/hard-evidence-does-london-get-too-much-arts-funding-22328 (accessed May 3, 2016).

99   "Cultural Gifts Scheme," *Arts Council England*, www.artscouncil.org.uk/what-we-do/supporting-museums/cultural-property/tax-incentives/cultural-gifts-scheme/#sthash.IC24lxS4.dpuf (accessed May 4, 2016).

100 "Finland," *Compendium: Cultural Policies and Trends in Europe*, www.culturalpolicies.net/web/finland.php?aid=812 (accessed May 3, 2016).

101 "France Announces Its 2013 Cultural Budget, 'Coalition pour la diversité culturelle,'" October 15, 2012, www.cdc-ccd.org/France-announces-its-2013-cultural?lang=fr (accessed May 3, 2016).

102 "France Cuts Its Culture Budget for 2013, While Germany Boosts Arts Spending," *Blouin ArtInfo*, November 13, 2012, http://blogs.artinfo.com/artintheair/2012/11/13/france-cuts-its-culture-budget-for-2013-while-germany-boosts-arts-spending (accessed May 3, 2016).

103 Eva Hershaw, "In Mexico, Artists Can Pay Taxes with Artwork," April 11, 2014, *The Atlantic*, www.theatlantic.com/international/archive/2014/04/in-mexico-artists-can-pay-taxes-with-artwork/360519/ (accessed May 3, 2016).

104 Ibid.

105 Andreas J. Wiesand, "Answers to Questions on Cuts in Cultural Budgets," *Norwegian Culture Magazine*, Edition 16-2013, Germany," culturalpolicies.net>, ISSN: 2222-7334 (accessed January 30, 2016).

106 Nina Siegel, "Dutch Arts Scene Is under Siege," *New York Times*, January 29, 2013 (accessed May 3, 2016).

107 "Regularly Funded Organisations Survey 2013/14," *Arts Council of Northern Ireland*, December, 2014, www.artscouncil-ni.org/images/uploads/publications-documents/RFO_Report_2013_14.pdf (accessed May 3, 2016).

108 "Life Changing: Where the Money Goes," *National Lottery*, www.national-lottery.co.uk/life-changing/where-the-money-goes?icid=sgp:na:co (accessed May 3, 2016).

109 "Home," *Konstnarsnamnden*, www.konstnarsnamnden.se/default.aspx?id=11309 (accessed May 3, 2016).

110 "Home," *Kulturrådet*, www.kulturradet.se/en/in-english (accessed May 3, 2016).

111 "Apply for Funding," *Nordic Culture Fund*, www.nordiskkulturfond.org/en/sog-stotte-0 (accessed May 3, 2016).

112 "National Endowment for the Arts Appropriations History," *National Endowment for the Arts – Open Government*, www.arts.gov/open-government/national-endowment-arts-appropriations-history#sthash.yTlekTCZ.dpuf (accessed May 3, 2016).

113 Paul Kiel, "The Bailout: By the Actual Numbers," *ProPublica*, September 6, 2012, www.propublica.org/ion/bailout (accessed May 3, 2016).

114 "Congress Completes Action on NY 2013 Appropriations," *National Science Foundation*, April 9, 2013, http://nsf.gov/about/congress/113/highlights/cu13_0409.jsp (accessed May 3, 2016).

115 Larry Rohter, "In Europe, Where Art Is Life, Ax Falls on Public Financing," *New York Times*, March 24, 2012; "Life Changing: Where the Money Goes," *National Lottery*, www.national-lottery.co.uk/life-changing/where-the-money-goes?icid=sgp:na:co (accessed May 3, 2016).

116 Ibid.

117 Ibid.

118 Ibid.

119 Andreas J. Wiesand, "Germany," Council of Europe/ERICarts: *Compendium of Cultural Policies and Trends in Europe*, 16th edn, 2013. culturalpolicies.net>, ISSN: 2222-7334.

120 Ibid.

121 State Policy Briefs, "National Assembly of United States State Arts Agencies, 2010," www.nasaa-arts.org/Advocacy/Advocacy-Tools/Why-Government-Support/WhyGovSupport.pdf (accessed April 22, 2016).

122 Daniel Reid, "An American Vision of Federal Arts Subsidies," *Yale Journal of Law & the Humanities*, Volume 21, Issue 2, Article 7, 2009, http://digitalcommons.law.yale.edu/cgi/viewcontent.cgi?article=1352&context=yjlh (accessed April 27, 2016).

123 Stern, Seifert, and Vitiello, "Migrants, Communities and Culture."

124 Nancy Groves, "George Brandis Will Have Final Say on Arts Funding, Draft Guidelines Suggest," *The Guardian* (Australia), July 1, 2015, www.theguardian.com/culture/2015/jul/02/george-brandis- (accessed May 3, 2016).

125 Ibid.

126 Frith.

127 Bob Shingleton, "Classical Music Should Not Be the Art of Compromise," *The Overgrown Path*, June 9, 2015, www.overgrownpath.com/2015/06/classical-music-should-not-be-art-of.html (accessed April 7, 2016).

128 Tania Branigan, "China Tightens Concerts Rules," *The Guardian* (UK), February 10, 2013, www.theguardian.com/world/2013/feb/10/china-tightens-concerts-rules (accessed April 7, 2016).

129 "Madonna Adds Her Voice to Critics of Russian Female Punk Rock Band Verdict," *Reuters*, August 18, 2012, www.reuters.com/article/2012/08/19/entertainment-us-russia-pussyriot-reacti-idUSBRE87H07X20120819 (accessed May 3, 2016).

130 Shingleton, "Classical Music."

131 Corinna da Fonseca-Wollheim, "Politics Is Personal, and Professional," *New York Times*, February 1, 2015.

132 Ibid.

133 Ibid.

134 Ibid.

135 Shingleton, "Classical Music."

136 Alex Ross, "Notes of Dissent," *New Yorker*, June 2, 2014.

137 Henry Fountain, "A Nation's Pride, Chided: As Globe Warms, Norwegians Turn Ambivalent on Statoil, Their Economic Bedrock," *New York Times*, December 13, 2014.

138 Ibid.

139 Ibid.

140 Zachary Woolfe, "Making the Case to Hear Nazi Song," *New York Times*, March 17, 2015.

141 Ibid.

142 Ibid.

143 Ross.

144 Ibid.

145 Ibid.

146 Rachel Donadio, "An Opera Fights Hungary's Rising Anti-Semitism," *New York Times*, October 23, 2013.

147 Ibid.

148 Ibid.

149 Ibid.

150 Ibid.

151 Ibid.

152 Ibid.

153 Robert Shingleton, "Classical Music's Ethically Compromised Funders," *The Overgrown Path*, December 14, 2011, www.overgrownpath.com/2011/12/classical-musics-ethically-compromised.html (accessed March 12, 2016).

154 Ibid.

155 "Corporate Social Responsibility," *JTI*, www.jti.com/how-we-do-business/corporate-social-responsibility/corporate-philanthropy (accessed May 3, 2016).

156 Shingleton, "Classical Music's Ethically Compromised Funders."

157 Ibid.

158 "Your National Lottery—Good Causes," National Lottery, www.lotterygoodcauses.org.uk/good-causes (accessed May 3, 2016).

159 Evan Powers, "Who Funds the Fine Arts (and Does It Matter)?" *The Crimson Cavalier*, www.crimsoncavalier.blogspot.com/2011/12/who-funds-fine-arts-and-does-it-matter.html (accessed May 3, 2016).

CHAPTER 2

Why Music Professionals Need to Think Like Entrepreneurs

CHAPTER OVERVIEW

In this chapter you will dig deeper into the meaning of "music entrepreneur." You will learn the various forms that entrepreneurship can take, and the difference between for-profit and nonprofit organizations. You will see *why* it's important for music professionals to think and act like entrepreneurs. Then you will gain the skills needed to learn *how* to think like an entrepreneur. The chapter concludes with a section of questions that will help you understand yourself from an entrepreneurial point of view. Two entrepreneurs are spotlighted: Andrew Cyr of the Metropolis Ensemble and Groupmuse founder Sam Bodkin.

KEY TERMS

Business model	Double bottom line
For-profit and nonprofit	The sharing economy
NGO	Growth mindset
Philanthropist	Crowdsourcing
Social entrepreneur	Crowdfunding
Intrapreneur	

A DEEPER MEANING OF "MUSIC ENTREPRENEUR"

The DNA of entrepreneurship is opportunity *recognition.* For artist-entrepreneurs and music business-entrepreneurs in the creative economy, we add the concept of opportunity *creation* to the definition. Music entrepreneurship demands that you understand the industry so well that, when you recognize opportunities in the marketplace, a new artistic creation will emerge as you fill that unmet need or desire in the marketplace.

In creative economy ventures, music professionals use entrepreneurial activity to bring music and other arts to audiences and fans in new and innovative ways. The entrepreneurial activities generate revenue that, in theory at least, will return to the artistic creators to make more art. Entrepreneurship within both the creative and the business sectors is the means by which artists and audiences find each other.[1]

"Entrepreneur" is a word that gets tossed around in the press, in colleges and universities, in books and magazines. It has become a catch-all phrase that has lost its crisp, precise meaning. Before we move further into this chapter, I would like to build a succinct definition that we can use in the context of the creative economies.

We examined these two aspects of entrepreneurship in Chapter 1:

- Entrepreneurs can create something of value from practically nothing, pulling together the right ingredients to start building an altogether amazing product or service.

- Entrepreneurs upend the status quo, which means turning upside down the traditional definitions, labels, and ways of doing things that can hinder an open-minded search for opportunity.

Here's a classic, elegant definition of entrepreneurship by Harvard Business School professor Howard Stevenson:

> Entrepreneurship is the pursuit of opportunity
>
> without regard to resources currently controlled.[2]

The British Council's Young Creative Entrepreneur Competition[3] defines a creative entrepreneur as someone working in the creative sector who:

- is able to demonstrate business success in the classic terms of business growth (profit, market share, employees) and/or in terms of her reputation (creativity, quality and aesthetic) among her peers;

- has developed a successful (in terms of impact and reach) social or nonprofit enterprise in this sector;

- has shown leadership in the industry by championing its development in her country;

- has developed initiatives (e.g., exhibitions, trade fairs, festivals) that develop and grow the market for this sector in her country.[4]

This is my definition:

> A music entrepreneur is someone who sees opportunity
>
> where others see only problems, and creatively channels
>
> his or her passion for music into a new business that challenges
>
> the status quo and has value in the public marketplace.

Changing lives, changing markets, changing the world—this is the work of an entrepreneur. Each of us has the power to dream, create, nurture, and build something of value from our great ideas, regardless of the resources we have at hand when that flash of inspiration strikes.

Characteristics of Entrepreneurs

Successful entrepreneurs run the gamut of personality types, from shy as a wallflower to as confident as Victoria Beckham. There are no specific personal characteristics needed for someone to choose an entrepreneurial path. In fact, entrepreneurship is a process, not a character trait. It is open to all kinds of people regardless of wealth (or lack thereof), level of tolerance for risk and ambiguity, or current business acumen. When an entrepreneur sees an opportunity, she pursues it regardless of the resources at hand. Entrepreneurs are *accustomed* to making do without resources.

One way to understand the characteristics of entrepreneurs and entrepreneurial situations is through the metaphor of jazz musicians. Unlike players in an orchestra, who play using a printed score and are led by a conductor, jazz musicians "improvise spontaneously in real time," explains business professor William Pendergast of California State Polytechnic University. "Jazz builds on minimal structure that allows maximum flexibility and adaptation . . . Jazz requires action and initiative. Passivity is not an option. Musicians climb out on a limb and push the edge of uncertainty. They follow where the music leads, sometimes stumbling, but learning from errors to create new musical opportunities . . . the essence of jazz is taking risks to explore novel, creative paths, inventing responses without a pre-scripted plan."[5]

Jon Burgstone, entrepreneur and founder of the Center for Entrepreneurship and Technology at the University of California, Berkeley, sums up the characteristics of an entrepreneur in this way: "Every time you want to make any important decision, there are two possible courses of action. You can look at the array of choices that present themselves, pick the best available option and try to make it fit. Or, you can do what the true entrepreneur does: Figure out the best conceivable option and then make it available."[6]

Types of Entrepreneurial Ventures

A business model describes the behind-the-scenes picture of how an organization creates, delivers, and captures value in economic, social, cultural, or other contexts.[7] There are many choices for entrepreneurs when it comes to selecting a formal business model for a venture. These will be discussed in detail later in the book. For now, we'll start with one of the first questions students usually ask: "What's the difference between a for-profit and a nonprofit business model?" (The terms "charity," "public benefit organization," and "nonprofit" will be used interchangeably throughout this book.) Both for-profit and nonprofit organizations serve the music industry and nurture entrepreneurial music professionals.

For-profit Ventures

For-profit business models rest on the foundation of creating products or services whose sales produce enough revenue to cover expenses, plus some amount of revenue above expenses, which is called profit. The profit can be used for growth or infrastructure, as dividend payments to investors, or for acquisition of other companies, to name a few.

Live Nation Entertainment, Inc. (Live Nation) is a global company with core businesses in event promotion, ticketing, sponsorship and advertising, and artist management. Live Nation Entertainment Inc. trades as LYV on the New York Stock Exchange.[8]

Live Nation has four divisions: Concerts, Ticketing, Artist Nation, and Sponsorship & Advertising. The Concerts division promotes live music events around the globe. It produces concerts in 33 countries that, each year, connect nearly 59 million fans to almost 23,000 events with more than 2,700 artists. It owns, leases, operates, and has booking rights for and/or equity interest in a large number of US entertainment venues. The Ticketing division is primarily an agency business that sells event tickets. The Artist

Nation division provides management services to music artists. The Sponsorship & Advertising division helps businesses connect with their customers by means of a sales force that facilitates relationships with sponsors.[9]

Live Nation Entertainment has a for-profit business model, meaning that it rests on the foundation of creating products or services where sales produce enough revenue to cover expenses, plus some amount of revenue above expenses, or profit.

Nonprofit Ventures

The underlying reason for creating a *nonprofit, public benefit, or charity organization* (to be referred to collectively as "nonprofit" for the purposes of this book) is to promote activities that serve the needs of communities. Governments recognize that nonprofits may be in some ways better positioned than the government to understand and provide for community needs. Nonprofits can often move more quickly than government in identifying and reacting to societal needs, and may be able to deliver services more efficiently and directly. Nonprofits can complement or supplement the role of the government in addressing social needs, or they can provide services that the government does not. In addition, in the provision of their services, most nonprofits are permitted to raise private funds.[10]

The term "nonprofit" confuses many people. It does not mean that the business spends more money than it takes in, or cannot earn more revenue than it has in expenses. Contrary to common belief, nonprofit organizations *can* make a profit, but the profit must be reinvested in the organization rather than distributed among the directors of the company.

In the nonprofit creative economy, the organizational mission rather than making money is the main focus. Governments generally offer exemptions from most forms of taxation to nonprofits. Donations made to a tax-exempt nonprofit organization may also be tax-deductible for the donor, which is another way that governments can encourage people to make contributions to charitable organizations.

The two key differences between a nonprofit and a for-profit organization are as follows:

- The owners of a nonprofit may not derive financial profits from the business (this is not the same thing as being paid a salary). All of the money earned by or donated to a nonprofit organization that is over and above its expenses must be used in pursuing the organization's objectives, not enriching its owners.

- A nonprofit organization is mission-driven rather than profit-driven.

Tatiana Rais is the founder and director of a nonprofit cultural center in Bogotá, Colombia, called Espacio Odeón: Centro Cultural. In 2014, she was a winner of the British Council Young Creative Entrepreneur Award, which celebrates young entrepreneurs who are creating exciting things at the intersection of culture and technology around the world.[11]

Rais' mission is to bring contemporary art in all its expressions to the people: visual, performance, theater, dance, video, and inter-disciplinary. Espacio Odeón is located in the community of La Candelaria, one of the poorest neighborhoods in Bogotá. Rais has created a space where neighborhood citizens have the chance to not just see art, but also to interact with artists and learn about art, culture, and its context within Colombia and the Espacio Odeón community.[12]

"In terms of culture, Bogotá is booming," says Rais. But, she explains, "there still is not enough investment and grant opportunities being offered through the public sector to satisfy the entire industry." To fill the gap, a network of alliances between nonprofit cultural organizations has developed in Bogotá, which helps the cultural economy to work together "to engage established audiences and surprise new ones."[13]

Espacio Odeón has a nonprofit business model that rests on its mission, which is to bring contemporary art of all types to its community of La Candelaria, Bogotá. The organization receives grants and other sources of revenue to supplement the sale of its products and services, which alone do not cover the organization's expenses.

Except for the distinguishing features of profit distribution and mission focus, nonprofits have quite a few aspects in common with for-profit organizations. Nonprofit enterprises work to accomplish their objectives, as do for-profit enterprises, so many business tactics and management techniques from the for-profit world also work well in nonprofit organizations. Looking from the outside in, it may be challenging to tell a well-run nonprofit organization from a successful for-profit company.

Philanthropy

Philanthropy is the term used to describe promoting the welfare of others, often expressed through donations of money to good causes.[14] Nonprofits all rely on philanthropists, both individual and corporate, to help them meet their budgets. In most cases, charities do not charge a market rate price—or do not charge at all—for their products and services, and seek donations to help cover their costs of doing business.

The International Index of Generosity

The proportion of people who make financial contributions to charity is significantly higher in countries offering tax breaks for giving, according to a recent study conducted by Nexus, McDermott Will & Emery LLP, and the Charities Aid Foundation, along with distribution partner NFP.

The "Rules to Give By Index," a global international index of government support for charitable giving, shows that the percentage of people donating money to charity is 12 percent higher in nations offering tax incentives to individuals than in those that do not.[15]

The study compared tax incentives and other aspects of charity law to people's likelihood to give, as measured by the Charities Aid Foundation's "World Giving Index," the international index of generosity. It found that the influence of tax incentives on giving does not depend on a country's level of economic development. Across the economic spectrum, according to the "World Giving Index," countries that offer tax incentives to individuals experience higher rates of philanthropic giving.[16]

Non-governmental Organizations (NGOs)

The term "non-governmental organization" (NGO) refers to a hybrid type of entrepreneurial company. (It may also be referred to as a "civil society organization" or CSO.) A NGO or CSO is a nonprofit group, independent from government, which is organized on a local, national, or international level to address issues in support of the public good.[17] Task-oriented and made up of people with a common interest, NGOs "perform a variety of services and humanitarian functions, bring public concerns to governments, monitor policy and program implementation, and encourage participation of public stakeholders at the community level."[18]

NGOs have an increasing global influence in today's world, affecting all areas of life. The Public Interest Registry (PIR) estimates that there are close to ten million NGOs worldwide. The number of UN-accredited multilateral NGOs alone rose from 40 in 1945 to 3,536 by the end of 2011.[19]

Examples of NGOs

Médecins Sans Frontières (Doctors Without Borders) was founded in Paris in 1971. It is an international, independent, medical humanitarian organization that delivers emergency aid to people affected by armed conflict, epidemics, healthcare exclusion, and natural or man-made disasters.[20]

Oxfam is an international confederation of 17 organizations in 92 countries that work together to build a future free from the injustice of poverty.[21]

The Wikimedia Foundation is dedicated to encouraging the growth, development and distribution of free, online multilingual content to the public. It operates some of the largest collaboratively edited reference projects in the world, including Wikipedia.[22]

Social Entrepreneurship

Another distinct type of entrepreneurship, called social entrepreneurship, focuses on finding creative solutions to important social problems. Social entrepreneurs combine their passion for creative problem-solving with business discipline, innovation, and determination in the service of resolving social issues. They improve systems, invent new approaches, and create solutions to change society for the better.[23]

Social entrepreneurs recognize that many governmental and philanthropic efforts have fallen short of the public's expectations, particularly in developing economies. Social entrepreneurs fill this gap with creative and sustainable ventures that help solve urgent community problems.[24]

Social entrepreneurs often commit their lives to changing the direction of their field. They are both visionaries and realists: most of all, they care about making their visions real in a practical way.[25]

We have always had social entrepreneurs, even if we did not call them that. They built many of the institutions we now take for granted.[26] People like Dr. Maria Montessori (Italy—developed the Montessori approach to early childhood education), John Muir (US conservationist—worked to establish US national parks), and Florence Nightingale (England—the founder of modern nursing) were all social entrepreneurs. Oprah Winfrey (US—entertainer, philanthropist, and broadcasting pioneer) and Muhammad Yunus (Bangladesh—founder of micro-finance institution Grameen Bank) are two contemporary social entrepreneurs.

Today, the term "social entrepreneur" is important because it implies a blurring of the lines between for-profit and nonprofit sectors. Social entrepreneurship encompasses not only creative nonprofit initiatives, but also for-profit organizations with a social purpose, such as for-profit community development banks, and hybrid organizations that combine nonprofit and for-profit elements: for example, homeless shelters that run businesses to train and employ their residents.[27]

Social enterprises are often referred to as having a "double bottom line" because they have the twin goals of effective social outcomes and making enough money to remain solvent. Of these two goals, mission-related impact is the overarching focus. To the casual observer, many social enterprises look, feel, and even operate like traditional businesses, but a closer look reveals the existence of the defining characteristics of a social enterprise: mission is at the center of business, with income generation playing an important but secondary role.[28]

On the whole, social entrepreneurs operate very similarly to business entrepreneurs; they must be connected to a specific unmet need, and able to secure capital and design a system that is self-sustaining. The difference, however, is a strong commitment to helping others in some way.[29]

Internal Entrepreneuring

Yet another specific type of entrepreneurship is known as internal entrepreneuring. At any given moment the world over, there are employees of companies who are thinking about innovative solutions to problems. Some of these employees may hope to establish an entrepreneurial outpost inside the company. If they succeed, these employees are called internal entrepreneurs, or intrapreneurs.

Guy Kawaski, author of many status quo-challenging books for entrepreneurs, has these recommendations for intrapreneurs in *The Art of the Start*:[30]

"Put the company first. Your motivation should remain the betterment of the company that employs you."[31]

"Stay under the radar. You want to be left alone until either your project is too far along to ignore or the rest of the company realizes that it's needed. The higher you go in a company, the more people want to maintain the status quo and their positions."[32]

"Find an internal champion. These are people who have paid their dues, are safe from everyday petty politics and have the attention and respect of top management. They may be idealists who want to see innovation in the company but have been ignored or trampled into corporate submission. Enlist these internal champions to help you make innovation happen."[33]

"Anticipate, then jump on, tectonic shifts. Whether caused by external factors like changes in the marketplace or internal factors such as a new CEO, large shifts signal changes and may create an opportunity for your efforts. Anticipate these changes and be ready to unveil new products or services the moment the environment shifts."[34]

"Dismantle when done. Once you've developed the new product or service for your company, dismantle the team and leave your outpost to remind everyone that you are still part of the larger organization."[35]

WHY *MUSICIANS* NEED TO THINK LIKE ENTREPRENEURS

There are many important reasons why music professionals need to think like entrepreneurs. First, the arts and cultural sectors drive economic evolution, according to Jason Potts, Senior Lecturer at the University of Queensland in Australia. In his paper entitled "Why Creative Industries Matter to Economic Evolution," Potts states that the creative industries are far from simply products for leisure time consumption: "Instead of thinking that the creative industries are an industry that produces a particular set of goods, they might be better modeled as producing a coordination service—namely the generation and facilitation of change."[36] In other words, music professionals working in the creative industries are a vital part of the process of global economic evolution.[37]

The process of economic evolution involves looking for opportunities where others see only problems. Creating something new and developing it to the point where it has value to others is one of the cornerstones of entrepreneurship. The creative industries contribute by providing new ideas that are then developed, often in collaboration with other industries, such as music merchandise created with 3D printers. The creative industries also provide the services to generate and develop new standalone ideas, particularly in publishing, TV, and radio.[38]

> ### *Pause and Reflect*
>
> In what specific ways can people who work in the creative industries contribute to new products and services in publishing, TV, and radio?

The creative industries play an increasingly important role in the growth of GDP[39] across the Americas. In the region's two largest economies—Brazil and the US—more than 10 percent of GDP comes from the creative industries.

In Argentina, Mexico, and Peru, the GDP contribution of the creative industries ranges from two percent to seven percent, suggesting the high growth potential of the sector.[40]

A second reason why music professionals need to think like entrepreneurs is to help address a severe shortage of creative workers in the global economy. In a recent research report by the Conference Board (Americans for the Arts), 85 percent of employers seeking creative employees said they could not find enough job applicants with creativity and innovation skills. The report showed that some employers believe creativity has less to do with finding solutions than with the ability to spot problems or patterns that others cannot see. Employers defined creativity in the workplace as "the integration of knowledge across different disciplines, the ability to originate new ideas, and being comfortable with the notion of 'no right answer.'"[41]

Creating a Sustainable Life

For the rest of this chapter we will focus on the third reason that music professionals need to think like entrepreneurs: to create a sustainable life in the creative economy.

The positive impact of entrepreneurs and new job creation in the world economy is well documented, but that's not the point of this book. I want to show you that entrepreneurship is more than a business practice that creates jobs. Even if you never start your own company, or work in the music industry, learning to think like an entrepreneur can be your personal, one-way ticket out of anxiety about your future, particularly in challenging economic times.

Globalization creates opportunities and threats. Digital technologies now allow music to be available in all territories at the same time in different platforms. Artists must build a global strategy for all parts of their career. This means music professionals must understand the business structure of music and approach it from the point of knowledge, flexibility, creative problem-solving, and opportunity recognition.

The downside of the often-heard comment "Today more music is heard by more people than ever before" is that anyone can become, to some degree, a "global artist." YouTube videos can go viral, spreading throughout the world in less than a day and catapulting a musical amateur to global internet fame—for a week or two. But our goal is creating satisfying and sustainable lives in this industry.

The ability to recognize opportunities and move quickly to exploit them will serve you well as a music professional, whether you start your own business or work for someone else, and whether you lead others or only yourself. Entrepreneurial thinking will expand your repertoire of ideas and options, both for the marketplace and for your professional development.

Here's what two creative industry entrepreneurs have to say about why you need to think like an entrepreneur:

Independent filmmakers Tom Putnam and Brenna Sanchez, founders of TBVE Films: If you're looking to take the step toward making your art your business, you better stay clear on that and treat it like a business. Use it as a mantra, use it as a [criterion] for decision-making. You've already invested your life in your art or your idea. Now you need to invest that much and more in your business, and you have to do it on a timeline. However great your art or idea, it is not a business until someone else wants to get in on it. Business is about giving the people what they want. If you are not always mindful of what they want, always, your business will fail. We're not talking about selling out here! All of this is said with the presumption that you'll stay true to your art.[42]

Performing artist-writer-arts advocate Seth Lepore: Self-producing one's work is a full-time job. When I was twenty-five I wasn't ready for what it would take to put myself out in the world in this capacity. I just wanted to create new works and perform them. All the business stuff freaked me out. After flailing about for almost a decade I realized that I had built up the skill set through various other jobs and life circumstances to actually go forward in this way, and my skin had thickened due to consistent rejection and indifference. My interest in so many subjects, my ability to juggle various administrative duties, to change focus quickly and see how things overlapped, to realize when to drop an idea that wasn't panning out . . . this way of being in the world wasn't scattered, it was actually entrepreneurial.[43]

SPOTLIGHT ON . . . GROUPMUSE: A TECH START-UP IN THE CLASSICAL MUSIC WORLD

Groupmuse is a social network that connects classical musicians with people who want to host chamber music house parties. Its mission is to create convenient opportunities for people to come together in the real world, in real time, to share a musical experience that is beautiful and profound.[44]

Groupmuse founder Sam Bodkin discovered the international hospitality service, couchsurfing.com, while traveling through Europe in 2007–8. "I had never seen anything like it. It seemed like such an unambiguously positive thing, connecting people who were willing to be generous with their space for the sake of a cultural exchange."[45]

In college, Bodkin became friends with a group of musicians who held practice sessions at each other's homes. "They played chamber music at a really high level and then they partied really hard. On the one hand it was a really good party, and [on] the other hand it had the life-affirming quality that only a great art experience can confer. I decided at that point that this is how classical music should be introduced to the rising generation, because we need not only great art and great beauty, we also need opportunities to come together and share something positive and meaningful."[46] He saw an opportunity to combine that experience with the couchsurfing.com concept, and the idea behind Groupmuse was born.

In its 2014–15 season, Groupmuse held more than 300 events. It has been featured in *TIME*, *The Guardian*, the *Boston Globe*, *NPR*, and many other media outlets.[47]

Groupmuse is a tech start-up in the classical music sector. It operates in what Bodkin describes as "this awkward middle-ground between the arts and nonprofit world and the start-up, for-profit world. When we were first getting started, we got a lot of skeptical looks from both sides. From the classic music patronage world we heard, 'What do you mean I'm not going to get a tax write-off?' It raises skeptical eyebrows.

In the start-up world, they're like, 'What do you mean? Classical music is where money goes to die.' That was really tough."[48]

At the beginning, Groupmuse was self-funded. Bodkin used personal savings and everyone who joined the project had outside jobs. Now Groupmuse is finding success in going the more traditional start-up funding route.[49]

Groupmuse's business model is similar to other start-ups in the world of the sharing economy. What makes it unique is that it's bringing the new approach of the sharing economy to a centuries-old art form.[50]

Bodkin's advice to arts entrepreneurs is as follows: "Talk the language of society. Don't assume that people already care about what you fight for. If they did, you wouldn't be necessary. Find reasons to make them care. For example: Let's stop talking about how classical music needs saving. That is entirely irrelevant to the people who don't care about classical music, which is most people. Let's talk about the ways in which our *society* needs saving and how we can make classical music its knight in shining armor. What does it look like when classical music wears shining armor?"[51]

Reflect and Discuss

In what other cities besides New York do you think the Groupmuse business model could work?

HOW TO THINK LIKE AN ENTREPRENEUR

Changing Your Mindset

Stanford psychologist Carol Dweck has spent decades researching achievement, failure, and success. In her book, *Mindset: The New Psychology of Success*, she convincingly demonstrates that one's frame of mind is a major influencer in determining who achieves her entrepreneurial potential and who does not.

Dweck asserts that people who believe intelligence is determined at birth have a *fixed mindset*. They are consumed by constantly proving to the world that they are talented and smart in all areas of their life. "Every situation calls for a confirmation of their intelligence, personality, or character," states Dweck. "Every situation is evaluated: Will I succeed or fail? Will I look smart or dumb? Will I be accepted or rejected?"[52]

Many young people find it personally challenging to overcome long-held beliefs and cultural pressures when it comes to dealing with failure. In some countries, failure is seen as a personal tragedy. It may be easier for North Americans to position failure as a badge of courage, particularly in the high-tech industry where the motto "Fail often to succeed sooner" is heard everywhere. But in cultures where stability and loyalty are highly valued, entrepreneurs may find a chilly reception to frequent job changes or innovations that are truly disruptive to an industry, such as the ride-sharing service Uber. Traditional ways of doing things may be cherished because they symbolize a regional or national identity.[53]

However, in entrepreneurship, as in science, a negative result can be just as important as a positive one. Just as it's important to discover that a certain drug isn't effective in curing cancer, vital information can come out of a failed artistic venture. When artists try something completely revolutionary that bombs at the box office, it can generate a lot of useful information. In both art and science, failure is a sign that the investigating process is at work.[54]

People who are not afraid to try a different way of doing things or speak up with new ideas have what Dweck calls *growth mindsets*. They believe that it is possible to become smarter over time because they understand that taking chances, trying new ideas, making mistakes, and correcting them are the tools that actually help grow entrepreneurial ability.[55] In the growth mindset, people want to become better at what they do, and they seek opportunities to challenge their abilities. They see personal setbacks as opportunities to learn and grow. Entrepreneurs need a growth mindset to flourish.

Reflect and Discuss

Watch these two videos by CD Baby founder Derek Sivers. Do you see yourself as a leader, a first follower, or something else altogether? Can you begin to see how looking at the world in a different way can change your perspective on the status quo?

"Leadership Lessons from Dancing Guy."[56]

"Japanese Addresses: No Street Names. Block Numbers."[57]

THE WISDOM OF "FAILING OFTEN TO SUCCEED SOONER"

Entrepreneurial thinking requires the ability to embrace mistakes as learning opportunities. Most of us try to avoid failing. We worry that we'll look foolish in front of our friends, or we'll lose money, disappoint people, or get a bad grade. When we are afraid of making a mistake, we become cautious and timid.

Many entrepreneurs believe that you can't succeed until you have experienced failure. On average, successful entrepreneurs have gone through 3.5 business failures. How can we achieve a balance between the wisdom gained from failing and the purposely naïve sense of adventure that remains vital to innovation?[58]

Fear of failing is a creativity-crusher. It inhibits boldness and innovation. In their *Harvard Business Review* publication, "The Wisdom of Deliberate Mistakes," authors Paul Schoemaker and Robert Gunther explain how traditional pedagogical practices have contributed to this anti-entrepreneurial situation. We tell children stories of famous people like Thomas Edison, the inventor of the electric light bulb, to show inspiring examples of people who failed for years before achieving their goals. Yet, as Schoemaker and Gunther point out: "Good grades are usually a reward for doing things right, not for making errors."[59]

Continuous learning requires going through continuous failures as well as successes.[60] At any given moment, most of us are involved with multiple projects, some of which will turn out well while others won't. That's the life of an entrepreneur. Fear of failure does not hold us back. In fact, the entrepreneur with a failed project is often the one to watch going forward.

Pause and Reflect

Watch the Derek Sivers video *Why You Need to Fail*. Then answer these questions based on your life experiences:

1. Give examples in your life when *deliberate* failure has been encouraged and rewarded. How did you view this concept? What was the outcome?

2. Give examples of *accidental* failures—when you tried something, didn't expect to fail, but did. What was your reaction? How did others react?

3. Reflect on "no pain, no gain" as a metaphor for "not failing, not learning" as it applies to your life, both personal and professional.

4. "If you're not failing you're not trying hard enough." Connect this quote from the video to your personal experiences with *music*.

A theater friend once told me that his motto was: "If you can't fix it, flaunt it." When the Broadway musical *Something Rotten!* failed to win a 2015 Tony Award (US), the creators of the musical embraced a controversial post-Tony marketing strategy: they flaunted their loss. The show placed notices on social media sites and in the *New York Times* declaring its status as "Loser!" in the competition for best musical. The ads noted other stellar shows of the past, such as *West Side Story* and *Wicked*, that did not receive a Best Musical Tony, but went on to memorable success at the box office. Kevin McCollum, the lead producer of the show, explained: "Very few shows have the confidence to go with the headline 'Loser!' but it illustrates that we're confident enough to acknowledge our loss and celebrate those that came before us."[61]

Right Brain/Left Brain

Author and former White House speechwriter Daniel Pink's powerful book, *A Whole New Mind: Why Right-Brainers Will Rule the Future*, delves deeply into the cognitive science of right brain/left brain characteristics. He bases his arguments on decades of data showing that the brain has two distinct hemispheres, each controlling different emotions and ways of thinking.

Pink argues that the world is moving away from an economy and society built on logical, linear, computer-like capabilities (left brain) to an economy and society built on the inventive, empathic, big-picture capabilities of the right brain. He feels that we are entering a new economic era, which he calls the Conceptual Age. We will need the capacity to detect patterns and opportunities, and to combine seemingly unrelated ideas into something new, if we are to succeed in the Conceptual Age.[62]

We know that we need both "sides" of the brain to function fully, even though we may find that we resort to one type of cognitive processing over the other, particularly in stressful situations. Look at the following worksheet. In the blank center column, write one or more of your day-to-day activities that employ the specific type of cognitive processing described in the right-hand column.

Pink cites the research of cognitive neuroscientists M. Jung-Beemna, E. M. Bowden, and J. Haberman at Drexel and Northwestern Universities (US). Their work shows that flashes of insight preceding "aha!" moments are accompanied by a large burst of neural activity in the brain's right hemisphere. An inspiration-centered

TABLE 2.1 *Left Brain/Right Brain Activities*[63]

TYPE OF COGNITIVE PROCESSING	ACTIVITIES THAT USE THIS TYPE OF COGNITIVE PROCESSING	BRIEF DESCRIPTION
Linear (Left brain)		Processes information from part to whole in a straightforward, logical progression.
Holistic (Right brain)		Processes information from whole to part; sees the big picture first, not the details.
Sequential (Left brain)		Processes information in order from first to last.
Random (Right brain)		Processes information without priority, jumps from one task to another.
Concrete (Left brain)		Processes things that can be seen or touched—real objects.
Symbolic (Right brain)		Processes symbols as pictures; likes to use letters, words, and mathematical symbols.
Logical (Left brain)		Processes information piece by piece using logic to solve a problem.
Intuitive (Right brain)		Processes information based on whether or not it feels right to know the answer, but not sure how it was derived.
Verbal (Left brain)		Processes thoughts and ideas with words.
Nonverbal (Right brain)		Processes thought as illustrations.
Reality-Based (Left brain)		Processes information based on reality; focuses on rules and regulations.
Fantasy-Oriented (Right brain)		Processes information with creativity; less focus on rules and regulations.

approach to innovation (those "aha!" moments) requires the ability and fortitude to experiment with novel combinations and to make the many mistakes that inevitably come with upending the status quo.[64]

Creative Problem-Solving

Cultivating a Growth Mindset

Your mindset determines how you see the world around you. Feeling stressed, tense, or anxious decreases your ability to tap into your creative self. On the other hand, feeling confident, relaxed, and open to new ways of thinking will energize your outlook on life. It takes work to change your attitude, but the benefits are enormous if you can do it.

Entrepreneurial thinking flows best when you're having fun or doing something out of the ordinary. Ever wonder why some companies that require lots of creative thinking from their employees have a room with scooters, a pool table, puzzles, Lego building blocks, and other toys? It's because that kind of environment wakes up our brains. We're able to tap into our playful selves, which are all too often buried underneath the pressure to behave like the adults we are. The designer Milton Glaser sums it up well: "There's a conflict between professionalism that calls for *minimizing* risk, while creativity *encourages* risk."[65]

A growth mindset opens you to a "What if . . . ?" attitude. It encourages you to question the status quo and imagine a completely new way of approaching problems. You'll find yourself asking "What if we tried it this way instead?" and "What would happen if we flipped that around?" The techniques in this chapter will help you create ideas big and small, practical and whacky, technical and artistic. Most importantly, you will abandon traditional ways of thinking and embrace an open, inquisitive approach to the world around you.

Don't just *read* this next section—*use* these techniques in order to master entrepreneurial thinking. You'll be flexing both the left (linear) and right (creative) sides of your brain as you work the exercises ahead.

Identifying Problems and Recognizing Opportunity

There's nothing more powerful than a creative mind with a powerful idea and the passion to make it a reality. Great ideas can bring about life-changing inventions, such as the cure for polio, the car, the internet, and the plane. Ideas can bring about game-changing technological disruption, such as railroads, radio, and smartphones. Some ideas even bring about massive social change, as did the concept of granting micro-loans to women in developing countries.

Think back over your morning. Did anything annoy you? Was there something that didn't work properly? What frustrated you because it was inefficient, poorly designed, or difficult to use? These are all excellent places to begin identifying problems that may turn out to be opportunities for entrepreneurial thinking.

After you've identified a few problems from your morning, complete this exercise:

- Write down the problem in a simple sentence of 15 or fewer words.

- Then write down for whom (besides you) this is a problem and why.

- If this is a massive problem, it may be too large to tackle as one piece. Break it down into its component parts and work on each part separately.

Explore the web for inspiration. One of my favorite inspiration sources is TEDTalks.

What if . . . .?
Yale professors and entrepreneurs Barry Nalebuff and Ian Ayres have written the blueprint for using simple methods and everyday ingenuity to come up with clever solutions to the world's problems. Their book *Why Not?* demonstrates how to generate great ideas by challenging a "that's just the way things are done around here" attitude with an open-minded "What if . . . ?" approach to problem-solving. I have adapted some of their structured methods of idea generation and problem-solving for our use in this book.

Problem-solving is a great way to look for ideas. It is a form of creativity and self-expression, allowing us to communicate and connect with one another. The satisfaction of helping people find a better way of doing things can be extremely rewarding.

Structured Problem-Solving Method #1: What Would Oprah Do?

Imagine you are Oprah Winfrey and have unlimited resources to solve problems. You are rich, have plenty of time, and access to the greatest geniuses in the world. How would you solve the problems listed below? Be bold. This is "blue-sky" brainstorming. Don't judge your ideas. Don't look for a realistic solution. Remove as many constraints as possible on your imagination:

Problem #1: The only time I can go to the gym is at lunchtime and it is always very crowded.

Problem #2: People in developing countries lack adequate and affordable health care.

Problem #3: (Use one of the problems you experienced this morning.)

Write down your ideas. Did you come up with some great blue-sky solutions?

Oprah Winfrey
Dave J Hogan/Getty Images

Structured Problem-Solving Method #2: The 99% Solution[66]

It's creative and fun to come up with solutions when we take money, time, and skill out of the equation. But as practical entrepreneurs, we know that there are real constraints in the marketplace. There's no point in bringing a product to market that will be affordable only to the handful of people in the world who are wealthy beyond measure.

We need to figure out a way to get most of the solution at a fraction of the cost. Nalebuff and Ayers call this "the 99% solution." Can you think of ways to get 99 percent of the benefits for only 1 percent of the cost? For example, if Oprah wants to create new programs for her TV network, she has the financial ability to hire well-known and expensive scriptwriters, producers, and actors. How can we get almost the same result at a fraction of the cost?

What if we try this: A young filmmaker has a great concept for a new film or TV show, but lacks deep-pocketed financial backing. Could he achieve 99 percent of the benefits for only 1 percent (or so) of the cost if he filmed his talented-but-not-yet-famous actor friends in a bare-bones film set with a green screen, and then created video episodes for the web? What other ideas can you suggest?

Structured Problem-Solving Method #3: Where Else Could This Work?
Another way to generate great ideas is to start with a solution that is working in one context, analyze why it's working, and then see if it could work in a completely different context.

Here's an example of a solution to the problem of high energy bills. In order to conserve electricity, many companies have installed motion-sensitive lights that turn off in five minutes if there's been no movement in the room.

What are the components that make this solution work?:

- The need to conserve valuable and expensive resources (electricity).

- The benefits of using the resource (it allows us to see in the dark).

- An understanding of human nature (many of us simply forget to turn off lights).

Could this solution work in a different context, such as safe drinking water, medicines, or gasoline?

Structured Problem-Solving Method #4: Would Flipping It Work?
Sometimes changing the order of key words in a sentence can help generate great ideas and creative solutions to completely different problems. Rearranging and flipping some of the words can produce startling images that are full of potential.

Here is a solution to a chronic urban problem: Public transportation reduces air pollution in cities.

What images do you see when the key words in the solution above are rearranged?

Air transportation in *cities* reduces *public* pollution.

What images do you see when we use the *antonym* of a key word in the sentence?

Public air *increases* cities in pollution transportation.

Try rearranging more key words and be open to the ideas you discover.

Spending Your Ideas

Ideas, like money, represent value only when they are "spent." Generating ideas is not a straightforward, sequential process, where one idea at a time pops into your head. Ideas and opportunities are flying in and out of your mind constantly. Some are acted upon, while others are put into the "maybe another time" file. Don't throw out any of your ideas. When your inspiration is having a dry spell, read through them all again. Timing is everything; only when the right factors are aligned can the arts entrepreneur "spend" the idea and turn it into a new venture.[67]

Kickstarter founder Perry Chen wondered if there was a way to know whether or not anyone would buy tickets to a show *before* he went to the expense of mounting a production. He asked: "What if we flip the usual model? Let's sell tickets *first*, and stage a show only if there's enough of a market." From this creative problem-solving approach, he launched the online crowdfunding site Kickstarter in 2009.[68] Users define a specific project, set up rewards for contributors, and announce a dollar target with a deadline for raising the money. If they don't meet their target, they get nothing.[69]

Crowdsourcing: A Revolution in Problem-Solving

The business world is eagerly embracing the benefits of weaving together the masses of humanity linked by the internet into a productive—and mostly unpaid—problem-solving workforce. Online communities share their knowledge, give support, and participate in the development of products and services that they care about. From crowd-generated ad campaigns to online record labels that let the fans sign the artists, crowdsourcing has given well-deserved dignity to the concept of amateurism.[70]

In the music world, the idea of crowdsourcing and crowdfunding are excellent examples of collective problem-solving. Crowdfunding used to be pretty simple. Artists, inventors, and filmmakers posted their ideas, and funders chipped in a few bucks to make something happen. Kickstarter was the cornerstone. In its first three years, the site helped launch more than 25,000 projects.[71]

Crowdfunding today is more than simply an innovative approach to income generation. It can help music professionals and arts organizations solve problems by creating opportunities to develop new audiences, test new ways of working, and generate advocacy and PR opportunities. In Belfast, the Oh Yeah Music Centre used Indiegogo to raise much-needed funds to refurbish its heavily used main gig space and rehearsal rooms. Even more importantly for the Center's growth, the project had two development aims. First, the organization launched a membership plan with frequent-user rewards as a means to encourage visitors to come back to Oh Yeah more frequently. Second, it offered rewards to corporate backers, such as an annual sponsorship package, in order to raise its profile as a venue to rent for private events.[72]

Threadless has found success in using the artistic crowd to solve the problem of finding great T-shirt designs. Artists submit their designs through the Threadless website, the community of users rates each design, and the top scoring designs are printed and sold. The winning artists can profit handsomely from their designs.[73]

Pick The Band is an online record label that solves the problem of how to involve fans in new band development. While the name may be a bit misleading—the fans only come into the picture after "a team of industry veterans" actually picks the band in an online audition process—the fans get to select the single, design the artwork, and make the video.[74]

In all of these examples, one sees a community of collective problem-solvers sharing knowledge for the pure pleasure of creating something from which they and others will benefit.[75]

Hands-On Problem-Solving for the Music Industry

Try to turn these "problems" into opportunities using the creative thinking work you've just done:

- In today's music marketplace, many people feel music should be free. Artists and the people who support them are scrambling to adjust to this new environment.

- The game-changing benefits of digital technologies have provided opportunities for every artist in the world to have a global presence. This is great for artists and for fans who want to discover new music. But it creates a challenging, crowded, and noisy marketplace in which artists are struggling to be heard. Some people say there is too much music available and it's impossible for anyone to separate signal from noise, sort through it all, and find music they love.

- There is increasing pressure on artists to tour in order to compensate for less revenue from recorded music sales. With live performance being one of the few consistently strong areas of the business, bands must find a delicate balance between risking over-exposure by appearing in a market too often, while keeping their ticket prices appropriate for their fans.

Using the skills and techniques you've learned earlier in the chapter, start with this industry challenge and generate ideas to solve it.

Artist acquisitions are disappointingly unprofitable more often than profitable . . . At an early stage, we have to make instinctive decisions because there is typically insufficient market feedback to rely on . . . Therefore, the successful signings must produce such a windfall that they subsidize those that are unprofitable.

(James Diener, CEO-President of A&M/Octone Records)[76]

Step 1: Restate the problem in ten words (or fewer) and write it down.

Step 2: Imagine you have unlimited resources to solve it. Apply blue-sky thinking to come up with great ideas. "What would Oprah do?"

Step 3: Apply the 99% solution. How can you solve most of the problem with only a fraction of the resources?

Step 4: Are there solutions to this general type of problem in any other industry that could be translated to the music industry?

Step 5: Try rearranging the words in your Step 4 solutions to stimulate your imagination.

Step 6: Try to solve the problem by comparing it to something unusual. Pull apart and recombine the essential elements, and look for unexpected connections and new relationships.

The music industry has abundant opportunities for entrepreneurial thinkers. What areas of the industry interest you the most? What are the problems you see in that sector? Use the skills and techniques you learned in this chapter to tackle one or two specific issues that you think may have the potential to grow into a business opportunity.

SPOTLIGHT ON . . . ANDREW CYR AND THE METROPOLIS ENSEMBLE[77]

Critics, musicians, and fans alike bemoan the death of classical music. But couldn't these times also be viewed as a tremendous growth opportunity for reaching new audiences and expanding the boundaries of our art form?

(Andrew Cyr, founder, Metropolis Ensemble)[78]

The idea for creating a chamber orchestra devoted to contemporary classical music came to Andrew Cyr in 2004. Cyr, a musician and conductor, was attending the opening night of a performance art installation. He was astonished at the number of young New Yorkers who clearly had an appetite for the arts. What was it about a gallery opening that attracted such an enthusiastic crowd? Why didn't classical music attract these same young people to attend classical music concerts?[79]

When he compared the two experiences, Cyr realized that gallery openings were opportunities for casual social interaction, eating, and drinking as well as an exchange of contemporary ideas about art and society. Classical concerts, on the other hand, required respectful silence from its audiences, with very little chance for mingling and socializing, and not very much new music.

Cyr's own professional experiences pointed to a related problem: The current classical music industry did not provide a supportive environment for talented emerging composers and artists devoted to creating and performing contemporary classical music. He wondered if there was a way to connect both these challenges and satisfy an audience hungry for cutting-edge art.

For an entrepreneur, identifying unmet needs in the marketplace is the first step. While most people saw only problems for the future of classical music, Cyr saw the potential in it. "Why not upend the status quo and try something new?" he thought.

Cyr's question gave birth to the Metropolis Ensemble, a professional chamber orchestra and ensemble devoted to broadening the audience for contemporary classical music. It began with Cyr's focus on finding creative solutions to fill the needs of audiences. This in itself was a revolutionary concept, as most classical ensembles take the "if we play it they will come" approach to their audiences.

Cyr spent the following year thinking about who, what, where, and how, arriving at the vision to expand the audience base for classical music and create new entry-points for young professional musicians and composers. His idea was that classical music could encourage social interaction just as rock 'n' roll does, without the formal trappings of a traditional concert experience. He spent the next year asking for advice from professionals from a diversity of fields to find collaborators who shared the same vision.

First, Cyr moved the performance stage to non-traditional venues like the nightclub Le Poisson Rouge in Manhattan. Non-traditional venues provide a more casual social environment where young audiences can enjoy eating, drinking, and watching the performance at the same time.

Next, he decided to set very affordable ticket prices in order to attract his target audience: the young arts enthusiasts.

Third, Cyr sought funding from private foundations and government arts organizations to launch the Metropolis Ensemble. According to him, for a nonprofit organization, finding enough supporters is the "life-blood to survival." He described the Metropolis' supporters as a gathering of people who come from different walks of life, not just other musicians or his friends. When asked how he managed to persuade people to support his innovative concept, he replied: "Asking for support is not about persuading anyone. It's just framing what you are doing in a way that resonates with an individual's values and passions."

Metropolis has successfully transformed the relationship between music, artists, and audiences with its new model for classical music. Esa-Pekka Salonen, the New York Philharmonic 2015–18 Composer-in-Residence, described the Metropolis Ensemble as "a great addition to the US music scene." John Corigliano, a Pulitzer Prize-winning composer, considers Cyr and his Metropolis Ensemble "the future of what we know as classical music."[80]

Cyr possesses traits that are common among successful entrepreneurs, such as creativity, determination, and perseverance. What makes him really different from others is his deep commitment to the quality of life and education of schoolchildren in his New York City community. One of Metropolis' projects is collaboration with the TEAK Fellowship, an organization that helps talented students from low-income families succeed at top high schools and colleges. Another Metropolis project is aimed at helping young composers hone their craft and gain exposure to the public, producers, and the larger music community.

Launching and sustaining a new venture takes a lot of hard work, and sometimes it helps to know that your efforts are appreciated. Working late one night in 2011, Cyr received an email from Avner Dorman, one of the composers on the Metropolis roster. Metropolis' first studio album had just been nominated for a Grammy in the "Best Instrumental Soloist with Orchestra" category.[81]

When asked whether the nomination changed his vision for the Metropolis, Cyr said:

> It changes both everything and nothing. It definitely says to the world at large that what the Metropolis Ensemble is doing is respected and recognized on a national platform. This really helps our composers and performers and amplifies the reach of our mission. It also has given our organization, which is young and emerging, instant credibility and fantastic branding, especially among those who are less familiar with classical music. Does it lead directly to new opportunities—perhaps not—but it does open many new doors and it will be forever part of our story.

Every year we see more and more people dream about founding a new business. Some of them actually start it, but only a few of them survive and even fewer of them finally make it a success. For Cyr, communication is critical to success: "The places where I've failed—and there have been many—seem to have been prompted or made worse by ineffective communication. In seeking solutions, the path has been always to understand how the failure occurred, and to find a way to communicate to others that you have learned how and why you made the mistakes in the first place, and that you've found a way forward."

There are several factors that make Cyr and the Metropolis Ensemble successful: a creative environment, an accurate identification of opportunity, innovative practices to fill the unmet needs in the classical music industry, and a "Why not *us*?" attitude that liberates them to try new things. For Cyr, a revolutionary in the world of contemporary classical music, the Metropolis Ensemble and its young, enthusiastic audiences are proof that there is a vibrant future ahead.

Pause and Reflect

What was the biggest reason for Cyr's failures? What did he change in order to learn from his mistakes?

So far, we've constructed a definition of *entrepreneur* that includes generating great ideas, bold thinking, an appetite for upending the status quo, an inspiration-centered approach to innovation, economic value, a growth mindset, and the ability to learn from failure. Now let's look at the value of entrepreneurial thinking for *your* life's mission.

WHO AM I? FINDING YOUR OWN VOICE AS A MUSIC PROFESSIONAL

Strive not to be a success, but rather to be of value.

(Albert Einstein, inventor and scientist)

Your Personal Mission

A personal mission is a short statement outlining what makes life meaningful for you and how you will focus your energy on it to create a sustainable life. How can you discover your mission? Start by noticing the things that are important to you *beyond* music. The goal is to look at yourself as a whole person, not just your musical self. Your list might include teaching, a spiritual path, family, your health, or your community activism. Whatever is important to you beyond music will allow you to fulfill your mission, even when you aren't making music. When you lead with your mission, you will be acting in the world as your authentic self. This will make you more powerful and more fulfilled.[82]

The following step-by-step guide adapted from Think Simple Now, an online personal development community, will help you get started in crafting your mission statement. While you're working on this, please keep in mind the following observation:

Writing or reviewing a [personal] mission statement changes you because it forces you to think through your priorities deeply, carefully, and to align your behavior with your beliefs. (Stephen Covey, author of *7 Habits of Highly Effective People*)[83]

A personal mission consists of three parts:

What do I want to do?

Who do I want to help?

What is the result? What value will I create?

Steps to Creating Your Personal Mission Statement

Step 1: The Nine Questions Exercise

Find a place where you will not be interrupted. Turn off your phone. Write down your answers to each question below, quickly and without editing:

1. What activities make you lose track of time?

2. What makes you feel great about yourself?

3. What qualities do you admire most in someone who inspires you?

4. What do people typically ask you for help in?

5. What would you regret not fully doing, being, or having in your life?

6. What were some challenges, difficulties, and hardships you've overcome or are in the process of overcoming? How did you do it?

7. What social or political causes do you strongly believe in or connect with?

8. How could you use your passions and values to serve and contribute to that cause?

9. What are your highest values? Select five from the list below and prioritize the words in order of importance.[84]

Achievement	Fitness	Passion
Adventure	Friendship	Performance
Beauty	Giving service	Play
Challenge	Health	Productivity
Comfort	Honesty	Primary relationship
Creativity	Independence	Respect
Curiosity	Intimacy	Security
Education	Joy	Spirituality
Empowerment	Leadership	Success
Environment	Learning	Time freedom
Family	Love	Variety
Financial freedom	Motivation	Other

Step 2
List action words that are meaningful to you.

Examples: accomplish, empower, encourage, improve, help, give, guide, inspire, integrate, master, motivate, nurture, organize, produce, promote, travel, spread, share, satisfy, understand, teach, write.

Step 3
Based on your answers to the nine questions above, list everything and everyone that you believe you can help.

Step 4
Identify your end goal. How will the "who or what" from Step 3 benefit from what you can do for them?

Step 5
Combine Steps 1–4 into two to three sentences. This is the first draft of your personal mission statement.

Find Your Own Voice

Today you are You, that is truer than true. There is no one alive who is Youer than You.

(Dr. Seuss)[85]

Mark Simpson is a UK composer and clarinetist, and a champion of contemporary music. In 2006, he won both the BBC Young Musician of the Year for his performance as a clarinetist, and the BBC Proms/*Guardian* Young Composer of the Year. He pursues these two careers simultaneously and is equally successful in both of them. Starting in 2016, he will serve a five-year stint as BBC Philharmonic Composer in Association.[86]

Describing some of the challenges that he faces in his process, Simpson explains: "I have a tendency to intellectualize what I do, to try to understand the process, what chords I use when, and what I want the listener to feel. When I get into those sorts of states, I tend to close up." So he turns for help to his colleagues, who tell him to trust in his instincts. "That kind of affirmation is really helpful," he states. "There are times when I need to listen to that voice, and know that I can do what I do, just by doing it."[87]

Speak Your Own Truth. Find Your Own Value

What is the value of your music or of any art you create? In general, value is defined by the opinion of the marketplace. Even if only one person is willing to buy your work, the work is considered to have value to society.[88]

Money is the physical representation of value in a capitalist society. There are ways to be "paid" other than money, but musicians have expenses, just like anyone else. The debilitating notion that you shouldn't be paid—since you are getting "free publicity" or a free dinner—does not serve anyone working in the creative economy. Artists should be paid with cash for their art if it is valued by society.[89]

Pause and Reflect

1. If you were paid in actual cash, what do you believe is the value of your music?[90]
2. Are the rates you set for yourself—including your time spent creating, the creative product, or service itself—what society believes its value to be or are your rates what you believe society thinks it is worth?
3. How do your own value judgments about the art you make, and the prices you set, affect society's opinion of your art?

The late *New York Times* writer and author David Carr taught a journalism course called Press Play at Boston University's communication school. Carr was an exceptional writer with a unique voice who generously shared his communication gifts with his students. In a class called Voice Lessons, he sought to teach students "how to quit sounding like everyone else and begin sounding like . . . yourself." Students were told to think about their personal experiences, things that happened in their lives. "Talk about those with a friend who can help you tease out the threads," he advised. "Your friends will say 'these are things that you have that no one else does, and you should channel that.'"[91] Carr's advice to his journalism students is applicable to anyone in any field who is trying to communicate something they feel deeply to other human beings.

You as Entrepreneur

Which description of "entrepreneur" suits you best?

- I think I would be most comfortable using my entrepreneurial skills as an employee of a company that was doing something I really believed in.

- I am passionate about a particularly daunting social problem and want to make meaning by creating and managing a venture to achieve sustainable social change.

- I want to make meaning by creating a venture that measures performance in profit and return rather than in social capital.

- I am firmly planted in the nonprofit/charity/ Public Benefit Organization (PBO) mindset and want to make meaning in the new venture I launch, but I'm not a social entrepreneur.

Kate Tempest
David Wolff-Patrick/Redferns/Getty Images

Believe in Yourself

Every business is about selling something. People have to believe in you to buy your product or service. And before others can believe in you, you have to believe in yourself. Developing self-belief, and cultivating it through both good and bad times, can be deeply motivating.[92]

At some point in life, we face the challenge of finding our own voice. Here are three stories that may have meaning for you.

Britain's Triple Threat

Kate Tempest is a young south London playwright, poet, rapper, and cross-genre talent who has a growing and fervent global following. Her boundary-crossing work has won some extraordinary awards. Her debut album, *Everybody Down*, was named one of the Mercury Prize's "12 Albums of the Year" (2014).[93] Each track on the album correlates with a chapter in her debut novel, *The Bricks That Built the Houses*. Her 2014 poetry collection, *Hold Your Own*, was described by *The Guardian* as "acute and insightful poems that lodge in the ear and sear themselves on the vision."[94] One year earlier, she received the £5,000 (US$7,446) Ted Hughes Award for innovation in poetry with "Brand New Ancients," an hour-long "spoken story" with orchestral backing. Tempest is the first poet under 40 ever to win the Hughes Award (she was 26 at the time).[95]

Some of Tempest's poems are deeply moving, autobiographical tales about being bullied at school and coming of age as a lesbian. "I was a weird gay woman in a homophobic, misogynistic culture. It took me a long time to be able—rather than just trying to hide all those parts of myself—to realize that actually it's OK."[96]

Tempest was thrilled to get a record deal (with Big Dada), and was astonished that people were listening to it on Spotify "because I've been trying to smash my way into the music industry for the best part of 12 years."[97]

Born Kate Calvert, she took the name "Tempest" because of how she feels onstage. "Her performances are incendiary," said singer Billy Bragg, who in 2010 invited her to participate in the Glastonbury (UK) performing arts festival. "She wasn't just singing or rapping. She was telling you stuff like her life depended on your understanding what she was saying."[98]

Stradivarius violin
PHILIPPE LOPEZ/AFP/Getty Images

Every Instrument Has a Voice

Georgian violinist Lisa Batiashvili feels the violin world has an unhealthy obsession with the instruments of Antonio Stradivari. "These great violins have so much personality. It's either in conflict or in harmony [with the violinist]." To young performers who feel that not having a first-rate instrument will hold back their career, she advises: "It's not about holding a Strad in your hand. It's about finding your own voice."[99]

Playing with Joy Again

The lessons from this sports story will resonate with many in the high-pressure music world.

As a Stanford University (US) soccer forward, Christen Press felt smothered by her apparent need to prove that she was a star. She had convinced herself that she had to live up to everyone's expectations by scoring every goal and leading her team to victory. "I hate soccer, I really hate soccer," she wrote on her personal blog. "There is just so much PRESSURE. It's making me miserable."[100]

When her league, Women's Professional Soccer, ceased operations in 2012, Press knew she had to get away from the win-at-all-costs American sports culture. She moved to Sweden to play with their

Kristen Press soccer
Mike Zarrilli/Getty Images Sport

women's pro league. Far from home, she could take a step back and examine her life. The internal voice that plagued her with self-doubt began to get softer. "And so, away from everyone, with nobody watching, I learned that my best is really good enough," she said. "I found my love of the game again. It was fun again."[101]

Press' alternative route saved her sports career but—more importantly—it revived her passion for the game. "It allowed me to play with joy," she said, "and that's the most important thing in the end."[102]

Tools for Building a Sustainable Life

Andrew Simonet, author of the essential book *Making Your Life as an Artist*, recommends repeating the following affirmations regularly to keep you on the path of building a sustainable life:[103]

- "I am building an artistic *life*, not an artistic *career*, step by step, thinking long-term and staying responsive to changing circumstances."

- "The success of other musicians is good for me. And mutual artistic support is worth more than money."

- "The world is hungry for noncommercial experiences, for moments of focus, connection, and insight instead of the profit-driven distraction provided by the entertainment industry."

- "I schedule non-work time in my day, my week, and my year. This is essential to my wellbeing and artistic growth."

- "With calm and focus, I work toward the art, the values and the life that I believe in."[104]

Opportunities Ahead

Where do you see opportunity for personal and professional growth as you begin to think of yourself as a 21st century music professional?

CONCLUSION

Entrepreneurial thinking and creative problem-solving are the tools you need to visualize the abundant opportunities that exist within the music industry. Music may be an emotional touchstone for all of us, but it cannot survive as an industry if people aren't willing to reach into their wallets and support it. This reality contributes to the constant struggle between music as art vs. music as commerce.

Learning to think like an entrepreneur can have an enormous impact on your life and the economic vitality of your community. Entrepreneurial thinking will be useful even if you don't use it to start a new venture. Every day we face problems large and small that need creative solutions. Having a growth mindset will help you be fluent and flexible in looking at the world in a new light.

Talking Back: Class Discussion

What has helped each of you find your own voice? Consider how you've changed in the past five years. What contributed to those changes? Can you identify areas where you need ongoing support in understanding your personal mission?

NOTES

1 Linda Essig, "The Ouroboros 2: What IS Arts Entrepreneurship Anyway?" *Creative Infrastructure*, March 13, 2014.
2 Eric Schurenberg, "What's an Entrepreneur? The Best Answer Ever," *Inc.*, January 9, 2012, www.inc.com/eric-schurenberg/the-best-definition-of-entepreneurship.html.
3 "About Us," *British Council*, www.britishcouncil.org (accessed May 12, 2016).
4 "Definition of a Creative Entrepreneur," *British Council: Poland*, www.britishcouncil.pl/en/programmes/arts/yce-competition/definition-creative-entrepreneur (accessed May 12, 2016).
5 William R. Pendergast, "Entrepreneurial Contexts and Traits of Entrepreneurs," presented at the 2004 ECI Conference on Teaching Entrepreneurship to Engineering Students, Monterey, CA, USA, http://dc.engconfintl.org/teaching/8 (accessed May 26, 2016).
6 Schurenberg, "What's an Entrepreneur?"
7 Alexander Osterwalder and Yves Pigneur, *Business Model Generation* (Hoboken, NJ: Wiley, 2010), 14.
8 "Live Nation Inc. Company Information," *New York Times*, topics.nytimes.com/top/news/business/companies/live-nation-inc/index.html (accessed May 12, 2016).
9 Ibid.
10 David Moore, Katerina Hadzi-Miceva, and Nilda Bullain, "A Comparative Overview of Public Benefit Status in Europe," *International Journal of Not-for-Profit Law*, 11(1) (2008), www.icnl.org/research/journal/vol11iss1/special_1.htm#_ftnref1 (accessed May 12, 2016).
11 "Interview with Tatiana Rais, Winner of the British Council Young Creative Entrepreneur Award 2014," Aesthetica, July 21, 2014, htttp://wwwaestheticamagazine.com/interview-tatiana-rais-winner-british-council-young-creative-entrepreneur-award-2014 (accessed May 12, 2016).
12 Ibid.
13 "Creative Economy: People —Tatiana Rais, YCE Winner," *British Council*, www.creativeconomy.britishcouncil.org/people/tatiana-rais (accessed May 12, 2016).
14 "Philanthropy," *Google Dictionary*, www.google.com/search?q=define+philanthropy&ie=utf-8&oe=utf-8 (accessed May 12, 2016).
15 "Global Campaigning for a Culture of Philanthropy," *Nexus*, www.nexusyouthsummit.org/programs/campaign (accessed May 12, 2016).
16 Ibid.
17 "Non-governmental Organizations, United Nations Rule of Law," www.unrol.org/article.aspx?article_id=23 (accessed May 12, 2016).
18 Ibid.
19 "Top 10 NGO's from the 100 Best List 2012 by *The Global Journal*," Miratel, July 27, 2012, www.miratelinc.com/blog/top-10-ngos-from-the-100-best-list-2012-by-the-global-journal (accessed May 12, 2016).
20 Ibid.
21 Ibid.
22 "Home," *Wikimedia Foundation*, https://wikimediafoundation.org/wiki/Home (accessed May 12, 2016).
23 "What Is a Social Entrepreneur," *Ashoka*, https://www.ashoka.org/social_entrepreneur (accessed May 26, 2016).
24 J. Gregory Dees, "The Meaning of 'Social Entrepreneurship,'" Stanford University Center for Social Innovation, October 31, 1998, http://csi.gsb.stanford.edu/the-meaning-social-entrepreneurship (accessed May 12, 2016).

25 What Is a Social Entrepreneur."

26 Ibid.

27 Dees, "The Meaning of 'Social Entrepreneurship.'"

28 Ibid.

29 Naomi Doraisamy, "Six Qualities of Social Entrepreneurs," *The Borgen Project*, May 2013, www.borgen project.org/6-qualities-of-social-entrepreneurs (accessed May 12, 2016).

30 Guy Kawaski, *The Art of the Start* (New York: Penguin, 2004), 19–23.

31 Ibid.

32 Ibid.

33 Ibid.

34 Ibid.

35 Ibid.

36 Jason Potts, "Why Creative Industries Matter to Economic Revolution," *Economics of Innovation and New Technology*, 18(7) (2009): 663–73.

37 Frank Rose, "The Father of Creative Destruction," *Wired Magazine*, Issue 10.03, March 2002, www.archive. wired.com/wired/archive/10.03/schumpeter.html (accessed May 12, 2016).

38 Ibid.

39 Gross Domestic Product—an indicator of a country's economic health.

40 "Executive Summary: The Economic Impact of the Creative Industries in the Americas," report prepared by Oxford Economics for the British Council, IDN, and Organization of American States, 2013.

41 James Lichtenberg, Christopher Woock, and Mary Wright, "Ready to Innovate," The Conference Board, Research report R-1424-08-RR, www.americansforthearts.org/sites/default/files/pdf/information_services/ research/policy_roundtable/ReadytoInnovateFull.pdf (accessed May 12, 2016).

42 "2015 Arts Entrepreneurship Awards Honorees," *Fractured Atlas*, www.fracturedatlas.org/site/blog/2015/ 02/23/2015-arts-entrepreneurship-awards-honorees/#TBVE (accessed May 12, 2016).

43 Seth Lepore, "Facing Facts: Artist Have to Be Entrepreneurs," https://www.facebook.com/erobinsonstudio/ posts/10153123403536195 (accessed May 12, 2016).

44 Jason Tseng, "Up Close with Arts Entrepreneurs: Groupmuse," *Fractured Atlas*, March 2, 2015, www.fracture datlas.org/site/blog/2015/03/02/up-close-with-arts-entrepreneurs-groupmuse (accessed May 12, 2016).

45 Ibid.

46 Ibid.

47 "About," *Groupmuse*, www.groupmuse.com/about (accessed May 12, 2016).

48 Tseng, "Up Close."

49 Ibid.

50 Ibid.

51 "Arts Entrepreneurship Awards Honorees," *Fractured Atlas*, www.fracturedatlas.org/site/blog/2015/02/23/2015- arts-entrepreneurship-awards-honorees/#GM (accessed May 12, 2016).

52 Carol S. Dweck, *Mindset: The New Psychology of Success* (New York: Ballantine Books, 2006), 6–7.

53 James B. Stewart, "A Fearless Culture Fuels Tech," *New York Times*, June 19, 2015.

54 Andrew Simonet, *Making Your Life as an Artist* (Manitoba, Canada: Artists U, 2014), www.artistsu.org/ making/#.V0t73ddeKr8 (accessed May 28, 2016).

55 Dweck, *Mindset*, 61.

56 http://sivers.org/ff (accessed 26 May, 2016).

57 http://sivers.org/jadr (accessed 26 May, 2016).

58 Simon Cronshaw and Peter Tullin, "Intelligent Naivety," www.slideshare.net/culturelabel/culturelabel- intelligent-naivety (accessed May 12, 2016).

59 P.J.H. Schoemaker and R.E. Gunther, "The Wisdom of Deliberate Mistakes," *Harvard Business Review,* June 2006.

60 Cronshaw and Tullin, "Intelligent Naivety."

61 Michael Paulson, "A Musical Spins a Tony Loss into an Ad Opportunity, *New York Times*, June 15, 2015.

62 Daniel H. Pink, *A Whole New Mind* (New York: Riverhead Books, 2006), 51–2.

63 The table is adapted from Carolyn Hopper, 'Practicing College Study Skills: Strategies for Success', 2009, http://capone.mtsu.edu/studskl (accessed May 26, 2016).

64 Ibid, 138.

65 Herb Meyers and Richard Gerstman. *Creativity—Unconventional Wisdom from 20 Accomplished Minds* (New York: Palgrave Macmillan, 2007), 122.

66 Barry Nalebuff and Ian Ayers, *Why Not?* (Boston: Harvard Business School Press, 2003), 17.

67 Cronshaw and Tullin, "Intelligent Naivety."

68 Kickstarter, "A New Way to Fund & Follow Creativity," www.kickstarter.com (accessed May 12, 2016).

69 Rob Walker, "The Trivialities and Transcendence of Kickstarter," *New York Times*, August 5, 2011.

70 Jeff Howe, *Crowdsourcing: Why the Power of the Crowd Is Driving the Future of Business* (New York: Three Rivers Press, 2009), 8, 14.

71 Lisa Waananen, "Three Years of Kickstarter Projects," *New York Times*, April 30, 2012, www.nytimes.com/interactive/2012/04/30/technology/three-years-of-kickstarter-projects.html (accessed May 12, 2016).

72 Oonagh Murphy, "What Can Crowdfunding Offer the Arts Beyond Money?" *The Guardian*, February 5, 2015, www.theguardian.com/culture-professionals-network/2015/feb/05/crowdfunding-arts-beyond-money (accessed May 12, 2016).

73 "How It Works," *Threadless*, www.threadless.com/how-it-works (accessed May 12, 2016).

74 "About the Label," *Pick The Band*, www.picktheband.com/index.php?cn=frontend/learnmore&id=the_label (accessed May 12, 2016).

75 Ibid.

76 Anita Elberse and Elie Ofek, "Octone Records," Harvard Business School Case #N9-507-082, July 13, 2007, 3.

77 This section by Yifan Qin and Catherine Radbill.

78 Information for this profile is based on interviews between Andrew Cyr and Yifan Qin in March and April 2011.

79 Bob Keyes, "Andrew Cyr Is Having a Classical Gas in NYC," *Portland Press Herald/Maine Sunday Telegram*, April 18, 2010, www.pressherald.com/life/classical-gas_2010-04-18.html (accessed May 12, 2016).

80 "About," *Metropolis Ensemble*, www.yciw.net/1/metropolis-ensemble (accessed May 12, 2016).

81 Katie Colaneri, "Andrew Cyr, Who Serves Hoboken's Our Lady of Grace Church as Music Director, Is up for a Grammy Award for Recording of Avner Dorman Concerto Made with His Metropolis Ensemble," *NJ.com*, December 4, 2010, www.nj.com/news/jjournal/hoboken/index.ssf?/base/news-2/1291447546263310.xml (accessed May 12, 2016).

82 Ibid.

83 Tina Su, "Life on Purpose: 15 Questions to Discover Your Personal Mission," *Think Simple Now*, www.thinksimplenow.com/happiness/life-on-purpose-15-questions-to-discover-your-personal-mission (accessed May 12, 2016).

84 Ibid.

85 "Dr. Seuss, Quotes, Quotable Quote," *Goodreads*, www.goodreads.com/quotes/3160-today-you-are-you-that-is-truer-than-true-there (accessed May 12, 2016).

86 Gavin Dixon, "Manchester International Festival: Mark Simpson discusses *The Immortal*," *Bachtrack*, May 1, 2015, http://bachtrack.com/interview-mark-simpson-immortal-manchester-international-festival (accessed May 12, 2016).

87 Ibid.

88 Heather Fenoughty, "What Is the Value of Your Music?" *Music Business UK*, March 19, 2009, www.heather-fenoughty.com/music-business/what-is-the-value-of-your-music (accessed May 12, 2016).

89 Ibid.

90 Ibid.

91 David Carr, "A Writer's Last Word on Journalism," *New York Times*, February 15, 2015.

92 Cronshaw and Tullin, "Intelligent Naivety."

93 The Mercury Prize promotes the best of UK and Irish music and the artists who produce it. This is done primarily through the celebration of the 12 "Albums of the Year," a shortlist from which an overall winner is selected.

94 Sarah Crown, "*Hold Your Own* Review—Powerful Poetry from Kate Tempest," *The Guardian*, October 31, 2014, www.theguardian.com/stage/2014/oct/31/hold-your-own-kate-tempest-poetry-collection-review (accessed May 12, 2016).

95 Sam Wolfson, "Kate Tempest: The Performance Poet Who Can't Be Ignored," *The Guardian*, April 10, 2013, www.theguardian.com/books/2013/apr/10/kate-tempest-performance-poet-cant-be-ignored (accessed May 12, 2016).

96 Rachel Donadio, "Kate Tempest, A British Triple Threat, Crosses the Pond," *New York Times*, March 6, 2015.

97 Ibid.

98 Donadio, "Kate Tempest."

99 Corinna da Fonseca-Wollheim, "Politics Is Personal, and Professional: Lisa Batiashvili on Violins, Ukraine and Valery Gergiev," *New York Times*, January 31, 2015.

100 Juliet Macur, "Christen Press Went Abroad and Found a Place on the U.S. Team," *New York Times*, June 11, 2015.

101 Ibid.

102 Ibid.

103 Simonet, *Making Your Life as an Artist.*

104 Ibid.

CHAPTER 3

Developing the 21st Century Global Music Professional

CHAPTER OVERVIEW

In this chapter you will learn how global music professionals are nurtured and developed. Classical rock star Lang Lang serves as an excellent example of a 21st century global music professional. You will be introduced to each major section of the music industry to learn how it contributes. Four global artists are profiled so that you can see how many ways there are of developing global music professionals. Canada is spotlighted as a country that is exemplary in nurturing and supporting its artists.

KEY TERMS

Music publisher

Licensing

A&R

Break an artist

Artist manager

Booking agent

Promoter/presenter

Talent buyer

Collecting society

NAMM

Canada's MAPL system

WHAT IS A GLOBAL MUSIC PROFESSIONAL?

Global music professionals in the 21st century are defined by the "hyphen." For example: Lang Lang is a pianist-cultural ambassador-fragrance developer-philanthropist. You may be a composer-music festival organizer.

As you can see, the definition of "music professional" today is fluid. You may feel certain that you know precisely what your musical path will be. And perhaps that will be so. But it is much more likely that you will find new paths to explore that are compelling and intriguing. Whether you attribute this to artistic development, career mobility, or curiosity about life, being open to opportunities is a vital mind-set for today's global artist.

The path to becoming a global music professional was never meant to be straight. It is up to you to define your life's mission and take action to carry it out. You will decide how to chart a path to sustainability, whether in the practice room or the record label boardroom—or both. The creative industries are inspired by and borrow from each other. You will explore other art forms and incorporate new points of view into your own work.

Artist-entrepreneurs understand that making business decisions is a creative endeavor. Music-business entrepreneurs know that their work is crucial to the production of new art.

"It Took Me Ten Years to Be an Overnight Success"

The desire to be a household name comes with a steep price, yet many young artists are focused here. The traditional measures of worldwide recognition include vast numbers of ticket sales, record sales, digital downloads, branding sponsorships, music commissions, winning a performance competition, performing in famous venues, touring the world, owning an indie record label, and managing Top 40 artists. We all know people who have reached this level of renown.

The reality is that today there are far fewer Artist and Repertoire (A&R) people looking for new talent, and far fewer people are being signed. Even though many musicians are waiting for something to happen, in the 21st century one needs to *make* something happen.

They say it takes ten years of dedicated, focused work to become an overnight success. The public becomes aware of artists when they burst into the mainstream, but rarely do we know about the rejected demos and bad business deals that litter an artist's uncertain path to the global stage.[1]

The Need for Professional Partnerships

No one is going to knock on your door and turn you into an overnight success. That doesn't happen. But there *are* people who will partner with you to move your work forward. And you already know many of them.[2]

Creative entrepreneurs need to find resources, connections, and audiences. You have to change the mindset that asking for help is akin to begging. There is only so much that you can do independently. Most people have no idea how many partnerships go into making an artist successful.[3]

Everyone you come into contact with is a potential partner, be they funders, presenters, music publishers, fans, or critics. When you find reliable partners—and in turn act as one to your colleagues—you have the foundation to reach your goals.

DJ Chuckie

AFP/Getty Images

A partner stands up for her own needs, while also considering the needs of the other person. Only a balanced alliance is good for everyone.[4]

As a music professional you have to build a business around yourself and take yourself to the marketplace. To do this, one needs to understand the creative economy inside-out in order to make the best decisions. Knowing how music is made, published, licensed, recorded, protected, and exploited are all required topics. Additionally, independent musicians must become fluent in venue operations, contracts, royalty payments, and ways to leverage fan relationships to maximize cash flow.[5]

If you uncouple the business side of music from the art of music, it is quite possible that you will wake up one morning to discover that you're losing money, or at best just breaking even. When your revenue streams don't cover your investments in instruments, studio time, and marketing, don't automatically blame it on the material or the market-place—it could well be your inattention to business. Copyrights, licensing, and publishing are all integral facets of the art of creating music. If you don't know how to fully monetize (make money from) your music, you will doom yourself to working a day job for the rest of your life.[6]

Workers in the creative economy thrive when their life is balanced, productive, and sustainable. Balanced means you have things in your life besides your work, like friends, family, hobbies, and community. Your life is productive when you lead with your personal mission statement. A sustainable life means you can work at what you love over the long term because you understand the business aspects of the music industry.

Clyde Sergio Narain, better known as DJ Chuckie, is a well-respected producer and DJ working in the Dutch house music scene. As a producer he's collaborated with Akon, 50 Cent, Lupe Fiasco, LMFAO, and many other artists.

Carving out a career in the music industry requires patience and a strong belief in your work, DJ Chuckie says. "Stick to your own beliefs and ideals instead of doing what you think is popular and expected of you. Stay patient and work towards becoming a more rounded artist, instead of looking to become as big as possible as soon as possible."[7]

As DJ Chuckie explains, building a strong network of contacts is an essential part of a career in music, and being visible in the music scene fosters those connections. "I go out and discover all this music and I start to meet other people who are as into it as I am," he says. "The deeper I get into the scene, the more people I meet. And you never know which people that you briefly met on the previous Saturday night will end up working with you professionally further down the line."[8]

DJ Chuckie's story shows the value of putting aside a fear of acquiring business skills. Global artists must develop an entrepreneurial mindset and understand how to see opportunities where others see only problems.

Build Your Team

The music industry functions like this:

Artist-entrepreneurs . . .	Music business entrepreneurs . . .	Music consumers . . .
↓	↓	↓
are the music creators and interpreters.	connect music creators with music consumers.	buy the music products and services.
They may be . . . songwriters, composers, arrangers, singers, orchestra members, solo performers . . .	They may be . . . artist managers, business managers, presenters, arts administrators, promoters, talent agents, booking agents, touring producers, publishers, sound engineers, rights management experts, collection society managers, digital music providers, music attorneys . . .	They may be . . . fans, audience, corporations, radio, television, digital broadcasting, film, video games, advertising agencies . . .

A global music professional draws from these (and many other) roles to create her "hyphenated" approach to a sustainable life in music. Partnerships and collaborations between these roles will ebb and flow throughout a career. Most artist-entrepreneurs find that having a team is a key element in their professional growth.

You have to *earn* your team by attracting people to your dream. They come on board to support you because they believe in you. Your team has to be confident that you are living your mission before they are inspired enough to be part of your professional life.

In the first edition of this book I frequently referred to "DIY" or "do-it-yourself" artists and entrepreneurs. I now realize that the phrase "DIY" is a disservice to the musical community. The truth is that the overwhelming majority of artist-entrepreneurs need a team of partners to help them build their music career. So, with thanks to author Dave Kusek, who coined the phrase, I will now encourage artist-entrepreneurs to participate in the "Do It With Others" (DIWO) movement.

Learn Your Craft

Artist-Entrepreneurs

Let's get the big myth out of the way first. It's impossible to have a sustainable life in music without putting in the time to learn the craft. The idea that a band breaks overnight or is discovered busking in the streets and becomes a star in a month is an enduring but misleading and romantic interpretation of reality.

For artist-entrepreneurs, there's nothing more important than learning your creative craft. Work with a teacher, coach, or mentor whose musical philosophy matches yours. Perform in public as often as possible to get invaluable feedback from your audience. Share your work, especially if it is still in-progress, and involve your audience/fans as partners. They do not expect perfection. Audiences want to be close to the creative action, so bring them into it and be open to what they have to say.

The rapid pace of music discovery today can be a double-edged sword for emerging bands and artists. A global buzz can erupt around an artist with lightning speed, making them the darlings of the social media world in a matter of days. However, the internet can thrust performers into the public spotlight long before they are ready to play a full set at the local bar, much less take on all that's required to have a solid music career.

To sustain a career over time, artist-entrepreneurs need to put in the hours honing their skills at writing great music, developing a unique sound, and playing in public. This can't be rushed. You can't cut corners. So hunker down and do the work.

Music Business-Entrepreneurs

For music business-entrepreneurs, your craft is helping artist-entrepreneurs connect with music consumers. That may sound simple, but the global music marketplace is complex. You will need to be fluent in all areas of the industry, from how to help an artist-entrepreneur hone her craft and find her unique voice to understanding how to monetize her music.

Just as importantly, you will foster an honest, trusting relationship with every artist-entrepreneur you represent or on whose behalf you work. Transparency in business actions and ethical decision-making are your two guiding lights. The music industry has for too long suffered at the hands of people who are dishonest, self-centered, and focused on profit at all costs. This will only end when music business professionals understand that they are *part* of the universe, not the center of it, and behave accordingly. Without your integrity, skill, and passion, the creative economy cannot thrive.

CREATING GLOBAL MUSIC PROFESSIONALS

Next we will take a closer look at how each major section of the music industry works to nurture and develop global artists. The information that follows can be viewed from both the artist-entrepreneur and the music business-entrepreneur perspective. Remember to be open to all the information, as it is very likely that your professional path will take you in and out of both of these worlds.

Colleges and Universities

Colleges and universities offer abundant opportunities for helping to develop entrepreneurs and musicians. In addition to formal musical and music industry study programs, there are business classes, workshops, master classes, public lectures, performances, concerts, theater, art, and, in general, a welcoming atmosphere that encourages curiosity about life. While there are degree programs and specialist schools, such as world-renowned music conservatories and entrepreneurship centers, it is entirely possible to benefit from the vast riches of these institutions as a community member or as a student.

Colleges and universities offer free or inexpensive tickets to opera, symphonic concerts, pop, rock, jazz, and chamber music events. Attend as often as you can to learn all types of music. See how professionals interact with their audiences. Notice their stage presence. Find a way to speak to performers, their managers, the concert presenter—anyone with whom you can learn more about the industry.

As a music student, you have a responsibility to get out into the community and show why the arts are important, says Joseph Pollisi, President of the Juilliard School (US). Community involvement is a crucial partnership in the development of young musicians.[9] If your school doesn't have a formal community outreach program, including gig-services, use your entrepreneurial abilities and create one.

There are music industry online resources, such as courses from the Berklee College of Music and Dave Kusek's "New Artist Model." For classical musicians, there is Musaic, a collaborative digital initiative between the New World Symphony, the Cleveland Institute of Music, the Curtis Institute of Music, the Eastman School of Music (University of Rochester), the Guildhall School of Music and Drama (London), the Manhattan School of Music, the Royal Danish Academy of Music, the San Francisco Conservatory of Music, the University of Missouri-Kansas City, and the University of Southern California. Musaic provides access to classical music instruction and conversations for students and performers alike.

Music Publishers

A music publisher collaborates with songwriters and composers to market and promote their songs, which results in exposure of songs to the public and an income stream to the composer/songwriter. Music publishers earn revenue from licensing the right (giving permission) to use an artist's songs. One of the areas of expertise that a songwriter taps into when signed to a publisher is the publisher's large network of professionals who work in the fields that use music, such as film, television, record labels, mobile phones, digital media, and advertising agencies. Music publishers will work to get the highest fee for use of their works in all media licensing deals.[10]

Music publishers "pitch" songs to record labels, movie and television producers and others who use music, then license the right to use the song and collect fees for the usage. The major functions of a music publisher include finding and supporting up-and-coming composers and songwriters; finding revenue-generating uses for the work generated by composers and songwriters; and keeping track of all monies owed by the clients who have licensed the music.[11]

Publishers often support new songwriters by providing co-writing opportunities, access to recording studios to create demos, and financial advances to help writers pay their bills so they can focus on songwriting. This type of partnership is very important to a writer's career. Co-writing in particular is helpful to young songwriters who are building a catalogue of songs, honing their professional and creative skills, and making connections to other writers in the industry.

The Recording Industry

Signing with a record label is a traditional partnership in artist development. Through A&R teams, labels help recording artists by opening the door for them to collaborate with songwriters, producers, sound mixers—all music professionals who can help an artist reach her full potential in connecting with her audience.

Ashley Newton, former President of Columbia Records US, says: "A&R in its purest form is identifying unique talent and encouraging them to dig deep and create remarkable artistry. Some artists are truly self-supporting in this respect while others require a level of expertise, resource and evangelical enthusiasm in order to realize their full potential."[12]

Labels partner with artists in every aspect of their development. Collaborations may include developing song tracks the artist has written, finding or commissioning new music, or creating a cover version of a song to show off the artist's distinct interpretation.[13]

Artists typically partner with both a manager and a lawyer in order to negotiate a recording contract. These deals have evolved quickly in the last few years due to the heavy loss of income from sagging record sales. Many record labels now offer greater upfront support to an artist in exchange for a share of revenues from a wide range of income streams.[14]

It can cost between US$500,000 and US$2 million to break (establish) an artist in a major recorded music market. Labels take the risk of investing in emerging artists through the payment of an advance, funding a recording, music video production, tour support, and promotional costs. Worldwide, the major labels combined have around 7,500 artists on their rosters. Tens of thousands more are signed to independent labels.[15]

Mini-Case Study: Lorde—Developing Young Talent

Some musicians, like violinist Anne Akiko Meyers, pianist Keith Jarrett, and pop star Justin Bieber, appear on the scene at a very young age. Ella Yelich-O'Connor, now known as Lorde, caught the ear of Universal

Music New Zealand when she was just 13 years old. Realizing that the usual approach to signing, nurturing, and developing a global artist would not be appropriate for such a young musician, Universal offered a development deal to Yelich-O'Connor (with her parents' approval) to give her time to have a reasonably normal childhood and continue with her studies.[16]

The young musician was introduced to producer Joel Little, who worked with her on her debut EP, *The Love Club*. Yelich-O'Connor decided she wanted to put her music on various social network sites but remain anonymous, not revealing her age or personal details. The track "Royals" was released under her stage name, Lorde, and immediately went viral. Part of the allure was the mystery surrounding the identity of this new artist.[17]

In the early days of Yelich-O'Connor's work, the label worked closely with her parents and management to protect her (at least for a while) from the pressures that global recognition can bring. Lorde's debut album, *Pure Heroine*, was a chart-topper in Australia and New Zealand. By the end of that year Universal stepped up promotion in Canada, the UK and the US, where the album reached the top five. Lorde chose to expand her touring commitments in 2014, and now has the freedom and maturity to work with whomever she chooses.[18]

Lorde
NBC Universal/Getty Images

Pause and Reflect

Put yourself in Yelich-O'Connor's shoes as a young teenager. How would you have balanced the professional opportunity and your growing-up process?

Legal Advisors

Trained legal advisors who are skilled in copyright law and business affairs for the music industry are valuable collaborators in developing global artists. In addition to advising the artist in negotiating contracts, including recording, publishing, or licensing, the legal advisor will draw up documents that guide in the formation and financial relationship of band members and ensembles.

Well-connected legal advisors can help the artist build partnerships in many areas, particularly in recording, sponsorship, and business affairs. Many top entertainment lawyers see themselves primarily as deal-makers, which can lead to the appearance of conflicts of interest. Lawyers are hired by studios, record labels, and publishers, while at the same time they are retained by artist clients who may have or want a relationship with one of those companies.

In situations that require litigation, an artist's legal team will advocate on her behalf. Copyright infringement lawsuits are common in the US, highlighting the tension between money and creative freedom.[19] While an artist may be reluctant to sue her record label for fear of unpleasant reprisals in the industry, a lawyer like Richard Busch, a partner in the Nashville firm of King & Ballow, has no such qualms. Busch is known as a tough-minded litigator who aggressively pushes against the status quo.[20] In one of the most important music industry copyright cases in years, Busch convinced a federal jury that Pharrell Williams' and Robin Thicke's 2013 hit "Blurred Lines" had too closely copied Marvin Gaye's 1977 song "Got to Give It Up." As a result, creative freedom advocates are concerned that the "Blurred Lines" verdict will hurt creativity by lowering the threshold of what counts as copyright infringement.[21]

Lang Lang
Kevork Djansezian/Getty Images Entertainment

SPOTLIGHT ON . . . CLASSICAL ROCK STAR LANG LANG

Born in Shenyang, China to parents whose own artistic careers had been thwarted by China's Cultural Revolution, Lang Lang's father and mother decided their infant son was going to be an international star. Lang Lang's father spent half his yearly salary to purchase the toddler a piano. While other children might have wilted under these high parental expectations, Lang Lang states: "I really didn't . . . feel the pressure at the time. Because I thought, I mean, I always played really good. And always got the first prize."[22]

At eight, Lang Lang said goodbye to his mother and comfortable lifestyle in Shenyang, and moved with his father to Beijing to study music. His mother stayed behind, the sole breadwinner for the family. It was a hard time for them, living in a sparsely furnished, unheated flat in a slum, sharing a bath with three other families. Lang Lang's constant practicing angered the neighbors. His father became moody and withdrawn.[23]

Lang Lang was fired by his first Beijing teacher, who said he had no talent. This crushed his father. In a fit of rage he told his son to kill himself, screaming: "You shouldn't live anymore—everything is destroyed." Understandably, Lang Lang melted under the pressure this time. "I hated everything: my father, the piano, myself. I got totally crazy."[24] For three months, he did not touch the piano. "We stayed in Beijing, I don't know why. Probably because having to go home would have resulted in shame for us."[25]

After more than a year of intense practicing, Lang Lang was admitted to the Beijing Conservatory, winning the International Tchaikovsky Competition for Young Musicians at age 13. He and his father finally left their slum apartment when he was 15, relocating to Philadelphia, Pennsylvania (US) to study with Gary Graffman at the Curtis Institute of Music.

Lang Lang became an "overnight star" when, at 17, he performed the Tchaikovsky Piano Concerto No. 1 with the Chicago Symphony Orchestra as a last-minute substitute for an ailing André Watts. Lang Lang says: "When we came to America, my father could see that the American system was much more relaxed. At that time he said he still believed in the Chinese way. But as we met different musicians from different countries, his opinion changed . . . his personality has totally changed, he doesn't push me anymore. When I turned 22, he let go."[26]

Lang Lang has grown up in full view of an international public. He has been called "one of the hottest artists on the classical music planet" by the *New York Times*[27] and has performed in every major concert hall in the world. He builds cultural bridges between the East and West, frequently introducing Chinese music to Western audiences, and vice versa.[28] He has played at the Olympic Games, the World Cup, and the Euro Cup finals.[29] Thanks to his Sony ambassadorship, he brought Prokofiev's Seventh Piano Sonata to the soundtrack of the multimillion-selling computer game *Gran Turismo 5* and *6*. His former record label, Deutsche Gramophone, promoted him as a rock star: "The future of classical music has arrived. His name is Lang Lang."[30]

Lang Lang has appeared on every major TV network, in a wide variety of news and lifestyle magazines, and has performed for dozens of political dignitaries. He has been the global brand ambassador of Sony Electronics, Audi Automobiles, Hublot watches, and Adidas, which added a limited edition Lang Lang-branded version of its Gazelle sneakers to its Originals line.[31] He is the only musician ever to have his name attached to a model of Steinway pianos.

Lang Lang's parents may have been satisfied with these remarkable accomplishments, but he has pushed further. His deep interest in music education thrust him into the role of professional music entrepreneur. He recognized an

Amazing Lang Lang fragrance launch
Alexander Koerner/Getty Images Entertainment

unmet need in the musical education marketplace and seized an opportunity to meet that need. In 2010 he created the Lang Lang International Music Foundation to further his goals of inspiring young pianists, building audiences through live performance, and expanding music education using technology.[32]

"Music is powerful," Lang Lang explains. "I want every child to have access to music experiences that ignite something wonderful inside of them, just as music delivered something incredible for me. My hope with my Foundation [is] to find a way to capture the potential that I see in music to positively transform lives and provide inspiration to kids around the world in a meaningful and sustainable way. I hope that my Foundation can help carry on my passion for music to encourage kids to engage in some way, any way, with any genre of music that touches them."[33]

The Foundation is much more than a vanity project for this musical superstar. Underlying its programs is the belief that music provides children with the ability to think critically and creatively, while discovering that, with discipline and persistence, they can achieve extraordinary results.[34]

The Foundation's 101 Pianists™ performances bring together 100 young pianists—plus Lang Lang—to show that piano playing doesn't always have to be a solitary endeavor. The event includes a master class and public performance, and has taken place in Paris, Berlin, London, Hong Kong, Rome, and other international cities.[35]

Despite all the sold-out performances and rock star hype, there are some in the music world who find fault with Lang Lang's exuberant performing style. The *New York Times* music critic Anthony Tommasini wrote that Lang Lang's "playing can be so intensely expressive that he contorts phrases, distorts musical structure and fills his music-making with distracting affectations."[36] Other music critics are bothered with his overt showmanship and his appearance, which includes a spiky hairdo and Versace-designed concert clothes.

And, as with all "products" in the marketplace, Lang Lang has competition. Considered the "other" super-star Chinese pianist, Yundi (born Li Yundi), is considered a rock star in his country. He burst onto the international scene by winning, at the age of 18, first prize at the 14th International Piano Competition, the youngest and first Chinese winner in the history of the competition.[37]

Lang Lang A Capitol Fourth 2015
Paul Morigi/Getty Images Entertainment

Yundi attracts millions of fans to his concerts, television shows, and on Weibo (China's Twitter), where he has more than 14.5 million followers. Along with his rival, Yundi is credited with unleashing "piano fever" in China that has motivated more than 50 million young Chinese to learn an instrument that until recently was banned as "decadent."[38]

Like Lang Lang, corporate sponsors flock to Yundi, including Rolex and Bang & Olufsen. However, Yundi is not shy about pointing out aesthetic differences between the repertoire of the two competitors. "I don't do crossover, I don't change my style," he states. "I share what I do with young people; if they want different music they can find it in a different area."[39]

Sensing an opportunity to encourage the rivalry, the Chinese media pits the pair against each other. While flashy Lang Lang is the Communist Party's and international favorite, the shyer—also seen as more poetic—Yundi is the Chinese people's favorite. As author and arts critic Norman Lebrecht summarizes: "Lang Lang is a global brand, Yundi a national dish."[40]

Some describe it this way: Lang Lang relishes the spotlight—and the rivalry. Yundi, on the other hand, has become increasingly adept at playing the marketing game, but would be happier without it. "Only music can define me," he says passionately.[41]

Yet the tug of commerce is a big part of this story. Music education, especially for piano and violin, is strong among middle-class families in China, as well as in Japan and Korea.[42] Today many of the world's finest classical musicians are East Asian by descent. Record labels are eager to penetrate this huge, emerging market for Western classical music.

Cited by *Time* magazine's Time 100 as one of the world's most influential people, Lang Lang was recognized as a symbol of the youth of China and its future.[43] With so much global pressure to live up to the accolades and honors, could his artistry pay the price?

Pause and Reflect

Why does Yundi speak disparagingly of "crossover" music?

When does the music suffer from an interpretation that is imbued with the performer's fame and personality?

How can an international superstar musician find time to devote to charitable causes? And what's the best way to choose those causes?

How does commercial sponsorship impact an artist's brand?

Live Events and Performances

Concert and event promotion are familiar to nearly everyone in the world as live music concerts, theatrical performances (operas, musicals and plays), ethnic festivals, choruses, music festivals, and many more. The primary activities of concert promotion include managing venues (arenas, outdoor theaters, clubs, performing arts facilities, auditoriums, and stadiums), organizing logistics for concerts, tours, shows, and festivals; promoting and marketing events; and booking talent, including musicians and performers, for events.

Performing live before an audience is the bedrock of artist development. It allows musicians to try out new material and get audience feedback. Performing regularly helps bands and ensembles to smooth out the rough edges and become a tight-knit ensemble.

Nearly all performers, aspiring artist managers, and sound engineers start off in small clubs that seat fewer than 200 people. The number and popularity of club- and theater-level concerts has risen as concert-goers use the internet as a tool for music discovery. Furthermore, musicians and other artists are increasingly using live events to generate revenue from sales of merchandise, including recorded music, T-shirts, and other branded items. Summer is typically a heavily booked time of the year for outdoor venues and music festivals, which are lucrative and popular. College and university presenters' seasons usually occur during the academic year of September through May.

Ticket sales are the traditional source of revenue for concert promoters. However, in recent years other revenue streams—such as sales of food and beverages, parking, merchandise, and VIP packages—have become essential to cover the costs involved in putting on a public event.

In the nonprofit sector, ticket sales for operators such as community arts centers, orchestras, and chamber music presenters cover only 40–65 percent of the costs of staging events. Many countries understand the cultural value of the creative arts and provide public funding. Nonprofit organizations also look to private individuals and corporations and foundations to cover their income gap.

Key Players in the Area of Live Events

An *artist manager* is one of the most important partnerships an artist-entrepreneur can have when forming her team. Managers are the individuals who remain focused on the big picture and the end goal of an artist. The artist manager coordinates projects that involve the artist, works with event presenters, promoters, booking agents, record labels, music publishers—anyone with whom the artist has a professional relationship. A well-connected artist manager can help artists find other team members, such as a business manager, a personal assistant, or a branding consultant.

There is no official training or degree that an artist manager needs before starting out. Many have worked their way up in other areas of the industry or have learned the ropes as a managerial assistant. Some managers decide to open their own businesses right off the bat and learn on the job. There are professional organizations around the world that help managers determine best practices, understand changing legislation and legal issues, and provide professional support. A few are listed below:

- International Music Managers Forum (IMMF).

- International Artist Managers. Association (IAMA).

- North America Performing Arts Managers and Agents (NAPAMA).

- Association of Artist Managers-Australia (AAM).

- European Association of Artist Managers (AEAA).

- International Network for Arts and Business (Japan).

- The Music Business and Music Production Companies in Japan (FMPJ).

A *booking agent* secures paying employment for an artist with whom she has a contract. A booking agent is very knowledgeable about venues and ticket pricing in specific territories. Global artists often have different agents for different areas of the world.

The *promoter* (known as the "presenter" in the classical world) selects the artists, organizes the event, and markets it independently of venues. A promoter bears a large share of the risk in mounting live events.

A *talent buyer* typically works as an employee of a venue. She will book the venue's entire calendar and oversee those shows plus any booked by outside promoters. Talent buyers are common in clubs and pop venues, but not in classical music.

Some artists who are just starting out will use online tools to do many of the above jobs themselves. However, at a certain point, artist-entrepreneurs may decide to bring others on to their team as their live shows and touring become more frequent and complex.

Mini-Case Study: Flume and E.D.M. Touring

Harley Streten of Australia, better known as Flume, began posting dance music (E.D.M.) tracks to SoundCloud in 2011. Flume's rise in popularity has paralleled the surge in interest in E.D.M., where young producers can achieve global renown through SoundCloud and other free streaming sites which produce millions of plays but little revenue. Since E.D.M. is rarely played on commercial radio stations, this usually lucrative income source was not available to Flume.[44]

In order to build a sustainable career, Flume and his managers created increased demand for his live shows—which pro-

Flume, at Governor's Ball 2015
C Flanigan/WireImage/Getty Images

vide more than 60 percent of his income—by piggybacking on well-known songs from Arcade Fire and Chet Faker. For example, Flume's remix of "You & Me" by the UK electronic duo Disclosure was used in a 2013 Lacoste commercial in France. Flume earned no money from it, but his remix became a viral hit. Later that year he played to a crowd of 40,000 at the Rock en Seine festival in Paris. According to his manager, Nathan McLay (who also is the founder of his Australian label, Future Classic), in 2014 the Flume business generated revenues in the low seven figures. The strategy seems to be working.

Pause and Reflect

Compare the role that fans play in Flume's success to the role of his remixes and commercial sponsorships. Are these partnerships equally important?

Collecting Societies

Performances—whether live or otherwise—generate performance royalties for artists who have affiliated with various collecting societies around the world. The issuing of licenses and collection of royalties from a wide array of performances[45] is managed internationally by organizations known by several different names, including authors' societies, collective management organizations, performing rights organizations, and collecting societies. They represent creators of music, visual arts, audiovisual, literary and dramatic works, and manage their rights on a collective basis.

When a songwriter or composer affiliates with a collecting society or performing rights organization, she is in fact giving the society the right to issue performance licenses for her songs. In exchange, the society will collect and distribute the revenue that is generated.

Unions and Professional Organizations

Young musicians just starting out often see union membership as restrictive, expensive, or just unnecessary. As artists move higher in the professional ranks, however, joining unions will be required, particularly if an artist signs with a booking agency. Most professional-level performing opportunities in concert touring, television, radio, and film are under the jurisdiction of a variety of unions, and require that artists be union members to work in that field.

Unions, trade organizations and professional organizations exist to support artists in the workplace. The relative strength of a union is largely dependent upon the size of its membership. The higher the number of members, the more validity the union has in being recognized as the collective representative of labor interests.

Union leaders negotiate on behalf of all of their members on any number of crucial issues in the workplace, including pay, working conditions, fair trade, health and wellbeing, and livelihood protection.

The International Federation of Musicians (FIM) is the international organization for musicians' unions, guilds, and professional associations, with 70 members in 60 countries throughout the world. It has created three regional groups, for Africa (FIM-AF: the FIM African Committee), for Latin America (GLM: Grupo Latinoamericano de Músicos), and for Europe (the FIM European group).

The American Federation of Musicians (AFM) of the US and Canada is a labor union representing the interests of professional musicians.

Key US Unions and Guilds

Actors' Equity Association (AEA)—a labor union representing US actors and stage managers working in the professional theatre.

American Guild of Variety Artists (AGVA)—a labor union representing performers in Broadway, off-Broadway, and cabaret productions, as well as theme park and nightclub performers.

American Guild of Music Artists (AGMA)—a labor union serving the interests of singers and dancers working in the opera, dance, concert, oratorio and recital fields.

Dramatists Guild of America—a professional association of playwrights, composers, and lyricists.

International Alliance of Theatrical Stage Employees (IATSE)—a labor union representing technicians, artisans, and craftspersons in the entertainment industry, including live theater, film and television production, and trade shows.

SAG-AFTRA—a labor union representing actors in feature films, short films, and digital projects.

Stage Directors & Choreographers Society (SDC)—a labor union representing directors and choreographers of Broadway national tours, regional theater, dinner theater, and summer stock, as well as choreographers for motion pictures, television, and music.

Writers Guild of America (WGA)—a labor union representing writers in the motion picture, broadcast cable, and new-media industries.

Union Issues at the Metropolitan Opera

In 2014 the Metropolitan Opera (US) and two of its unions signed a deal that just barely managed to avoid a prolonged labor strike. The Met's endowment had been decreasing for years due in part to over-spending on operating expenses. The Met's board refused to begin an endowment fundraising campaign until significant decreases in operating expenses were agreed upon by both sides.

Prior to the final agreement, the Met's management had been engaged for months in rancorous financial talks with the stagehand's union, the International Alliance of Theatrical Stage Employees (IATSE), and a few other unions of artisans and craftspeople. Hanging over the discordant negotiations was the sobering reminder of the recent bankruptcy of its former Lincoln Center neighbor, the New York City Opera. The compromises on both sides prevented the kind of crushing labor battle that afflicted the Minnesota Orchestra (US), where management locked out the musicians from performing for 16 months.[46]

Key Performing Arts Organizations

Both artist-entrepreneurs and music business-entrepreneurs may join professional organizations that provide an inside look at how the music industry operates. Many such organizations have online information and resources for their members. Attending a conference hosted by a professional organization is an excellent investment in gathering knowledge, building skills, and meeting people in the field.

The Association of Performing Arts Presenters (APAP) is the national service, advocacy and membership organization for presenters of the performing arts. The annual APAP New York City conference is the world's leading booking conference for the performing arts industry. APAP has more than 1,600 national and international members.

Chamber Music America is a US association of professional chamber music, with an annual conference in New York City.

The European Orchestras Forum is led by the French Association of Orchestras and represents orchestra professionals from 35 countries.

The League of American Orchestras has a membership of 800 North American orchestras, from world-renowned symphonies to community groups, and from summer festivals to student and youth ensembles. It is involved in advocacy and leadership advancement for managers, musicians, volunteers, and boards through its conferences and events, *Symphony* magazine, and website.

The National Association for Campus Activities (NACA) is a network of regional US booking conferences for college and university campus entertainment programs. The conferences attract international booking agencies as well as self-represented artists.

Key Music Conferences for Artist- and Music Business-Entrepreneurs

There are probably as many annual music conferences as there are music festivals in the world. The following small representation of conferences is based on a listing by Moses Avalon, a music business author, artist advocate, court-recognized music business expert, blogger, frequent guest speaker and workshop leader, and founder of the Moses Avalon Company.[47]

KEY MUSIC CONFERENCES

NAME OF CONFERENCE	COMMENTS
AES (Audio Engineering Society)	Good if you're looking for an internship at a recording studio or want to meet producers who are shopping for gear.
ASCAP EXPO	If you need to meet songwriters, go here. Great mentor sessions with top pros make it worth the price of admission.
Billboard	The stalwart industry magazine puts on at least a dozen conferences each year.
Canadian Music Week	Conferences, trade exhibition, award shows, film festival, comedy festival, and Canada's biggest New Music Festival.
CMJ	College radio people. Good for making promo inroads.
Digital Hollywood	Good hunting for just about everything.
Digital Entertainment World	A great integration of creative types and technocrats.
MIDEM (Marché International du Disque et de l'Edition Musicale)	Expensive but worth the price if you're looking to license your music catalogue.
NAMM	Lots of gear. H.O.T. Zone (hands-on-training) and other educational opportunities.
New Music Seminar	Good blend of business-to-business and educational opportunities.
SXSW (South by Southwest)	Lots of showcase opportunities. Top execs abound if you can find them in the crowd.
TAXI Road Rally	Opportunities for unsigned artists, songwriters and composers who want revenue-producing deals.
LAMC (Latin Alternative Music Conference)	Small but very potent. Panels are in English.
MUSEXPO	The UN of music conferences. Executive hunting ground. European meet 'n' greet.
MusicBiz (run by NARM—National Association of Recording Merchandisers)	A great backdoor way to meet label people on the marketing side. Managers galore.
Pollstar Live!	Venue promoters. Get on a better tour. Meet managers of top acts. Powerful, often overlooked, opportunity.
Sundance Film Festival	Avalon's top-ranked music conference is a film festival. Why? You'll stand out and be one of the only music people in the room.
San Francisco MusicTech Summit	For music, business, technology, developers, entrepreneurs, investors, service providers, journalists, and organizations that work with them in a getting-business-done environment.

Broadcasting

One of the most opportunity-laden areas for entrepreneurial innovation and partnerships today is the convergence of broadcast communications media—TV, internet service providers (ISPs), video, radio, podcasts, smartphones, games, social media, advertising, and apps. The internet is not only revolutionizing the business of media; it has upended the way we think about and interact with it, as well.

Regional mass media like network TV and radio are now available on and augmented by an explosion in global content found on internet services like Spotify, Vevo, YouTube, Netflix, and Amazon. The opportunities for artistic discovery have increased exponentially.

Mini-Case Study: Artist "Passenger" Partners with Traditional Media

British singer-songwriter Mike Rosenberg, better known as Passenger, and his indie label Inertia Records needed a strategy to build on the artist's small but enthusiastic fanbase in his adopted country of Australia. Joining forces with German independent label Embassy of Music in 2012, Passenger and his partners created a plan to launch his career in continental Europe. The strategy? Traditional radio.[48]

Embassy wanted to build Passenger's following in smaller markets before breaking the artist in Germany. So it partnered with Sony Music Netherlands to launch a campaign in the Netherlands. "German radio is really fragmented," said Embassy's music director Konrad von Löhneysen. "It's hard to create an impact with an unknown artist from a standing start. The radio market is far smaller in the Netherlands. Working closely with a top Dutch radio plugger, we helped get 'Let Her Go' to Number 1 in November 2012. That was the turning point." With this success, Passenger and his partners now had a platform to reach the German market. Again the team decided to focus on radio as they turned their efforts to Germany.[49]

"Let Her Go" topped the German singles chart in February 2013, subsequently reaching number 1 in Austria, Belgium, Sweden, Switzerland, Australia and New Zealand, and reached Number 2 in the UK. Passenger's story shows that breaking artists using traditional media like radio is still an important element in an overall marketing strategy.[50]

Audiences and Fans

Fans and audiences play a huge role in deciding which artists make it in today's music world. They

Mike Rosenberg "Passenger"
Frank Hoensch/Getty Images Entertainment

buy tickets, come to your concerts and shows, and use social media to talk about you and your music. The explosion of social media has spawned a global non-stop surveillance culture. Fans are interested not only in the artist's music; they want to know about the artist's lifestyle, family, vacations, struggles with their weight, and dust-ups with friends or ex-spouses. Artists are brands, companies in their own right that have to keep their customers—the fans—happy, informed, and hungry for their products and services.

Musical Instrument and Recording Equipment Suppliers

Many of us started our musical journeys as children with either private lessons or in school programs. Many traditional musical instrument retailers are strong community partners in fostering a love of and skill in music for both children and adults. Retailers who remain strong are focused on improving customer loyalty and promoting the benefits of expert advice and hands-on interaction with customers who want to try before they buy. Physical stores are usually the most convenient way for customers to purchase items needed quickly, such as replacement strings, reeds, and drumsticks. Instrument repairs and modifications is another area that is well-served by retail establishments. The sale of high-value antique instruments remains a robust market because stringed orchestral instruments are expensive.

The National Association of Music Merchants (NAMM) in the US and in Russia is the major trade association serving the US$17 billion global music products industry. NAMM and NAMM-Russia hold massive trade shows each year, where thousands of people seek out the newest innovations in musical products, recording technology, sound, and lighting.

Students and young entrepreneurs are encouraged to attend the popular trade shows. NAMM U and TEC Tracks are two special programs for students offered by NAMM to provide opportunities in music business and in pro audio education for recording and live sound.[51]

Producers

A music producer collaborates with an artist to guide a recording from start to finish. In partnership with the artist's manager, record label, and studio engineer, a producer helps the artist with everything from song choice, structure, and arrangement to the actual performance that gives each recording its distinct aural personality.[52]

Producers come from different backgrounds and experiences. They may be songwriters, or musicians with a music theory and instrumental background. Whatever their background, they must be proficient in the nuts and bolts of the recording process. One of a producer's most valuable roles is helping the recording artist and session musicians maintain perspective throughout the recording process.[53]

Marc Kinchen is a house and dance music producer from Detroit, Michigan (US). He has worked with artists like Celine Dion, Lana Del Ray, Enrique Iglesias, and Will Smith, and with the legendary producer Quincy Jones. He tells aspiring music producers: "Surround yourself with people you trust, whether they are friends, supporters or business people. Ask everyone questions. If you have a favorite DJ or producer, see who handles them and try to get a meeting. Put a record out, do remixes on spec and offer to help in the office of your favorite label for work experience. Being loyal and nice pays off in so many ways. It makes for a more pleasant life and it helps you develop long-term relationships—99 percent of the people I started out with are still friends and we still help each other in some way."[54]

Failure and Criticism: A Necessary Part of Creating 21st Century Global Music Professionals

Failure is a fear we all have. It keeps us from taking the risks we know we should and it often forces us to give up on our ambitions.

But failure is a huge opportunity for growth. Building a life as a music professional comes with a few risks, so setbacks and failures are unavoidable. Having a thick skin helps, but if we change our mindset to view each failure as a growth opportunity, we will become stronger musicians and human beings.[55]

Each of us defines failure in different ways. No band or composer is going to turn every idea they come up with into a legendary hit. Music business-entrepreneurs may miss an opportunity to sign the next Katy Perry. There are going to be hours and dollars wasted in the studio on a song that just never works. It's important to leave behind creative ideas that don't work. Find your strengths and build on them. Embrace failure as part of the creative process.

Being Receptive to Criticism Enables Growth

Young musicians don't always understand that listening to feedback from an audience can help them grow. It's okay to not be perfect—no one is. It's not okay, however, to deny your flaws and refuse to grow.[56]

It may seem that some music critics are overly harsh, and everyone has an opinion about your work. Be open, receptive, and gracious when you're critiqued. Stay humble. Be grateful that someone took the time to listen to your music and give you honest feedback.[57]

SPOTLIGHT ON . . . CANADA: DEVELOPING 21ST CENTURY GLOBAL ARTISTS

Canada's music history has been strongly influenced by outside countries, particularly its nearest geographical neighbor, the US. In order to help its own musicians flourish and achieve worldwide recognition, Canada has developed a very strong support network of funding, opportunities, awards and programs. With the mid-20th century introduction of the MAPL system, Canadian artists are flourishing both at home and abroad. Canada is a model in demonstrating how to develop the 21st century global music professional.

Government Funding to Artists and Arts Organizations

The Canadian government supports its individual artists and organizations in many ways. One of the most important is through funding.

The Canada Council for the Arts supports more than 20,000 professional artists and arts organizations through grants, prizes and its Public Lending Right program. In 2011–12, it awarded more than US$157 million in funding, or approximately US$5.25 per Canadian citizen.[58] To put this into perspective, the US spends approximately US$0.41 per citizen[59] and Australia spends roughly US$228 per citizen.[60]

The Canada Council directly supports individual artists' research, creation, professional development, travel, and market development. Direct support is also available to artists who are employed and paid professional fees by organizations receiving Canada Council operational funding.[61]

Nonprofit organizations of all sizes receive support from the Council. In 2014 it funded special projects from 1,633 arts organizations. In addition, 1,000 arts organizations located in 156 Canadian communities received annual and multi-year operating funding.[62]

Assisting Canadian Talent on Recordings

The Canada Music Fund (CMF) provides more than US$18,640,595 in annual funding for the creation and worldwide promotion of Canadian music.[63] This part of Canada Council funding is administered by FACTOR for the English-language sector of the music industry and *Musicaction* for the French-language sector. FACTOR stands for the Foundation Assisting Canadian Talent on Recordings. It funds the production and licensing of sound recordings by Canadian artists, as well as activities to support the commercialization of those sound recordings. The assistance is wide-ranging and includes marketing and promotion, touring and showcasing, and video production and digital content.[64]

FACTOR is a major contributor to regional Canadian music conferences like the East Coast Music Awards and Breakout West. It also supports major music events such as Canadian Music Week, the Juno Awards, North by Northeast, Pop Montréal, and the Halifax Pop Explosion.[65]

FACTOR provides financial support to touring artists and event producers who have an international presence. In addition to international tour support for bands and ensembles, it funds event producers who organize showcases for Canadian talent at the biggest international music markets, like MIDEM in France and South by Southwest in the US.[66]

Helping Young Music Entrepreneurs

Along with its record company, Coalition Records, the full-service Canadian company Coalition Music includes artist management, music licensing, online creative, and publicity departments. It also offers 10-week skills development workshops for artist-entrepreneurs and other industry stakeholders, with mentoring by some of the best songwriters, producers, booking agents, lawyers and accountants in the industry.[67]

The Canada Music Fund has a Music Entrepreneur component that provides assistance to Canadian music publishing firms, music industry national service organizations, and sound recording firms.

Canada's Walk of Fame Emerging Artists Programs and Scholarships sponsor a mentorship program for Canadian musicians aged 10–35. The Grand Prize includes private recording studio time, industry mentorship opportunities, a cash award, and performance opportunities in Canada's Walk of Fame Events.[68]

Canada's MAPL System

By law, the Canadian Radio-television and Telecommunications Commission (CRTC) mandates that 35 percent of all radio content must come from Canadians. What makes a song Canadian? The four elements used to qualify songs as Canadian are Music, Artist, Performance and Lyrics (MAPL). The MAPL system is designed to

K'naan @ Sundance—Canadian

Mat Hayward/Getty Images Entertainment

increase the exposure of Canadian performers, lyricists, and composers to Canadian audiences, and to strengthen the Canadian music industry in the areas of artistic content and production.[69]

To qualify as Canadian content, a musical selection must generally fulfill at least two of the following conditions:

M (music): the music is composed entirely by a Canadian.

A (artist): the music is, or the lyrics are, performed principally by a Canadian.

P (performance): the musical selection consists of a live performance that is recorded wholly in Canada, or performed wholly in Canada and broadcast live in Canada.

L (lyrics): the lyrics are written entirely by a Canadian.[70]

The CRTC's Radio Regulations define a Canadian as being one of the following:

- A Canadian citizen.

- A permanent resident as defined by the Immigration Act 1976.

- A person whose ordinary place of residence was Canada for the six months immediately preceding their contribution to a musical composition, performance, or concert.

- A person licensed to operate a radio station.[71]

Music Tourism

The Canadian Tourism Commission (CTC) incorporates music, festivals, and cultural events into its global tourism marketing strategy. Domestically, it works to encourage young people to travel within Canada. Internationally, it works closely with Festivals and Major Events Canada to encourage foreign tourists to attend Canada's many music festivals. One event of note that acknowledges the official bilingual status of Canada is the Games of La Francophonie, an international event held every four years in a French-speaking country for youth in culture and sports competitions.[72]

Uniquely Canadian Music Festivals

Boots and Hearts is the largest country music festival ever to be hosted on Canadian soil. It is a three-day celebration in Bomanville, Ontario.[73]

Canada's Walk of Fame Festival programs 100 percent Canadian entertainment from all genres (music,

Sarah McLachlan—Canadian
Dimitrios Kambouris/Getty Images

film, dance, and comedy), ranging from emerging talent to internationally recognized stars.[74]

Folk on the Rocks takes place in Yellowknife, North West Territories (NWT) and features 24 hours of programming with performers, food, and creative works from artists from the NWT, Nunavut, and beyond.[75]

Hillside Festival has been going for 32 years in Guelph, Ontario and, besides its eclectic mix of artists, is known for its innovative green initiatives, like the solar-powered stage, dishwashing stations, and trike-powered transport.[76]

A country as vast as Canada has a lot of really big festivals to match its size, including:

- Montréal International Jazz Festival (Montréal).
- Squamish Valley Music Festival (British Columbia).
- Cavendish Beach Music Festival (Prince Edward Island).
- Edmonton Folk Festival (Alberta).

Shania Twain—Canadian

Dimitrios Kambouris/Getty Images Entertainment

Professional Associations

Canada has hundreds of professional music associations that support its professional musicians. A few of note are the Canadian Recording Industry Association (CRIA), which represents foreign multi-nationals and major independent music companies, and the Canadian Independent Record Production Association (CIRPA) for independent Canadian companies. There are also provincial industry associations, such as the Association québécoise de l'industrie du disque, du spectacle et de la video (ADISQ) and the Alberta Recording Industries Association.

Finally, there are associations representing musicians, publishers, and creators at both the national and provincial levels, such as the Canadian Music Creators Coalition, La Société Professionnelle des Auteurs et des Compositeurs du Québec (SPACQ), and the Songwriters Association of Canada (SAC).[77]

Broadcasting

The Canadian Broadcast Corporation, known as CBC/Radio-Canada, is the country's public radio, television and digital broadcaster. It has both French and English services. Canada's Broadcasting Act requires that each element of the Canadian broadcasting system contribute to the creation and presentation of Canadian programming. To comply, broadcasters offer funding initiatives that provide support, promotion, training, and development of Canadian musical and spoken word talent, as well as music journalism.[78]

There are eight CBC radio channels, including the English-language network Radio 2, featuring classical, jazz, world beat, and pop,[79] and ICI Musique, a French-language, predominantly Canadian line-up of music and cultural programming in genres ranging from classical, jazz and vocal to world and new music.[80]

CBC is the television arm of the Canadian Broadcast System (its French-language counterpart is Ici Radio-Canada Télé). CBC is the producer of the hit reality show *Dragons' Den*, in which aspiring entrepreneurs pitch business ideas to a panel of venture capitalists in the hopes of securing business financing. *Dragons' Den* has opened the eyes of millions of Canadians to entrepreneurship, business risk, and the start-up process.[81] *The Big Decision*, a spinoff show on CBC, takes viewers inside companies at a business tipping point, revealing the struggles and tensions that characterize entrepreneurial companies.

According to the CBC, "*Dragons' Den* is more than a TV show. It's a cultural force propelling Canada in its long, slow march from Resources Nation to Entrepreneurial Nation."[82]

Provincial Funding for Music

In addition to federal funding, many of Canada's 10 provinces and three territories provide assistance to the creative industries. The province of Ontario has the largest music marketplace in Canada, generating 82 percent of the industry's value. These revenues come from music publishing, sound recording studios, record production, and record distribution.[83]

The Ontario Ministry of Tourism, Culture and Sport funds both the Media Development Corporation (for the province's numerous types of media, including music) and the Ontario Music Fund. Ontario record labels, music publishers, artist management firms, and other companies have access to public funding through the Ontario Sound Recording Tax Credit.[84]

In addition to directly supporting its domestic music businesses, the Ontario Media Development Corporation provides assistance for the music industry to have a presence at international events like London Calling, UK, MIDEM, POPKOMM, and SXSW.[85]

Public Recognition for Its Music Communities

Canada is well represented at the international level by some of the world's top classical musicians. Angela Hewitt, James Ehnes, Ben Heppner, Marc-André Hamelin, Measha Brueggergosman, and Yannick Nézet-Séguin perform regularly in the most prestigious concert venues and as guests of today's leading orchestras.

There is strong national interest in predicting the next Canadian classical music stars.[86] Each year CBC/Radio-Canada announces its "30 Hot Canadian Classical Musicians under 30." The list is compiled with advice from conservatories, music competitions, and professional training programs all over the country. The musicians range in age from 8 to 28. The 2014 list included pianist Jan Lisiecki from Calgary (age 19), tenor Owen McCausland from St. John, New Brunswick (age 24), and harpist Antoine Malette-Chénier from Gatineau, Québec (age 23).[87]

Canada's Walk of Fame is an annual, widely promoted, and televised event that acknowledges the achievements of successful Canadians in the areas of athletics, music, theater, playwrights, film, and television. The Canadian Music Hall of Fame "recognizes Canadian artists who have attained commercial success while having a positive impact on the Canadian music scene at home and around the world."[88] Among other criteria, Walk of Famers must "represent the essence of the Canadian identity: Peace Loving, Diverse,

Harmonious, Socially Responsible, Creative, Confident, Innovative, and Successful." The award consists of a maple leaf star embedded in 13 designated Toronto sidewalks on King and Simcoe Streets.[89]

The *JUNO Awards* are presented annually to exceptional Canadian musical artists and bands to acknowledge their artistic and technical achievements in all musical genres. New members of the Canadian Music Hall of Fame are inducted as part of the Juno Awards ceremonies, which are presented by the Canadian Academy of Recording Arts and Sciences (CARAS).[90]

Ben Heppner—Canadian

Anne Cusack/Los Angeles Times/Getty Images

Canada's "Bollywood"

"Bollywood," a lighthearted mash-up of the words "Hollywood" and "Bombay," refers specifically to the Hindi-language films produced in Mumbai (formerly Bombay), India, the heart of the South Asian film industry. The term "Bollywood" has come to represent Indian cinema as a whole.[91]

Some prominent Indian film directors are filming in North America to capitalize on its large South Asian population and well-developed film infrastructure. Since the 1990s, there has been an upsurge in Indian-produced films shot in such "exotic" locations as Vancouver, Toronto, Calgary, Niagara Falls, and even Hamilton, Ontario. A typical example is the film work of Akshay Kumar, an action star of Indian cinema, who has made three of his popular "Khiladi" movies in Toronto, and starred in other films shot on location in Montréal, Calgary and Vancouver. So popular is Kumar with Canadian South Asian audiences that he was named the brand ambassador for the Canada Tourism Commission in India in 2010. He was invited to meet with Prime Minister Stephen Harper and Indian Prime Minister Manmohan Singh during the 2010 G20 summit in Toronto. In recognition of the growing importance of Canada to Indian film producers, Toronto hosted the International Indian Film Academy Awards, dubbed the Bollywood Oscars, in 2011.[92]

Oh, Canada!

Canada is a massive country with hundreds of internationally known achievers. However, many of us don't realize that these famous people are actually Canadian. To help set the record straight, I've based the following list on a compilation by Dr. Jeffrey Rosenthal, Professor at the Department of Statistics, University of Toronto.[93] I have included only those Canadians involved in the music industry in the interest of saving space:

Bryan Adams (musician and songwriter; Grammy award winner; writer of the international hit "(Everything I Do) I Do It for You")

Paul Anka (singer and songwriter; writer of the song "My Way")

Arcade Fire (rock band; won the 2011 Grammy for Album of the Year)

Bachman-Turner Overdrive (BTO) (rock group; writers of the songs "You Ain't Seen Nuthin' Yet" and "Takin' Care of Business")

The Band (rock group; performed extensively with Bob Dylan)

Barenaked Ladies (rock group; writers of the song "If I Had a Million Dollars")

Justin Bieber (teen international singing sensation)

Paul Brandt (country singer; CMA 2005 Global Artist of the Year)

Michael Bublé (pop/jazz singer; won a 2007 Grammy award)

Canadian Brass Quintet (formed in 1970 in Toronto)

Robert Charlebois (French-language singer and songwriter)

Leonard Cohen (poet, singer, and songwriter)

Holly Cole (jazz singer; especially popular in Japan)

Celine Dion (ballad singer; many huge hits, including "Where Does My Heart Beat Now")

Dennis Doherty (musician; founding member of "The Mamas & the Papas")

Drake (Grammy-winning hip-hop artist)

Percy Faith (composer and bandleader; initiator of the "easy listening" genre)

Maynard Ferguson (classical trumpeter)

David Foster (music producer of Whitney Houston, Barbara Streisand, The Corrs)

Maureen Forrester (classical singer)

Nelly Furtado (singer and songwriter)

Glenn Gould (leading classical piano player)

The Guess Who (rock band; writers of the song "American Woman")

Ben Heppner (classical singer)

K'naan (musician; writer of World Cup anthem "Wavin' Flag")

Diana Krall (bestselling jazz singer)

Anton Kuerti (classical pianist)

k.d. lang (rock/country singer and songwriter)

Daniel Lanois (musician and producer of Bob Dylan, U2)

Avril Lavigne (rock singer and songwriter)

Gordon Lightfoot (folk singer and songwriter)

Guy Lombardo (big-band leader; 1929–62 performer of "Auld Lang Syne" in New York on New Year's Eve)

Louis Lortie (classical pianist)

Natalie MacMaster (Cape Breton fiddler and international performer)

Loreena McKennitt (Celtic-style musician)

Sarah McLachlan (rock singer and songwriter; Lilith Fair organizer)

Men Without Hats (rock group; performers of international Top 10 song "The Safety Dance")

Abe "Honest Abe" Mirvish (philanthropic businessman who developed Toronto's King St. Entertainment District)

Joni Mitchell (folk singer and songwriter)

Alanis Morissette (rock singer and songwriter; won seven Grammy awards)

Anne Murray (pop singer of the mega-hit "You Needed Me")

Zara Nelsova (classical cellist)

Oscar Peterson (legendary jazz piano player; won seven Grammy awards)

Raffi (children's music composer and performer)

Stan Rogers (folk singer and songwriter)

Rush (progressive rock/heavy metal group; received "Living Legend Award" from London's *Classic Rock* magazine)

Paul Shaffer (band leader on David Letterman's *Late Night* television show)

Sam "Sam the Record Man" Sniderman (entrepreneur who helped shape Toronto's international music scene)

Hank Snow (country singer; released the mega-hit "I'm Movin' On" in 1950)

Shania Twain (country singer and songwriter)

John Vickers (classical singer)

Gilles Vigneault (French-language singer and songwriter)

Roch Voisine (French-language rock singer)

Neil Young (singer, musician, and songwriter)

Opportunities Ahead

Of the long list of institutions, organizations, and music industry sectors that are dedicated to developing the 21st century global music professional, which five do you think might contain opportunities for you within the next 12–18 months?

CONCLUSION

The major sections of the global music industry help create and sustain both artist-entrepreneurs and music business-entrepreneurs in different ways. Most DIWO music professionals will create a team to help them after achieving a certain level of renown. Lang Lang, Lorde, Flume, and Passenger are all excellent examples of global artists. Canada stands out as an exemplary country in its devotion to the development of 21st century global music professionals.

 Talking Back: Class Discussion

It's not easy to think about failing as a necessary part of professional development. How could educational institutions—from kindergarten through graduate school—help students see value in taking creative risks without fear of being penalized for failing?

NOTES

1 Tyler Allen, "Three Branding Lessons from Music's Biggest Superstars," *SonicBids*, http://blog.sonicbids. com/3-branding-lessons-from-musics-biggest-superstars (accessed May 12, 2016).

2 Andrew Simonet, *Making Your Life as an Artist* (Manitoba, Canada: Artists U, 2014).

3 Ibid.

4 Ibid.

5 Yannick Ilunga interviewing Dave Kusek, "TJS 029: Music Business and the New Artist Model with Dave Kusek," *The Jazz Spotlight*, www.thejazzspotlight.com/tjs-029-music-business-new-artist-model-dave-kusek (accessed May 12, 2016).

6 Sam Friedman, "Three Important Lessons You Learn When Your Band Fails," *SonicBids*, http://blog.sonic bids.com/3-important-lessons-you-learn-when-your-band-fails#at_pco=smlrebv-1.0&at_si=55997ff54d6 0bfa3&at_ab=per-2&at_pos=3&at_tot=5 (accessed May 12, 2016).

7 Jack Oughton, "What Does It Take to Be a Music Producer?" *The Guardian*, May 5, 2013, www.theguardian. com/careers/music-producer-career-advice (accessed May 12, 2016).

8 Ibid.

9 Evan Fine, "Examining the Artist's Role as Citizen," *Juilliard Journal*, www.juilliard.edu/journal/examining-artists-role-citizen (accessed May 12, 2016).

10 James Crompton, "Music Publishing in the US," IBIS World Industry Report 51223, December 2014.

11 Ibid.

12 "How Record Labels Invest," *IFPI*, www.ifpi.org/how-record-labels-invest.php, (accessed May 12, 2016).

13 Ibid.

14 "Investing in Music," *Pro Music*, www.pro-music.org/resources/investing_in_music.pdf (accessed May 12, 2016).

15 Ibid.

16 "Case Study: Lorde," Nurturing and Developing Talent, *IFPI*, www.ifpi.org/nurturing-and-promoting-talent/ed-sheeran (accessed May 12, 2016).

17 Ibid.

18 Ibid.

19 Ben Sisario, 'Lawyer Rocks Music Industry Again," *New York Times*, March 16, 2015.

20 Ibid.

21 Ibid.

22 Rebecca Leung, "Lang Lang: Piano Prodigy," *CBS News*, January 7, 2005, www.cbsnews.com/news/lang-lang-piano-prodigy (accessed May 12, 2016).

23 Rosanna Greenstreet, "Lang Lang: 'I'd Play the Piano at 5am,'" *The Guardian*, June 17, 2014, www.theguard ian.com/lifeandstyle/2011/may/14/lang-lang-piano-china-father (accessed May 12, 2016).

24 Ibid.

25 Ibid.

26 Ibid.

27 Daniel J. Wakin, "Increasingly in the West, the Players Are from the East," *New York Times*, April 4, 2007, www.nytimes.com/2007/04/04/arts/music/04clas.html?_r=0 (accessed May 12, 2016).

28 "Carnegie Hall Presents, Lang Lang Bio," Carnegie Hall, February 4, 2014, www.carnegiehall.org/calendar/2014/2/4/0800/PM/Lang-Lang (accessed May 12, 2016).

29 "One of the Few True Classical Superstars Who Can Sell Out a Large Venue," *San Francisco Classical Voice*, www.sfcv.org/artist-profiles/lang-lang (accessed May 12, 2016).

30 Leung, "Lang Lang."

31 Hazel Davis, "Crossover Stars Fuel Branding Interest in Classical Music," *Billboard*, August 9, 2008, 14.

32 "One of the Few True Classical Superstars."

33 "A Message from Lang Lang," *Lang Lang International Music Foundation*, www.langlangfoundation.org (accessed May 12, 2016).

34 "Music Education, Success in Society," *Lang Lang International Music Foundation*, www.langlangfoundation. org (accessed May 12, 2016).

35 Ibid.

36 Anthony Tommasini, "Lang Lang: His Life So Far," *New York Times*, www.nytimes.com/2008/11/28/arts/music/28lang.html?pagewanted=1&_r=0 (accessed May 12, 2016).

37 Julia Llewellyn Smith, "Lang Lang? We've Never Met," *The Telegraph*, June 2, 2014, www.telegraph.co.uk/culture/music/classicalmusic/10863146/Lang-Lang-Weve-never-met.html (accessed May 12, 2016).

38 Ibid.

39 Ibid.

40 Ibid.

41 Ibid.

42 Ibid.

43 Herbie Hancock, "Lang Lang," *TIME*, April 30, 2009, http://content.time.com/time/specials/packages/article/0,28804,1894410_1893836_1894420,00.html (accessed May 12, 2016).

44 Ben Sisario, "An Artist Climbs: The Metrics Say So," *New York Times*, February 2, 2015.

45 The definition of "performance" includes live performances at concert or other venues, staged theatrical productions, and performance royalties from the broadcasting of music on TV, radio, cable and satellite, at sporting events, restaurants or bars, in commercial establishments, and online, satellite, and wireless streaming and downloading.

46 Michael Cooper, "In Labor Deal at Metropolitan Opera, a Surprise Finale: Both Sides Give in to Cuts," *New York Times*, August 19, 2014.

47 Moses Avalon, "19 Music Conferences Ranked: Worth the Cost of a Waste of Time?", April 18, 2011, www.mosesavalon.com/19-music-conferences-ranked-worth-the-cost-or-a-waste-of-time/ (accessed May 12, 2016).

48 "Working in Partnership: Passenger and the Embassy of Music," IFPI Digital Music Report 2014, 29.

49 Ibid.

50 Ibid.

51 "Educational Sessions," National Association of Music Merchandisers, http://namm.org/summer/2015/educational-sessions (accessed May 12, 2016).

52 Cliff Goldmacher, "Producers: What They Do and Why You Should Consider Using One," *BMI*, October 29, 2009, www.bmi.com/news/entry/Producers_What_They_Do_Why_You_Should_Consider_Using_One (accessed May 12, 2016).

53 Ibid.

54 Oughton, "What Does It Take."

55 Friedman, "Three Important Lessons."

56 Ibid.

57 Ibid.

58 "Canadian Music Industry Celebrates Ongoing Renewal of the Canada Music Fund," *CIMA*, www.cimamusic. ca/canadian-music-industry-celebrates-ongoing-renewal-of-the-canada-music-fund (accessed May 12, 2016).

59 "National Endowment for the Arts Appropriations History," *National Endowment for the Arts—Open Government*, www.arts.gov/open-government/national-endowment-arts-appropriations-history#sthash. yTlekTCZ.dpuf (accessed May 12, 2016).

60 "4172.0—Arts and Culture in Australia: A Statistical Overview, 2014," *Australian Bureau of Statistics*, www. abs.gov.au/ausstats/abs@.nsf/Lookup/4172.0main+features82014 (accessed May 12, 2016).

61 "Economic Action Plan 2014," *Canada Council for the Arts*, www.actionplan.gc.ca/en/initiative/canada-council-arts#sthash.8UzVMZ9R.dpuf (accessed May 12, 2016).

62 "Annual Report 2014," *Canada Council*, www.canadacouncil.ca/~/media/images/annual%20reports/2014/ pdfs/en/2014-mdna-ccfa-annual-report.pdf?mw=1382 (accessed May 12, 2016).

63 "Canadian Music Industry Celebrates."

64 "What FACTOR Funds," *FACTOR*, http://factor.ca/resources/forapplicants/whatfactorfunds#.VdYlv0VeKr8 (accessed May 12, 2016).

65 Ibid.

66 Ibid.

67 "Artist Entrepreneur Program," *Coalition Music*, www.coalitionmusic.com/education.php?p=courses (accessed May 12, 2016).

68 Bram Conshor, "Canada's Walk Of Fame Announces Return of Emerging Artist Music Mentorship Program," *Music Canada*, March 4, 2015, www.musiccanada.com/news/canadas-walk-of-fame-announces-return-of-emerging-artist-music-mentorship-program (accessed May 12, 2016).

69 "The MAPL System—Defining a Canadian Song," *Canada Radio-television and Telecommunications System*, www.crtc.gc.ca/eng/info_sht/r1.htm (accessed May 12, 2016).

70 Ibid.

71 Ibid.

72 "Arts and Culture," *Canadian Heritage, Festivals and Performing Arts*, www.pch.gc.ca/eng/1268168281111. (accessed May 12, 2016).

73 "Canadian Music Festival Guide 2015," *Indie 88*, www.indie88.com/canadian-music-festival-guide (accessed May 12, 2016).

74 "Canada's Walk of Fame Festival," *See Toronto Now*, www.seetorontonow.com/annual-events/canadas-walk-of-fame-festival/#sthash.B6fYtOOS.dpuf (accessed May 12, 2016).

75 "Home," *Folk on the Rocks*, www.folkontherocks.com (accessed May 12, 2016).

76 "Home," *Hillside Festival*, www.hillsidefestival.ca (accessed May 12, 2016).

77 Ontario Media Development Corporation, "Industry Profiles: Music," www.omdc.on.ca/collaboration/ research_and_industry_information/industry_profiles/Music_Industry_Profile.htm (accessed June 27, 2015).

78 "Who We Are—Our Services," *CBC-Radio Canada*, www.cbc.radio-canada.ca/en/explore/who-we-are-what-we-do/our-services (accessed May 12, 2016).

79 Ibid.

80 Ibid.

81 Denhette Wilford, "Canada TV: Dragons' Den Season 9 CBC," October 14, 2014, www.huffingtonpost. ca/2014/10/14/dragons-den-season-9-cbc_n_5982772.html (accessed May 12, 2016).

82 "Season 9 —Dragons' Den," *CBC*, www.cbc.ca/dragonsden (accessed May 12, 2016).

83 Ontario Media Development Corporation, "Industry Profiles: Music," www.homdc.on.ca/collaboration/ research_and_industry_information/industry_profiles/Music_Industry_Profile.htm. (accessed May 12, 2016).

84 Ibid.

85 Ibid.

86 Robert Rowat and Michael Morreale, "30 Hot Canadian Classical Musicians under 30, 2013 Edition," www.music.cbc.ca/#!/blogs/2013/8/30-hot-Canadian-classical-musicians-under-30. (accessed May 12, 2016).

87 "Home," *Canadian Music Hall of Fame*, www.canadianmusichalloffame.ca (accessed May 12, 2016).

88 "Nominations," *Canada's Walk of Fame*, www.canadaswalkoffame.com/inductees/nominations#sthash.ghWdMX1F.dpu (accessed May 12, 2016).

89 "Home," *Canada's Walk of Fame*, www.canadaswalkoffame.com/#sthash.ov2G5BMo.dpuf (accessed May 12, 2016).

90 "Home," *Juno Awards*, www.junoawards.ca/#sthash.m9VKjq3f.dpuf (accessed May 12, 2016).

91 "Bollywood in Canada," *Canadian Encyclopedia*, www.thecanadianencyclopedia.ca/en/article/bollywood-in-canada (accessed May 12, 2016).

92 Ibid.

93 Jeffrey Rosenthal, "Famous Canadians," www.probability.ca/jeff/canadians.html (accessed May 12, 2016).

PART 2

Opportunities Ahead

CHAPTER 4

Opportunities Ahead: Branding and Marketing

> The possibility of privileged access to the glamorously inaccessible is one of the greatest marketing lures there is these days.[1]
>
> Ben Brantley, American journalist and theater critic

CHAPTER OVERVIEW

Articulating your authentic brand and communicating it to the public are two of the most important aspects of entrepreneurship. Your (or your business') unique qualities and strengths will set you apart from others in the marketplace. Building a loyal fan- or customer-base, keeping them engaged with content marketing, thanking them for their loyalty, and making it easy for them to tell others about you will help you create a rewarding and sustainable business as a music entrepreneur. Three marketing case studies at the end of the chapter are designed to give you practice in branding and marketing.

KEY TERMS

Personal brand	Rebranding
Product category	Creative niche
Cultural tastemaker	Content marketing
Brand influencer	Target market
E.D.M.	Marketing plan
Soberoo	Consumer value proposition

INTRODUCTION TO BRANDING

Creating a brand is at the heart of building a powerful marketing program. Everything that you do contributes to the process of brand-building.[2] Brands are the essence of the company in the minds of consumers.

Consumers use brands to differentiate between products and services when they are about to make a purchase. Branding is an efficient, time-saving way to help customers make purchasing decisions. The adage "Nothing happens until somebody sells something" has a new corollary: "Nothing happens until somebody *brands* something."[3]

Your branding program helps customers sort through a crowded marketplace and find your product or service. With a strong brand, your value is crystal clear to consumers, unique and distinct from your competitors' value.[4]

Creating a Personal Brand

At this point you may be feeling queasy about the concept of personal branding because it feels like self-promotion. For some it may feel gimmicky or inauthentic. But personal branding doesn't mean manipulating people or giving them an over-inflated idea of who you are. Personal branding is the process of being clear about your most authentic self and your natural strengths. When you know this, you can be incredibly efficient at expressing who you are and what you stand for to friends, colleagues, and customers.[5]

"Brand you" is the sum of your innate strengths and preferences, which are baked into your genes and stamped into your brain. Your authentic attributes—the way you think, act, and express yourself—are consistent over time and with your friends, family, and colleagues. For example, if you are highly expressive, people can depend on you to bring energy and enthusiasm to a task and happily share your work. If you are reserved, people understand that when you do speak you will say something thoughtful and succinct. If you are a peace-maker, people know you will bring a calming presence and affable attitude to the conversation.[6]

How can you figure out what are your natural strengths? See if you can recall a moment when you were so engrossed in a project or activity that you lost all track of time; when you felt like you were "in the zone" and people told you that you were doing a great job. Moments like these show you were working in your greatest strengths and passions.[7]

Ask those who know you: "What am I good at? What do you come to me for? What information do I give you?" Your strengths might include empathy, individualism, problem solving, enthusiasm, compassion, or coming up with great ideas. When you are engrossed in your strengths, you are completely engaged in your work and in life.[8]

A key to finding your personal brand is to understand why you are doing what you do, and how that fits in with your life's purpose and mission.[9] For musicians, think about the dimensions of audience engagement *beyond* brand development that make your music socially impactful. For whom are you performing? What kind of audience/fan responds to the feelings you express through your music? Get comfortable with the fact that you will not appeal to every person. Trying to be everything to everyone will cause you to feel frustrated and self-doubting. Figure out what kind of listener will engage with you and your music so that you can target your message authentically and confidently.[10]

When you ask friends and colleagues for help in understanding your personal brand and how to market it, know the difference between advice and support. You want seek out supporters, not advisors. Advice comes from someone else's worldview; it's what they would do if they were in your shoes. On the other hand, supporters will help you make decisions that resonate with your strengths, goals, and passions.[11]

Everyone has a personal brand; most just don't know it. Simply put, personal branding is the most important way to proactively control your career development and how the marketplace perceives you. Whether you like it or not, people form perceptions of you in every interaction, including social media. You want to take control of your personal brand with thoughtful and intentional communication.[12]

Consider your behavior on social media. "People often tweet and update without any perspective about themselves," explains Gina Trapani, cofounder of ThinkUp, a subscription service that analyzes how people communicate on Twitter and Facebook. "That's because Facebook and Twitter and other social networks suggest a false sense of intimacy. They tend to lower people's self-control. They worm into your devices, your daily habits and your every free moment, and they change how you think."[13]

ThinkUp helps create mindfulness and awareness of what one says on social media, with the goal of behavioral change. The problem with social media is people act without thinking. There's a "knee-jerk thoughtlessness and lack of empathy that one has because you're online . . . and you're not looking at people's faces," says Trapani.[14] Indeed, it often seems as if outrage is the *lingua franca* of our social media age.[15]

Keep in mind that every post and tweet impacts your personal brand, which in turn has an effect on potential clients, fans, funders, and even employers. You're never more than a few keystrokes away from an embarrassment that could damage your brand and your professional life.[16]

Creating a Brand for Products and Services

Some professional marketers recommend finding one or two words that describe your product or service in such a way as to instantly differentiate them from your competitor's brand. For example, when someone is shopping for a new car and safety is the primary consideration, the brand Volvo will come to mind. If you want a premium electric automobile, the Tesla is probably the first brand you will consider. Both Volvo and Tesla brands are in the "automobile" category, but each has a unique strategy for helping a potential customer find the right car for her needs.[17]

Another marketing tactic is to narrow your brand's focus, which gives the impression that you are a specialist in the category. For example, 75 years ago most people shopped for kitchen utensils in a grocery or hardware store, which also sold ladders, garden tools, canned beans, eggs, and brooms. American entrepreneur Chuck Williams turned his Sonoma, California, hardware store into a French cookware shop in the 1950s and called it Williams-Sonoma. Williams narrowed the focus of his hardware store and branded it to mean "high-end kitchen goods and sophisticated prepared food from France."[18]

Creating a New Category

If your product or service doesn't fit into one specific category, consider announcing a new category in which you are the first. For example, Uber was the first in the category of ride-sharing services. To build a brand in a category that doesn't exist, describe your brand using words such as "first" or "pioneer." Then promote the category, not your brand.[19]

Brands are built with publicity—what others say about you and your product or service for free.[20] It's a lot easier to get some publicity by announcing a new category than it is to announce yet another brand in an existing category. Customers are keenly interested in new categories that will help them solve their problems, whether it's getting groceries delivered to their home in one hour (Instacart) or a home thermostat that they can control from their smartphone (Nest).

Google showed the world how to promote a brand by creating a new category that solved a lot of people's problems:

Narrow the focus of your brand (for example, Google) to a new category (intuitive internet search engines). Then make your brand name stand for the category ("Google it") while at the same time promoting the benefits of the *category*, not the brand:[21] "Don't struggle to find what you're looking for in the vast sea of internet data, use an *intuitive* search engine."

What happens after you create a new category? Inevitably there will be followers. But the arrival of competition creates even more noise in the marketplace, which gets publicity for the category. Media attention will help increase consumer interest and sales for everyone in the category.[22]

A great brand—whether it is personal or business—isn't a collection of half-truths and exaggerations. It is authentic. Claims to authenticity are a brand's credentials, and in the consumer's mind, credentials guarantee that the brand will perform as promised.[23] A great brand provides exceptional customer service and exceeds its customers' expectations.

Choosing a Name

By far the most important branding decision you will make is the name you choose for your product or service. The name will carry you through the early months and years of establishing the unique concept and value of your new product or service. After the excitement wears off, however, what remains in the mind of your customers is whether or not they trust your brand name and how they perceive the brand names of your competitors.[24]

As an example, the term "xerography," a mash-up of two Greek words meaning "dry writing," was coined by the Haloid Photographic Company in 1958 to differentiate its new process for printing images using an electrically charged drum and dry powder toner. The Xerox 914 was the first one-piece plain-paper photocopier in the brand new category of plain-paper copiers, and it sold in the millions.[25] But now all copiers are plain-paper copiers, and Xerox doesn't even make stand-alone copiers anymore. So what's left? The brand name. Xerox still means "copier" to most of us, as in, "I'm going to Xerox this and send you the original," not "Canon" it or "Ricoh" it, the names of two competitor copiers.[26]

If *you* are your company and have an unusual name, consider making that your brand name. If others are likely to have your name, or your name has an awkward translation or meaning in another language, consider creating something that is a combination of part of your name and the unique word that describes your brand. Again, your goal is to help customers find you, not someone who has the same name.[27]

Another way to differentiate your brand in a marketplace of similar products or services is to position it as a high-end or luxury product. This is a delicate balance because you must have something in your brand that justifies its higher price compared to your competitors. To consumers, high-priced goods and services convey exclusivity and higher quality.[28] The customer who carries a Lana Marks Cleopatra clutch doesn't do so to hold more lipsticks; she carries it to let other people know she can afford a US$250,000 handbag.[29]

Social media and an effective online presence are essential marketing and branding tools today. As soon as you can, purchase the domain name that corresponds to your brand name and secure a Facebook page, Twitter account, Google+ account, and whatever other medium of communication that can be personalized. Consider setting up a social media management system, such as Hootsuite or Buffer, so that you can post information to all your accounts at the same time. Building a professional-looking website has gotten a lot easier with platforms like WordPress or Weebly. If you think blogging will help you make a strong emotional connection between your brand and your customers, set one up in less than an hour using WordPress.[30]

Brands and Music

> If handled well, the brands of music professionals are a powerful antidote to the often hollow brands of commerce. The challenge is to leverage this value without damaging the very integrity that makes it special.[31]
>
> Simon Cronshaw and Peter Tullin, founders of Remix

Businesses have understood for a long time how associating their brand with music can speak effectively and directly to the consumers they want to reach. Some companies have moved beyond the traditional means of support—tour sponsorship and licensing songs for ad campaigns—and have created actual recording labels and studios to support indie musicians. Often the advertising and production budgets of these companies exceed the support that major labels can give their artists.[32]

So what's in it for the companies? They're all eager to embrace under-the-radar, next-big-thing musicians, hoping that some of the bands' hip, cool fans will become their fans too.

High-profile examples of a commercial, non-musical brand trying to double as cultural tastemaker by starting a record label include the TV cable network Adult Swim (Adult Swim Singles),[33] beverage company Mountain Dew (Green Label Sound),[34] and energy drink company Red Bull (Red Bull Records).[35] Brewery Stella Artois has Polaris, which is both a record label and the "biggest annual chill-out event" in Denmark.[36]

Clothing maker Levi Strauss has a site called "Unzipped" that explains its culture, sustainability, and social progress (and we thought it only sold jeans). At the moment the site is featuring "8 Music Artists Who Live in Levi's" with the goal of "celebrating the way music influences our everyday style." Artists include The Vaccines, Haim, Kavka Shishido, and Local Natives.[37]

Converse Rubber Tracks is the 5,200-square-foot space in Brooklyn, New York, that holds a sleek recording studio built by the beloved sneaker company in 2010 for indie musicians.[38] In its daily operations, Rubber Tracks provides free, no-strings-attached recording time to indie bands that couldn't otherwise afford professional studio time with world-class engineers and producers. It also hosts pop-up recording studios all over the world—Brazil, Germany, China, Mexico, and the US—with no Converse shoe promotion expected in return.[39]

Converse CMO Geoff Cottrill explains why the company supports music: "Lots of brands use music, and they borrow equity and they try to make their car or their phone or their products cool by associating it with music. We have been really fortunate over the years that musicians themselves have sort of adopted our brand. It goes back to the '50s. Through the iconic punk era, all of these great artists adopted us, and we've been kind of passed down from generation to generation."[40]

In other words, Converse thinks of musicians and artists as its core consumer instead of someone from whom it can borrow the "cool" factor. "As a marketer, when you figure out who your core consumer is, your job is to obsess over them and serve them," says Cottrill. "What's wrong with the music business is that everybody is fighting over ownership split. We make sneakers. We don't want to be in the music business. We don't aspire to run a record label."[41]

For some, the overt and ubiquitous commercialism at music festivals is a stark reminder that music cannot pay its own way. Securing corporate sponsorship is the goal of every musician and festival organizer. Due in large part to changing consumer preferences of streaming rather than owning music, the value of music itself has plummeted.[42]

When music moved into the cloud, not much of the revenue went with it. So the global corporate world has stepped in to fill the financial hole, hoping to piggyback on one of music's most coveted assets—its hip, youthful demographic. Has the situation devolved into letting shoe and snack food companies decide what is artistically worthy? "Anybody who wonders about the impact of big companies as cultural gatekeepers need only go see a studio blockbuster," remarked critic David Carr.[43]

Brand Name Troubles

Electronic dance music is a broad range of percussive electronic music genres produced largely for nightclubs, raves, and festivals. Dance music is generally used in the context of a live DJ mix, where the DJ creates a seamless selection of tracks by segueing from one recording to the next.[44]

The term "E.D.M." refers to the increasingly commercial American electronic music scene. In this context, E.D.M. does not refer to a specific genre, but serves as an umbrella term for several genres, including techno, house, trance, hardstyle, dubstep, drum and bass, trap, and their emerging subgenres such as hardstyle and moombahton.[45, 46, 47]

This is one of the reasons why "E.D.M.," the latest term being used to describe dance music, is problematic. Many resent the term's clear commercial connotation. One reason for this consolidation of classification may be the economics behind the global multi-day, multi-stage dance-music festivals that attract hundreds of thousands of attendees. Finding one catch-all term for the various subgenres of E.D.M. helps simplify the festivals' marketing efforts. Thus, "E.D.M" is shorthand for getting the message to prospective ticket buyers that they can expect "such varied artists and sounds as the sing-along music of Avicii, the taunt techno of Carl Cox, and the destructive dubstep of Skrillex" at any one festival.[48]

Drugs and Audience Deaths Mar the Brand

Its drug-drenched history and concert-goer deaths are two more aspects of E.D.M. that have marred the brand. Mike Bindra and Laura de Palma, two of the founding members of the US dance music community, have been involved since the late 1980s when the music was found primarily in the pre-dawn hours of warehouse clubs of New York, Chicago, and Detroit. Due to its roots in the repressive US gay scene of the 1970s, most of the music stayed in hiding on the turntables of DJs like Frankie Knuckles and Junior Vasquez.[49]

"We had a clear vision all along to take the music out of the darkness and into the light of day," said de Palma. "We'd been to Ibiza"—the Spanish ravers' island—"and knew that it didn't have to be played in blacked-out clubs at 2 in the morning." Bindra and de Palma founded Made Event in New York, which has presented Electric Zoo since 2009.[50]

In a relatively short period of time, electronic dance music has morphed into a "Balearic Island bacchanal to a largely middle-class, US$6.9 billion cultural phenomenon."[51] In 2013, E.D.M. was the fastest-growing music genre in the US. Media entrepreneurs and corporate sponsors such as SFX poured massive amounts of money into festivals like Electric Zoo. The scene has also spawned an educational platform called the International Music Summit (IMS), which is dedicated to electronic music, DJing, and other popular art forms. IMS sponsors major events in Ibiza, Los Angeles, and Singapore.[52]

The year 2014 was a particularly troubled one for the E.D.M. brand, with at least six deaths reported at North American festivals. Following the deaths of two Electric Zoo attendees in 2013, and 2014's early shutdown due to inclement weather, Bindra and de Palma's Made Event has now partnered with the SFX Entertainment subsidiary ID&T (a well-known Dutch festival promoter) to rebrand and redesign the festival as Electric Zoo: Transformed.[53]

In the public soul-searching following the deaths, DJs and promoters pointed out that fans had died at other famous festivals like Bonnaroo and Woodstock. Others noted that when it came to the safety of twenty-somethings looking for a party, there was only so much that a festival manager could do. In 2013, "Electric Zoo's safety measures included 70 emergency technicians, 15 paramedics, five trauma nurses, two physicians and a team of guards on pneumatic lifts with binoculars and night-vision goggles."[54]

Attempts at Brand Resuscitation

"We encourage organizers to acknowledge the drug use, because not acknowledging it is negligent," says Missie Wooldridge, Executive Director of DanceSafe, a nonprofit that works with electronic music event organizers in the US and Canada. "It's usually an uphill battle. They're fearful of any potential legal liabilities in working with us. It's easier for them to just say, 'This is a drug-free event.'"[55]

In Toronto, a nonprofit called Trip works on harm reduction at festivals. Lori Kufner, Trip's coordinator, said it primarily helps people who are having a "bad trip," leaving the emergency work to professionals. "We do a lot of reminding people to drink water, and we keep an eye on the dance floor," Kufner said. "We try to catch people before things get bad."[56]

As the number of summer festivals continues to expand, the presence of volunteer sober groups is spreading. Transcending genre and geography, similar support communities have spread to more than a dozen festivals. Soberoo is a group of clean & sober music fans who have chosen to remain drug- and alcohol-free at Bonnaroo and other music festivals. The sober music scene was started by a group of Grateful Dead fans in the 1980s who wanted to enjoy the music without falling back into their old drug and alcohol excesses. The called themselves the Wharf Rats, after a Grateful Dead song about a down-and-out wino, and used yellow balloons to find each other at concerts. So-called yellow balloon communities began appearing at other jam band events — Phish has the Phellowship, while Widespread Panic has the Gateway. By 2008, Bonnaroo's promoters acknowledged the movement and gave it a clearly marked tent that houses an information table and three or four daily meetings run by volunteers throughout the weekend events.[57]

The idea of bringing drug- and alcohol-free tents to the world of dance music began much later. In 2014 Insomniac Events, the company sponsoring Electric Daisy Carnival in Las Vegas, created the first support space at an E.D.M. event, called Consciousness Group. Says one young E.D.M. fan: "When I first got into recovery, I thought my life was over. How could I ever go to a rave or a festival? I would watch the live-streams of Ultra"—another E.D.M. event—"in my room, and I thought that was the closest I was going to get."[58] Consciousness Group and other such movements make it possible for sober E.D.M. festival-goers to get the support they need while enjoying the music live.

Pause and Reflect

How has your perception of the E.D.M. brand been influenced by the negative press it has received due to drugs and deaths at music festivals?

Brand Influencers

Many advertisers who want to connect with young audiences have turned to so-called influencers: video and social media stars who have thousands of online followers. Advertisers believe that using influencers helps build brand credibility and emotional connections between their brand and potential customers. The tactic has become quite popular with media companies like Viacom and Tumblr.[59]

Advertisers measure how engaged consumers are with content that comes from influencers in likes, comments, re-tweets and shares. AT&T reported that engagement per post on its Instagram feed had increased about 250 percent since it hired influencer Dave Krugman, a photographer who now has nearly 200,000 Instagram followers.[60]

The advertising firm BBDO New York hired Krugman to work on its social media campaigns. "Social isn't just an add-on anymore," said John Osborn, President and Chief Executive of BBDO New York. "Social is really core to all ideas, and the way to build credibility through social is through authenticity and through influence."[61]

Pause and Reflect

Do you pay more attention to a product or service that's endorsed by an influencer on social media? Is this an area of marketing that interests you?

Grenco Science, a technology company in the vaporizer category whose product is called the G Pen, shows another way to harness the power of celebrity. Since its launch in 2012, Grenco's marketing strategy has included co-branding with artists, musicians, and clothing and lifestyle companies. Its bestselling product is a blue-and-white pen covered by a street map of Snoop Dogg's favorite hangouts in Long Beach, California. Grenco's founder, Chris Folkerts, says collaborations with musicians and bands who are outspoken smokers is a natural fit. Beyond the celebrity endorsement, Grenco has encouraged artists and established lifestyle brands to redesign and customize their own pens and packaging.[62]

Rebranding and Brand Rehabilitation

America's most powerful radio broadcaster, Clear Channel Communications, introduced its iHeartRadio app in 2008 as an online outlet for the company's 800+ stations. Now iHeartRadio has become such a central part of Clear Channel's efforts to rebrand itself as a multiplatform media company that "iHeart" was selected as the new identity of the entire operation, with the brand built into practically everything Clear Channel does. The 2014 rebranding is an effort to influence the public's perceptions of the company for the digital age, where traditional radio is being upstaged by digital companies like Pandora and Spotify.[63]

There are plenty of stories of how the "in real time" pace of social media has wreaked havoc with a star's brand. But one such casualty, singer Miley Cyrus, has shown the world that social media also can work to rehabilitate a damaged brand. Cyrus' twerking with Robin Thicke at the MTV Video Music Awards in 2013 caused Twitter to explode, as stunned users posted an average of 306,100 tweets per minute commenting on the performance.[64] The public reaction was largely negative.

Cyrus made deft use of Twitter and Instagram to help reclaim her popularity with the news media and her fans. Over the next year she openly embraced her twenty-something sexuality, framed it as youthful rebellion, and shared the fun times with fans on Instagram. Other efforts at brand rehab included hosting *Saturday Night Live* and visiting a homeless center in Hollywood where she met Jesse Helt, who accepted Cyrus' Video of the Year award for "Wrecking Ball" on behalf of homeless youth at the MTV Video Awards in 2014.[65]

Pause and Reflect

The 2015 US copyright lawsuit over the song "Blurred Lines" provided a rare window into an unseemly and embarrassing side of the music industry. Testimony and pretrial documents revealed lurid details of drugs, unearned songwriting credits, and intentional deception of the news media employed as a standard promotional practice.[66] Do you think this has improved or damaged the entire music industry's brand?

INTRODUCTION TO MARKETING

Marketing your brand to potential stakeholders—including fans, sponsors, co-writers, and merchandise purchasers—is an activity that you will begin once your brand is in place. As you can see from the previous section, you may need to adjust or even rehabilitate your brand from time to time. The following key concepts will give you a broad overview of the field of marketing to help you create a plan to keep your brand in the public eye.

One of the first marketing concepts to explore is determining who is your customer. We began working on this in the previous section and now we are going to expand it further. When I ask creative people to tell me who their ideal customer is, many hesitate or blurt out "well, pretty much anyone who likes music." But such a non-specific, unfocused image of your ideal customer makes it very difficult to create an effective strategy.[67]

David Guetta

Ethan Miller/Getty Images Entertainment

Mini-Case Study: David Guetta—Marketing Strategies for Building Global Hits

David Guetta is one of the most popular dance music artists in the world. A French musician who has been recording and DJ'ing for more than 20 years, Guetta and his team have successfully used music streaming platforms to build his worldwide success.

When it comes to deciding when and where to launch a music campaign, artists rely heavily on the massive amount of data that is generated from streaming services and other online sources. Guetta "is very hands-on in deciding which tracks he wants to promote and works closely with us on his promotional campaigns," says Bart Cools, executive vice president of dance music marketing at Warner Recorded Music. He says that Warner and Guetta monitor data to see which of his tracks are making an impact in specific territories and are worth additional marketing expenditures.[68]

For example, Guetta and Cools looked at encouraging data coming in from Germany a few months before Christmas 2014. Combining that with the knowledge that the fourth quarter typically is the biggest for recorded music, they decided to invest in additional marketing in Germany, which was not Guetta's strongest territory. The risk paid off. Guetta's album, *Listen*, became a top five Christmas hit that year.[69]

Streaming music platforms have become a major piece of dance music artists' marketing strategies. Says Cool: "We issued the track, 'Bad,' as a pre-release for the album primarily for his core fans, and thanks to streaming services we were able to get millions of streams with something that is not a traditional radio-friendly hit."[70]

Guetta's team uses different strategies to generate a hit in different territories. "When David is active we tend to promote four or five tracks a year in Europe and Australia, whereas in the US we'll probably go for fewer, maybe two or three, because it can take five to nine months to work a track to become a top 40 radio hit," explains Cools. "Some markets are cautious, such as Germany where mainstream radio might be hesitant to play it, but you have to plan on a global basis."[71]

Your Creative Niche

Finding your creative niche and targeting your marketing to a defined audience are the next two key marketing concepts to tackle. In marketing terms, a niche is a small, focused area of a marketplace. When you narrow your focus, you create an opportunity to bond more closely with a specific type of music consumer.[72]

Sound and voiceovers for ads in the multi-faceted and nuanced Hispanic market is an example of a niche market. Jaime Zapata and Raquel Ramirez saw an opportunity to cater to the Spanish-language ad market in California (US). So they founded Tono Studios, a commercial audio company in California, to create sound specifically for advertisements in Spanish. The challenge of serving the Hispanic advertising market goes beyond recording, mixing, and editing. An ad must be culturally authentic.[73]

The term "Hispanic" is a broad term used to describe a diverse population of people from more than 20 countries, each with its own traditions, dialects, and slang. "If the writer is from Mexico and didn't take into account that the ad is not just for people who are Mexican, it will not be the same, even if it is in perfect Spanish," Zapata explains. Tono itself has six full-time employees representing Argentina, Colombia, Mexico, and Peru.[74]

Content Marketing

A specific type of marketing, known as content marketing, can be an effective way of serving existing customers and attracting new ones. Content marketing was developed as a way to combat the growing sophistication of consumers' ability to ignore traditional ads.[75]

The premise is that content marketing looks and feels less like an ad to be ignored and more like valuable information that a customer will want to absorb. Information is "valuable" if people *want* to consume the information rather than trying to avoid it.[76]

In short, content marketing is the art of communicating with your customers and prospects without appearing to sell them something. Instead of pitching a product or service, content marketing is perceived as information that makes a buyer smarter and better informed. In theory, if businesses deliver consistently "valuable" information to potential customers (content marketing), they will ultimately become loyal purchasing buyers of the product or service.[77]

Infographics, podcasts, and short-form videos are all examples of content marketing. Infographics generally are vertical graphics that include statistics, charts, graphs, and other information. Infographics may contain a lot of data, but their visual presentation is much friendlier than reading the same data written out in a couple of paragraphs. Podcasts are a growing and relatively new form of content marketing. Michael Hyatt, author of the bestselling book *Platform: Get Noticed in a Noisy World,* has a podcast on his website that is viewed 250,000 times a month. He says: "A podcast gives you visibility in a completely different world—primarily iTunes. I have had scores of new people say they had never heard of me until they stumbled onto me in iTunes."[78] YouTube is, of course, one of the best and most enduring examples of how content marketing can be very effective using short-form videos.

Know Your Customer

As a content marketer, it's crucial to understand how your potential customers use digital content if you are planning to communicate with them online. To better understand how digital content consumption differs by generation, the content marketing agency Fractl,[79] together with customer relationship management company BuzzStream,[80] surveyed more than 1,200 people from these three generations:

- Millennials (people who were born between 1981 and 1997).

- Generation X (born between 1965 and 1980).

- Baby Boomers (born between 1946 and 1964).

Here is a brief overview of what they learned:[81]

- Percentage of each generation engaged in online content for 20+ hours per week:

  - Millenials: 20 percent.

  - Generation X: 22 percent.

  - Baby Boomers: 27 percent.

- Time of day each generation consumes the most online content:

  - Millenials: 8PM–Midnight (35 percent).

  - Generation X: 8PM–Midnight (35 percent).

  - Baby Boomers: 9AM–12 Noon (22 percent) and 6PM–8PM (15 percent).

Three Women
Marcio Eugenio/Shutterstock.com

- Primary devices used for viewing online content:

  ◦ Millenials: Laptop (35 percent), Desktop (28 percent), Mobile (26 percent), Tablet (9 percent).

  ◦ Generation X: Laptop (39 percent), Desktop (36 percent), Mobile (27 percent), Tablet (8 percent).

  ◦ Baby Boomers: Laptop (43 percent), Desktop (39 percent), Mobile (7 percent), Tablet (11 percent).

- The most and least consumed types of content were consistent across all generations:

  ◦ Most favorite content types: blog articles, images and comments.

  ◦ Least favorite content types: quizzes, webinars, flipbooks (and memes for Baby Boomers).

- All generations agreed that 300 words is the ideal length for articles.

- Facebook is the social platform used most often by all three generations for sharing content.

- Images are by far the preferred visual content for all three generations (the choices included videos, memes, GIFs, infographics, charts/graphs, slide shares, trend analyses, and flipbooks.) For Baby Boomers and Generation X, videos were a close second choice, while memes (virally transmitted cultural symbols or social ideas) were the next favorite for Millenials.[82]

The Tween Market

Children aged 10–14 are known as "tweens," a market that has the power to buy enough concert tickets, music, and merchandise to make their favorite singers stars. In the US, tweens account for nearly US$200 billion in spending each year, of which approximately 10 percent is music-related.[83] The Walt Disney Company was an early adopter of a marketing strategy for tweens, using its television series and Radio Disney in the early 2000s to appeal to this age group. When Disney artists like Taylor Swift, Miley Cyrus, and Demi Lovato became pop stars, Disney realized that its vast experience in cross-marketing could be influential in the music industry.[84]

Now music marketing to tweens is a US$17 billion annual industry. In a twist on traditional thinking, music has become the major content delivery system, not simply one of the industry's products. Demi Lovato doesn't just sell songs; she has her own makeup, clothing, and nail polish lines. And her best customers are her overwhelmingly female tween audience.[85]

By age 12, most girls are working hard to be like the teenagers they see on TV and in school. Tween girls are very active consumers and heavy users of social media. Their pop idols understand this and extensively use social media to communicate with their fans. And, as their tween fans grow up, artists like Swift, Lovato, and Cyrus must try to keep them close while reaching out to the newest crop of 12-year-olds.[86]

A recent study suggests that by age 33, most people no longer seek out new music. Ajay Kalia, product owner for taste profiles at Spotify and blogger at Skynet & Ebert, notes in the study that our interest in discovering new pop music is keen until age 25, then drops off steadily into our thirties until we've settled into an unhip groove.[87]

Kalia's study shows that, on average:

- while teens' taste in music is heavily dominated by new pop music, this proportion drops steadily through peoples' twenties, before their tastes "mature" in their early thirties;

- men and women listen similarly in their teens, but after that, men's mainstream music listening decreases much faster than it does for women;

- at any age, people with children listen to smaller amounts of currently popular music than the average listener of that age.[88]

How can you use this information for marketing your music product or service? Every single thing you know about your target audience will help you focus your marketing resources efficiently and appropriately.

Keeping Fans Close

If you want to stay in touch with your audience in a low-tech way, consider using an email platform, such as Mailchimp or Constant Contact, so you don't have to use your personal email account. A software platform like Topspin Media is very musi-

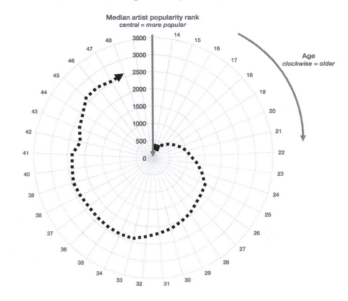

Infographic by Ajay Kalia: #1 "On average, peoples' music taste evolves quickly"

April 22, 2015, Skynet & Ebert, skynetandebert.com/author/amkalia/

cian-friendly. It helps you communicate with your fans and can connect them to your online store.[89]

Sites like Bandcamp can help your fans find and purchase your music and merch. Bandcamp has useful features like allowing you to monitor real-time sales statistics and make tie-ins and bundled offers with music and merch. Nearly all global currencies are accepted, and Bandcamp submits US, Canadian, and international sales reports to SoundScan every week. Bandcamp currently takes a commission on sales.[90]

Most of us humans are drawn to goals and rewards. Encourage your fans and customers to stay in touch by rewarding them with a loyalty program. We are all familiar with restaurants and retail shops that offer something free after a specific number of visits or dollar amount of purchases. Musicians can offer inexpensive yet effective rewards such as a shout-out at a concert, meet and greets, exclusive access during rehearsals, or a personally written song for loyal supporters.[91]

For example, Smoke Sessions, a new record label founded by the New York City jazz club Smoke, rewards its customers by inviting them to become part of live recordings. The musicians play their best when the house is full, and customers love being in on the action of a live recording.[92]

Get Your Fans and Audience Involved

Former Israeli rock star Yoni Bloch wanted to create a scripted music video that would let viewers make certain choices as the story unfolded. But the technology did not exist, so Bloch and his band members developed it themselves and created the video for US$2,000. That technology is now the basis for Interlude, a company Bloch helped found in 2010 that is a challenger to YouTube. "Our basic idea was that instead of building one curated ride, we would let creators build a playground and let other people do it," he said.[93]

Bloch's video technology also led to a new joint venture with Warner Music Group called Interlude Music, which is home to stars like Coldplay and Bruno Mars. Artists who've made Interlude videos include Bob Dylan, Wiz Khalifa, and Coldplay.[94]

Yoni Bloch

Slaven Vlasic/Getty Images Entertainment

For Warner and advertisers that use Interlude, the appeal of the technology lies in how it lures people to be more active viewers. A more engaged audience yields higher ad rates, plus Interlude's complex narratives offer ways for producers to incorporate brands into the videos (for a fee).[95]

Digital Media Marketing in Opera and Classical Music

In the fall of 2014 the great American mezzo-soprano Joyce DiDonato made digital history in the worlds of opera and classical music. A fan-sponsored online campaign went viral and propelled DiDonato, who is adept with social media, onto the field of Kauffman Stadium in Kansas City, Missouri (US). She sang the national anthem in a World Series game featuring her hometown baseball team, the Royals. The unexpected online response by her fans grew so big that for the first time she could not keep up with her accounts on Twitter and Facebook. "Maybe they'll click over," she said, hoping that some baseball fans will start listening to opera.[96]

A few days later, DiDonato's New York City recital of Venetian-themed songs made history as the first Carnegie Hall concert streamed free over the internet.[97] The classical website Medici.tv filmed DiDonato's recital and made it available free for 90 days after the performance. Medici.tv offers free access to live concerts and replays, but charges for access to its archive of 1,400 performances.[98]

Orchestras and opera houses around the world are finally beginning to use music streaming as a marketing tool. Forced to consider alternatives to the traditional economics of classical recording and broadcasting, arts administrators are embracing new media cautiously. Clive Gillinson, Executive and Artistic Director of Carnegie Hall, explains: "The way it used to work is that performances promoted media, and it was through media that artists made money, with big recording contracts, with TV . . . It is now exactly the opposite model. So, essentially, media promotes performances. Every artist is making their living in the concert hall."[99]

Joyce DiDonato at baseball game

Ron Vessely/Major League Baseball/Getty Images

Mini-Case Studies: Introduction to Marketing Plans

Sam Smith: Getting Nearly Everything Right

British singer-songwriter Sam Smith swept into the international music scene seemingly overnight, picking up four Grammy Awards in 2015, including Best New Artist and Record of the Year, and two BRIT Awards. Here is a brief look at the marketing strategies that Smith and his team used to get him to the top.

Joyce DiDonato

Hiroyuki Ito/Hultan Archive/Getty Images

Smith's first New York concert, in August 2013, was at the 250-seat Mercury Lounge, with all tickets priced at US$12. Seventeen months later, he sold out the 18,200-seat iconic Madison Square Garden in less than five minutes. His astonishing ascent shows what can still happen in the music industry when a marketing plan clicks and the artist is ready to fly.[100]

Smith signed with Capitol Music Group in 2012 and was given the rare opportunity to take time to find his feet musically before producing an album. In one early collaboration, producer Naughty Boy invited Smith to lay vocals over one of his tracks. The result was "La La La," which came out on Smith's

Sam Smith Grammys

Jason LaVeris/FilmMagic/Getty Images

twenty-first birthday and became a hit.[101]

Smith's debut album, *In the Lonely Hour*, was completed in December 2013 and Capitol decided to take the lead single "Money on My Mind" to radio. Simultaneously Smith was awarded the BRITS 2014 Critics' Choice award, which put him in the company of previous winners Adele, Emeli Sandé, and Tom Odell.[102]

The buzz started to build. In order to quickly put Smith before a wider audience, Capitol devised a novel marketing concept – the UK's first live TV ad. The ad aired in May 2014 and featured Smith performing the single "Stay With Me" live from the Camden Roundhouse (London). "Stay With Me" sold more than two million copies, pushing the album *In the Lonely Hour* into the million-plus sales category.[103]

From an appearance on *Saturday Night Live* to business details like the management of digital sales, Smith and his label executed a comprehensive, well-timed marketing plan. "He is the perfect new artist in this world we live in," said Steve Barnett, chairman of Smith's label. "Five years ago you could not have done what we did in the last six months."[104]

The Piano Guys: Carving Out a New Marketing Path

The marketing strategy for the Piano Guys can best be described as "carving out a new path with a delicate machete."[105] The four-man group (a pianist, cellist, videographer, and producer) has become a YouTube sensation with its videos of classical and pop mash-ups performed at places like the Great Wall of China, the Christ statue in Rio, and a film set of the Batcave. Their YouTube channel has well over 3 million subscribers.[106]

Everything about this group, from its music to its marketing strategy, upends the traditional approach.[107] Its back-story is compelling. Paul Anderson, a piano shop owner in a small southern Utah town (US), wanted to sell more instruments in an unconventional way. He had heard of something called YouTube and decided to take a chance on using music videos as a sales pitch.[108] He assembled a team of friends to help write copy, stage, and film the performances, put the videos on YouTube, and watched in astonishment as they went viral. Anderson turned out to be a master at content marketing.

In 2012 the Piano Guys secured a very unusual contract with Sony Music. Sony distributes their music internationally and the musicians have complete creative control. Instead of paying royalties to the Piano Guys—the traditional label deal—Sony shares the profits with the Piano Guys as partners. Long before Sony, however, the band had created a productive and successful marketing and music-making process that included making 20 videos using their own funds. Since partnering with Sony, the band has released five albums and 30 more videos.[109]

In true cross-genre fashion, the Piano Guys' music is hard to fit into any specific category. They combine songs and music from composers as diverse as Michael Jackson, Mozart, One Direction, Disney, and Vivaldi. Their target audience is families with children. The band's layered and comprehensive marketing plan includes both social media and traditional forms of publicity.[110]

The Piano Guys have found an authentic, unique way to connect with a niche audience. They advise young classical musicians hoping to be noticed on YouTube to "crank out consistent, quality content. Listen to your audience's feedback, but always stay true to your passion."[111]

Jay Z: Answering "What's in It for Me?"

The bumpy marketing effort surrounding the launch of Jay Z's music streaming service Tidal underscored the importance of a basic marketing truth: no matter how famous the pitchman, the product must answer the ordinary customer's question "what's in it for me?" "The whole announcement seemed geared toward other artists," said the late Dave Goldberg, former Chief Executive of Survey Monkey. "What is the consumer value proposition? Why should I sign up for Tidal when I can sign up for Spotify?"[112]

The company had misjudged the average music consumers' interest in the issue of fair royalties for artists. "If felt like a bit of a lecture," said Amy Thomson, manager of DJ acts like Axwell and Ingrosso. "If you choose to make such a big point about how artists are paid, you should make sure that the person on the other side of that debate cares."[113]

Ways to Stand Out in a Crowded Marketplace

As this section comes to a close, let's explore some general concepts and strategies that are important to include in every marketing plan.

Build on Your Current Community . . .

Spread your message by asking your current customers to recommend you or your company to a friend. Word of mouth may be low-tech, but it's still an effective method.

. . . Then Say "Thanks" in a Special Way

"A 'thank you' can change someone's day, so that's why we have been surprising our customers across Canada, to say 'TD Thanks You,'" said Tim Hockey, President and CEO of TD Canada Trust.[114] The bank put its philosophy into action with its "TD Thanks You" marketing campaign, which included giving 300,000 twenty-dollar gift certificates to its clients. While this level of thanks may not be within every business' reach, taking the time to thank someone for being your customer always resonates in a special way.[115]

Work Your Personal Strengths

The best way to stand out is to take what's already working for you and do more of it. Build on your strengths by noting which parts of your marketing plan are the most effective. This will help you remain a trusted and reputable brand to your customers.[116]

PRACTICE YOUR BRANDING AND MARKETING SKILLS

The following case studies are designed for you to practice your branding and marketing skills. The questions that follow each case will help you think about how you would determine the brand, identify the primary audience/fanbase, and design a marketing campaign. This is all hypothetical, of course, and there is no right or wrong way of going about it. Refer to the earlier pages in the chapter to help you work through each case in a logical way. Use your creative thinking ability, be bold, and have fun.

Case #1: Taylor Swift

The path of a creative entrepreneur was never meant to be straight. You may be doing perfectly well in your current endeavors when you notice that your artistic curiosity has been pulling you in a different direction. How do you decide whether or not to explore this opportunity? How might a change affect your brand and your relationship with your customers and fans?

Taylor Swift Red *Tour w/Ed Sheeran*
Gareth Cattermole/TAS/Getty Images Entertainment

In 2012, Taylor Swift was one of the most famous country singers in the world when she jolted fans by releasing her album *Red*, which featured synth-pop songs and even a bit of dubstep instead of the familiar country twang. Why did Swift risk alienating her millions of loyal fans, plus every person and radio station in Nashville, by leaving country music behind? This was the question on everyone's lips.

Swift has an unwavering sense of who she is and an uncommon determination to express that through song lyrics. Since the tender age of 10, she had a plan to reach her dream of becoming a country music recording artist. Why country music for a young woman who grew up in Pennsylvania? Country music lyrics tell stories—livin', lovin' and leavin' stories. Swift connected with these songs and the expressiveness of the artists in telling the stories to their fans.

A Setback and a Challenge

But Swift's path to realizing her dream was not straight. No one on Nashville's Music Row was interested in an 11-year-old girl named Taylor the day she dropped off her demo CD of LeAnn Rimes and Dixie Chicks cover songs. Swift's first trip to Nashville was a bust in terms of getting signed to a label.

Swift returned to Pennsylvania. She realized that cover songs and karaoke didn't really express who she was musically and wasn't going to get her where she wanted to be. So she decided to learn how to write her own music and play the guitar. For the next two and a half years, she kept herself on a rigid schedule of music lessons and songwriting every day after school until 9PM. Finally, after getting enthusiastic support from her friends and playing every fair and festival she could find, she talked her parents into moving the family to Nashville, where she finished high school.

There Swift continued to develop her songwriting skills and began to build a loyal fanbase. Two of her earliest fans were country singing legend Dolly Parton and Bruce Springsteen, both highly successful songwriters and music entrepreneurs. They recognized Swift's ability to attract fans and keep them close with her endearingly old-fashioned form of romanticism. "I want to make people feel things when they hear my music," Swift explains.[117]

Swift's songwriting material comes from her life experiences and her authentic, accessible earnestness and craft. She states: "When you're growing up and essentially publishing your diary for the world to read, you end up incorporating new themes as these themes become evident to you in your own life."[118]

Her Target Audience

Swift's primarily female fan base of teens and early twenty-somethings "are discovering the music that tells them how they are going to live their lives and how they should feel and how it's acceptable to feel," she says. "I think that's kind of exciting."[119] Even now, as the top-selling *pop* artist in the world, she still takes time to respond to messages from her fans and send thank-you notes to radio stations that play her music.

There have been other country stars who successfully switched genres—Pink, Katy Perry, Darius Rucker, and Alanis Morissette—and a few whose changes weren't quite as successful (Garth Brooks and Jessica Simpson). But, from the start, "Swift's easy mastery of contemporary country tropes, like the slight twang in her voice and that subtle pedal steel, suggested she'd quickly feel limited by the genre."[120] In fact, the 2008 "Love Story," Swift's first pop hit, was available in two versions. The original had acoustic instrumentation and targeted a country audience, while the mix for mainstream pop listeners included electric guitars. "You Belong With Me" had an even bolder electric guitar presence. It was a well-thought-out strategy that kept her options open while she decided which path she would ultimately choose—country or pop.[121]

By 2012, it was clear that Swift wasn't interested in a crossover stance – she wanted to dominate the pop marketplace. So she teamed with Swedish megapop producer Max Martin (Britney Spears, Katy Perry, Avril Lavigne) and his frequent partner Shellback to create her first Number 1 hit, "We Are Never Ever Getting Back Together Again." Many considered this Swift's breakup song to country music.[122]

A New Direction

If there were any lingering doubts, Swift's 2014 blockbuster hit video "Shake It Off" set things straight. Seeming to taunt and defy her former country music roots, she danced with innocent but clearly deliberate ineptitude. "Shake It Off" was the final gem in her well-deserved Queen of Pop crown.[123]

Michael Martin, head of Programming and Music Initiatives at CBS Radio, says that Swift will always have crossover appeal on radio "as long as she keeps writing songs that speak to her target audience, which is female." And for Swift, that audience is a major consumer of today's mass media pop radio.[124]

"She's a young, 24-year-old female," Martin said of Swift. "She's writing a song that talks to women and says, 'I don't care what other people think. I don't care what they say.' She's empowering the audience, and that's a great message to send to any audience, regardless of format."[125]

As Swift explains it when talking about her latest album, *1989*:

> I've always implemented different kinds of sensibilities from different genres in my music and that's been something I've been proud of. I've always wanted an album that had a very distinctive sound, and this one is very synthesizer-based and automated drums and layered vocals. I think that the most authentic thing to do, and the most authentic way to approach it was to be honest about what it was.[126]

The Best Choices Are Bold Choices

"This time around I've chosen the brave and bold way of going about things," said Swift. "Because with this album [*1989*] I've completely changed the sound of everything I've done until now. So it's interesting to not be afraid of that. You know, I

Taylor Swift 1989 *Tour*
Jeff Vinnick/Getty Images Entertainment

don't want to hurt people's feelings, I don't want to betray Nashville, whatever, but essentially it comes down to challenging yourself as an artist."[127]

Marketing Questions to Consider

1. Can you tell, by listening to Taylor Swift's songs from 2006 to 2012, that she was exploring pop music even while planted firmly in Nashville's country music scene?
2. What is Swift's brand? Has it changed with her genre shift?
3. Imagine that you are one of Swift's trusted advisors in the time period of the album *Red's* release (2012). How would you advise her to move forward (pretend you don't know the outcome)? Design a comprehensive marketing plan for Swift as she prepares for her next album.

Case #2: South African Hip-Hop

South African hip-hop reached a turning point in its bid for worldwide recognition when hip-hop veteran K.O. won Record of the Year at the MTV Africa Music Awards, South Africa's equivalent of the Grammys. It was the first time in the award program's 21-year history that a hip-hop recording had reached this level of prominence.[128]

K.O.'s award-winning song "Caracara" is a bass-heavy ode to a VW camper van that was popular with black people in the 1990s for cruising through the townships. The track, which also featured Kid X, "was unashamedly South African in both subject and execution. Delivered in a mix of languages, dealing with a subject that the nation could love, and using a beat that owed as much to the electronic intensity of South Africa's dance scene as to any American hip-hop." The song demonstrated to the judges that South African hip-hop had come of age on its own terms.[129]

"The texture of our beats used to be foreign—it was like we were trying to do what Jay Z or Drake were doing in America," K.O. said. "So when we finally made the decision to use our own cultural influences to create what is now South African hip-hop identity, we found it was more appealing not only to fellow South Africans but also beyond our own borders. We now have traction in Nigeria, in East Africa, Central Africa."[130]

K.O. on red carpet at 2015 MTV Africa Music Awards

Gallo Images/Getty Images

A Golden Age

Hip-hop artist AKA, whose single "All Eyes On Me" was the first South African hip-hop tune to be A-Listed on 1Xtra (a BBC radio network),[131] thinks this may be "a golden age" for hip-hop in his country. He describes a new sense of pride among South African musicians in approaching their own cultural heritage. "Right now I think we're going through a revival of sampling our own music, and pushing our own music, as opposed to sampling international artists," he said. "Sampling is different now, we don't sample George Benson or the Temptations. Now we're looking to artists like Brenda Fassie or Fela Kuti."[132]

South Africa has a national fascination with house music. It is played everywhere from nightclubs to taxis and banks. South Africa's homegrown version of house music is known as Kwaito, which is a combination of house rhythms with rap vocals. Many feel Kwaito is the true South African version of hip-hop.[133] The Kwaito beat is heavy and synth-driven, a party music "sound" that is meant for club dancing.[134]

Hip-Hop's Early Days in South Africa

The development of South African hip-hop began in the 1990s. P.O.C. was one of the first on the scene. P.O.C.'s politically tinged lyrics caught the attention of the apartheid government and they were banned from performing.[135]

Hip-hop pioneers Skwatta Kamp played an important role in the South African hip-hop industry. Their 1997 album *Washumkhukhu,* along with their enormously popular single "Umoya" from the album *Experience South Africa,* were high points in the development of the country's hip-hop industry.[136]

Yet another hip-hop era was ushered in by Teargas with their 2004 song, "Go Away." The group, made up of artists K.O., Ma-E, and Ntukza,[137] chose its name in a deliberately provocative manner. It is a reminder of the June 16, 1976 Soweto Youth Uprising, when young South Africans marched against apartheid and were greeted with teargas and rubber bullets.[138] Using the name Teargas in 2004 was a way to focus South Africa on its post-apartheid struggles.[139] The group won the "Best Rap" award for their album *Dark or Blue* at the 2010 Africa Music Awards.[140]

Other influential hip-hop artists who served as stepping stones along the way include HHP with the song "Music and Lights" and Khuli Chana with "No More Hunger."[141]

A New Direction

In 2011 Teargas decided to take a new approach to hip-hop. Ma-E and K.O. set up a label called Cashtime Records to support new artists.[142] In addition to a bestselling solo album from K.O. and the big club hit, "uGogo" from Ma-E, Cashtime is responsible for finding and nurturing South Africa's hottest new talent, including Kid-X, Maggz, Moozlie, Riky Rick, and Boss Zonke. Their collective sound "took the deep electronic soundscapes of Kwaito and slowed them down to a slinking hip-hop tempo."[143] The new generation of artists appears eager to help the distinctly South African brand of hip-hop take on the world.

Marketing Questions to Consider

1. How does South African hip-hop express the cultural and political history of the country? How has it broken away from American influences to find its own unique voice?
2. Cashtime is a lifestyle brand as well as a record label. What other companies or groups are helping to build the excitement of South Africa's burgeoning hip-hop movement?
3. Taking into consideration the grassroots nature of the music, design a brand and marketing plan for expanding into new markets for South African hip-hop.

Case #3: The Baalbeck Festival, Lebanon

One of the Middle East's oldest arts institutions, the Baalbeck Festival, takes place deep within Lebanon's Bekaa Valley, a Hezbollah stronghold 11 km from the Syrian border. Since 1956, the summer festival has presented dance, theater, and music in the Temple of Bacchus, which UNESCO calls "one of the world's finest examples of imperial Roman architecture."[144]

The Gods Are Near

The festival has hosted many world-class productions, including the Old Vic Theatre Company, the Ballet Rambert, and the New York Philharmonic. Then, in the 1970s, jazz came to Baalbeck, following a series of stormy showdowns at committee meetings about the suitability of its unorthodox rhythms. Ella Fitzgerald, Nina Simone, Miles Davis, and Dizzy Gillespie took to the stage. Herbie Hancock looked around at the crumbling temples and declared: "I feel near the gods when I'm here."[145]

But the ancient site now finds itself a hostage to modern geopolitics.[146]

Music and Rocket Fire

While all festival promoters around the world face challenges, Baalbeck must contend with some extraordinary situations that are out of its control: rocket fire, crowds of refugees, soldiers, and war. For nearly 20 years, starting in 1974, the Festival fell silent as the country collapsed into civil war. Picking up the pieces after such a long hiatus required courage and diplomacy. Potential visitors are discouraged from traveling to this war-torn area. Baalbeck's location makes it very challenging to persuade world-class artists to come and perform.[147]

One artist who is not fearful is Nihad Haddad, better known as *Fairuz*, a Lebanese singer who is among the most widely admired and deeply respected living singers in the Arab region. On the night of Fairuz's pre-opening performance at Baalbeck in 2006, shelling began. She refused to stop her show, hoping that the shelling would end quickly. But eventually she was persuaded to leave the stage and take cover backstage, where she was briefly trapped. Military intervention was needed to bring her to a safe place.[148]

Lebanese diva Fairuz
Anadolu Agency/Getty Images

We Still Exist

In 2013 the festival was forced to relocate at the last minute to an abandoned factory near Beirut due to heavy fighting in nearby Syria. Baalbeck's President, Nayla de Freige, explains that the Baalbeck Festival is a national project where everyone is involved, "including the ministries of culture and tourism, the prime minister and the president—when we have one." For de Freige and many others, it's a matter of national pride to keep the festival running. "The idea," de Freige says, "[is] simply to say that we still exist."[149]

Security forces at Baalbeck Int'l Festival
JOSEPH EID/AFP/Getty Images

Marketing Questions to Consider

1. With such a long history and ancient venue as its home, Baalbeck already has a solid brand. Do you think it should stick with that or consider rebranding, given the politics of the region?
2. Based on your answer to question #1, create a marketing plan for Baalbeck's next season of events. If you want, go ahead and select the artists as well. Be sure, however, that the artists, brand, and marketing efforts are all in alignment.

Opportunities Ahead

The public uses brand identities to help them make choices in a noisy and crowded consumer marketplace. What opportunities do you see for your music and/or your musical venture as you begin to build your authentic brand?

CONCLUSION

Discovering your personal brand is the first step in understanding how you can serve your customers. Choosing a name that represents your authentic self and shows how you're different from your competition is key. Marketing your product or service to the public involves finding a creative niche, knowing your customer, using content marketing, and keeping your fans close. The value of marketing plans was demonstrated with examples from Sam Smith, The Piano Guys, and Tidal. The three practice marketing plans gave you an opportunity to practice your branding and marketing skills with Taylor Swift, the South African hip-hop scene, and the Baalbeck Festival in Lebanon.

 Talking Back: Class Discussion

Consider all the aspects of building a marketing plan for a global artist. You know that there are major cultural, political, social, and economic differences in each of the world's major music markets. How can you learn about those differences and reflect your understanding in a global marketing plan?

NOTES

1 Ben Brantley, "Review: Helen Mirren Stars in 'The Audience' on Broadway," *New York Times*, March 9, 2015, www.nytimes.com/2015/03/09/theater/review-the-audience-with-helen-mirren-opens-on-broadway.html (accessed May 16, 2016).
2 Al Ries and Laura Ries, *The 22 Immutable Laws of Branding* (New York: HarperCollins, 1998), 2.
3 Ibid, 3.

4 Ibid, 4.

5 Jeff Haden, "One Word That Defines a Great Personal Brand," *Inc.*, August 6, 2012, www.inc.com/jeff-haden/the-one-word-that-defines-a-great-personal-brand.html/3 (accessed May 16, 2016).

6 Geil Browning, "What Your Brain Has to Do with Your Brand," *Inc.*, June 25, 2012, www.inc.com/geil-browning/personal-branding-what-your-brain-has-to-do-with-your-brand.html (accessed May 16, 2016).

7 Erin Arvedlund "Personal Brand Is in Your Strengths," *Philadelphia Inquirer*, February 8, 2015.

8 Ibid.

9 Laura Garnett, "How to Build a Great Personal Brand," *Inc.*, July 26, 2013, www.inc.com/laura-garnett/how-to-build-a-great-personal-brand.html (accessed May 16, 2016).

10 Ibid.

11 Ibid.

12 Mark Suster, "Your Personal Brand Matters," *Inc.*, July 24, 2013, www.inc.com/mark-suster/your-personal-brand-matters.html (accessed May 16, 2016).

13 Farhad Manjoo, "Get to Know Your Social Media Persona," *New York Times*, January 1, 2015.

14 Ibid.

15 Nate Chinen, "An All-Year Season of Discontent in Jazz," *New York Times*, December 31, 2014.

16 Manjoo, "Get to Know"

17 Ries and Ries, *The 22 Immutable Laws*, 40.

18 Ibid, 7, 8.

19 Ibid, 68.

20 Ibid, 7.

21 Ibid, 69–71.

22 Ibid, 70.

23 Ibid, 50–54

24 Ibid, 74–77.

25 Claudia H. Deutsch, "Xerox Hopes Its New Logo Doesn't Say 'Copier,'" *New York Times*, January 7, 2008.

26 Ries and Ries, 74–78.

27 Geoffrey James, "Create Your Personal Brand: Eight Steps," *Inc.*, April 23, 2013, inc.com/geoffrey-james/create-your-personal-brand-8-steps.html (accessed May 16, 2016).

28 Ries and Ries, *The 22 Immutable Laws*, 61.

29 "Top 10 Most Expensive Handbags in the World: Louis Vuitton, Hermes & Chanel," *Finances Online*, www.financesonline.com/top-10-most-expensive-handbags-in-the-world-louie-vuitton-diamonds-crocodile-skin (accessed May 16, 2016).

30 James, "Create Your Personal Brand."

31 Simon Cronshaw and Peter Tullin, "Intelligent Naivety," www.slideshare.net/culturelabel/culturelabel-intelligent-naivety (accessed May 16, 2016).

32 Ben Sisario, "Looking to a Sneaker for a Band's Big Break," *New York Times*, October 6, 2010.

33 "Adult Swim Singles," *Adult Swim*, www.adultswim.com/music/singles-2014 (accessed May 16, 2016).

34 "Green Label," *Green Label*, http:/www.greenlabel.com (accessed May 16, 2016).

35 "Home," *Red Bull Records*, www.redbullrecords.com (accessed May 16, 2016).

36 "Labels: Stella Polaris Music," *Resident Advisor*, www.residentadvisor.net/labels.aspx (accessed May 16, 2016).

37 "8 Music Artists Who Live in Levi's," *Unzipped*, February 17, 2015, www.levistrauss.com/unzipped-blog/2015/02/musicians-live-in-levis (accessed May 16, 2016).

38 "Converse," www.converse.com (accessed May 16, 2016).

39 Evie Nagy, "How Converse Supports Musicians without the Brand-Sponsor Ick Factor," *Fast Company*, April 3, 2014, www.fastcompany.com/3028602/most-creative-people/how-converse-supports-musicians-without-the-brand-sponsor-ick-factor (accessed May 16, 2016).

40 Ibid.

41 Ibid.

42 David Carr, "A New Model for Music: Big Bands, Big Brands," *New York Times*, March 16, 2014, www. nytimes.com/2014/03/17/business/media/a-new-model-for-music-big-bands-big-brands.html?_r=0 (accessed May 16, 2016).

43 Ibid.

44 Mark J. Butler, *Unlocking the Groove: Rhythm, Meter, and Musical Design in Electronic Dance Music* (Bloomington: Indiana University Press, 2006), 32–33.

45 Drew Millard, "Is 'E.D.M.' a Real Genre?" *Vice*, www.noisey.vice.com/en_ca/blog/is-E.D.M.-a-real-genre (accessed May 16, 2016).

46 Andrew Ryce, "RA Roundtable: E.D.M. in America," *Resident Advisor*, September 11, 2012, www.resident advisor.net/feature.aspx?1709 (accessed May 16, 2016).

47 FACT Team, "The FACT Dictionary: How 'Dubstep,' 'Juke,' Cloud Rap' and Many More Got Their Names," *FACT*, July 10, 2013, www.factmag.com/2013/07/10/the-fact-dictionary-how-dubstep-juke-cloud-rap-and-many-more-got-their-names/6 (accessed May 16, 2016).

48 Joshua Glazer, "Etymology of E.D.M.: The Complex Heritage of Electronic Dance Music," *Medium*, October 10, 2014, www.medium.com/cuepoint/etymology-of-edm-the-complex-heritage-of-electronic-dance-music-d3e3aa873369 (accessed May 16, 2016).

49 Alan Feuer, "A Year after Drug Deaths, the Electric Zoo Music Festival Tries Again," *New York Times*, August 15, 2014.

50 Ibid.

51 Ben Sisario, "Sillerman's Failed Bid, Debts and Growing Losses Test SFX Investors' Patience," *New York Times*, August 24, 2015.

52 Ibid.

53 Matt Medved, "Electric Zoo Festival Announces Full 2015 Lineup," *Billboard*, May 27, 2015, www.billboard. com/articles/columns/music-festivals/6576130/electric-zoo-festival-2015-lineup (accessed May 16, 2016)

54 Feuer, "A Year After."

55 Brian Platt, "Music Festivals Need Better Strategies for Party Drugs, Health Advocates Say," *The Star*, August 9, 2014, www.thestar.com/news/gta/2014/08/09/music_festivals_need_better_strategies_for_party_drugs_health_advocates_say.html (accessed May 16, 2016).

56 Ibid.

57 Joe Coscarelli, "Raving Sober: Remembering the Music in the Morning," *New York Times*, June 4, 2015.

58 Ibid.

59 Sydney Ember, "Cool Influencers with Big Followings Get Picky about Their Endorsements," *New York Times*, August 3, 2015.

60 Ibid.

61 Ibid.

62 Erika Allen, "A Campaign Where Smoke Means Fire," *New York Times*, July 9, 2014.

63 Ben Sisario, "Clear Channel Renames Itself iHeart Media in Nod to Digital," *New York Times*, November 14, 2014.

64 Laura M. Holson, "A 'Blurred Lines' Boomerang," *New York Times*, October 26, 2014.

65 Ibid.

66 Ben Sisario, "Side Issues Intrude in 'Blurred Lines' Case," *New York Times*, March 2, 2015.

67 Home, Heather Fenoughty, composer, www.heather-fenoughty.com (accessed May 16, 2016).

68 International Federation for the Phonographic Industry, "2015 Report."

69 Ibid.

70 Ibid.

71 Ibid.

72 Bob Baker, "Niche Music Market: 7 Great Examples," www.bob-baker.com/buzz/niche-music-markets-7-great-examples (accessed May 16, 2016).

73 Sarah Max, "Selling Marketers a Spanish Accent That Doesn't Sound Faked," *New York Times*, March 26, 2015.

74 Ibid.

75 Josh Steimie, "What Is Content Marketing?" *Forbes*, September 19, 2014, www.forbes.com/sites/josh steimle/2014/09/19/what-is-content-marketing (accessed May 16, 2016).

76 Ibid.

77 "Getting Started," *Content Marketing Institute*, http://contentmarketinginstitute.com/getting-started (accessed May 16, 2016).

78 Ibid.

79 Homepage, *Fractl*, http://frac.tl (accessed May 16, 2016).

80 Homepage, *BuzzStream*, http://buzzstream.com (accessed May 16, 2016).

81 Kelsey Libert, "How Millennials, Boomers, and Gen X-ers Respond to Content Marketing," *Inc.*, July 17, 2015, www.inc.com/kelsey-libert/how-content-marketing-engagement-differs-by-generation.html (accessed May 16, 2016).

82 Ibid.

83 John Schaefer, "Unlikely Savior for the Music Industry: Your 12-Year-Old," *WNYC*, March 12, 2015, www.wnyc.org/story/12-year-old-pod (accessed May 16, 2016).

84 Ibid.

85 Ibid.

86 Ibid.

87 Jose Alvarez, "Study Suggests People Stop Listening to New Music after Age 33," *Digital Trends*, April 30, 2015, www.digitaltrends.com/music/people-stop-listening-to-new-music-after-age-33 (accessed May 16, 2016).

88 Ajay Kalia, "'Music Was Better Back Then': When Do We Stop Keeping Up with Popular Music?" *Skynet & Ebert*, April 22, 2015, www.skynetandebert.com/author/amkalia (accessed May 16, 2016).

89 Andrew Hall, "16 Must-Have Online Tools for Indie Musicians," *SonicBids Blog*, http://blog.sonicbids.com/16-must-have-online-tools-for-indie-musicians (accessed May 16, 2016).

90 "Fee Structure: Bandcamp for Artists," *Bandcamp*, http:// bandcamp.com/artists (accessed May 16, 2016).

91 John Grossman, "Using Smartphones and Apps to Enhance Loyalty Programs," *New York Times*, January 28, 2015, www.nytimes.com/2015/01/29/business/smallbusiness/using-smartphones-and-apps-to-enhance-small-business-loyalty-programs.html (accessed May 16, 2016).

92 Nate Chinen, "Jazz Clubs Recording Their Own Sound," *New York Times*, November 12, 2014.

93 Ben Sisario, "YouTube Challenger Lets Music Fans Call the Shots," *New York Times*, December 22, 2014.

94 Ibid.

95 Ibid.

96 Michael Cooper, "On the Infield or Onstage, a Diva Is But a Click Away," *New York Times*, November 3, 2014.

97 Ibid.

98 "Subscription," *Medici TV*, www.medici.tv/#!/subscribe (accessed May 16, 2016).

99 Cooper, "On the Infield"

100 Ben Sisario, "The Crowds Stay with Him, and Grow," *New York Times*, February 8, 2015.

101 International Federation for the Phonographic Industry, "2015 Report."

102 Ibid.

103 Ibid.

104 Ibid.

105 "About," *The Piano Guys*, www.thepianoguys.com/thepianoguys (accessed May 16, 2016).

106 Leslie Kaufman, "A Musical Mash-Up Plays Well on the Web," *New York Times*, October 8, 2014.

107 Ibid.

108 "About," *The Piano Guys*.

109 Kaufman, "A Musical Mash-Up."

110 Elizabeth David, "The Piano Guys Share the Secrets of Their YouTube Success," *Classic FM*, May 5, 2015, www.classicfm.com/artists/piano-guys/guides/youtube-interview/#5SjWKAxtucwjbrUy.97 (accessed May 16, 2016).

111 Ibid.

112 Ben Sisario, "Music Streaming Service Seeks to Regain Footing," *New York Times*, May 2, 2015.

113 Ibid.

114 Stan Phelps, "TD Bank Turns ATMs into Automated Thanking Machines," *Forbes*, July 30, 2014, wwwforbes.com/sites/stanphelps/2014/07/30/td-bank-turns-atms-into-an-automated-thanking-machines (accessed May 16, 2016).

115 Ed Zitron, "8 Outside the Box Marketing Ideas Your Business Should Try in 2015," *Inc.*, June 16, 2015, www.inc.com/ed-zitron/8-outside-the-box-marketing-ideas-your-business-should-tryin-2015.html (accessed May 16, 2016).

116 Ibid.

117 Taylor Swift. *AZQuotes.com*, 2015, www.azquotes.com/quote/863142 (accessed May 16, 2016).

118 Jack Dickey, "The Power of Taylor Swift," *Time*, November 13, 2014.

119 Ibid.

120 Keith Harris, "Trace Taylor Swift's Country to Pop Transformation in 5 Songs," *Rolling Stone*, September 9, 2014, www.rollingstone.com/music/lists/taylor-swift-country-pop-transformation-20140909 (accessed May 16, 2016).

121 Ibid.

122 Ibid.

123 Ibid.

124 Annie Reuter, "Taylor Swift Leaves Country Radio Behind for Mass-Appeal Pop," *Radio.com*, August 25, 2014, www.radio.com/2014/08/25/taylor-swift-leaves-country-radio-behind-for-mass-appeal-pop (accessed May 16, 2016).

125 Ibid.

126 "Taylor Swift Explains Her Move to Pop in *CMT Hot 20* Interview," *CMT*, www.cmt.com/news/1731531/taylor-swift-explains-her-move-to-pop-in-cmt-hot-20-interview/ (accessed May 16, 2016).

127 Michelle McGahan, "5 Things We Learned from Taylor Swift's British Vogue Interview," *Pop Crush*, October 1, 2014, www.popcrush.com/taylor-swift-british-vogue-interview/?trackback=tsmclip (accessed May 16, 2016).

128 Ian McQuaid, "South African Hip-Hop," *Red Bull Music Academy*, May 1, 2015, http://daily.redbullmusicacademy.com/2015/05/south-africa-hip-hop-feature (accessed May 16, 2016).

129 Ibid.

130 Ibid.

131 "Home," *Radio1xtra*, www.bbc.co.uk/1xtra (accessed May 16, 2016).

132 McQuaid, "South African Hip-Hop."

133 Ibid.

134 Gregg Diggs, "Five Kicking Songs from the Kings of Kwaito," *NPR Music*, June 30, 2010, www.npr.org/templates/story/story.php?storyId=128014019 (accessed May 16, 2016).

135 Ibid.

136 "SA Hip-Hop Fans Mourn Skwatta Kamp's Flabba Habedi," *Destiny Man*, www.destinyman.com/2015/03/09/sa-hip-hop-fans-mourns-skwatta-kamps-flabba-habedi (accessed May 16, 2016).

137 "Local Personalities—Teargas," *Show Me*, www.showme.co.za/durban/interactive/local-personalities/teargas (accessed May 16, 2016).

138 Isha Sesay and Mark Tutton, "The Image That Changed the Course of South Africa's History," June 16, 2010, www.cnn.com/2010/WORLD/africa/06/16/soweto.uprising.photograph (accessed May 16, 2016).

139 McQuaid, "South African Hip-Hop."

140 "Local Personalities—Teargas."

141 Ibid.

142 Bernice Maune, "'No Transparency or Credibility': Why Rappers K.O, Kid X are Not Taking Part in SA Hip-Hop Awards," *Times Live*, November 12, 2014, www.timeslive.co.za/entertainment/2014/11/12/no-transparency-or-credibility-why-rappers-k.o-kid-x-are-not-taking-part-in-sa-hip-hop-awards (accessed May 16, 2016).

143 McQuaid, "South African Hip-Hop."

144 Harriet Fitch Little, "Baalbeck Festival, Lebanon," *Financial Times*, July 25, 2014, www.ft.com/cms/s/2/bf322ad2-10c5-11e4-b116-00144feabdc0.html (accessed May 16, 2016).

145 Ibid.

146 Jsaline Lannoy, "Lebanon: The Difficulties of Being a Social Megaphone," *Festival Bytes*, June 11, 2015, www.festivalbytes.eu/lebanon-social-megaphone/ (accessed June 30, 2015).

147 "History," *Baalbeck*, http://baalbeck.org.lb/history (accessed May 16, 2016).

148 Little, "Baalbeck Festival."

149 Ibid.

CHAPTER 5

Opportunities Ahead: Global Rights Management

Disclaimer: This chapter is intended to provide an introduction for non-specialists or newcomers to the subject of copyright and related rights. It explains in layperson's terms the fundamentals underpinning copyright law and practice. It describes the different types of rights which copyright and related-rights law protects, as well as the limitations on those rights.[1] For specific answers to and detailed guidance on deeper aspects of international copyright issues, please refer to the World Intellectual Property Organization (WIPO) website and its publications.

CHAPTER OVERVIEW

This chapter provides a comprehensive look at copyright law within the context of intellectual property as it has developed around the world. While each country has its own specific laws, in general copyright protection is given to the owner of original works of music. The challenges of global rights management are explored. We have spotlighted Cape Verde, a tiny African island that is working to build its unique music into an economic engine. The chapter concludes with a musician's guide to avoiding copyright infringement.

KEY TERMS

Exploit a musical work	Fair use
Public domain	Royalties
Berne Convention	Neighboring rights
WIPO	The two copyrights in music
World Trade Organization	'Works for hire'
Public performance	Creative Commons

THE RIFF THAT CHANGED HIS LIFE: PHIL MANZANERA

We will begin our exploration of global rights management and copyright with a story. British composer and guitarist Phil Manzanera, a fairly laid-back sort of guy, learns that a riff he wrote for guitar in 1978 has been sampled on a new album by two American superstars.

Manzanera's tale is one of the best ways I know to demonstrate why music professionals need to be fluent in the laws of global rights management. Manzanera told his story to Emily Jupp of *The Independent* (UK)[2] and I have excerpted it below.

Manzanera got a call in 2011 that went like this: "Yeah, it's Roc-A-Fella records here calling you from New York," the voice said. "Just want to tell you that Jay Z and Kanye West have sampled your guitar on their new album."[3]

While most of us would have been flabbergasted, Manzanera took it in his stride. "People always get me mixed up with Ray Manzarek from the Doors, so I thought that's what they'd done. To check it was definitely my riff, they played it down the phone to me, and it was a riff I'd written for a tune called 'K-Scope' in 1978."[4]

Manzanera wondered how anyone could have found this riff on an obscure, out of print album. He learned that a musician named 88-Keys spends his time in record shops looking for vinyl gems that have largely been relegated to the bargain bins. 88-Keys brought Manzanera's riff to Kanye West's attention, who, along with Jay Z, decided to use it in the song "No Church in the Wild" from their next album.[5]

"The genius thing is, they slowed it down," Manzanera explains. "What nobody knows is that it's not just a guitar playing. I've got this huge harmonica: it's about a foot long and you blow this one note along with the first beat of every bar and it creates this weird sort of slightly sinister riff. When it's slowed down, that combined with that guitar low note creates this very special sound."

A few months later, Jay Z and Kanye West's album *Watch the Throne* was released and quickly went platinum. "No Church in the Wild" is the first track on the album, "so the first thing you hear on Jay Z and Kanye's album is my riff, and yet they probably don't even know who I am," marvels Manzanera. "I'm owed six figures. Six figures plus, which is more than I've made in the past 15 years with [my band] Roxy . . . it really reassured me about all of my beliefs, why I'm doing what I'm doing and the power of music. Things come and go—fame, fortune—I'm not interested in that. I just do what I do because I love music. But it felt like someone, somewhere up there in the ether, has said: "You know what? You've been doing stuff for ages, had ups and downs—you can have that now.'"

Manzanera says he's a typical musician: "Years ago a rapper called Ice-T [phoned] and said, 'I've sampled your thing,' and I just said, 'Ah yeah brilliant, thanks, bye!' I had no idea you could get some money from it. I don't know what happened with that, I'll have to Google it."[6]

Manzanera's riff is like a friend, following him everywhere. It's been used in the films *Safe House* and *The Great Gatsby*, in a Superbowl commercial, and on TV shows. The riff has had more than 57 million hits on Spotify.

Phil Manzanera
Guitarist Magazine/Future/Getty Images

"The ironic thing is I played that riff five times in 1978 and I've got to learn to play it now," explains Manzanera. "When Jay Z slowed it down, they put it in E-flat. But for a guitarist E-flat is so hard to play. So there are people from the Berklee College of Music, incredibly technical people, playing it [on YouTube videos] . . . So I've done a little YouTube clip showing people how to play the definitive version. It's terribly easy if you play it in A."[7]

Pause and Reflect

Why do you think that sampling snippets of someone else's recording and using it on your own recording is such a big deal to artists and record companies? Can you suggest a way to balance artistic freedom (the art) with the financial rewards of copyright ownership (the commerce)?

How Copyright Law Affects the Music Industry

Understanding the Two Copyrights in Music

When it comes to music, there is copyright protection for the song itself (the music and lyrics, also called the underlying composition) and separate copyright protection for the recording of a particular performance of the song.

The following examples illustrate how there can be two separate copyrights for what might appear to be the same work.

Ownership of a CD and the right to use it publicly are two separate issues. When you purchase a CD, you are, in effect, given a license only for private use of the CD in your home. The license does not carry with it the right to perform the CD outside the home, unless the site where the CD is performed is properly licensed for performance.

The same is true for films. Neither the rental nor the purchase of a movie carries with it the right to show the movie publicly outside the home, unless the site where the movie is used is properly licensed for public exhibition.[8] The legal compliance requirement does not change if admission is free, if the facility or organization is commercial or nonprofit, or if there is a governmental agency involved. However, there is an educational exemption that allows a film or CD to be performed in certain types of teaching.[9]

Whose Music Is It, Anyway?

Who has rights in a particular creative work? Usually the rights belong to the person who created the work, but there are important exceptions:

- Songwriters as employees: Copyright law states that an employer owns the copyright to the music written by her employees. These compositions are known as "works for hire."

- Commissioned works: If a composer is engaged to write a work for a person or an organization, the rights to the new work are owned by the person or entity that engaged the composer to create the work.

- Assignment of copyright: Copyrights can be sold, given away, divided up, and bequeathed. For example, unless otherwise specified, each person in a four-member band owns 25 percent of each song they compose together. One band member can decide to give his sister half of his copyright to a song as a birthday gift. For that particular song only, there would be five owners. Three band members will own 25 percent. The band member who gave his sister half his copyright to the song will own 12.5 percent, and so will his sister.

CHALLENGES IN GLOBAL RIGHTS MANAGEMENT

Music rights management is a complex and essential area to understand. It revolves around the ownership of copyright and how the work is exploited. We will build on this basic definition in the pages ahead.

Money flows from the user of a creation (such as a composition, song, or recording) to the owner of it. This simple statement is what drives the music industry across all genres and countries. In fact:

The key to making money in today's music industry

is ownership of rights and their effective global management.

The legal foundation for music rights management is copyright law. While each country has its own specific laws, in general, copyright protection is given to the owner of original works of music, art, photography, books, plays, broadcasts, and sound recordings. If someone creates a work as an employee, then the employer owns the copyright. As a copyright owner, you can give away your rights to someone else, or you can give someone permission to use the work while you retain the ownership.

The term "rights management" refers to an important legal concept known as copyright or authors' rights, depending upon the country or region.

A license, or permissions agreement, is a form of contract law that represents an agreement between someone who wants to use a copyright-protected work (a film, song, image, or text) and the rights holder (someone who owns the copyright and its exclusive rights). In most cases money will be exchanged between the two parties when the agreement is signed. There are many different types of licenses that can be granted. The key elements that determine which license is appropriate are the nature of the work under consideration, who is asking for the license, how the work will be used, and for how long the potential user wishes to have the right to exploit it.[10]

Key players in global rights management include music publishers and music collecting societies (also known as performing rights organizations or PROs). These two groups of professionals work on behalf of their musician, songwriter, and composer clients. Their activities include licensing the intellectual property of their clients and ensuring that royalties are collected for its use. Royalties are payments made to creators, publishers, and PROs by rights users. Money is earned in a variety of ways, such as when music is downloaded (purchased), heard on Pandora (streamed), sold on an album, performed in a live concert, used in an advertisement or movie, and played on terrestrial radio, television, or through other media outlets. Three common types of licenses issued by publishers and collecting societies are mechanical licenses, performance licenses, and synchronization (synch) licenses.[11] These will be explained in more detail later in this chapter.

Traditional publishers serve their clients in the areas of music acquisitions, creative development, and rights management. They focus on the side of the music industry that deals with copyrights for recordings. A music publisher's job is to find ways to use a writer's music, keep track of the revenue earned through the song's usage, and distribute a portion of the money to the writer. Publishers traditionally owned the economic rights of a composition or song for the legal length of copyright term in their country or region. The contracts between publisher and composer are usually long in duration and exclusive.

Collecting societies, or PROs, traditionally have focused on the side of the music industry that deals with copyrights for songwriting rather than copyrights for recordings. The definition of performing is quite broad and includes music that is streamed online, played on the radio, or performed in public. The societies have both individual and publishing clients. PROs issue performance licenses and collect royalties on behalf of both their composer/songwriter clients and their publishing clients. Music publishers usually belong to all collecting societies around the world. Songwriters and composers may belong to one collecting society per country or region. Contracts between songwriters and collecting societies are therefore non-exclusive and usually are less than five years in duration. Songwriters do not assign their copyrights to the collecting societies.

The disruptive technology of the internet and its impact on music has caused significant anxiety, opportunity, and change in the field of global rights management. Royalties are paid based on sales of music. The significant weakening of music purchases has negatively affected the royalties from mechanical licenses (the copyrights for the recording side of the industry). For decades, this royalty source was the primary source of revenue for the music industry. In fact, most people felt that the recording industry *was* the music industry. In the current industry climate, musicians, publishers, and PROs are looking to performance royalties to help stem the losses. As consumers show their preference for music access (streaming) over music ownership in the exploding field of digital media, more and more performance licenses are being generated, which, in turn, produce increases in performance royalties.

The globalization of the music industry is another challenge for rights management. Today there are three multinational companies that together control roughly 50 percent of the global recording and publishing areas of the industry, and compete on a global scale. The three major record labels, Sony Music Entertainment (Japan), Universal Music Group (a division of the French company Vivendi), and Warner Music Group (Russia), each own a major publishing company: Sony/ATV Music Publishing, Universal Music Publishing Group, and Warner/Chappell Music, respectively. The increasing trend of distributing and promoting music in new, foreign markets has further added to the industry's globalization.

The field of global rights management and licensing is hobbled by the lack of an international infrastructure and consistent international regulation in the digital intellectual property arena. Currently, publishers must engage in the arduous process of negotiating contracts and making deals with companies one-by-one for each country in which they operate. This creates a tangled web of often-conflicting laws, languages, regulations, and traditions.[12]

Finally, while there is a great deal more opportunity for music to be heard and licensed worldwide today, digital music delivery has cast a long shadow on the music industry. With music being omnipresent and easy to acquire without paying for it, music has been devalued in the public eye to the point where most consumers feel it should be free. Thus, there has been a massive social change caused by the global technological disruption of digital music.

The website Pro-Music contains useful links for locating global music licensing companies as well as links to worldwide organizations dealing with legal, copyright, and intellectual property issues.

WHO OWNS THE MUSIC? GLOBAL COPYRIGHT ISSUES

Copyright law is the bedrock of the music industry in the US, the UK, Europe, and most countries or territories. Strong legal systems are in place to enforce these laws, with unpleasant consequences for those who run afoul of them. Given the differences in the culture of law-making compared to the culture of technological innovation, it is not surprising that international laws lag behind the technologies that give us the ability to communicate and exchange ideas rapidly around the globe.

The struggle to keep copyright laws current with technology is not a new challenge. In the late fifteenth century, the game-changing invention called the printing press gave unprecedented access to information at rapid speed and (relatively) low cost. Prior to this, documents were copied by hand, a lengthy and laborious task that made the cost of books out of reach for most people. At the time, neither a book nor its author had copyright protection.

How things have changed in 600 years!

Intellectual Property

I have found that examining copyright law within the broader context of intellectual property rights and global trade agreements is a good place to begin exploring the impact of copyright law on the creative economy.

Intellectual property can be divided into two branches:

- industrial property, which protects inventions; and
- copyright, which protects literary and artistic works.

Industrial property law exists to protect inventions and industrial designs through patents. Industrial property also covers trademarks, service marks, commercial names and designations, and protection against unfair competition.[13]

Copyright, the second branch of intellectual property, exists to protect artistic creations and technology-based works such as computer programs. Copyright literally means the right to make copies of a work, which is one of the exclusive rights of a copyright holder. The expression "author's rights" refers to the creator of the artistic work. Most countries recognize that the author has a bundle of specific rights to which she has the exclusive rights to exercise.[14]

There is an important difference between the protections embodied in the two types of intellectual property. These differences pertain to inventions as well as to literary and artistic works. In non-legal terminology, *inventions* may be defined as new solutions to technical problems. These new solutions are considered *ideas*. Inventions protected under patent law do not require that the invention be represented in a physical embodiment. Therefore, inventors are protected against any unlicensed use of the *idea* embodied in their invention.[15]

On the other hand, copyright law protects only the *form of expression of ideas*, not the ideas themselves. Types of creative expression that are protected by copyright law can include the choice and arrangement of words, musical notes, color, and shapes. Therefore, copyright law protects the owner of property rights against those who copy or otherwise use the *form of expression* in which the original work was expressed by the author.[16]

For example, the words and music in a blues song (the *expression* of an idea) are protected, but the song's 12-bar, I-IV-V chord structure is not protected. That's because the universally recognized structure of a traditional blues song is considered a building block—an *idea*—for all blues songs. Copyright law protects the owner against unauthorized use of the expression of her artistic work; it does not protect the idea.

Legal protection for inventions and for literary and artistic works is provided differently, as you might expect. Industrial property law protects the *idea* itself. There is a lengthy and vigorous review of an inventor's design before a patent is issued, granting the inventor exclusive rights to her design for 20 years in most countries and regions. When the term of protection ends, the idea becomes part of the public domain, free for everyone to use.

By contrast, the duration of protection for literary and artistic works under copyright law can be much longer than in the case of protection of the ideas themselves. This is because legal protection of literary and artistic works under copyright prevents only unauthorized use of the *expressions* of ideas. Thus, the law demonstrates that it is important to allow public access to the *ideas* themselves more quickly than to the *expression* of those ideas. Since a created work is considered to be protected as soon as it exists, it is not necessary to publicly register it.[17]

After the legal period of protection granting exclusive rights to copyright owners, the invention or artistic work goes into what is called the "public domain." Works and inventions in the public domain are free for anyone to use for any purpose they choose. This gives citizens access to ideas and expressions of ideas to create new inventions and artistic products.

Intellectual property is a valuable export—and thus revenue producer—for many countries, particularly the "developed nations." While the discussion of and action upon international agreements regarding intellectual property protection across borders is an ongoing dialogue, the actual creation of laws and their enforcement is a highly political process. As in any negotiation, the outcome is influenced by the relative strength of those at the bargaining table.

International copyright agreements greatly simplify the conditions under which their member countries offer protection to foreign works. However, there does not exist an "international copyright" that offers identical protection to rights owners throughout the world. The national laws of each country still prevail in cases involving unauthorized use.[18]

Global Treaties and Conventions

Countries have exchanged ideas, goods, and services for centuries. By the early nineteenth century, many countries had copyright and neighboring rights laws in place to protect the intellectual property of its citizens when in their home country. It wasn't until the 1870s that discussions concerning international protection of intellectual property began in earnest.

Throughout this chapter, you will read the word "convention" many times. In this context the term refers to formal agreements between countries, not to the more familiar use of the word to mean a meeting where a large group of like-minded people come together over a period of several days to discuss shared academic or business issues.

The issue of international copyright protection was addressed at the *Berne (Switzerland) Convention* for the Protection of Literary and Artistic Works in 1886. The Berne Convention has been revised many times since it was completed in Paris in 1896. It now has more than 150 member countries and is administered by the World Intellectual Property Organization (WIPO).

The purpose of the Berne Convention is to help its member nations obtain international protection of their right to control and receive payment for the use of their creative works, including:

- novels, short stories, poems, and plays;

- songs, operas, musicals, and sonatas; and

- drawings, paintings, sculptures, and architectural works.[19]

The Berne Convention is based on the concept that countries should give an equal amount of copyright protection to the works of foreign citizens as the countries give their own citizens' works. For example, if a French copyright owner sues for an authorized use of her work (known as an infringement) occurring in another country that is also a member of the Berne Convention, the foreign country's copyright law will be applied. This is important in an increasingly global world of trade because it acknowledges the rights of sovereign nations to create their own laws while underscoring the importance of global protection of intellectual properly.[20]

The World Intellectual Property Organization (WIPO)

WIPO was established in 1967 by the WIPO Convention. It promotes intellectual property protection throughout the world through cooperation among countries and in collaboration with other international organizations. In 1974 it became a specialized agency of the United Nations. Currently, it serves 184 member states and administers 24 treaties. It is based in Geneva, Switzerland.[21]

Under WIPO's auspices, two important new treaties were finalized under the Berne Convention which brought copyright protection into the digital age: the WIPO Copyright Treaty (WCT) for authors, and the WIPO Performances and Phonograms Treaty (WPPT) for performers and phonogram producers. The WCT and the WPPT were adopted by the international community in 1996 and were implemented in the US in the Digital Millennium Copyright Act (DMCA) of 1998.[22]

WIPO administers the following international treaties on copyright and related rights:

- the Berne Convention for the Protection of Literary and Artistic Works;

- the Brussels Convention Relating to the Distribution of Program-Carrying Signals Transmitted by Satellite;

- the Geneva Convention for the Protection of Producers of Phonograms Against Unauthorized Duplication of Their Phonograms;

- the Rome Convention for the Protection of Performers, Producers of Phonograms and Broadcasting Organizations;

- the WCT;

- the WPPT.[23]

Stevie Wonder at WIPO

FADEL SENNA/AFP/Getty Images

The World Trade Organization and the TRIPS Agreement

The extent of protection and enforcement regarding intellectual property rights varies widely around the world, which can contribute to tension in some international economic relations. The failure to adequately protect intellectual property internationally is considered an unfair trade practice. So in the 1980s, many countries began including copyright protections in their multinational trade-based agreements. The World Trade Organization (WTO) was created in 1995 to help its member governments sort out the trading problems they encountered with each other. WTO agreements provide the legal ground rules for international trade.[24]

The WTO's Agreement on Trade-Related Aspects of Intellectual Property Rights (TRIPS) introduced intellectual property rules into the global trading system for the first time. The TRIPS agreement requires all members to comply with the key provisions of the Berne Convention. It includes protections against unauthorized copying of sound recordings and provides a specific right to authorize or prohibit commercial rental of these works.[25]

Since coming into force, TRIPS has received a good deal of criticism from developing countries, non-governmental organizations, and academics, particularly in the area of public health.[26] While at first glance this may seem to have little to do with the music industry, the controversy surrounding TRIPS sheds light on a consistent dilemma in the area of protection of intellectual property: Is it possible that the laws intended to encourage creativity and innovation by giving rights-holders a temporary monopoly on commercial exploitation of their work actually restrict the use of knowledge? How do the differences in the fundamental values of cultures and societies impact this discussion?

Some highly respected individuals, among them Joseph E. Stiglitz, former chief economist of the World Bank and a recipient of the Nobel Memorial Prize in Economic Sciences, speak bluntly about what they see as gross inequities caused by TRIPS. Here is an excerpt from an article entitled "Trade Agreements and Health in Developing Countries," published by Professor Stiglitz in *The Lancet* (January 31, 2009): "The fundamental problem with the intellectual property (patent) system is simple: it is based on restricting the use of knowledge. There is no extra cost associated with an additional person gaining the benefits of knowledge. Restricting knowledge is thus inefficient, but the patent system also grants (temporary) monopoly power, which gives rise to enormous economic inefficiencies."[27]

The discussion in this chapter of international treaties involving intellectual property rights is very brief. WIPO is an excellent source of full texts, summaries, and lists of countries that ratified the international intellectual property treaties and agreements.

For students who wish to explore the topic in depth, I recommend the general WIPO website and these two sources in particular:

- "Summaries of Conventions, Treaties and Agreements Administered by WIPO."

- An illustrated and very user-friendly timeline of major world events and WIPO treaties from 1883 to 2002.

Rights Protected by Copyright Laws

There are two broad types of rights under copyright law: economic and moral. Economic rights acknowledge the right of owners to enjoy financial reward from the use of their works. Moral rights allow the author to take certain actions to preserve the personal link between herself and the work.[28]

Most copyright laws state that the author or rights owner has exclusive rights to authorize or prevent certain acts in relation to her work, including:

- Rights of reproduction, distribution, rental and importation;
- Rights of public performance, broadcasting, communication to the public and making available to the public;
- Translation and adaptation rights; and
- Moral rights.[29]

Rights of Reproduction, Distribution, and Rental

As its name implies, the right of the copyright owner to prevent others from making copies of her work without her authorization is the most basic right protected by copyright law. Some national laws include a right specifically to authorize distribution of copies of works. The right of distribution of a particular copy usually terminates upon the copy's initial sale or transfer of ownership.[30] For example, if you are the copyright owner of a recording and you sell it to a record shop, the shop owner may resell it or give it away as she chooses, without consulting you.

When technological advances made it easy to copy works in sound recordings and audiovisual works, legislation to protect the right to authorize rental of copies of works became another exclusive right of ownership. This right helps protect the copyright owner's exclusive right of reproduction.[31]

The Right of Public Performance

Under many national laws, the definition of public performance is quite broad. It includes any performance of a work at a place where the public is or can be present, or at a place not open to the public, but where a substantial number of people outside one's family and close acquaintances are present. The broad definition of right of public performance encompasses live performances of a work, such as an orchestra concert, as well as performance by means of recordings. The idea that recorded music playing in a grocery store is considered a performance may seem a bit strange. In fact, any musical work is considered publicly performed when a sound recording of that work (still referred to as "phonogram" in legal terms) is played over amplification equipment.[32]

The Right of Broadcasting

Broadcasting rights cover "the transmission for public reception of sounds, or of images and sounds, by wireless means, whether by radio, television, or satellite." Cable transmission is an example of communication to the public.[33]

Translation and Adaptation Rights

Making a translation or adaptation of a copyright-protected work requires authorization from the rights owner. Since both a translation and an adaptation are themselves protected by copyright, someone wishing to publish a translation or adaptation must receive permission from *both* from the owner of the copyright in the original work *and* from the owner of copyright in the translation or adaptation.[34]

Moral Rights

The Berne Convention requires member countries to grant to authors:

- The right to claim authorship of the work (also called the right of paternity), and

- The right to object to any distortion or modification of the work, or other derogatory action in relation to the work, which could be prejudicial to the author's honor or reputation (sometimes called the right of integrity).[35]

These rights are generally known as the moral rights. The Berne Convention requires them to be treated separately from the author's economic rights and to remain with the author even after she has transferred her economic rights. For example, a film producer or a publisher may own the economic rights in a work, but it is only the individual creator who has moral interests at stake.[36]

Limitations on Rights

While all countries place certain limitations on rights, not all countries agree on what those limitations are. Here are a few examples:

- Exclusion from copyright protection of certain categories of works. In some countries, including the US, works are excluded from protection if they are not fixed in tangible form.

- Specific acts of exploitation that may be carried out without the rights owner's authorization. There are two basic types of limitation in this category:

  ○ free (or fair) use, which allows use of the work without authorization and compensation; and

  ○ non-voluntary licenses, which require that compensation be paid to the rights owner for non-authorized uses.[37]

Examples of free (or fair) use include:

- Quoting from a protected work, provided that the source of the quotation and the name of the author are mentioned, and that the extent of the quotation is compatible with fair practice,

- Use of works for teaching purposes, and

- Use of works for the purpose of news reporting.[38]

In the US, "fair use" is a gray legal area that is the basis of legal disputes. The concept of fair use takes into account additional factors such as the nature and purpose of the use, the type of work that is used, the amount of the work used in relation to the work as a whole, and whether or not the fair use will adversely affect the commercial value of the original work.[39]

The Berne Convention recognizes two non-voluntary licenses that permit the mechanical reproduction of musical works and broadcasting without the permission of the rights owner—but with compensation. Today there are many alternatives to a non-voluntary license for rights owners to authorize the public to use their works, including collective administration of rights and Creative Commons.[40]

Pause and Reflect

Reaching back to a time when borrowing a master's music was a compliment, not a "Blurred Lines" case of copyright infringement, Lyrica Chamber Music and Metropolis Ensemble recently commissioned 16 composer colleagues to write a contemporary equivalent of Robert Schumann's *Davidsbündlertänze* (a set of miniature dances woven together into a lyrical piano suite). The 16 composers were asked to write short pieces in the spirit of Schumann. Some came up with works to be played in-between Schumann's original pieces. Others transformed one of Schumann's miniature dances into something altogether new. The commissioned work, entitled "New Dances of the League of David," was performed at Le Poisson Rouge in New York City, a venue known for its enthusiasm for contemporary music of all genres.[41]

Schumann's compositions are in the public domain. What would have been different about this commission if *Davidsbündlertänze* were still under copyright protection? Who owns the copyright for the work "New Dances of the League of David?"

Duration of Copyright

Copyright is not a right that exists in perpetuity for individual or corporate copyright owners. In general, copyright protection begins from the moment the work is created (and fixed in a tangible medium under some national laws) and lasts until a specific period of time after the death of the author. This allows the author's heirs to benefit economically from exploitation of the work after the author's death. In many countries, including those that are signatories to the Berne Convention, the duration of copyright is the life of the author plus no fewer than 50 years after her death. There are works where it is not possible to base copyright duration on the life of an individual author, including anonymous, posthumous, and cinematographic works. In these cases the Berne Convention establishes the timeframe for copyright protection. There is a trend in a number of countries toward lengthening the duration of copyright. The European Union (EU), the US, and several others have extended the term of copyright to 70 years after the death of the author.[42]

Termination Rights in US Copyright Law

The 1976 US Copyright Law granted a 35-year Termination Rights opportunity for songwriters, recording artists, and other artists, allowing them to regain control of their work after 35 years. (There are a few strings attached, such as the artists must apply to terminate at least two years in advance.) The Termination Rights provision applies to most songs created after 1978. This issue has become a source of concern for both publishers and record labels as they face the prospect of losing valuable works.

Ownership and Transfer of Copyright

As you are beginning to see, copyright law is dense and nuanced because it covers such a wide variety of works that generate income for creators, heirs, corporations, and other owners. In general, the creator of a work is its first owner, but there are important exceptions. The Berne Convention contains rules for determining initial rights ownership in cinematographic works. In some countries, including the US, for a work created by an individual who is employed for the purpose of creating that work, it is the employer, not the creator, that is the initial rights owner. However, moral rights always belong to the individual author of the work, no matter who owns the economic rights.[43]

One nuance of copyright law that can be confusing is the fact that economic rights are fungible; that is, they are freely exchangeable in whole or in part. Rights owners may transfer or sell any percentage up to 100 percent of the economic rights to their works, as they wish. Reasons for an author to consider transferring their rights include:

- Rights transfer is a required element of a contract with a music publisher, in exchange for payments tied to the actual exploitation of the work (royalty payments).

- The author wishes to bequeath various percentages of a work to friends or heirs.

- The rights owner wishes to make a charitable contribution in the form of royalties from the exploitation of her work.

Transfers of copyright may take one of two forms: assignments and licenses. An assignment is a transfer of a property ownership, whereas under a licensing agreement, the rights holder retains ownership, but gives legal permission for a third party to carry out some of her economic rights. Under an assignment, the rights owner may authorize or prohibit specific activities that are part of her bundle of exclusive rights under law.

Some countries prohibit the transfer of copyright by assignment. In that case, only licensing is permitted, usually for a specific period of time and for a specific purpose. Licenses may be exclusive—meaning the rights holder will not allow any other party to carry out the licensed activities—or non-exclusive, where the rights holder allows many parties to carry out the licensed activities. For example, a songwriter who owns the rights to a work may grant an exclusive license to a music company to serve as the only legal distributor of the physical recorded song in specific global territories. Simultaneously, the songwriter may grant a non-exclusive license of the same song to a film producer for use in a movie, which means the songwriter reserves the right to license the same song for use in other films, videos, TV ads, and so forth.[44]

A rights owner may choose to forgo economic gain from her work by allowing it to be used or adapted by the general public, sometimes with restrictions such as "for non-commercial uses only." Examples of this are the open source movement, which specializes in creating computer programs, and Creative Commons, a global nonprofit organization whose licenses provide a standard way for content creators to grant someone else permission to use their work.

Royalty Rates

The music industry is engaged in an ongoing and lengthy legislative battle to update its policies regarding copyright, licensing, and royalty rates, due to the massive market changes caused by digital music distribution. At present, performance and songwriting royalty rates are based on the medium through which a song is played. In the US, terrestrial (land-based) radio stations are required to pay songwriting royalties but not performance royalties. Satellite and internet radio services must pay both. However, a significant source of the turmoil is due to the revenue minimums each type of service is required to pay. Pandora and other internet radio stations must pay a minimum of 25 percent of their annual revenue in performance royalties, whereas satellite radio companies must pay approximately 8 percent.[45]

Understandably, Pandora and others want their minimum payment to be closer to what satellite operators pay. This has put Pandora in the crosshairs of musicians and those who represent them. When a song is played on Pandora, it must pay royalties to the performers and rights owners. Pandora wants to decrease the amount it must pay—a significant percentage of its operating costs—which means that musicians and rights owners would receive less money when their songs are performed on Pandora.

In the US, terrestrial radio and television broadcasters do not pay performance royalties. The steep decline in the past decade of revenue from sales of music is driving musicians and those who represent them to press for change. They want terrestrial broadcasters to pay performance royalties, just as internet, satellite, and cable broadcasters do, so that artists are more equitably compensated for airplay of their music.

Enforcement of Rights

It is commonly understood that without appropriate means to enforce copyright laws, infringement will continue unabated. The Berne Convention contains very little guidance on rights enforcement. However, market forces themselves have brought about dramatic changes in national and international enforcement standards in recent years. Technological advances have made it very easy to make perfect copies of digital information, including music, which has increased the occurrence of both authorized and unauthorized transmission of copyright-protected works. Since international trade in intellectual property is such a massive economic sector worldwide, countries are motivated to adopt new national and international ways of enforcing and protecting the rights of intellectual property owners from infringement. The WCT requires enforcement procedures to be spelled out in the laws of its Contracting Parties. The laws must contain guidelines for effective action against any infringement as well as remedies to prevent or deter further infringements.[46]

Related (or Neighboring) Rights

Related rights protect the legal and economic interests of persons and legal entities who contribute to making works available to the public. If certain types of subject matter do not qualify as works under the copyright systems of all countries, a copyright-like property right is granted if the subject matter contains sufficient creativity or technical and organizational skill. The law of related rights states that those types of subject matter deserve legal protection, as they are *related* to the protection of works of authorship under copyright. In general, the exercise of related rights does not affect the protection of copyright.[47]

Traditionally, related rights have been granted in these three categories:

- performers;
- producers of phonograms;
- broadcasting organizations.

The *rights of performers* are recognized because they give life to the works through their individual interpretations. Performers' rights include the right to withhold consent of recording, broadcasting, and reproducing recordings of their performances under certain circumstances. Some countries also grant moral rights in the work to performers who want to protect their name, image, and reputation.[48]

Producers are granted rights in phonograms in recognition of the importance of their creative, financial, and organizational contributions to a recording project. Additionally, producers have a keen interest in and the resources to take action against infringing activities, such as making and distributing unauthorized copies. More and more countries are granting a right of rental for phonograms (or audiovisual works for performers) to performers and producers.[49]

The *rights of broadcasting organizations* are acknowledged due to their justified interest in controlling the transmission and retransmission of their broadcasts, and their role in making works available to the public. Broadcasting organizations are given the rights to authorize or prohibit re-broadcasting, fixation, and reproduction of their broadcasts.[50]

As in the case of copyright, national laws allow use in specific situations of copyright-protected performances, phonograms, and broadcasts in certain situations, such as teaching, scientific research, private use and short excerpts used in reporting current events. Related rights as performances may be granted to the unwritten and unrecorded treasury of folkloric or traditional cultural expressions in developing countries, as these are often brought to the public's attention through performances. As mentioned earlier, those countries that work diligently to protect intellectual property rights stand to benefit from the rapidly expanding international trade in rights-protected intellectual property goods and services.[51]

Spotlight on . . . Cape Verde, Africa

Leveraging Culture and Creativity for Sustainable Development

Thanks to its blend of cultures, history, and races, the music from the tiny African island of Cape Verde is rich and varied. Even the names of its distinct musical styles—batuque, morna, and funana—are evocative. Cape Verde's most important natural resource is its music and culture. The country's leaders are fully on board to exploit the economic potential of the island's music. Prime Minister Jose Maria Neves spoke about Cape Verde at a WTO conference in 2013, stating: "The future of our country's [music and arts] lies in our capacity to create, our capacity to innovate."[52]

Cape Verde is strategically located between Africa, Europe, and the Americas, which gives it a competitive advantage in creating a sustainable development model based on its creative economy and tourism.[53] The Kriol Jazz Festival,

Farro Gaita, Cape Verde musician

Judith Burrows/Hulton Archive/Getty Images

founded in 2009, attracts international talent, including Grammy-winning US singer Esperanza Spalding and acts from Luxembourg and Brazil.[54]

To help its creative economy workers compete in the global music industry, the country sponsors an annual conference and networking event called the Atlantic Music Expo. The Expo attracts local musicians and their management teams to attend workshops and talks on the intricacies of the business of music. Organizers say that the greatest economic benefits of the Expo lie in preparing Cape Verde's artists and musicians to tour the world and spread the word about their country. Tourism is expected to account for 20 percent of the country's GDP by 2024.[55]

Pause and Reflect

How can Cape Verde achieve its economic goals using its creative industries? Is there a model that exists for this strategy anywhere else in the world?

Global Copyright Reform

The UK

With a diversity of stakeholders ranging from consumer associations to industry, from digital rights activists to universities, research centers, and libraries,[56] and from national to international organizations, the clamor for copyright reform is mounting worldwide. Acknowledging the crucial importance of intellectual property as an economic driver and catalyst for growth, former British Prime Minister David Cameron accepted all of the recommendations contained in the May 2011 report, *Digital Opportunity: A Review of Intellectual Property and Growth* by Professor Ian Hargreaves. Cameron had commissioned the report and selected Hargreaves, an Oxford-trained digital communications scholar and a professor at Cardiff University, Wales, to chair the committee.

Hargreaves explained that his recommendations were "designed to enhance the economic potential of the UK's creative industries and to ensure that the emergence of high technology businesses, especially smaller businesses, in other sectors is not impeded by our IP laws."[57] Cameron and his government accepted Hargreaves' recommendations in full.

Perhaps as an outgrowth of the Hargreaves Report, the UK is currently building a comprehensive online resource called the Copyright Hub. In addition to helpful information about copyright and licensing laws, a plan is under way to create a database in which a user can easily find out the author, origin, and cost of licensing a particular work. But the Hub's greatest asset may be that it will allow creators to maintain control of their work, including what kind of licenses to offer (i.e., non-commercial use, commercial website, social media account, or personal use) and the compensation they would like to receive.[58]

The EU

In a digital borderless world, the EU's patchwork of national laws can create confusion and frustration as people try to navigate copyright laws. Despite political claims that the EU is the world's largest single market, EU citizens cannot access the same content across the region. Spotify was not available in every EU Member State for four years after its launch due to the difficulty in reaching agreements with each

Member State on fees and licenses. Some say the best approach for a European innovator is to move to the US to launch her company in order to take advantage of the real single market there and the "fair use" approach to copyright. Starting a business in the EU involves expensive legal fees, years-long procedures, and unpredictable results in European court cases.[59]

A group of copyright-reform activists have banded together as the Copyright For Creativity (C4C) and have issued a "Copyright Manifesto" detailing how the EU should support innovation and creativity through copyright reform. They want governments to create a true digital single market for the EU. C4C's website states that current copyright law is perceived as being "no longer fit-for-purpose by most stakeholders, except for those that benefit from the flaws of the current system."

C4C's Copyright Manifesto identifies four of these flaws and proposes solutions:

1.	The flaw: an *outdated* framework, based on a reality from 2001 that has long since changed	The solution: a *copyright review that simplifies and modernizes* the rules to bring them into line with today's reality and comprises a flexible norm to cope with future evolutions
2.	The flaw: a Directive that creates *no harmonization*, hence weakening any attempt to truly distill a digital single market	The solution: a harmonization based on a *mandatory list* of limitations and exceptions, which enables both users and businesses to understand their rights and obligations across the EU
3.	The flaw: the duration of copyright protection is *too long*	The solution: a *shortening* of duration that does not extend beyond what international treaties require and a faster transfer to the *public domain*
4.	The flaw: a *dysfunctional* implementation and enforcement of the rules	The solution: a *review* of the implementation and enforcement, based on demonstrated harm and the rule of law, including an in-depth reassessment of private copy levies and the preservation of intermediary liability rules

The US

In February 2015 the US Copyright Office issued a comprehensive report entitled "Copyright and the Music Marketplace." The Copyright Office has previously reported that the outmoded rules for licensing of musical works and sound recordings are an area in significant need of reform. The 245-page report was the result of a year-long effort to study the existing music marketplace and offer "a series of balanced recommendations to improve it."[60]

The report focused on best practices for ensuring that creators of musical works and sound recordings are compensated fairly for their work, especially in regards to licensing. The biggest issues to overcome in achieving this goal are:

- lack of transparency in the industry;
- no central authoritative music database; and
- different data being managed by different stakeholders.[61]

The report's recommendations included a complex concept comprising a public database to which government, private citizens, and existing licensing organizations would contribute. The proposed database would be maintained by a nonprofit general music rights organization (GMRO), which was neither named nor created in the report. The entire project would be funded through a mix of licensee royalty surcharges, administrative fees, and unclaimed royalties.

Creative Commons

Creative Commons is a global nonprofit organization that is working to balance current copyright laws and creative work on the internet. Its website provides a set of copyright licenses and other tools that give individual creators and corporations a simple, standardized way to maintain their rights while allowing certain uses of their work. In fact, this type of license is often called a "some rights reserved" approach to copyright. Creative Commons has collected a vast pool of content—a digital commons—that can be copied, distributed, edited, remixed, and built upon, all within the boundaries of international copyright law.[62]

TOOLS FOR THE DIWO (DO IT WITH OTHERS) MUSIC ENTREPRENEUR: A GUIDE TO AVOIDING COPYRIGHT INFRINGEMENT

Why Permission Is Needed

When using or adapting works protected by copyright, permission is required because rights owners are given an exclusive bundle of rights in conjunction with the exploitation of their work. The rights owner can decide whether or not she wants to grant permission for you to use or adapt her work, and what conditions she will set. If you do not agree to those conditions and use the work anyway, you may become involved in unpleasant and costly litigation involving infringing legal rights. It's best to understand your responsibilities and abide by the rights owner's conditions when you are contemplating use of a copyright protected work.[63]

Getting permission and the proper license also ensures that creators get paid for their work. When someone ignores copyright, the copyright holder is deprived of royalties (payment for use of their work). Clearly, if people don't get paid for their work, the creative industries will struggle to exist.[64]

You may be infringing copyright if you do any of the following without paying or having permission (this list is not comprehensive):

- download films from the internet;
- make copies of DVDs;
- download images from the internet and use them on your website;
- perform live or play recorded music in public;
- photocopy and distribute parts of a book, newspaper, or magazine.[65]

Music Uses That Require Permission

In order to legally use protected material, you need permission from the people who wrote the music (composers, lyricists, and music publishers) *and* from the people who performed and recorded it (performers and record labels). It's quite likely that you will need to spend some time researching the rights owners and contacting more than one organization for permission.[66]

Here are common uses that require permission for legal use:

- Playing music (including music on TV and radio) in your business for your staff, customers, visitors, and at events.

- Covering someone else's work in a new recording.

- Sampling music for use in a new recording.

- Using someone else's music in a new work (such as a soundtrack to a video, photo show, or podcast).

- Using recorded music in a program that will be broadcast via terrestrial, satellite, or internet TV or radio.

- Sharing music or music videos, even if you have purchased a copy, via websites, emails, or by converting MP3 files to CDs.

If getting permission to use an existing work proves to be too difficult or expensive, consider using one of the numerous commercial organizations that provide audio collections (music and sound clips) that can easily be licensed for a variety of uses. One such organization is Getty Images, which has a music section on its website where licenses may be purchased to download audio clips for a variety of different uses. Pay close attention to the terms of the license so that you understand and abide by the terms of usage (including any limitations) and avoid possible copyright infringement.[67]

Remember, if you do not have permission to use a work—either because you cannot find the copyright owner or the owner has denied your request—you must use another work for which you can get permission. If not, you will be in violation of copyright law.

For Composers, Songwriters, Lyricists and Arrangers

There are organizations that will register your creative work for you for a fee. Keep in mind that registration only proves that your work existed on a certain date (the date of registration). It does not prove that you are the original creator and will be of minimal help if you find yourself embroiled in infringement litigation. However, registration makes it easier for people to find and contact you if they are seeking permission to use your work.[68]

Another way to help protect and exploit your work is to place the copyright symbol (©), your name, and the year of first publication on it. Not only will this remind people that the work is protected, it will also give them a date from which they know the copyright period begins. Marking your work with a steganographic identifier (a digital watermark) is another excellent tool. For digital works, also embed metadata to help identify the work as yours. A service such as Creative Barcode can help you create a quick response (QR) code-based digital time-stamp.[69]

Pause and Reflect

John Fogerty, lead singer of Creedence Clearwater Revival (CCR), was sued in 1994 by Fantasy Records for plagiarizing himself in his song "The Old Man Down the Road." In other words, Fantasy Records thought "The Old Man Down the Road" (which Fogerty recorded as a solo act) sounded too much like CCR's song "Run Through the Jungle" (to which Fantasy owned the rights). Even though Fogerty won the case, for years afterward he refused to perform and record anything from the CCR catalog to avoid having to pay royalties for playing his own songs. Listen to the two songs and see if you can hear the similarities.

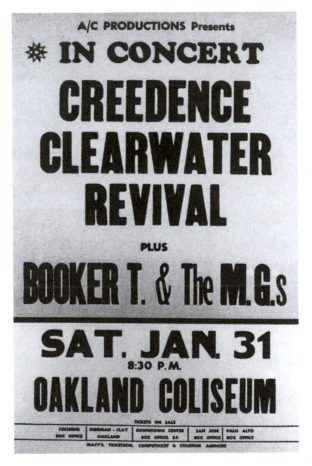

Concert poster Creedence Clearwater Revival

GAB Archive/Redferns/Getty Images

Opportunities Ahead

Sit back and recharge your right brain. It can be challenging to find opportunities for entrepreneurial thinking in the music copyright sector. For inspiration, watch a few of the videos on "Creativity & Culture, Science & Innovation" from Duke University's Center for the Study of the Public Domain. You'll find talks by professors at top law schools and from organizations including Creative Commons, Knowledge Ecology International, and Research on Innovation.[70]

CONCLUSION

Intellectual property law is made up of two areas: "industrial" property, which deals with inventions and patents, and "copyright," which focuses on literary and artistic creations. Most nations want to encourage the intellectual creativity of their citizens in order to advance the country's social, cultural, and economic goals. Intellectual property laws attempt to balance the economic rights of individuals and society. Artist- and music business-entrepreneurs can benefit from learning how to avoid copyright infringement and possible litigation.

Since the early nineteenth century, countries have gathered to discuss the complex issues of international trade and intellectual property. These conventions, such as the Berne Convention, can last for many years. International dialogue and, ultimately, agreement on any legal topic requires discussion, patience, sensitivity to vast cultural, economic, and legal differences, lobbying, and perseverance. Two organizations that work in this area are WIPO and the WTO.

Talking Back: Class Discussion

Explore these resources for research and discussion about copyright:

- "Copyright and Fair Use," Stanford University Libraries. Contains copyright case opinion summaries, copyright news, legislation, and a lively blog.[71]
- "Music Copyright Infringement Resource," sponsored by UCLA and Columbia Law Schools. A website packed with information about music copyright infringement cases from the mid-nineteenth century forward.[72]

NOTES

1 "Understanding Copyright and Related Rights," *WIPO*, www.wipo.int/about-ip/en/ (accessed May 17, 2016).
2 Emily Jupp, "Phil Manzanera on Jay-Z, Kanye West and the Riff That Changed His Life," *The Independent*, March 23, 2015, www.independent.co.uk/arts-entertainment/music/features/phil-manzanera-on-jay-z-kanye-west-and-the-riff-that-changed-his-life-10128766.html (accessed May 17, 2016).
3 Ibid.

4 Ibid.

5 Ibid.

6 Ibid.

7 Ibid.

8 "Understanding Copyright," *Movie Licensing USA*, www.movlic.com/k12/copyright.html (accessed May 17, 2016).

9 Ibid.

10 "An Introduction to Copyright," *The Copyright Hub*, www.copyrighthub.co.uk/find-out/what-is-copyright (accessed May 17, 2016).

11 James Crompton, "Music Publishing in the US," IBIS World Industry Report 51223, December 2014.

12 Andrew Johnson, "Sound Recording & Music Publishing in the UK," Ibis World Industry Report J59.200, December 2014.

13 "Intellectual Property," *WIPO*, www.wipo.int/edocs/pubdocs/en/intproperty/909/wipo_pub_909.pdf#page=22&zoom=auto,419,610 (accessed May 17, 2016).

14 Ibid.

15 Ibid.

16 Ibid.

17 Ibid.

18 "Understanding Copyright and Related Rights."

19 Ibid.

20 Ibid.

21 "Intellectual Property."

22 Ibid.

23 Ibid.

24 "What Is the WTO?" *World Trade Organization*, www.wto.org/english/thewto_e/whatis_e/wto_dg_stat_e.htm (accessed May 17, 2016).

25 "Intellectual Property."

26 Katia Gomez, "Inside the TRIPS Agreement," *Prospect: Journal of International Affairs at the University of California San Diego*, October 2009, www.prospectjournal.ucsd.edu/index.php/2009/10/inside-the-trips-agreement (accessed January 15, 2012).

27 Joseph E. Stiglitz, "Trade Agreements and Health in Developing Countries," *The Lancet*, January 31, 2009, 373: 363–65.

28 "Understanding Copyright and Related Rights."

29 Ibid.

30 Ibid.

31 Ibid.

32 Ibid.

33 Ibid.

34 Ibid.

35 Ibid.

36 Ibid.

37 Ibid.

38 Ibid.

39 Ibid.

40 Ibid.

41 Anthony Tomasini, "An Exclusive Schumann Club, Open for Members," *New York Times*, March 24, 2015.

42 Ibid.

43 Ibid.

44 Ibid.

45 Gavan Blau, "Musical Groups & Artists in the US," IBIS World Industry Report 71113, December 2014.

46 "Understanding Copyright and Related Rights."
47 Ibid.
48 Ibid.
49 Ibid.
50 Ibid.
51 Ibid.
52 Eoghan Macguire, "The Tiny Island Paradise Where 'People Breathe Music,'" *CNN*, April 15, 2015, www. cnn.com/2015/04/13/travel/cape-verde-music-economy (accessed May 17, 2016).
53 Ibid.
54 "About," *Kriol Jazz Festival*, www.krioljazzfestival.com (accessed May 17, 2016).
55 Macguire, "The Tiny Island "
56 "The Copyright Manifesto," *Copyright4Creativity*, January 2015, www.copyright4creativity.eu/wp-content/ uploads/2015/01/C4C-Copyright-Manifesto-20150119.pdf (accessed May 17, 2016).
57 The (UK) National Archives, Intellectual Property Office, "The Hargreaves Report Shows Potential to Boost Economy," http://webarchive.nationalarchives.gov.uk/20140603093549/www.ipo.gov.uk/about/press/press-release/press-release-2011/press-release-20110518.htm (accessed May 27, 2016).
58 Cori Stedman," Could the UK's Copyright Hub Provide a Template for Simple Rights Use?" *WHYY*, April 8, 2015, http://pbs.org/mediashift/2015/04/could-the-uks-copyright-hub-provide-a-template-for-simple-rights-use/ (accessed May 17, 2016).
59 "The Copyright Manifesto."
60 "Copyright and the Music Marketplace: A Report of the Register of Copyrights," February 2015, copyright. gov/docs/musiclicensingstudy/copyright-and-the-music-marketplace.pdf (accessed July 24, 2015).
61 Ibid.
62 "About," *Creative Commons*, https://creativecommons.org/about (accessed May 17, 2016).
63 Ibid.
64 Ibid.
65 Ibid.
66 Ibid.
67 Ibid.
68 Ibid.
69 Ibid.
70 http://web.law.duke.edu/cspd/video (accessed May 27, 2016).
71 http://fairuse.stanford.edu (accessed May 27, 2016).
72 http://mcir.usc.edu (accessed May 27, 2016).

PART 3

Music Revenue Streams

CHAPTER 6

Revenue Streams: Global Performing and Licensing

CHAPTER OVERVIEW

In this chapter we will examine the two broad areas of the performance sector that produce revenue streams for artist-entrepreneurs: performance royalties and live events. Entrepreneurial artists, bands, promoters, presenters, and producers tell the story of the live music industry. A proliferation of online tools is helping DIWO artist-entrepreneurs manage their shows and tours. For many groups, however, this is only a short-term strategy.

KEY TERMS

CISAC	Consent decrees
Blanket license	Technical rider
Secondary ticket market	Artist manager
Recoup	Booking agent
Paper the house	Sound technician
Ancillary spending	Talent buyer
Live Nation	Legal advisor
AEG	Presenter/Promoter

INTRODUCTION TO PERFORMANCE RIGHTS

There are two broad areas of the performance sector that produce revenue streams for artist- and music business-entrepreneurs. The first area is performance royalties from the broadcasting of licensed music on TV, radio, cable, and satellite, at sporting events, restaurants, or bars, in commercial establishments, and wireless and satellite streaming and downloading. The second area that produces revenue streams for entrepreneurs is live performances at concert halls or other venues, and staged theatrical productions. Revenue comes from ticket sales, VIP ticket packages, performance fees to artists, corporate sponsorships, venue rentals, merchandise sales, and all other ancillary products such as food, beverages, and souvenirs, parking, and facility taxes.[1]

PERFORMANCE ROYALTIES: A REVENUE STREAM FOR THE 21ST CENTURY GLOBAL PROFESSIONAL

In order for revenue to flow from the many types of performances described above to the creator and rights holder, rights must be identified and licenses issued. These services are provided by organizations known as authors' societies, collective management organizations, performing rights organizations, and collecting societies. They represent creators of music, visual arts, audiovisual, literary, and dramatic works, and manage their rights on a collective basis.[2]

In order to perform a work protected by copyright, permission must be granted directly from either the rights holder or an organization involved in rights management (a licensing body). A collecting society is a type of licensing body which grants rights on behalf of multiple rights holders in a single ("blanket") license for a single payment. Generally speaking, rights holders will join a collecting society and give the society permission to license their works for exploitation (to earn money). The collecting society charges a fee to the user for the license, from which it deducts an administrative charge before distributing the remainder to the rights owner as royalties.[3]

When a songwriter or composer affiliates with a collecting society or performing rights organization, she is in fact giving the society the right to issue performance licenses for her music. In exchange, the society will collect and distribute the revenue that is generated from the music's exploitation. No copyright ownership changes hands when a writer signs with a collecting society.[4]

In his Foreword to the 2015 Global Collections Report of the International Confederation of Societies of Authors and Composers (CISAC), electronic music pioneer and CISAC president Jean Michel Jarre summarizes why global collective management of rights is beneficial to creators:

> Alone, we are vulnerable, but when we combine our strengths, via the societies that represent us and protect our works, we have a voice. Authors' rights ensure us rewards for our creative endeavors. Creators are the singular force behind the works—films, paintings, songs, books, poems, pictures—that millions around the world enjoy. Yet we are often at the mercy of groups that control the channels of distribution of our works. This is acutely felt in today's digital ecosystem where creators are the most fragile element. For this reason, we rely heavily on our authors' societies and CISAC to take care of our interests.[5]

Key Terms and Definitions in Licensing

Authors' Societies

Also referred to as Collective Management Organizations (CMOs), authors' societies represent creators of music, visual arts, audiovisual, literary, and dramatic works, and manage their rights on a collective basis.

Collections

The money collected by an authors' society before deducting administrative costs.

Collective Management Organization (CMO)

An organization that manages rights for a variety of rights holders. Also known as performing rights organization (PRO) and collecting society.

Reproduction/Mechanical/Reprography Rights

The right to make a copy of a work protected under authors' rights/copyright. The term "Mechanical Rights" is typically used to describe the rights obtained by record producers in order to make a sound recording of a musical work. "Reprography" is used in the context of reproduction of literary and printed works.

Performing Rights

The right to communicate a copyright work to the public, whether by way of live performance, radio broadcast, cable transmission or dissemination via digital platforms such as streaming.

Private Copying

Creating a copy of rights-protected work by an individual, for private and personal use (for example, copying from a CD to an iPod). Acts of private copying are, in some countries, subject to a tax that is applied to blank media and storage devices.

The UK: Performance Licensing

The two main collecting societies for music in the UK are PRS for Music and Phonographic Performance Limited (PPL). PRS manages the rights of songwriters, composers, and publishers, while PPL manages the rights of record producers and performers. It is not uncommon to need a license from both PPL and PRS to get complete copyright coverage for such activities as playing recorded music (records, CDs, jukebox, or the radio) in a public space, such as a pub, shop, workplace, or theater.[6]

Europe: Performance Licensing

Music licensing has traditionally been handled on a country-by-country basis in Europe. Individual copyright owners would assign the worldwide exploitation rights in their works to their country's collecting society, which would then license copyright works on its members' behalf. Most national collecting societies have agreed to participate in what are known as reciprocal representation agreements. This means that each society is able to offer the repertoire of all the artists represented by all the collecting societies participating in the reciprocal agreements.[7] It is a complex process that is fraught with the possibility for human error.

As a result of complaints about practices by collecting societies, the European Commission in 2008 handed down a decision that allowed individual writer/publisher members of the European collecting societies to choose which society will represent them throughout Europe. This meant that writers and publishers were no longer restricted only to their country's collecting society and could "shop around" for the best deal. The change was implemented to encourage competition in the European rights management marketplace.[8]

Despite these and other efforts, every entity offering music services within the EU still needs many licenses from different collecting societies. The repertoire of each society is constantly changing and fragmented. Multiple societies can represent different shares in the same recording. And, to complicate things even further, some major labels have made deals with new digital entities for exclusive exploitation rights of their holdings rather than work with the various national collecting societies.[9]

Warner-Chappell was the first major publisher to grant each of the European collecting societies the ability to license its repertoire on a pan-European basis. This was a step forward in achieving the goal of having the major European collecting societies able to grant multi-territory, multi-repertoire licenses, particularly in relation to the major pop repertoires. In the Warner-Chappell deal, licensees are now able to obtain comprehensive mechanical and performing rights licenses for music in publishers' repertoire from any number of European collecting societies on a non-exclusive basis. Many feel that a Warner-Chappell type of change in the EU as a whole would introduce competition into the music licensing marketplace, greatly reduce compliance costs for businesses which commercialize music content across Europe, and provide consumers with greater choice and better access to a wide range of music services.[10]

CISAC

CISAC is a network of 230 author's societies (CMOs) in 120 countries. Author's societies issue licenses and collect royalties on behalf of their author and publisher members for the use of their works. In most countries, author's societies collect royalties and issue licenses for music uses that require performance, mechanical, and synchronization licenses. (The US is an exception to this.)

CISAC represents more than three million creators from around the world who are working in the areas of music, audiovisual, drama, literature, and visual arts.[11] The collecting societies for the top ten international music markets are:

US (ASCAP, BMI, SESAC)

Japan (Jasrac)

Germany (Gema)

UK (PRS, PPL)

France (SACEM)

Australia (AMCOS and APRA)

Canada (Socan)

Italy (Siae)

Brazil (Ecad)

South Korea (Komca)

Trends in Worldwide Collections

- Live performance and digital uses of music are replacing recorded music as the primary revenue producers for worldwide collection societies.[12]

- Performing artists now must rely more heavily on their live performances as a revenue source and are touring for longer periods of time. The live music sector continues to grow as a result, bringing greater revenue to songwriters for the live performances of their works.[13]

- Emerging, high-growth and heavily populated countries such as those of the BRICS nations (Brazil, Russia, India, China, and South Africa) are expected to produce significantly larger revenues in the years ahead, in part due to wider internet accessibility and the rapid adoption of internet and mobile services.[14]

- Indonesia, South Africa, Pakistan, and Nigeria are replacing developed markets such as the US, Japan, the UK, and Germany as the markets generating the most new money from smartphones.[15]

- Collections from digital use of creative works increased by 25 percent from 2012 to 2013, but still only represented 5 percent of overall global collections, indicating an opportunity for significant growth.[16]

Challenges in Worldwide Collections

- There is inequity among the European collecting societies regarding live music licensing. Some societies receive more than 7 percent of the ticket value to compensate writers for their contribution, whereas others receive 3 percent or less.[17]

- The base on which the compensation for writers is calculated often excludes the fastest growing live music revenue streams, such as "at the event spend" or the secondary ticket spend (where tickets are re-sold by fans or by professional scalpers).[18]

- Growing internet penetration and the use of smartphones in emerging countries brings new opportunities for content providers, while at the same time increasing the likelihood that illegal copyright usage will continue to depress collections.[19]

The US: Performance Licensing

Until now, performance royalties in the US were collected separately from mechanical royalties, and digital uses of music were collected by yet another organization, SoundExchange. (Since 2014, SoundExchange revenues are counted as digital sales rather than performance rights income.)[20] Performing rights organizations ASCAP and BMI, which together represent more than 95 percent of the music available in the US,[21] are restricted by law to collecting only performing rights royalties. The Harry Fox Agency had served as the primary US collector of mechanical rights since its creation in 1927 by the National Music Publishers Association (NMPA).

However, now that performance royalties are king of the royalty marketplace, major changes in the US PROs may be at hand.

Spurred on by the reality that mechanical licenses for recorded music are no longer the huge revenue generator they once were, SESAC, the smallest of the three major US PROs and the only one not bound by law to collect only performing rights royalties, purchased the Harry Fox Agency from the NMPA in 2015.[22] SESAC now has the ability to issue both performance and mechanical licenses, which will enable it to be more efficient in managing the many overlapping kinds of licenses required for digital platforms.[23]

Consent Decrees

ASCAP and BMI are still governed by decades-old regulatory agreements with the Justice Department, known as consent decrees. The consent decrees restrict how these two PROs negotiate with companies and individuals using music. ASCAP and BMI offer blanket licenses, which give a user access to everything in their catalogs. Thus, they are unable to turn down a request for music by a user or charge a higher royalty rate for a specific work or song. As online outlets like Spotify and Pandora grow, songwriters and music publishers are complaining that the old rules result in unfairly low royalty rates.[24]

Three key elements comprise the consent decrees. First, the decrees established a royalty distribution system mandating a 50/50 split between songwriter and publisher, with the songwriter's share going directly to her without first passing through the publisher's account. This means that writer's royalties cannot be held against an unrecouped advance (one that is not paid back) given to the writer.

Second, the decrees specified that performance rights users could license music either through a blanket license or on a per program basis. The decrees prohibited the issuing of a license that "discriminates in license fees or other terms and conditions between licensees [who are] similarly situated."[25]

Third, the consent decrees required ASCAP and BMI to grant a license upon the licensee's request, even if a rate had yet to be agreed to, and established an arbiter in cases when the collecting society and licensee were unable to agree on a royalty rate.[26]

For decades, the publishing industry has fought to loosen the stranglehold of the consent decrees, claiming that the rate-setting procedures established by laws fashioned in 1941 are the source of the unacceptably low rates currently paid for the public performance of a composition. With the tectonic shifts in the music business landscape moving from downloading music (sales) to lower revenue-producing streaming music, the stakes have risen dramatically for publishers and the collecting societies.

ASCAP, BMI, and the publishers want more licensing flexibility and the consent decrees updated at the very least, if not eliminated altogether. Some of the major publishers are threatening to withdraw from ASCAP and BMI, which would weaken those two PROs and make the music licensing environment even more inhospitable.[27]

Pandora, along with TV and radio broadcasters, take the other side of the argument. They argue that regulation is needed to prevent anticompetitive behavior and to keep music licensing costs from becoming prohibitively high. Many composers and songwriters are quite vocal about their frustration with the low payments they receive from Pandora.[28] According to Sony/ATV executive Marty Bandier, one million streams of a song on Pandora yields approximately US$60 in royalties. "This is a totally unacceptable situation and one that cannot be allowed to continue," he protests.[29]

Sony/ATV music publishing was the first major publisher actually to try withdrawing its *digital* rights from the PROs in order to negotiate higher royalty rates directly with digital music services. However, the copyright rate courts ruled that publishers' membership in the PROs was either all in or all out; publishers and songwriters had to give their PRO all rights or no rights in relation to issuing licenses to users. Sony/ATV's petition to remove only its digital rights was rejected.[30]

A federal judge dealt a blow to ASCAP and major music publishers in 2014 by ruling that Pandora's royalty rate of 1.85 percent of total revenue would remain unchanged. At the time of this writing, Pandora is appealing a court ruling that requires it to pay 2.5 percent of its total revenue to ASCAP rival BMI.[31]

In response to complaints from all areas of the music industry, the US Department of Justice is in the process of reviewing the consent decrees governing ASCAP and BMI. Any changes would put millions of dollars in royalties into play and would significantly alter the music industry landscape.[32]

It seems unlikely that the consent decrees will be completely abolished in order to placate the music publishers and PROs. However, there are concerns among composers and songwriters that changes in the consent decrees could eliminate the currently mandated 50/50 split between publisher and writer, with the writer's share being paid directly to her. If collective licensing is abolished or weakened by the elimination of blanket licensing from ASCAP and BMI, independent publishers and songwriters could see much lower royalty rates for uses of their works.[33] And licensees would undoubtedly experience higher rates for use of the vast catalogs held by the major publishers, as licensees would have to make direct deals with those very powerful companies.

While this may not adversely affect large, deep-pocketed corporate music users, entrepreneurs who launch new online music ventures could face prohibitively high licensing costs, potentially stifling competition and innovation in the marketplace. Ironically, these were two of the reasons why, in 1941, the Department of Justice instituted the consent decrees in the first place.

Pause and Reflect

What opportunities for artist- and music business-entrepreneurs do you see in this complex situation? Could you suggest how the consent decree issues could be resolved in a way that is favorable to all parties?

More Turmoil in the Royalty Marketplace

Music industry veteran Irving Azoff's new music publishing venture, Global Music Rights, has moved into the marketplace with the goal of controlling superstar songwriters' catalogs. Global Music clients include members of Journey, Fleetwood Mac, and Soundgarden; Pharrell Williams and Benny Blanco; and the estates of John Lennon and Ira Gershwin. Like SESAC, Global Music Rights is not governed by the consent decrees that control ASCAP and BMI. This means that Global Music has enormous flexibility in negotiating the cost to use works in its catalog and the ability to refuse to license a song. As existing affiliations with ASCAP or BMI expire for Global Music Rights clients, many of the industry's most popular songs may disappear from radio, TV, and digital music services if Azoff's licensing price isn't met.[34]

ASCAP Has a Great Year

As ASCAP fights to relieve the stranglehold of the decades-old consent decrees, it finds itself able to collect and distribute more money than ever to its songwriters. In 2014, it collected just over $1 billion in revenue, the first time that it or any collecting society has reached that level. It tracked 500 billion song performances, a 100 percent increase over the previous year. And its payments to author members increased nearly 4 percent compared to 2013.[35]

One of the reasons for the surge in collections is the rapid growth of online music delivery services. According to Nielsen, the amount of streaming in 2014 through services like Spotify and YouTube increased 54.5 percent compared to the year before. Another reason for the revenue increase is that ASCAP has increased its technological ability to identify each of these 500 billion performances and collect licensing revenue from them. According to ASCAP, it was able to identify 30 times more songs in 2014 than it did in 2013. The result was good news for its writers: ASCAP paid nine times more songwriters for their work.[36]

The Differences between Collecting Societies and Publishers

There are two main differences between collecting societies and music publishers.

- Collecting societies are not publishers; rather, they serve as the publisher's *agent* for performance licenses. Performing rights organizations license, collect, and distribute money earned through performance licenses. They send the performance royalties (less a small administrative fee) to both their publisher members and to their writer members.

- Writers do not give up any of their copyrights when signing with a PRO. This is in contrast to a traditional agreement between a publisher and writer, where the writer may be required to assign a percentage of her copyright to the publisher.

LIVE EVENTS AS A REVENUE STREAM

No musician I know is making their living from selling their music. Everyone's making their living from touring and playing shows.[37]

(Nicholas Jaar, founder of the subscription-based "serial label" Other People)

Live events and promotion involve everything to do with putting on a show or event, from booking the event through to staging it. Live events can be indoors or outdoors, one-off events or tours, and small- to large-scale productions.

What is it that makes live events so compelling? Nothing can come close to the feeling of being in the same physical space as the performers and other audience members. It's an experience that ignites all our senses. The most memorable concerts feel spontaneous. We can sense the musicians feeding off each other's energy and folding us into a riveting, visceral experience.[38]

These moments are few and far between for most concert-goers. In the classical realm the emphasis on technical mastery and the sheen of perfection can get in the way of artistic risk-taking. Besides, why bother to leave the house when great recordings are as easily accessible as a YouTube search?

A 2015 performance by Nadja Salerno-Sonnenberg and the Philadelphia Orchestra provided the answer: we go to live events because of the value of surprise and its magical effect on our emotions. The program looked quite ordinary on paper: a respected violinist in a warhorse concerto. But Salerno-Sonnenberg made the Mendelssohn Violin Concerto in E minor into such a completely personal statement that "it left the impression it might never happen again," stated critic Peter Dobrin. "Without being extreme or eccentric, the violinist essentially rewrote a good deal of the work's performance tradition . . . and she created a world within a world that

Nadja Salerno-Sonnenberg
Hyoung Chang/Denver Post/Getty Images

seemed almost a portrayal of some specific event in the composer's emotional life. Competent violinists abound. Convincing individualists we should hold close."[39]

Think back on all the concerts you've attended and name the one that defined you. Describe that moment during the show when you had a flash of recognition: "*This* is who I am, now I get what my life is about."

At first glance, the live music sector may not seem to be a rich environment for innovation. The basic idea—musicians performing for an audience—has been around for hundreds of years in one form or another. The digital revolution has impacted it, of course, but that's not what drives this sector. The essence of a live show is personal, face-to-face communication between the artist and the fans. We may be able to watch a live event in real time on a movie screen or in an online social media environment, but so far we haven't figured out how to download the three-dimensional electricity and excitement we feel at a concert.

The entrepreneurs in the live events sector are the bands and artists themselves. The best of them find innovative ways to connect with their fans, keep their ticket prices reasonable, and give unforgettable, life-changing shows. In this section we'll take a look at the how the industry works today and how some entrepreneurial musicians are shaping its future.

Getting Started

While it may seem a bit random that some bands and ensembles have longevity in the marketplace and others don't, there are compelling similarities in the story of musicians who have staying power. Knowing the basic business structure of the live music industry is, without a doubt, the single most important factor in determining how long an ensemble or band can prosper.

If you're an artist-entrepreneur, you need songs to play and people who will listen to them. Every band starts out playing small gigs, often with only two or three people in the audience—their moms and friends they've bribed with free drinks. It's a humble beginning.

At some point the band or ensemble will decide they need to step up the pace and join the legions of musicians who hit the road. Touring is the proving ground for bands. If they can draw a crowd, get some buzz going, and keep those crowds growing, they have a good chance of getting some mainstream attention.

DIWO musicians begin their touring careers by doing all the work: planning a (somewhat) logical tour route, finding the right-size venues with the right vibe, and contacting the people at the venues who will book them. At this point in their careers, a DIWO band will get a non-negotiable deal from the venue. That could be US$5 per head from anyone who comes to see their band specifically (there's a sign-in sheet at the door), 20 percent of the door before the band's set, or "here's 30 tickets, keep the money from any you sell."[40]

Rich Nesin, a veteran concert tour and production manager in New York City, has this story about his band: "My own little cover band has yet to play a live gig . . . we're still rehearsing every week. Yet, there are neighborhood bars and restaurants that will pay us as much as five hundred dollars, if we can a) play the night and b) guarantee 20–25 people who will come in to eat, drink, and clap loudly for us. That's not a formula for success as an original band, but it shows the lack of negotiating at this level."[41]

Then there are all the other arrangements, like finding a van, someplace to sleep, and money to buy food and gas. Did we mention marketing? The only reliable way for DIWO bands to get an audience is to spread the word on their own.

Everybody starts off this way and it's a lot of hard work. At some point, most bands and ensembles hope to find somebody else to do this for them.

Building Your Team

Many musicians work with industry professionals like artist managers and booking agents who are highly skilled at this very thing. The tricky part is that agents get paid a commission, or percentage, of what the band earns on each gig they book. And a manager gets a commission on each gig *plus* other things the band makes money from, such as product endorsements, being on a TV show, and merchandise sales.

Why would any manager or agent want to take on a band that's getting paid in free beer? The answer—most people wouldn't. Until they're actually making enough money from their music to share with a booking agent (traditionally a 10 percent commission) and a manager (15–20 percent commission), the band or ensemble is on their own. Sounds harsh, but remember—it's a business.

Let's do the math:

Hypothetical #1

Band gets paid $100 for a gig

10 percent to booking agent = $10

20 percent to manager = $20

Band splits $70 four ways = $17.50 each.

Hypothetical #2

Band gets paid $1,000 for a gig

10 percent to booking agent = $100

20 percent to manager = $200

Band splits $700 four ways = $175 each.

And the numbers above don't include the cost of transportation, eating, sleeping, paying taxes, and buying strings for your violin or guitar.

Many artist-entrepreneurs feel the first person they need on their team is a *manager*, the professional who oversees all aspects of an artist's career. This includes brand management and artist PR; touring and sponsorship; helping the band secure a recording partner; dealing with the ensemble or band's personal problems; and long-range planning for their career. Managers typically receive 15–20 percent of the artist's earnings on concerts, merchandise (merch), sponsorships, and other revenue streams.

Touring makes up a large part of professional musicians' revenue and most (serious) bands tour for months or even a year at a time. An artist and her manager will decide how often to play each music market in order to keep fans' interest high and avoid playing too soon in the same place.

Some artist-entrepreneurs employ a *booking agent* to get them paying gigs. In association with the artist, her manager, and attorney, the booking agent will route the tour, find the appropriate venues, and then negotiate dates and fees. Experts in the art of the deal, they have a vast knowledge of the venues and talent buyers in the regions where the artist wants to tour.

As the show begins to take shape artistically and technically, the booking agent will begin looking for venues along the projected tour route. The ideal venue will have a vibe that matches the band's brand and image, and can accommodate the technical needs of the show. Seating/standing capacity, stage size, tech specifications, fly space, wing space, loading dock, parking for trucks, lighting and electrical—these are among the many venue variables that a booking agent considers when routing a tour.

Another member of the artist-entrepreneur's trusted inner circle is her *lawyer*. As bands begin to seek representation by a manager or booking agent, they will be expected to sign legal agreements stating the terms of each relationship. The band or ensemble will need to consult a skilled entertainment attorney before saying "yes" to anyone. In fact, a lawyer could even be the best guide to the right manager or agent for a band, as lawyers are paid to be an advocate for their client's goals. An experienced attorney who knows the music industry will be invaluable in giving her clients an unvarnished view of the pros and cons of all situations.[42]

In some US states, notably New York and California, professionals such as booking agents are required to have a talent agency license in order to procure work for performers. This is very important to remember if you are doing business in those two states and any others that require such a license.

Strictly speaking, a *talent buyer* represents a client. That client can be:

- a bar or a club;

- a concert promoter, such as SJM Concerts in the UK or New York's Bowery Presents, which utilizes many venues of all sizes and in a variety of markets;

- a giant corporation, such as Microsoft, that wants talent for large meetings or events;

- a college or university, acting as the "middle agent" between an act and the school;

- a larger venue. Nowadays more and more venues are getting into self-promoting, or even co-promoting with local promoters, as the competition to bring business into a venue gets stiffer.[43]

Talent buyers have valuable knowledge of the entertainment tastes and ticket-buying habits of their communities. For the highly competitive top level of artist shows, buyers in the same market often bid against each other in order to get the superstar to play in their venue. This can lead to some risky contractual revenue splits with the artist, as the buyer tries to outbid her competitors.

A *promoter* (also called a presenter) has one of the riskiest jobs in the industry. She must sell enough tickets to cover the costs of putting on the show, plus make a bit of profit to stay in business. Occasionally, a show will have such weak advance ticket sales that the artist, manager, and promoter decide to cancel rather than risk losing money and causing embarrassment for the artist. Sometimes, however, it's necessary to carry on and, in order to make the house look fuller, the promoter will paper the house (give away tickets in special promotions).

There is a saying in the live concert industry that sums up the risk that promoters take: "There are no bad shows, only bad deals." The show itself could be great, but its success is all in the deal. If everyone makes money, then the promoter made the right deal. Financial success isn't always based on what the sellable capacity is of the venue, but rather what the act is worth in a specific market.[44]

A promoter/talent buyer may own the venue(s) she books, or she may just rent various spaces as needed. Owning a venue opens up a lot of possibilities for additional revenue, including parking fees, food and beverages, merch, and renting out the venue when the promoter isn't using it.

Sidney Mills, Steel Pulse

Ilya S. Savenock/Getty Images Entertainment

"Steel Pulse played in Austin [Texas] a few years back, a market we had been struggling in for years," explains Rich Nesin, the band's production manager. "Rather than go to the same room we had been doing poorly in, we took a smaller guarantee for a smaller room (one that was harder to put our show into) for a Monday night, to boot. We walked out with double the money, a packed house, and a story to rebuild on in the future."[45]

The *sound technician* is the person who will be controlling the mixing board at the venue, monitoring the speakers, and making sure the room sounds as good as it can. Sound techs will conduct soundchecks and possibly even work the lights if the venue is small.

For Music Business-Entrepreneurs

For students just starting out as music business-entrepreneurs, it helps to have some experience. Here are a few entry-level jobs where you can learn how live events and promotion work from the inside:

Event promotion—supporting staff publicity activities, contributing to the production and distribution of publicity for live events, assisting in the production of press releases, and presenting live event ticket sales information.

Booking agents—assisting in the details of finding artists paying work, researching and assessing the appropriateness of venues, and contributing to the preparation of contracts.

Venue—maintaining the booking calendar, updating holds and cancelations, supporting licensing and permissions applications, and contributing to preparation of contracts.

Stage crew—supporting load in, breakdown, and load out of equipment for a live event, and safely supporting the set-up of the stage, instruments, sound, and lighting for the live event.

Global Players in the Live Events Marketplace

Two of the largest companies involved in live events are Live Nation Worldwide and AEG Live.

Live Nation Worldwide has a market share of approximately 17.1 percent. In 2013 the company produced more than 240,000 events in 33 countries, generating US$6.5 billion in total revenue. The company owns or controls 128 venues in North and South America and Europe, including amphitheaters, theaters, clubs, arenas, and festival sites. Live Nation operates in five business segments: concerts (concert promotion and venue operations), sponsorship, ticketing, e-commerce, and artist management. In 2011 Live Nation acquired Big Champagne Media Measurement, a data and analytics company.[46]

AEG Live is the entertainment segment of the Anschutz Company, one of the world's largest sports and entertainment presenters, with an estimated market share of 4.8 percent. In addition to AEG Live, the Anschutz Company owns several music industry subsidiaries, including Goldenvoice and the Messina Group. AEG owns numerous major venues in the US, as well as a number of sports franchises, including the Los Angeles Kings National Hockey League team, the Manchester Monarchs American Hockey League team, and several Major League Soccer teams.[47]

Through AEG Events and AEG Live, the Anschutz Company books, manages, and promotes the ESPN X Games, HBO Boxing events, and the Grammy Awards, among others. It produces and promotes internationally acclaimed music festivals, including the New Orleans Jazz and Heritage Festival, and the Coachella Valley Music and Arts Festival.[48]

Ticketing

Although global live music revenue is forecast to rise in the next five years, income from ticket sales is likely to grow faster than sponsorship revenue, according to Ibis World forecasts. Live music ticket sales revenue from for-profit organizations will generate US$23.69 billion in 2019, compared with US$20.51 billion in 2014, which is equivalent to a compound annual growth rate of two percent. A significant technological innovation known as Smart wristbands made a major impact on the live music sector in 2014, offering concerts and festival attendees easy access to events as well as cashless on-site payments.[49]

The forecast for global nonprofit organizations is that the urgency for revenue from private sources will increase in importance as public funding falls. Over the five years to 2020, funding for the global nonprofit creative economy is expected to shrink as countries continue to struggle with an economic slowdown. Consumers may become even more price-conscious as the downturn drags on, putting pressure on music organizers to price events to compete with other forms of entertainment and leisure time recreation.[50]

The artist's performance fee and popularity, the cost of staging and promoting the event, and the uniqueness of the event being held are all major contributors to ticket prices. For example, if a disbanded group reunites for a tour, demand for tickets will be high and could then support ticket prices that are much higher than the current industry average. Promoters and artists generally work to find the sweet spot in ticket pricing, which means charging the highest possible ticket price while still selling out the venue. Important factors to consider in a pricing strategy include the number of the artists' performances offered in the venue, the duration of the tour, ticket prices of comparable shows in the market, and the exclusivity of the venue.[51]

Ticket pricing begins with the promoter, who bundles it into her offer to the booking agent along with other parts of the deal, such as the artist's guarantee and percentage-of-ticket-sale structure (e.g., $200,000 plus 90 percent of ticket sales). To get to the range of individual ticket prices for the event, the promoter will prepare a mathematical model of potential expenses and revenue. The expense factors include the guarantee for the artist, production costs, venue rental, licensing fees to collecting societies, sound and lighting, local stage labor, catering, show-specific needs (i.e., advertising and marketing, barricades, security, rentals, and piano tuner), and variables such as insurance costs. The revenue factors include an educated guess on what sort of business the act will do and what the promoter feels comfortable risking.[52]

The booking agent, artist, and manager evaluate the offer based on a variety of factors, such as: is it the right venue and the right promoter? How does it compare to competing offers? Is the ticket price within the acceptable range of the artist's fans?

Occasionally, an artist will set a maximum ticket price for her tour, or a flat price across the tour, and the promoter's offer must then be submitted to fit that mold. But that is more the exception than it is the rule. Young bands with a college-age fanbase, metal bands, and artists like Bruce Springsteen who want to keep tickets reasonably priced for their fans are the most likely to take that route.[53]

It is easy to see how the ticket pricing and all other parts of the deal go round in circles for a period of time before an offer gets formally confirmed. But eventually, one will arrive at numbers that everyone can agree with and a show gets confirmed.[54]

The ticketing industry consists of primary and secondary sellers. Buying a ticket from a primary seller, such as the venue itself, means the ticket came from the original ticket inventory.

The secondary ticket marketplace comprises tickets that are being resold by someone who purchased them from the original ticket inventory. There are formal secondary sellers (StubHub, TicketLiquidator, and Vipaco international ticket brokerage) and informal sellers (friends, people standing outside the venue on the night of the show, or ticket scalpers who try to sell their tickets for more than the face value). The price of a ticket on the secondary market is set by the seller and her best guess as to what price the market will bear. If the show is sold out and demand is high, people without tickets may be willing to pay a lot more than the price on the face of the ticket in order to get into the show.

Some artists and managers are disparaging about the secondary ticket market. They worry that it is driving up the cost of tickets for fans who cannot find tickets on the primary market. Managers also resent the fact that the artist does not receive any of the money from a ticket that is sold on the secondary market.

On the other hand, some industry people argue that the secondary market is a fair way to determine ticket prices. It's like an auction: whoever is the highest bidder gets the ticket.

The secondary market is a lucrative but controversial area. Today, many artists participate in it by selling VIP ticket packages, which include special souvenirs, meet & greets, photo ops, and early entry into a venue. This is done through the fan club or by ticket agencies that specialize in such things. Almost all of these deals give the fan something more than they would have gotten for the same price ticket on the open market.[55]

Trying to Find an Ethical Ticketing Route

It's sometimes difficult to give something away for almost nothing. The rush tickets program of the Metropolitan Opera (Met) in New York City is subsidized by the Agnes Varis Trust, which makes up the difference between the US$25 rush ticket and its full cost, which can run into hundreds of dollars. This arrangement allows the Met to benefit from the ability to offer an affordably priced ticket to someone who might not otherwise be able to attend, while also taking in the full price of the seat.[56]

The Met has been going through daunting financial challenges. With a house of 3,800 seats, there are often hundreds of unsold tickets for each performance. In theory, the Met could sell those tickets at the last minute at a discount. Opera lovers could gain entry to a performance and the Met would make at least some money.[57]

This raises an ethical dilemma. Would it be fair to allow last-minute ticket purchasers to buy cheaper tickets than those who paid full price weeks or months in advance, such as the Met's season subscribers?

Like many nonprofit music organizations, the Met is trying to expand its audience, particularly to young people. It has a student rush ticket option that is not subsidized and applies only to certain performances. The student rush program raises an ethical question as well. Is it fair to those who paid full price to be sitting next to a student who purchased an unsubsidized ticket? Peter Gelb, the Met's General Manager, says sympathetic patrons understand that the goal is to bring in young audiences to opera. But an online survey revealed that the same people were receiving the rush tickets night after night, and some were even scalping them.[58]

An attempt at setting up a lottery did not solve the problems, so this was replaced with a first-come-first-served online program. Customers were allowed up to two tickets for a single performance every seven days, which is tracked by a computer technology ticket-monitoring service. When it reviewed the data, the Met found about 1,000 new ticket purchasers who were not previously in the company's records, suggesting that the program just might be fulfilling its original goal of bringing new audiences to opera.[59]

The Money Comes in . . .

In recent years the contractual split of ticket revenue between the artist and the promoter/buyer has moved aggressively to favor the artist. The most common split is 85/15, where 85 percent of the ticket revenue goes to the artist and the remaining 15 percent to the talent buyer. Some superstar artists can command revenue splits of 90/10.

There are a few typical deal types for how bands are paid—a flat fee; a straight percentage of ticket sales; and various combinations of the two, the most common being a fee plus a percentage of ticket sales. In classical music the deals are primarily flat fee.

Revenue from ancillary sales—merchandise, food, beverages, parking, sponsorships, ticketing surcharges, and VIP packages—has become increasingly important to the financial success of pop and rock shows, but not so much for classical events. Ancillary revenue is now so vital to the profit or loss of a show budget that a promoter and venue may go ahead with a weak-selling show because they know that the band's fans will spend a lot of money on food, beverages, and merchandise. For early-career bands, T-shirt and CD sales often make the difference between making or losing money on a show.

Even some of the ancillary revenue that was traditionally the promoter's is now shared with the artist, such as parking fees and ticket surcharges. An interesting fact that most people don't realize is that ticketing companies, such as Ticketmaster, return some of the ticket surcharge revenue to the promoter or venue in exchange for being the exclusive provider of ticket services.

> ### Pause and Reflect
>
> What information about customers does a ticketing company collect at the point of sale? How could this information be used by the ticketing company, the promoter/venue, the artist, and others?

The details of how a band, soloist, or ensemble will be paid are spelled out in a performance contract, along with the technical and hospitality requirements for putting on the show. Some DIWO bands are nervous about asking for a formal contract because they're afraid that the talent buyer will just laugh and find somebody else to play. That does happen, of course. But it's always better to have even the simplest written agreement outlining everyone's expectations.

The backstage or technical rider, presented to promoters by every touring act, details specifications on stage design, sound systems, lighting, as well as the artist's requirements—from travel and billing to dressing room accommodations and meals.

Made famous by Van Halen's contractual demand that brown M&M's be plucked from the group's candy bowl, the rider often reflects the personality of an artist. The website The Smoking Gun maintains an ever-expanding list of 300+ riders, covering performers from Frank Sinatra and U2 to Lady Gaga and Kenny G.[60]

U2

Kevin Mazur/WireImage/Getty Images

. . . And the Money Goes Out

DIWO artist-entrepreneurs usually won't have much of a budget for show design. However, once a band starts to break and adds industry professionals to its team, the band will try to find the money to add production value to its shows.

As they begin tour discussions, the artist and the manager will have a vision of what they want the tour to look like. If they have the budget, a high priority will be hiring a variety of professionals, such as a production manager, stage and lighting designer, choreographer, and costume designer to help them put together an exciting show for the fans, consistent with the artist's brand. Shows can be very complex, with high-tech and sophisticated special effects and literally tons of equipment. The design of the show influences its cost, which, in turn, is a large factor in deciding how tickets will be priced.

The technical complexity and size of a show will determine how many trucks will be needed to haul everything that is traveling on the tour. Key players on the road may include an accountant, the tour manager, production and stage managers, riggers, carpenters, sound and lighting techs, backline techs (formerly called roadies), bus and truck drivers, security personnel, production assistants, plus dressing room and wardrobe assistants. Local crews provided at each venue may include stagehands, truck loaders, more riggers and electricians, audio and lighting specialists, additional security personnel, and spotlight operators.[61]

From a promoter or presenter's perspective, the costs that go into putting on a show can include the artist's fee, venue rental and production costs, advertising, PRO or collecting society licenses, ushers, security, insurance, catering, box office, technical crew, and equipment rental. These costs can and do fluctuate if problems arise during the load-in or load-out of a show. If ticket sales fall short, the promoter may lose money on the event.

Venues

Key Terms and Definitions for Venues

Amphitheater

An outdoor venue with a combination of fixed and lawn seating for 5,000–30,000 ticket holders.

Arena

A multi-purpose indoor facility with average seating capacity between 5,000 and 20,000.

Club

An indoor venue built primarily for music events, but that may also include comedy clubs. Capacity is generally less than 1,000 seats and often without full fixed seating.

Marquee Event

An event having or associated with the name recognition and drawing power of one whose name appears in bright lights on a venue and as the headline act in marketing materials.

Stadium

A multi-purpose, often open-air facility that has 30,000 seats or more.

Theater

An indoor venue built primarily for musical and theatrical events. Capacity is generally 1,000 to 6,500 seats.

According to Ibis World Reports, there has been substantial growth in the music theater and club-level event sector in the past five years, including increased spending per person at shows (called ancillary spending or "per-cap") on food, beverages, merchandise, and upgrade purchases. Events held at theaters and clubs are often considerably more affordable to attend than arena and amphitheater shows, making them attractive to consumers who are price-sensitive. Additionally, online music discovery is helping new artists book successful tours in these smaller venues.[62]

In the Northern Hemisphere, companies that promote music (as opposed to sports and other performing arts) typically see higher operating income in the second and third quarters of the financial year because promoters take advantage of outdoor venues, many of which provide a platform for lucrative summer festivals. Conversely, promoters that own theaters typically see higher operating income and demand during the first, second, and fourth quarters of the calendar year because the theatrical touring season typically runs from September through April.[63]

Mini-Case Study: China's Concert Etiquette Challenges

One of the unexpected obstacles China faces today as it aspires to be a cultural power is proper concert etiquette at Western classical music concerts. Deng Xiaoping's campaign of reform in 1978 launched China's rise to prosperity and with it a demand for culture, particularly Western classical music.[64]

Zheng Xiaoying, the renowned 86-year-old female conductor of the China National Opera House, remembers the first performance in China by the Berlin Philharmonic Orchestra. It was October 1979, and the Beijing Capital Gymnasium was filled with people who were just emerging from the dark days of the Cultural Revolution. Conductor Herbert von Karajan refused to begin the concert until the whole hall was silent. "Many people were late, and we waited for a long time," Zheng said. "Everyone held their breath because we all knew what he was waiting for."[65]

Tan Dun, composer

Roberto Serra—Iguana Press/Redferns/Getty Images

In traditional China, concerts were often held in restaurants and teahouses, where enthusiastic applause and loud cheers from the audience would erupt when performers successfully hit a high note. Even as recently as 2009, audiences could be seen eating oranges during performances in the newly constructed National Centre for the Performing Arts (NCPA) near Tiananmen Square in Beijing.[66]

In the past decade, local governments have spent billions of yuan building grand performance venues across the country, which have hosted some of the world's finest ensembles and orchestras. Government underwriting and corporate sponsorships help keep ticket prices affordable for mainland Chinese concert-goers to attend Western classical music concerts. Music education, especially in piano and violin, is strong among middle-class families in China, as well as Japan and Korea—and many of the world's finest classical musicians have East Asian heritages. Composer Tan Dun and pianists Lang Lang and Li Yundi are among those who have gained international fame.[67]

However, more than 30 years after the Cultural Revolution ended, concert etiquette remains a challenge for China. Some attribute it to the lack of formal national education about Western music. Ke Hui, a Beijing-based music critic, is sympathetic to audiences, stating that change would take time and patience. "They have no knowledge about it, just like jaywalking, waiting in a queue and travelling abroad—these are totally new experiences for many mainlanders," Ke Hui said.[68]

Change, in some places, is under way. At the NCPA, announcements are made before each concert reminding the audience about concert manners. NCPA management also works with Beijing schools in music education and theater etiquette, providing 1,090 courses to 616,000 people in 2014 alone, according to China Daily, the leading English-language news organization in China.[69]

Mini-Case Study: Can a Concert Hall Unite a Wealthy Neighborhood and Its Struggling Suburbs?

The Philharmonie de Paris opened in January 2015 with a daunting mission: to break down age-old cultural and social barriers to classical music. The hall is on the edge of the Parc de la Villette in the 19th Arrondissement in northeast Paris, a symbolic dividing line between the wealthy center of Paris and its largely poor and working-class suburbs.[70]

The hall's programming, location, and architectural design are carefully aimed at reaching out to the residents of Pantin—a densely populated town of 50,000 residents and historically a home to waves of immigrants. The nearby suburbs to the north and east of Pantin, home to four million people, have seen years of violence and riots. The question on everyone's minds after years of political wrangling, infighting, cost overruns, and work stoppages is whether the Philharmonie will become "a temple of sound that brings égalité [equality] to classical music."[71]

Most of Paris' well-known cultural institutions are in the center of town, and many aging Parisian concert-goers are hostile to the idea of traveling to a suburb for a musical experience. The Philharmonie's President, Laurent Bayle, says "this is the first signature, cultural building of grand Paris in this area . . . the Seine River has always defined the axis of other cultural institutions," such as the Louvre, the Musée d'Orsay and the Opéra Bastille.[72]

There are many heavy-hitters in the classical music world taking up permanent residence in the Philharmonie, including the Orchestre de Paris and Ensemble Intercontemporain (a major international contemporary music group). Les Arts Florissants (a Baroque vocal and instrumental ensemble) and two other orchestras will perform there regularly. In a nod to the goal of attracting the residents of its neighborhood, the hall will program world music, jazz, hip-hop, and electro-pop. Care has been taken to offer inexpensive tickets for weekend family concerts, and musical outreach programs will take place in Pantin and other suburbs.[73]

National Centre for the Performing Arts, Shanghai

MARK RALSTON/AFP /Getty Images

Lang Lang at New Philharmonie of Paris

JACQUES DEMARTHON/AFP/Getty Images

But change can be difficult for everyone. More than 11,000 people have signed a petition demanding that classical music remain in the heart of Paris. Some say that the Philharmonie is difficult to reach by public transport and is expensive by taxi. "What we resent is a government institution turning a deaf ear [to our concerns about classical music leaving the area]" says one of the petition's signers.[74]

There is equal hesitation to embrace this new venue in Pantin and the suburbs. Pantin's mayor says many residents have little interest in Parisian cultural attractions, even the famed Louvre Museum. The mayor calls the Philharmonie "good news" for the neighborhood, but worries that developing a taste for classical music "is a long learning process that will take time to attract people."[75]

Paavo Jarvi, music director of the Orchestre de Paris, acknowledged that there will be members of its subscription audience who will not venture to the new hall: "Sometimes it is hard to convince people to take the leap because it is inconvenient, but on the other hand, it will be a magnificent hall and, in a way, a once-in-a-lifetime opportunity."[76]

Mini-Case Study: Adapting Spaces for Classical Music

Michael Tilson Thomas, the music director of the San Francisco Symphony, had long been hoping to start a concert series in which his musicians would play smaller-scale repertory in a casual, club-like atmosphere. The challenge was finding the right venue in one of the world's most expensive cities. In late 2013 he realized that the solution might just be in his own Davies Symphony Hall. He sought the help of Meyer Sound Laboratories, manufacturers of high-end audio products that can enhance the acoustics of an existing hall or space.[77]

The result was SoundBox, an experimental performance space inside Davies Symphony Hall. SoundBox was transformed from an industrial backstage cavern into a cozy venue with food and a bar, and acoustics that can change at the whim of curators and fans. It has become a draw for the 21-and-over crowd looking for late-night music, mingling, and cocktails.[78]

How did this miracle happen? Tilson Thomas had a Meyer "Constellation" system installed, which uses microphones, a digital-audio platform, and loudspeakers to sample the noise of a room, modify it, and send it back to the room. The venue's seating area has sound-absorbing panels on the walls that are disguised as an attractive façade. The system's digital processor is tucked discreetly into a back room and is controlled with a tablet. Tilson Thomas explains that the cost of installing the Meyer "Constellation" was far below the real estate market rate for a new club-size venue in downtown San Francisco.[79]

Meyer systems are becoming a fixture of the global classical world. Even Vienna's staid Musikverein uses Meyer components for performances that include narration. Meyer systems are not a substitute for the vaunted acoustics of some of the world's greatest halls, but they are helping to make classical music a more adaptable and flexible art form.[80]

Mini-Case Study: A Solution for Venue and Neighborhood Noise Restrictions

Shortly after he discovered "quiet clubbing" on a cruise with his family, entrepreneur William Petz saw an unmet market need and launched Quiet Events, a company that puts on soundless concerts. Now, two and a half years later, Quiet Events hosts as many as 600 people a night in New York and has 3,000 headphones in circulation across the country.[81]

Known as "silent discos' in Europe, two side-by-side DJs spin completely different sets that can only be heard through each clubber's personal wireless two-channel headphones.[82] The DJs compete with each other to see who has the most listeners (each channel has a different color light on the headphones). The music may be blaring through your headphones, but when you take them off, it's completely silent. The scene can be amusing, as you watch people singing along to music only they can hear, and breaking into spontaneous dance routines with those who happen to be on the same channel.[83]

It was the renowned Glastonbury Festival, under pressure from complaints about noise from its surrounding neighborhood, that hosted the first major silent disco in 2005. A few American festivals followed. Now the silent disco is making appearances at weddings, parties, and bars as a way to allow guests to enjoy the music without running afoul of noise and curfew restrictions.[84]

Mini-Case Study: Philadelphia and Detroit Are the New Brooklyn

The Galapagos Art Space, a performance center and cultural staple in Brooklyn (US) for nearly 20 years, closed in 2014 due to rising rental prices. Robert Elmes opened Galapagos in 1995 as a bar and performance venue when Williamsburg was a dodgy, nondescript section of Brooklyn.[85] As often happens after artists move into an area, the neighborhood became attractive to hip singles and young families, who contributed to Williamsburg's slow but inevitable gentrification and ever-increasing real estate prices.

Many emerging artists who have been priced out of New York are beginning to move to cities like Philadelphia, where costs are considerably lower and there is a healthy and vibrant arts community. Philadelphia is a 90-minute train ride from New York and, as the home to the Curtis Institute of Music and the Philadelphia Orchestra, has been a cultural draw for years.

Somewhat surprisingly, in the past few years Detroit, Michigan, has caught the attention of artists and musicians, despite its image as a forlorn, blighted city and its 600-mile distance from New York. Elmes and his wife have purchased nine buildings totaling about 600,000 square feet in Detroit's Corktown neighborhood and nearby Highland Park. "[In Detroit we will have] the opportunity to go back to the early years of our venue and recreate the success that we had, and the impact that we had on a growing community," Elmes said.[86] Its expansive, empty spaces and lower cost of living draws both established and younger artists who are seeking new outlets and resources, and—in the unlikely city of Detroit—find inspiration and a receptive community for their abundant ideas.[87]

Pause and Reflect

Could you be adventurous enough to move to a city like Detroit for the sake of your art? Besides space and affordable rent, what other qualities do you consider essential in a place for you to feel comfortable and inspired?

Touring

There are enormous challenges for artists who want to tour globally. Passports, visas, tax obligations, currency, shipping, transportation, language, and cultural differences all contribute to the stress of moving about in different regions of the globe. Even if a tour only takes place in one country, there can still be challenges, particularly in countries that are vast, such as Russia, Canada, Australia, and the US. With heightened security measures at the borders, touring internationally takes meticulous planning. Most experienced tour managers will advise artists to seek assistance from professionals in each country through which the tour is routed. They can provide invaluable help in advising on everything from visas and border crossings to ticket sales and merchandise shipping.

Traveling with Instruments

Air travel is unpleasant for many people, but for musicians traveling with valuable instruments, it can be traumatic. Airline policies have been in place for years stating they accept instruments as carry-on luggage. But today, when so many flights are fully booked and passengers are loath to check their bags, the overhead baggage compartments fill up quickly. So, when a musician tries to board carrying an instrument in a case, she frequently is told she must gate-check her instrument because it is too large to fit in the overhead compartment. As every professional musician knows, instruments placed in the cargo hold can easily be damaged.[88]

One widely reported incident yielded a viral protest song and video, "United Breaks Guitars," by the Canadian musician Dave Carroll. In 2008 Carroll was forced to check his guitar on a United Airlines flight and it arrived badly damaged. An entrepreneur at heart, Carroll turned his protest videos into a book and now has a career as a speaker on customer service.[89]

The US Transportation Department, responding to requests from the American Federation for Musicians labor union (AFM), has issued a new rule that addresses this problem. Since March 2015, airlines are now required to treat instruments just like any other passenger's carry-on bag. The new rule may reduce the number of arguments and anxiety between musicians and flight attendants.[90]

Nataly Dawn, lead singer, Pomplamoose

Fred Hayes/Getty Images Entertainment

Musicians traveling with large instruments, such as cellos, must purchase an extra seat. And musician organizations in the US and Europe are trying to find a solution to problems encountered with international endangered species laws, such as ivory and hardwoods used in instruments made decades ago and now deemed endangered.[91]

SPOTLIGHT ON . . . INDIE BAND POMPLAMOOSE'S 2014 TOUR

I introduced the entrepreneurial indie band Pomplamoose in the first edition of this textbook. Pomplamoose is a quirky collective of San Francisco Bay area musicians, anchored by Nataly Dawn and Jack Conte. They broke onto the scene in 2008 with irreverent music videos shot in Conte's house, and quickly became blog darlings for their humorous covers of Beyoncé's "Single Ladies (Put a Ring on It)" and Lady Gaga's "Telephone."

Pomplamoose's approach to its career shows the basic elements of entrepreneurship: opportunity, creativity, innovation and a "what if?" attitude. The band has consistently charted its own path, steering (mostly) clear of the traditional music industry. In the first edition I noted that we didn't know if Pomplamoose would have lasting success as a band, but it sure was working hard at it in 2012.

Just in time for this book's second edition, member Jack Conte posted a story on Medium[92]—a collaborative internet site for people to connect through original stories and ideas—entitled "Pomplamoose

2014 Tour Profits (or Lack Thereof)," shortly after its 28-day, 23-city US tour ended. Conte's open, frank account of the high and low points give a gritty taste of what it's really like to be a 21st century music professional.

"Being in an indie band is running a never-ending, rewarding, scary, low-margin small business," Conte explained. He went on to describe the months-long planning, which included renting equipment, booking hotel rooms, and assembling a crew. Band co-leaders Conte and Dawn financed the upfront investment primarily with credit card debt well before the first ticket sold. They would be traveling with four musicians, a front of house engineer, and a tour manager, all of whom would be paid weekly during the tour. They built the budget for the tour themselves, hoping that their revenue and expense projections would be close to realistic.[93]

The final cost to produce and execute the tour was US$147,802. The largest expenses were production, hotels and food, travel (gas, airfare, parking, and tolls), salaries and per diem (US$20 payments to each musician and crew member every day during the tour), insurance, commissions to their booking agency, High Road Touring, for planning the four-week tour, and merchandise manufacturing, supplies, and shipping.[94]

Ticket and other income helped to offset the expense of tour production and execution. Ticket revenue accounted for 72 percent of tour income. Other sources included merch sales and sponsorship. Pomplamoose earned $135,983 in total tour income.[95]

Conte said that the band's goals for the tour were "to put on a wild and crazy rock show . . . be invited back to every venue, and [have our fans] bring their friends next time. The US$11,819 loss was an investment in future tours." Dawn and Conte consider themselves fortunate to be making a living from their music. Pomplamoose earns money each month via iTunes, Loudr,[96] and its Patreon[97] page. Dawn and Conte each draw a monthly salary of approximately US$2,500. Any money left over is reinvested in the band or saved for the next big tour.[98]

Conte's point in publishing the financial details of the 2014 tour was to illuminate the reality of how professional artists today are making a satisfying and sustainable life in music. "We, the creative class, are finding ways to make a living making music, drawing webcomics, writing articles, coding games, recording podcasts," Conte explains. "Most people don't know our names or faces. We are not on magazine covers at the grocery store. We are not rich, and we are not famous. We're entering a new era in history: the space between 'starving artist' and 'rich and famous' is beginning to collapse. The 'creative class' is no longer emerging: it's here, now."[99]

Pause and Reflect

What information in the account of Pomplamoose's tour surprised you? Is the band's business model viable in the long run, in your opinion? Why or why not?

TOOLS FOR THE DIWO (DO IT WITH OTHERS) ENTREPRENEUR: PERFORMING AND LICENSING

Technological innovation has created a veritable online industry of platforms and business tools for DIWO musicians. Artists who are savvy and persistent about marketing themselves, and have realistic expectations about what these tools can do for their career, can certainly use them to increase their chances of being discovered and build a stronger fanbase.

But converting page views and video hits into significant income is unlikely for most artist-entrepreneurs who are just getting started. DIWO sites and services are best viewed as effective *distribution* partners, helping bands strengthen their brand and get music and merch into the hands of people who want to buy it.

The Sharing Economy

The sharing economy is a vibrant but largely untested marketplace where both artist- and music business-entrepreneurs can find opportunities. Sharing economy businesses, like GroupMuse, Airbnb, and Uber, have workers who are pioneers of a new type of workforce that, not unlike DIWO musicians, experiences unpredictable fluctuations of income.

"Workers, young and old, value having some certainty over their hours and earnings. When you take that away you create enormous uncertainty and stress," states Thomas Kochan, a professor at the MIT Sloan School of Management who teaches an online course about the future of work.[100]

Here are some tips and ideas to help DIWO artist-entrepreneurs take a little stress out of their lives.

Staying Organized

SherpaShare is an app that helps people who gig keep track of their income and expenses in order to analyze how much they're actually making per hour. It was designed to help ride-sharing drivers for Uber and Lyft, and can work just as well for freelance musicians. The *Road Trip* app helps touring musicians keep track of mileage and fuel economy. *Artful.ly* is an online system to manage your tickets, donations, and contacts. It's a simple, elegant way to keep track of events, people, and your everyday work.[101]

Online Booking and Gig Help

- GigMasters—a booking resource for artists and talent buyers.

- GigMaven—a free and user-friendly booking website for musicians.

- Gigwish—collects votes from your fans to help you convince venues, promoters, and booking agents to hire you.

- G2.fm—connects bands and musicians with venues by sharing their music.

- Live Music Machine—a booking resource for musicians.

- MusiGigs—a private beta service that helps artists get booked by connecting venues directly to bands.

- OnlineGigs—a booking and promotional tool with a large, detailed venue database.

- ReverbNation's Gig Finder—helps musicians locate venues that have booked similar artists.

- Sonicbids—the largest online booking service for musicians, bands, managers, and promoters, as well as corporations and organizations looking to book artists.

- SplitGigs—a social web app that helps emerging artists find other artists with whom to exchange and share gigs.[102]

Touring Promotion

Here are five essential places to list information about your upcoming tours so that people can find you and buy tickets:[103]

- Bandsintown—easy to integrate with Facebook or use its app to build a strong stand alone community.

- Songkick—similar to Bandsintown.

- Eventful—its social media platform, Demand it!, lets fans request artists for performances in specific locations.

- Meetup—helps you organize a local group or find one of the thousands already meeting up face-to-face.

- Bachtrack—a classical event finder and reviewer.

Broadcast Your Gigs

Livestream is an integrated live video platform. It lets you monitor audience engagement, get real-time 24/7 event-based support, and get pointers on event production from filming to web development.[104]

Start Your Own Streaming Service

Sub Pop is among the most prominent indie labels experimenting with subscription models that connect them directly to their fans. Labels like Fool's Gold, Jagjaguwar, and Secretly Canadian have signed on with social platform Drip.fm to try and attract fans with exclusive music, a sense of community, and an intimate connection with bands and artists. Some digitally savvy musicians are starting their own services to appeal directly to their fans, like Nicolas Jaar's Other People and Ryan Hemsworth's Secret Songs.[105]

Get Paid More for Your Gigs

Many musicians are resigned to playing shows for free or even having to pay to play.

They say things like "Everyone has to pay their dues," or "I just do it because I love music." This type of thinking is counter-productive for anyone who wants to make a living with her art.

Here are suggestions to help you overcome self-defeating thoughts and get paid more for your gigs.[106]

Step 1: Change Your Mindset

You have a skill that you've perfected with years of practice. There is a market for your carefully crafted skill and, like any tradesperson, you deserve to be compensated for your work. Understand that in people's minds there is a correlation between product price and level of quality. A low price point is associated with a product of lesser value. Price your concert tickets so that people know that they can expect a correspondingly high value in return. And remember—venues do not exist without performers. You are helping venues to solve one of their biggest challenges—getting people into their place to spend money.[107]

Step 2: Get to Know the Venue Owner and Your Audience

Ask a friend to "audit" four of five of your performances to see how your audience interacts with your music. Record how many people come in, their average length of stay, what they buy, and whether or not they are engaged with your show. You can develop your gig value by calculating the gross profit your audience brought into the venue. Get to know the venue owner in person if possible. Ask her what her biggest challenges in running her business are and figure out a way you can help her with them. Just by listening to her and showing interest in her business, you will stand out from all the other musicians who pass through town. Use the knowledge you've gained about your audience and the venue owner to prepare your show and setlist, and the strategy for your presentation and proposal.[108]

Step 3: Close the Deal

Create a brief presentation that outlines how you will provide value to the venue with your shows. In addition to bringing in paying customers, your value may include new methods of marketing their brand or helping the venue promote new products or services to the audience. Think of yourself as a partner rather than a supplicant asking for work. Meet with the owner and make your presentation about why you should be hired for a monthly gig at this venue (or whatever it is you want). Include the ways you can bring value to her business. State your fee calmly and with confidence. Be prepared for her counter-offer. Know on which points you can be flexible. Do not sell yourself short. You are demonstrating that you are an investment worth the price. You are laying down the foundation for a lasting and sustainable career with patience and polite persistence.[109]

Opportunities Ahead—Thinking Like an Entrepreneur

What areas of the online music world strike you as the most promising for you and your music venture? Give your reasons and explain how you would get started in taking advantage of the opportunities.

SPOTLIGHT ON . . . GLOBAL MUSIC FESTIVALS

Music festivals have become big business around the globe. What began in Europe as city celebrations of summer, agriculture, and local talent has grown into a financial juggernaut, featuring every conceivable type of music, art, food, and location.

Some of the European festivals date back hundreds of years. Known as "folk festivals," many are still in existence. The Fiera della Frecagnola in the southern Italian mountain village of Cannalonga began around 1450.[110] The Annaberger Kät in the town of Annaberg-Buchholz in Saxony, Germany, will celebrate its 500th anniversary in 2020.[111] The Three Choirs Festival in the UK, one of the world's oldest classical choral music festivals, celebrated its 300th anniversary in 2015.[112]

Classical, rock, jazz, and E.D.M. now dominate the global scene, attracting large numbers of young people for multi-day experiences that (usually) focus on music. Following Europe's lead, North America burst onto the big-festival marketplace with the launch of Coachella in 1999. Before that, large American outdoor summer concerts and festivals were primarily in amphitheaters, with expansive lawns and some fixed seating. In fact, many classical summer music festivals can still be found in amphitheaters. The Boston Symphony Orchestra has the Tanglewood Music Center, the Chicago Symphony Orchestra has the Pavilion at Ravinia, the Cleveland Orchestra has the Blossom Music Center, and the Aspen Music Festival has the Benedict Music Tent.

While the economics of classical music and commercial summer music festivals are somewhat different, the overall goals are the same: to bring great music to an inviting, beautiful place where people can enjoy themselves outdoors in summer. Each festival strives to build a powerful identity, draw large crowds, and find significant sponsorship funding.

Newport Folk Festival

Douglas Mason/Getty Images Entertainment

Global Proliferation

During the summer, the sheer number of commercial music festivals can be staggering. On the second weekend in July 2015, for example, there were major events in Slovakia, Norway, Serbia, the Czech Republic, Spain, Portugal, England, Switzerland, and Hungary. When it assembled its annual listing for 2015, industry trade publication *Pollstar* featured 1,500 festivals in 70 countries, says *Pollstar* president and editor-in-chief Gary Bongiovanni.[113]

"Festivals have become a huge part of American culture," says Pasquale Rotella, chief executive of Insomniac, promoter of Electric Daisy, which began as a rave in 1997 and now draws more than 400,000 people in a single weekend. "When we first started, it was really foreign—all people could remember was Woodstock. It made it really difficult to explain. That's no longer true."[114]

Good Profit Margins

Music festivals can be highly profitable for the presenters/ promoters who sell the tickets, control the ancillary revenue streams (such as food, beverages, and merchandise), and

Aspen Music Festival Tent

Leigh Vogel/Getty Images Entertainment

Sziget Festival, Hungary

Didier Messens/Redferns/Getty Images

Wickerman Festival, Scotland

Ross Gilmore/Redferns/Getty Images

offer VIP ticket packages. "Profit margins on a good festival are vastly better than a regular night at Jones Beach," explains Steve Martin of the APA Agency in New York City.[115]

The festival business continues to grow in importance because of its potential to make money. Coachella is the most profitable festival in the US, with tickets selling out within 20 minutes of the season's opening announcement. In 2014 Coachella sold tickets to the value of $78.3 million, far more than any other festival, according to *Pollstar*.[116] Goldenvoice, which produces the festival, expanded Coachella to two weekends in 2012, a move that raised eyebrows but is now being replicated by other events. Bonnaroo also sold out in 2014, with regular tickets ranging from US$224 to $269, and a pair of VIP tickets—which included parking and camping perks, exclusive lounges, and viewing areas—going for US$1,449.50.[117]

Corporate Sponsors

One reason for the growth of festivals has to do with the integration of corporate brands and music in a practice known as experiential marketing. Music has become a significant player in helping to convey the brand's message as companies seek effective ways to monetize consumers' emotions.[118] Sponsorship dollars are plentiful when a corporation sees a strong connection between how it wants to be perceived by consumers and a specific music festival's ethos. Multi-day summer music festivals with tens of thousands of potential customers roaming around with money in hand are irresistible to marketers from deep-pocketed companies.[119]

With so many festivals around the world and so many entertainment options from which to choose, it's clear that the festival model continues to represent the best value for music fans.

Award-Winning Festivals

The European Festivals Association is the umbrella organization for festivals across Europe and beyond. Its 2014 awards were decided by a combination of public vote and industry juries, with a total of 1.2 million votes cast from more than 350 festivals in 35 different European countries. Here are their awardees:[120]

The European Festival Awards Winners 2014

Hungary, Sziget Festival, Best Major Festival

Belgium, I Love Techno, Best Indoor Festival

UK, Glastonbury, Best Line-Up

Montenegro, Sea Dance Festival, Best Medium-Sized Festival

The Netherlands, Down the Rabbit Hole, Best New Festival

The Netherlands, Mojo/Loc Festivals, Health & Safety Innovation Award

Spain, Primavera Sound, Artists' Favorite Festival

Poland's Tauron Nowa Muzyka, Best Small Festival

Denmark, Roskilde Festival, Green Operations Award

Primavera Festival, Spain
PYMCA/Universal Images Group/Getty Images

The following music festivals were named "Europe's Best Classical Music Festivals" by *Time Out* magazine:

The Puccini Festival, Lucca, Italy

Lucerne Festival, Lucerne, Switzerland

Bayreuth Festival, Bayreuth, Germany

Festival de Wallonie, Wallonia, Belgium

MITO SettembreMusica, Milan and Turin, Italy

The Helsinki Festival, Helsinki, Finland

Steirischer Herbst Festival, Graz, Austria[121]

Roskilde Festival, Denmark
Yulia Christensen/Redferns/Getty Images

Time Out's global music team named "The 50 Best Music Festivals in the World" for 2015. The top scoring festival in each of the 18 countries mentioned were:

Primavera Sound, Barcelona, Spain

Glastonbury, Somerset, UK

Coachella, Indio, California, US

Pentaport Rock Festival, Incheon, South Korea

Sziget, Budapest, Hungary

The Garden Festival, Tisno, Croatia

Yerevan (Armenia) Music Festival
Pacific Press/LightRocket/Getty Images

Montreux Jazz Festival, Canada

Andadolu Agency/Getty Images

Leonard Bernstein at Tanglewood, 1968

The Estate of David Gahr/Premium Archive/Getty Images

Splendour in the Grass, Byron Bay, Australia

Baleapop, Saint-Jean-de-Luz, France

Roskilde, Roskilde, Denmark

Vive Latino, Mexico City, Mexico

Fuji Rock, Niigata Prefecture, Japan

Fusion Festival, Larz, Germany

Way Out West, Gothenburg, Sweden

Meadows in the Mountains, Rhodopes Mountains, Bulgaria

Lake of Stars, Mangochi, Malawi

Montreux Jazz Festival, Montreux, Switzerland

Tomorrowland, Boom, Belgium

Mutek, Montréal, Canada[122]

Here are the "Top Ten US Classical Festivals" as identified by Sinfini Music in the UK:

Aspen Music Festival, Aspen, Colorado

Bard Summerscape, Annandale-on-Hudson, New York

Bravo! Vail, Vail, Colorado

Caramoor, Katonah, New York

Tanglewood, Lenox, Massachusetts

Ojai, Ojai, California

Mostly Mozart, New York City

Glimmerglass, Cooperstown, New York

Santa Fe Chamber Music Festival, Santa Fe, New Mexico

Ravinia, Highland Park, Illinois[123]

Here is a listing of some of the most prominent UK music festivals:

Aldeburgh Festival, Suffolk

Bath International Music Festival, Bath, England

Cheltenham Music Festival, Cheltenham, England

Edinburgh International Festival, Edinburgh, Scotland

Glyndebourne Opera Festival, East Sussex, England

The BBC Proms, London, England

St. Albans Organ Festival, St. Albans, England

Swaledale Fetival, Swaledale, Arkengarthdale and Wensleydale, England

Moving across the world, here are the "Big Three" in Japan:

Fuji Rock Festival, Naeba Ski Resort, Yuzawa, Niigata

Summer Sonic, Makuhari Messe convention complex in Chiba City

Rising Sun Rock Festival, Tarukawa Wharf, Ishikari Bay New Port, Otaru, Hokkaido

Queen Elizabeth & Benjamin Britten, Aldeburgh Festival, 1967
Peter Dunne/Hulton Archive/Getty Images

The Benefits of Festivals to Young Performers

Music festivals are an efficient way for young performers to build an international audience base, with their in-person, social experience of music discovery.[124] Keisza, a 26-year-old singer and dancer whose viral hit video "Hideaway" got her an invitation to play at Governors Ball (US), says she likes the challenge of playing in front of an audience that doesn't know her. "For me, festivals are where I can really see growth as a performer," she said, "because if people aren't your fans, they don't let you get away with as much. Your own fans will love you even if you mess up."[125]

If young, untested artists and bands get a good time slot at a festival and play effectively to a big crowd, it can make the difference between just surviving and thriving as a musician. "A festival pays three and a half or four times more than the average club show," says Dylan Baldi of Cloud Nothings, who played Bonnaroo, Pitchfork, and several European festivals in

Fuji Rock Festival, Japan
The Asahi Shimbun/Getty Images

Picnic at Glyndebourne Opera Festival, England

Oli Scarff/Getty Images News

recent summers. "We're still a small-scale band, but the festival shows make you realize what happens when you try to become more popular."[126]

Coachella has achieved a reputation as one of the top destination festivals in the world, which in turn makes it a solid anchor date for a world tour. It's also a great place for an artist to get attention and build buzz. "It almost matters too much," said Flying Lotus, a producer and DJ who has appeared at Coachella multiple times. "This is one of those festivals where the whole world is watching."[127]

The hope that a casual festival encounter will turn into new professional opportunity is a strong lure for young musicians. Many spend their time at music festivals in an exhausting jumble of performances, interviews, handshaking, and trying to meet industry execs.[128]

Many bands are eager to pay their own way to festivals, hoping to attract the attention of anyone who thinks they have potential and offers them an opportunity. The South By Southwest Festival (SXSW) hosts approximately 2,000 bands, solo performers, rappers, and DJs in Austin, Texas (US), for five packed days each spring. In 2015 the Prettiots, a baby band from New York, was one of the groups that self-financed their trip to SXSW. The Prettiots' manager, Asif Ahmed, has a track record for finding breakout bands—the Yeah Yeah Yeahs and TV on the Radio—and taking them to SXSW over the years. "When you're a band this young, it's a necessary evil—spending money to eventually make it," he explained. Ahmed detailed their expenses: US$1,000 in gas plus US$3,000 to rent the van with insurance, US$1,500 to hire someone to manage the tour, US$500 for bargain hotels along the way, and US$2,500 for four nights at an Airbnb accommodation. With incidentals and a US$15 per diem for each band member, the trip cost the unsigned Prettiots approximately US$10,000.[129]

The Prettiots' goal in attending SXSW was to find a label to release their debut album. When they arrived at SXSW, they already had a professionally produced music video, a full promotional team, and a few write-ups in fashion magazines. With ten tour dates on the route from New York to Austin, Ahmed predicted that, with luck, the band members might take home around US$1,500 each.[130]

A follow-up story in the *New York Times*, entitled "Paying Their Own Way to SXSW Worked Out," highlighted the Prettiots' adventure. In fact, the band did meet a few music supervisors who might be able to place their songs in commercials, TV shows or film trailers. "We definitely drummed up some industry interest. That was the entire goal, trying to get signed," said Kay Kasparhauser, the band's lead singer.[131]

Festival Food Competes with the Music

A welcome development at many festivals is the outpouring of interest in culinary consciousness. Delicious, creative food is now a focal point at hundreds of festivals around the world. Some say the

London street food scene spearheaded the movement. Others attribute it to what young fans expect from a festival. "It's a generation that grew up with the Food Network," said Sang Yoon, 42, a California entrepreneur and chef. "They grew up watching chefs as TV stars, and without a doubt, that's had an impact."[132]

The food scene at some festivals is nothing less than a love fest between chefs and musicians. Musicians on the road tweet and blog about amazing meals they've had in out-of-the-way locations.[133] Fans post pictures of their duck hot dog with pickled cabbage and black garlic on Instagram. A recent UK festival boasted a menu that included soft shell crab burger with bacon jam, and the cheese curd and gravy-based Canadian fast food poutine.[134] At some American festivals like Bonnaroo, Outside Lands, and Lollapalooza, it almost feels as if the music is secondary to ever-growing menus featuring culinary curators and food trucks.[135]

"It doesn't matter who's playing at jazz fest [New Orleans Jazz & Heritage Festival]," says Zach Brooks, a veteran of the radio business whose blog and podcast, *Food Is the New Rock*, recently featured an episode entitled "Vegan Black Metal Chef Episode 1 Pad Thai." "You spend most of your time eating, anyway."[136]

SXSW showing Pandora stage

Rachel Murray/Getty Images Entertainment

Industry Consolidation

Music festivals are a big business and some of the biggest players—Live Nation Entertainment, AEG Live, and SFX Entertainment—are moving aggressively to buy up major outdoor events. This means that more promoters are coming under the control of a handful of large corporations. Promoters like C3 Presents and Ultra have expanded heavily in South America, Australia, and Europe. Big, deep-pocketed festival operators have built a global network for booking talent and finding sponsorship deals.[137]

The expansions and investments have become as complicated as the relationships in a blended family. Live Nation controls more than 60 festivals around the world, including the iconic Bonnaroo in Manchester, Tennessee (US). In 2014 Live Nation bought a 51 percent stake in C3 Presents (the company behind Lollapalooza and Austin City Limits). In 2013, Live Nation bought a controlling stake in Insomniac, the promoter responsible for the dance-music festival Electric Daisy Carnival. Founders Entertainment, the independent promoters of New York's Governors Ball, co-produced FarmBorough with Live Nation in 2015.[138]

AEG Live controls 16 festivals, including Coachella, Bumbershoot, Supersonica, and the New Orleans Jazz & Heritage Festival. In 2007 Goldenvoice, the company behind the Coachella Valley Music and Arts Festival, entered into a joint venture with AEG's Hangout Music Festival in Gulf Shores, Alabama to co-produce Stagecoach, a Coachella country music offshoot, in Indio, California. This partnership is the latest move in a nationwide expansion for Goldenvoice, a subsidiary of AEG Live, and for the broader Coachella brand. In 2014 Goldenvoice created a similar partnership with the Firefly festival in Dover, Delaware.[139]

SFX Entertainment became a serious competitor with Coachella by amassing a portfolio of dance music events around the world.[140] It controls, among others: Electric Zoo in New York; Tomorrowland in Chattahoochee Hills, Georgia; Mysteryland USA in Bethel, New York; and Sensation in Amsterdam, the Netherlands.[141]

The Festival Booking Process

Large festivals begin booking their acts for the next year immediately after the festival ends. There is a lot of competition in the booking process. Festivals compete with each other for talent as well as with free municipal events, such as parties in public squares, concert series in parks, and national summer holiday celebrations. For a festival to secure a top artist line-up, it has to start early, even if this means paying thousands of dollars in guarantees to hold the dates. Booking music festivals can devolve into a kind of silent bidding war as talent buyers keep upping their offers as more bids come in.[142]

Ali Hedrick, a veteran agent at Billions, a high-profile US booking agency, explains that booking agents tend to give festivals that book early price quotes that presume a band's appearance will be a one-off (a concert that is the only one in that geographic area at that time, after which the artist will return to her home base). This multiplies the cost several times over. It's a tough call for talent buyers who know they'll be paying an inflated price to ensure that they can announce the headliners as early as possible. "I have to quote money based on everything being a fly-in," states Hedrick. "If you have 12 people touring with a band, you have to say that's three full days of salary for 12 people to come into your city," she says. "You're going to have maybe US$25,000 extra just because it's a one-off. But for the festival, it's an investment in selling tickets."[143]

Major festivals like Coachella and Lollapalooza routinely sell out within hours of announcing their line-ups. A festival's ability to sell tickets so quickly is a newsworthy event that guarantees that the performers will get a lot of media attention. This fact gives the festival tremendous leverage in negotiating with the publicity-hungry acts. One of the ways in which this leverage is exerted is in something called a radius clause in the festival's booking contract. A radius clause typically prohibits bands from performing at any other show—no matter how small—within a specific number of miles from the festival location and within a specific time period of the festival date.[144]

Air Traffic Control

The use of the restrictive radius clause in a booking contract has made it quite complex to route and book bands' summer tours. Booking agency William Morris Endeavor (WME) has created a separate department devoted exclusively to making bands' deals with festivals and managing their touring routes. "It's like playing air traffic control," says WME's Kirk Sommer, agent for the Killers and the Arctic Monkeys. "You have to think about how playing Governors Ball in June could affect another [event in the New York area] in the fall."[145]

How do talent buyers predict what will be popular by the time their festival comes around? Jack Trash, CEO of SIMshows (Summer Set Music & Camping Festival, Somerset, Wisconsin, US), explains: "Given the time in advance that we book acts, everything we look to with trends is like a year in advance. We pay attention to all kinds of indicators, from blogs to charts to social media activity and a wide variety of other items. Sometimes we get lucky with acts, and sometimes it works the other way around." A good track record for predicting who the next hot band or soloist will be gives a festival cachet and is a real draw for festival crowds.[146]

It's a delicate balance for festivals to find and book underground artists before they become big names, secure the headliners that fit within the festival's artistic parameters and brand, and still book the classic acts that pioneered the industry and can appeal to the nostalgia crowd as well as excite the new fans. Chuck Flask, Artist Coordinator for Paxahau Event Production and Management, says that preserving the Movement Music Festival (Detroit, Michigan, US) tradition is very important. However, Movement's social media team reaches out to engage the fans in selecting their line-up. "We have a very passionate group of fans that trust our vision and know that we work really hard to provide them with an experience that is unlike any other," says Flask.[147]

Curated Stages

Record label- and artist-curated stages are becoming more common across the festival landscape. Fans of a specific band or artist, or even a label, may be more willing to try out a festival they are not familiar with if the band or artist is appearing there, thereby giving the festival a thumbs-up stamp of approval. In turn, festivals will send record label news from their label partners to the fans, making them feel that they are getting exclusive information. Curating a stage is a creative way for artists and labels to showcase their music. Having different-themed or curated stages provides the customer with the opportunity to enjoy a range of experiences.[148]

Routing acts from festival to festival is an important component of the business for Sam Hunt, a talent seller (booking agent) at the Windish Agency in Chicago. Each year, Hunt suggests an assortment of bands to different festivals, basing his recommendations on what's realistic for that market, the amount of money the festival might have to spend, and how many fans one event can accommodate. "Sometimes you don't need to be the absolute cream of the crop [to succeed]," he explains. "Not every car is a Rolls Royce . . . but they still get you from Point A to Point B." He says it's important to understand each client's status and budget so that he can offer them a line-up they can afford and that will help them build their brand. But at the end of the day, his job is to find paying gigs for his artists.[149]

The Role of the Music Festival Production Manager

While the following description of the duties, skills, and responsibilities of a production manager apply primarily to classical music productions, there are key elements that are applicable to commercial music festivals as well.

A production manager is the link between the artistic program and the organization. She is responsible for supervising the practical and technical aspects of the production process.

The artistic director will define the overall musical concept of the festival. There may be a thematic element—for example, the Mostly Mozart Festival or the anniversary of a composer's birth or death. The artistic director may select specific pieces to be performed, or allow the guest performers and ensembles to create their own program. As in commercial music festivals, planning begins at least 12–18 months in advance, given the lead-time needed to book classical performers and opera singers.

Once the artistic program has been defined, the realization and implementation of it begins. The artistic vision needs to be analyzed and translated into a practical and realistic production plan. At this point, the production manager enters the scene. She is tasked with translating the artistic director's vision into a smooth, efficient process that comes to fruition in a successful public performance.[150]

A production manager works closely with the festival's artistic programmer, the artists, staff, venue, production/technical team, and other employees and collaborators to ensure the smooth running of the festival. A qualified production manager needs to have managerial skills (managing budgets, technical riders, travels, working plans, oversight of assistants and personnel) and so-called hard competencies, such as financial, technical, and organizational skills.[151]

The production manager also needs competencies related to the artistic vision of the festival. It is vital for her to know how to deal with artists, to build and maintain a good relationship with them, to understand the artist's way of working, and to develop creative solutions—all this to ensure the artistic vision is realized. Efficient artist management—including organizing travel and accommodation, welcoming, guiding, and working with the artists—is essential to get the artistic creation on stage for an audience.[152]

The production manager and her team are responsible for carrying out the vision of the festivals' artistic directors and the artists within the given technical framework. In addition to management and financial skills, the production manager must have detailed knowledge of all related disciplines, including:

- production disciplines (scenic, wardrobe, lighting, sound, projection, automation, video, pyrotechnics, stage management);

- interconnection of these disciplines during the production process;

- procurement of staff, materials and services, freight, customs coordination, telecommunications, financial management, work relations, logistics, information technology, government liaison, venue booking, scheduling, operations management, and workplace safety.[153]

Festival Revenue Streams

Most music festivals depend on four major revenue streams: tickets, ancillary spends, VIP packages, and sponsorships or municipal grants. People pay to see bands or experience the "festival atmosphere," while companies pay to associate their brand with (and expose their brand to) hip young people with disposable income.[154]

Tickets

If a festival survives its first few years and begins selling out its ticket inventory, the festival model can become a significant revenue source for its investors. In 2014 Coachella had a total combined sold-out attendance for both weekends at 96,500 per day for a total of 579,000 and a gross of US$78.332 million, according to numbers reported to *Billboard* Boxscore. The weekend following Coachella, Goldenvoice produced the Stagecoach country music festival at the Empire Polo Grounds, which drew 63,400 per day for a total attendance of 190,200. The total gross for Stagecoach was US$18.615 million. All in all, the combined three weekends at the Empire Polo Grounds saw a total paid attendance of 769,000, resulting in a gross of US$96.947 million.[155]

Ancillary Spends

Fans' purchases of food and beverages, parking, VIP packages, "glamping" fees (glamorous tent camping), and all the other ancillary revenue streams can be even more lucrative than ticket revenue.[156]

Promoters have a captive audience of tens of thousands at multi-day festivals, with an average per-person spend of US$678, according to recent figures from a UK survey.[157] An average spend usually includes festival tickets, food and beverages, travel, non-food at festivals, and accommodation (including camping). The promoter assumes a lot of financial risk in putting on a festival, but the pay-off can be worth it.

VIP Packages

"Watching some guy get a pedicure in an air-conditioned tent is so not rock & roll."[158]

VIP packages for concerts began in the 1990s when stars, promoters, and Ticketmaster executives created a "golden circle" program for high-priced prime seats. Over time, the price gap between the cheapest and the most expensive tickets has grown exponentially, effectively separating the haves from the have-nots. For example, regular tickets for the 2014 Beyoncé/Jay Z stadium shows cost as little as US$35, while platinum seats cost US$1,750.[159]

Festivals began offering VIP packages in the last ten years. Bonnaroo's first VIP tickets cost around $600 and included showers and a buffet. As prices have risen, VIP packages can be counted on to generate approximately 5–10 percent of a festival's overall revenue.[160]

At Bonnaroo in 2014, well-off fans could purchase the "Roll Like a Rockstar" package, which, for US$30,000 per group, provided a bunk in an air-conditioned tour bus and three gourmet meals a day. At the Alabama festival Hangout, the beach in front of the main stage sported private hot tubs that were available for US$1,600 each. At New York's Governors Ball, a cabaña for 16 people cost US$30,000 and included free beer, light catering, air-conditioned bathrooms, access to four lounges, and a concierge.[161]

Coachella's 2014 VIP package cost US$3,250, which included a shuttle to the side of the stage from the nearby air-conditioned safari tent, which had a couch with throw pillows, wooden flooring, a queen-size bed, and electrical outlets. VIP fans also could drink at a private bar, use private restrooms, swim in a private pool, and get advice from a personal concierge.[162]

Sponsorships and Municipal Grants

Corporate sponsorships and municipal grants make up the fourth main revenue source for festivals.

Sponsors are eager to associate their brand with festivals that attract the type of people who they feel reinforce their brand's image. Representatives roam around the festival grounds passing out product samples. Some sponsors spend thousands of dollars on infrastructure, production, drinks, and talent to create miniature villages filled with their goods. At festivals worldwide, sponsors offer prizes to concert-goers who take photos in front of company-branded backdrops and tag them on social media.[163] In Brazil, Rock in Rio covers about half its budget through a variety of deals that invite corporate brands into the festival in exchange for placing Rock in Rio's logo on hundreds of products.[164]

According to AdAge, budgets for these types of experiential marketing rose as much as 10 percent between 2013 and 2014.[165] The availability of so much sponsorship money is largely possible because of shifts in corporate marketing tactics. Companies like Scion, Mountain Dew, Tylenol, and Nike are eager to pay to be positioned with bands that reinforce their brands. Brands curate festival stages or even run their own record labels to create an association in the consumer's mind that the brand is just as hip and edgy as the art.[166]

Nile Breweries Limited, part of SABMiller, the world's second-largest brewer,[167] is one of the major sponsors of live music in Uganda. Nile uses experiential marketing to connect its different brands with different types of music. Under its Nile Gold Crystal Malt Lager brand, it supports the annual Nile Gold Jazz Safari in Kampala, while under its Club Pilsener brand, it sponsored the inaugural Club Pilsener Music Megafest in Kampala.[168]

The enormous number of global music festivals has put a strain on the sponsorship marketplace, which apparently has its limits. Festival producers are now vying with each other for corporate dollars. Making the case that *their* festival experience offers the best value for the brand—in exchange for lots of money—is one of a producer's most important jobs.[169]

Some festivals benefit from municipal or arts grants. For example, after a four-year hiatus, Knoxville's Big Ears festival returned in 2015 with the help of a long-term grant from the Aslan Foundation, a group with assets of nearly US$100 million that is "focused on preserving and enhancing the natural beauty, assets and history of the Knoxville area." The Aslan Foundation's US$300,000 contribution to Big Ears helped revive the festival and boost it into the black for the first time.[170]

The Mad Decent Block Party, a festival that started as an actual block party outside of record label Mad Decent's office in Philadelphia, uses sponsorship dollars to help keep ticket prices low. "The average price of our tickets is US$30, and the early bird ticket was US$20," said Andrew McInnes of TMWRK, who helped organize the event. "At some of the larger festivals, that would easily be a US$80 to $300 ticket. That's all due to sponsorships. We make an effort to make it affordable." A high ticket price, he adds, would keep out Mad Decent's core fanbase.[171]

That is something Seattle's Bumbershoot understands well. The festival, which takes place in downtown Seattle every Labor Day, has remained committed to its nonprofit mission since it was founded in 1971. Bumbershoot pioneered corporate sponsorship in the mid-1980s, using the funding to keep ticket prices low. "If you look at the price of Bumbershoot versus other festivals, we've stayed true to that desire to eliminate economic barriers to entry," explained Jon Stone, executive director of One Reel, the producer of Bumbershoot. He estimates that ticket sales make up about 60 percent of Bumbershoot's revenues, with sponsorship accounting for 30 percent, and concessions and vendors making up the rest.[172]

"In the '70s and '80s, festivals were the realm of pirates and crazy people, but as time went on in the late '90s and 2000s the rest of the corporate world caught up, and now it's just business," states Stone. Stone says that being nonprofit "is a philosophy, not a tax status." Instead of focusing on profits, Bumbershoot is dedicated to exposing attendees to the arts, which was the City of Seattle's mission when it started the festival. As a city festival, Bumbershoot reserves about a third of its musical programming space for local acts. It seems to be a good strategy.

Liliana Saumet of Bomba Estereo at Bumbershoot Festival
Suzi Pratt/FilmMagic/Getty Images

Both Macklemore and Ryan Lewis, two of the festival's break-out success stories, played Bumbershoot's small stages for years.[173]

From the Sponsor's Perspective

As head of brand experiences marketing for Mercedes-Benz, Stephanie Zimmer was not interested in partnering with music festivals. So what bothered her about music events that attracted tens of thousands of brand-conscious young people? Toilets, dirt, and mud. Finally, though, in 2015 Mercedes-Benz announced that it would sponsor the US version of Rock in Rio, which takes place not in an open field with portable toilets, but on 40 acres alongside the Las Vegas strip. Named City of Rock, it was built at a cost of US$25 million, paid for by MGM Resorts International.[174]

"Mercedes-Benz values best-in-class customer experience," Zimmer explained. "Rock in Rio is not your typical dust-and-dirt festival. The space will be . . . an immersive, clean experience." The Mercedez-Benz presence at Rock in Rio includes naming rights on a secondary stage and an amusement ride.[175]

Festival Expenses

The costs involved in putting on a major music festival can be considerable. One of the largest expenses is fees for top artists. It's an economic reality that high demand and competition for headliner talent leads to increases in talent costs.

How are those fees set? When considering how to price their clients' services, artist managers start by calculating the total amount of revenue potential for an event. It begins with ticket prices, multiplied by the number of people attending the event (for example, US$300 festival tickets × 50,000 people = US$15 million). Add income from VIP packages (a conservative 7 percent of revenue) and a percentage of ancillary revenue (from food, beverages, camping fees, and merchandise—calculate at US$678 per attendee) and you can see how festivals can afford to pay headliners up to US$4 million.[176]

As recording sales revenues have declined in recent years, musicians have turned to live shows as a major source of income. Music festivals offer a chance to earn a good fee without having to do the work to set up a concert tour and sell all the tickets. "For the last few years, they've been very lucrative for artists," says Allen Bargfrede, the executive director of Rethink Music, a research group at the Berklee Institute for Creative Entrepreneurship. "[Festivals] pay well, it's a flat fee, and you have a built-in audience. It's an easy gig."[177]

With so many festivals around the world competing with each other to book similar bands within a small window of time (summer), many acts are able to command a higher price than they would normally receive for a date in the same market if the concert were booked outside the festival time period. These inflated fees are another reason touring bands are so eager to play festivals: they can use the high payout from being a headliner on a festival as an anchor date for a longer tour.[178]

OutKast, for example, headlined a 40-festival tour in 2014 to mark its 20th anniversary comeback. In a matter of hours, André and Big Boi were announced as headliners for Governors Ball, Hangout, Firefly, CounterPoint, Big Guava, and Coachella. Many in the industry worried that this could become a new reality in booking top artists.[179]

Festival promoters guaranteed OutKast 40 big paydays and a hassle-free touring schedule no matter how many tickets were sold. Again, economics comes into play as one debates whether or not it was worth it for so many festivals to pay a huge fee to have OutKast as a headliner. Will their fans willingly pay a higher ticket price since their tour was both a reunion and, possibly, a farewell? "For the good bands, there's always going to be demand if you're away a long time," says Charles Attal, a partner with C3 Presents, which produces Lollapalooza and Austin City Limits.[180]

Develop a Niche

It's hard work but, given the crowded festival scene, promoters need to develop a niche to attract audiences if they don't have the budget for the "festival headliner du jour." Labyrinth, in Naeba Greenland, Niigata Prefecture, Japan, is a good example of this. The techno fest is carefully curated, attendance is capped at a few thousand people, and its offers something unique: a high-end Funktion One sound system that attracts tech nerds and musicians who appreciate its magic.[181]

The bigger festivals that aren't yet name brands and feature a jumble of bands with no apparent focus are the most likely to feel pressure to book the big-name headliners. Gary Richards, the veteran promoter and DJ who founded Hard Events, states: "Headlining-artist guarantees aren't impacting the broader artist lineups, but they are getting out of control and affecting the entire festival budget. They can't just constantly increase and increase. Eventually, something has to give."[182]

Electronic Cash Kings 2014

Just for fun, let's take a look at what some of the top electronic music acts are pulling in. Forbes compiles an annual list of the world's highest-paid DJs, entitled "Electronic Cash Kings." The numbers include earnings from live shows, merchandise sales, endorsements, recorded music sales, and external business ventures. Sources of the data include Songkick, *Pollstar*, the RIAA, managers, promoters, lawyers, and some of the artists themselves. All earnings are in US dollars and were calculated for the 12-month period from June 1, 2013 to June 1, 2014:[183]

1. Calvin Harris—US$66 million

2. David Guetta—$30 million

3. (TIE) Avicii—$28 million

3. (TIE) Tiesto—$28 million

5. Steve Aoki—$23 million

6. Afrojack—$22 million

7. Zedd—$21 million

8. Kaskade—$17 million

9. Skrillex—$16.5 million

10. Deadmau5—$16 million

11. Hardwell—$13 million

12. (Tie) Armin Van Buuren—$12 million

12. (Tie) Steve Angello—$12 million[184]

Mountains of Trash

Talent is the biggest line-item on a festival's expense sheet. Other major costs can include venues and grounds, lighting and sound, amplification equipment and Jumbotrons, insurance, security, and sanitation. Tackling the tons of trash left behind by festival-goers is a major headache and expense for most pop festivals and a growing concern for environmentalists.

The UK nonprofit "A Greener Festival" estimates that 20 million cigarette butts are left behind on the fields of the Glastonbury music festival every year, along with tent stakes and even entire tents. Sales of bottled water are a huge moneymaker for festivals and they generate mountains of trash. The single most effective tactic to reduce festival trash is for festivals to stop selling bottled water, which is precisely the route that Oregon's Pickathon Festival and California's Lightning in a Bottle have taken.[185]

Festivals around the world are coming up with ways to minimize their impact on the environment. For example, Roskilde Festival 2014 partnered with the Stop Wasting Food movement in Denmark to collect excess food from the many food stalls on-site. The food was prepared, packed, frozen, and handed over to a number of homeless shelters and crisis centers in Denmark. In total, 27.5 tons of food was donated to the charities, the equivalent of 50,000 meals.[186]

Is the Festival Boom a Bubble?

The fierce competition for more impressive and expensive headlining acts will mean higher ticket prices for consumers, which some fear will be the breaking point for the entire festival model. Again, we need to look at the economics behind the problem. The supply of festivals is at an all-time high, but no one knows if that's necessarily true of demand. For large multi-day festivals to succeed, thousands of people have to be able to afford to buy the tickets. If demand doesn't increase, higher ticket prices may push some concert-goers out of the market altogether.[187]

DJ Calvin Harris

Chelsea Lauren/WireImage/ Getty Images

DJ Tiesto

Tim Mosenfelder/Getty Images Entertainment

DJ Armin Van Buuren

Andrew Chin/Getty Images Entertainment

DJ Kaskade

Josh Brasted/FilmMagic/Getty Images

Glastonbury trash

OLI SCARFF/AFP/Getty Images

Andrew Morgan, a booking agent in Billions' Chicago office, says there's no quicker way to see if the festival model is a bubble about to burst than to "perpetuate a cycle of one-upmanship that attaches ticket prices to a rocket." Morgan feels that there eventually will be too many festivals for any given market to sustain. "There are only so many US$300 festivals that people can go to, if any at all," he says. "That might be the thing that eventually breaks the camel's back—not too many festivals, but too many festivals that are too expensive for a demographic. As soon as it starts happening, it sours ticket buyers, and it sours artists. [Then] that's it."[188]

Despite the fact that many festivals set new records each year for how quickly they sell out (for example, all 135,000 tickets for Glastonbury 2015—including the 15,000 coach plus ticket packages—sold out in just 25 minutes),[189] there is talk about whether or not the festival boom is actually a bubble about to burst. Some recent closures and postponements contribute to this uneasy feeling.

In the US

In 2012 Live Nation spent millions planning and staging the first of its five promised annual mega-festivals on Harriet Island (St. Paul, Minnesota). It was an expensive flop, leading the giant concert promoter to back out of its multi-year commitment to the city and put River's Edge on "indefinite hiatus."[190]

After announcing in 2013 that it was adding a second weekend of the 2014 Sasquatch! Music Festival, one of Washington State's most important annual rock events, Live Nation canceled the festival two months before it opened, citing slow ticket sales. "The fans did not support it, but continue to embrace the traditional Memorial Day Weekend event," said Jeff Trisler, president of Live Nation Northwest. "Message received, lesson learned and we move forward."[191]

AC Entertainment put Asheville, North Carolina's Mountain Oasis on indefinite hold in 2014, noting on its website that "the success necessary to sustain the venture has eluded us."[192]

In the UK

Several long-established festivals dropped off Britain's calendar in 2015, including Sonisphere, Global Gathering, Oxegen, Wakestock, RockNess, and Wildwood. The reasons ranged from "weak ticket sales" to "we weren't able to secure high quality headliners." Others claimed they were just taking a year off. This is not unusual in the UK. Many festivals, including the mother-of-all-festivals Glastonbury, take a brief sabbatical.[193]

"It sometimes takes years of development to get these events into profitability," says Bob Roux, Live Nation's co-president of US concerts. Festival entrepreneurs are finding that building a festival on niche music, like jam bands or electronic-dance DJs, is no longer an easy job. "There's a lot more politics and a lot more investment to make something happen," says Pasquale Rotella, the impresario behind Electric Daisy Carnival.[194]

"Everybody is chasing the same acts. They're in demand all over the world," says Pollstar's Gary Bongiovanni. "That's probably the greatest threat to the festival business: that we're maxing out on events we can produce with the available talent." Others attribute the problem to oversupply, a spike in headliner fees caused by competition for the same bands, and to the lack of differentiation on festival line-ups.[195]

A More Personal Experience

To those who say that festivals have peaked, Stuart Galbraith, CEO of the UK festival promoters Kilimanjaro Live, says: "I'd be careful not to jump to that conclusion. If you actually sit down and do the research, there are more people going to festivals in the UK and Europe than ever before. But what's becoming evident is that the customer is looking for something more personal—a boutique experience rather than a mega-festival."[196]

A critic from *Digital Music News* agrees. In an article entitled "Large Music Festivals Are OVER," Nina Ulloa compares her experiences at FORM, a 500-person weekend festival near Phoenix, Arizona (US), and at Governors Ball, a 55,000-person weekend festival on Randall's Island between Brooklyn and Manhattan. FORM, sponsored by Hundred Waters, took place at Arcosanti, an "urban laboratory focused on innovative design, community, and environmental accountability." Ulloa had "no intention of pitting the two against each other, but there was a stark difference: one festival was extremely inspiring and the other was incredibly draining."[197]

Ulloa explains that there were barriers to entry for both festivals. FORM was free, but prospective attendees had to fill out a questionnaire beforehand, and not everyone who applied was invited. Governors Ball had a US$275 price tag, which was an economic barrier to many.[198]

FORM was only open to those who were serious about experiencing the weekend. The musical line-up was compact and the crowd was respectful of others, cleaned up after themselves, and kept their alcohol in check. By contrast, Governors Ball was open to anyone who purchased a ticket, and most of the 55,000 attendees seemed bent on satisfying their every hedonistic desire.[199]

The bottom line: FORM is an inspirational retreat, while Governors Ball is a music festival designed to make money. They are very different entities with totally different business models. However, the comparison shows that smaller, specialized festivals can provide an inspiring experience for both fans and artists. Perhaps that may be the future of music festivals.[200]

Pause and Reflect

Do you feel that the competition for headlining artists at music festivals will eventually drive ticket prices so high that the "festival bubble" will burst? What creative problem-solving techniques could you use to propose a solution?

CONCLUSION

Demand for live concerts has remained strong, even during the prolonged economic downturn. Artists who are entrepreneurial understand how to position themselves in the market, stay close to their fans, and give spectacular shows are building a base to have sustainable lives in music. Most artists whose career attains some level of success decide to build a team of supporters, which could include a booking agent, artist manager, or business manager. It is important for artists to be well-matched to the venues in which they perform. The talent buyer and concert promoter play key roles in introducing new artists and supporting tours. The ticketing area of the live concert business abounds with opportunities for the entrepreneurial thinker. The financial risks involved in touring can be daunting, but the face-to-face excitement of a live concert makes it worthwhile for both artists and fans.

 Talking Back: Class Discussion

There are literally hundreds of potential revenue streams to explore in the global performing and licensing sector. Do you find the legal complexity daunting as you try to wrap your head around how to exploit performing and licensing for a new venture? If so, what tools are available to help you get started?

NOTES

1 Nick Petrillo, "Concert & Event Promotion in the US," March 2015, IBIS World Industry Report 71133.
2 Ibid.
3 "Guidance: Licensing Bodies and Collecting Societies," www.gov.uk/licensing-bodies-and-collecting-societies (accessed May 19, 2016).
4 Ibid.
5 "Foreword," CISAC Global Collections Report 2015, 3.
6 Ibid.
7 Eirini Zafeiratou, "Single Digital Market—Collecting Society Issues: The Vodafone View," https://www.vodafone.com/content/dam/vodafone/about/public_policy/position_papers/collecting_society_issues.pdf (accessed May 28, 2016).
8 Ibid.
9 Ibid.
10 Ibid
11 CISAC Report 2015, 2. A complete listing may be found at http://cisac.org/Our-Members (accessed May 19, 2016).
12 Ibid.
13 Ibid.

14 Ibid, 22.
15 Ibid, 41.
16 Ibid, 5.
17 Ibid, 37.
18 Ibid.
19 Ibid, 40.
20 Richard Smirke, "Seven Takeaways from IFPI's Study of the Global Music Market Last Year," *Billboard*, April 20, 2015, www.billboard.com/articles/business/6538815/seven-takeaways-from-ifpi-recording-industry-in-numbers (accessed May 19, 2016).
21 Ben Sisario, "Music Publishing Deal Driven by Shift from Sales to Streaming," *New York Times*, July 7, 2015.
22 Ibid.
23 Ibid.
24 Ben Sisario, "ASCAP Topped $1 Billion in Revenue Last Year, Lifted by Streaming," *New York Times*, March 3, 2015.
25 Griffin Davis, "Conflict over Consent Decrees," *Music Business Journal*, Berklee College of Music, October 2014, www.thembj.org/2014/10/the-conflict-over-consent-decrees (accessed May 19, 2016).
26 Ibid.
27 Ben Sisario, "New Venture Seeks Higher Royalties for Songwriters," *New York Times*, October 29, 2014.
28 Ibid.
29 Maya Kosoff, "Pharrell Made Only $2,700 in Songwriting Royalties from 43 Million Plays of 'Happy' on Pandora," *Business Insider*, December 23, 2014, www.businessinsider.com/pharrell-made-only-2700-in-songwriter-royalties-from-43-million-plays-of-happy-on-pandora-2014-12 (accessed May 19, 2016).
30 Sisario, "New Venture Seeks Higher Royalties."
31 Ibid.
32 Ben Sisario, "Justice Department Plans to Begin a Review of Music Licensing Rules," *New York Times*, June 4, 2014.
33 Davis, "Conflict over Consent Decrees."
34 Sisario, "New Venture Seeks Higher Royalties for Songwriters."
35 Sisario, "ASCAP Topped $1 Billion."
36 Ibid.
37 Jonah Bromwich, "Independent Music Labels and Young Artists Offer Streaming, on Their Terms," *New York Times*, July 7, 2014.
38 Vivien Schweitzer, "Seeking an Intimate Sound across a Cavernous Expanse," *New York Times*, November 24, 2014.
39 Peter Dobrin, "Orchestra, Violinist Full of Surprises," *Philadelphia Inquirer*, March 23, 2015.
40 Telephone conversation between Rich Nesin and Catherine Radbill, September 3, 2011.
41 Ibid.
42 Nesin, telephone conversation.
43 Ibid.
44 Ibid.
45 Ibid.
46 Nick Petrillo, "Concert & Event Promotion in the US."
47 Ibid.
48 Ibid.
49 "Music: Key Insights at a Glance," Global Entertainment Media Outlook, *PwC*, www.pwc.com/gx/en/global-entertainment-media-outlook/assets/2015/music-key-insights-6-technology.pdf (accessed May 19, 2016).
50 Petrillo, "Concert & Event Promotion."
51 Ibid.
52 Nesin, telephone conversation.
53 Ibid.

54 Ibid.

55 Ibid.

56 Anthony Tommasini, "Discounted Tickets: A Test for the Met," *New York Times*, January 6, 2015.

57 Ibid.

58 Ibid.

59 Ibid.

60 "Backstage," *The Smoking Gun*, www.thesmokinggun.com/backstage (accessed May 19, 2016).

61 Nesin, telephone conversation.

62 Petrillo, "Concert & Event Promotion."

63 Ibid.

64 Laura Zhou, "Off Notes: Lessons in Etiquette for China's Classical Music Concertgoers," *South China Morning Post*, International Edition, May 19, 2015, www.scmp.com/news/china/society/article/1802690/notes-lessons-etiquette-chinas-classical-music-concertgoers (accessed May 19, 2016).

65 Ibid.

66 Ibid.

67 Ibid.

68 Ibid.

69 Ibid.

70 Doreen Carvajal, "A Concert Hall in Paris Aims to Bridge Divides," *New York Times*, January 14, 2015.

71 Ibid.

72 Ibid.

73 Ibid.

74 Ibid.

75 Ibid.

76 Ibid.

77 Alex Ross, "Wizards of Sound, Retouching Acoustics, from the Restaurant to the Concert Hall," *The New Yorker*, February 23, 2015.

78 "The Space," *SoundBox,* http://sfsoundbox.com/the-space (accessed May 19, 2016).

79 Ross, "Wizards of Sound."

80 Ibid.

81 Malarie Gokey, "Have You Been to a Headphone Party? Why Quiet Events Are Making a Lot of Noise," Digital Trends, August 16, 2014, www.digitaltrends.com/music/quiet-events-headphone-party (accessed May 19, 2016).

82 Ibid.

83 Gokey, "Have You Been to a Headphone Party?"

84 Courtney Rubin, "Subsonic Boom," *New York Times*, June 18, 2015.

85 Colin Moynihan, "Born in Brooklyn, Now Making a Motown Move," *New York Times*, December 8, 2014.

86 Ibid.

87 Melena Ryzik, "Ready for a Renaissance," *New York Times*, July 16, 2015.

88 Joe Sharkey, "A Musician's Lament? Carrying on the Instrument," *New York Times*, January 13, 2015.

89 "United Breaks Guitars," *Dave Carroll Music*, www.davecarrollmusic.com/music/ubg/story (accessed May 19, 2016).

90 Sharkey, "A Musician's Lament?"

91 Ibid.

92 Home page, *Medium*, https://medium.com (accessed May 19, 2016).

93 Jack Conte, "Pomplamoose 2014 Tour Profits (or Lack Thereof)," *Medium*, November 24, 2014, https://medium.com/@jackconte/pomplamoose-2014-tour-profits-67435851ba37 (accessed May 19, 2016).

94 Ibid.

95 Ibid.

96 Home page, *Loudr*, https://loudr.fm (accessed May 19, 2016).

97 Home page, Patreon, https://www.patreon.com (accessed May 19, 2016).

98 Conte, "Pomplamoose 2014."

99 Ibid

100 Natasha Singer and Mike Isaac, "An App That Helps Drivers Earn the Most from Their Trips," *New York Times*, May 9, 2015.

101 "Artful.ly," *Fractured Atlas*, https://www.fracturedatlas.org/site/artfully (accessed May 19, 2016).

102 "Ten Resources that Help Musicians Book Gigs Online," Hypebot, http://hypebot.com/hypebot/2010/09/10-resources-that-help-musicans-book-gigs-online.html (accessed May 19, 2016).

103 Andrew Hall, "16 Must-Have Online Tools for Indie Musicians," *SonicBids Blog*, http://blog.sonicbids.com/16-must-have-online-tools-for-indie-musicians (accessed May 19, 2016).

104 "Products/Solutions," *Livestream*, http://livestream.com (accessed May 19, 2016).

105 Bromwich, "Independent Music Labels."

106 William Tait, "How Musicians Can Get Higher Pay for Live Shows," *Music Think Tank*, www.musicthinktank.com/blog/how-musicians-can-get-higher-pay-for-live-shows.html (accessed May 19, 2016).

107 Ibid.

108 Ibid.

109 Ibid.

110 "News," *Casalvelino*, October 9, 2008, http://casalvelino.net/news/eventi/bollito_di_capra_alla_fiera_della_frecagnola_di_cannalonga_000511.shtml (accessed May 25, 2016).

111 "Annaberg KÄT—The Biggest Fair in the Ore Mountains," *Berg- und Adam-Ries-Stadt Annaberg-Buchholz*, www.annaberg-buchholz.de/en/TourismusENG/annaberg-kaet-en.php (accessed May 25, 2016).

112 "About Us," *Three Choirs Festival*, www.3choirs.org/about-us (accessed May 25, 2016).

113 Ian Mount, "Music Festivals: From Peace and Free Love to Startup Pitches and Corporate Consolidation," *Fortune*, June 19 2015, www.fortune.com/2015/06/19/music-festivals-from-peace-and-free-love-to-startup-pitches-and-corporate-consolidation/ (accessed May 25, 2016).

114 Steve Knopper, "How Coachella, Bonnaroo and More Festivals Revamped the Music Industry," *Rolling Stone*, May 13, 2014, www.rollingstone.com/music/news/how-coachella-bonnaroo-and-more-festivals-revamped-the-music-industry-20140513#ixzz3h0cP1Emg (accessed May 25, 2016).

115 Ben Sisario, "Live Nation Buys Controlling Stake in Bonnaroo Festival," *New York Times*, April 29, 2015.

116 Ben Sisario, "Coachella Festival Fends off Rivals with Fresh Acts and Eye on Style," *New York Times*, April 13, 2015.

117 Melissa Locker, "From Coachella to Made in America, Multi-act Music Festivals Are Big Business," *Fortune*, July 3, 2013, www.fortune.com/2013/07/03/how-music-festivals-make-money (accessed May 25, 2016).

118 Grayson Haver Currin, "Why the Summer Music Festival Bubble Is About to Burst," *Wondering Sound*, www.wonderingsound.com/feature/too-many-summer-music-festivals (accessed May 25, 2016).

119 Ibid.

120 "EFA-Giving Festivals a Voice," *European Festivals Association*, www.festivalinsights.com/2015/01/european-festival-awards-2014-winners-announced (accessed May 28, 2016).

121 Yolanda Zappaterra, "Europe's Best Classical Music Festivals," *Time Out*, www.timeout.com/travel/features/1273/europes-best-classical-music-festivals (accessed May 25, 2016).

122 Mike Curle, Brent DiCrescenzo, and *Time Out* editors, "The 50 Best Music Festivals in the World," *Time Out*, May 14, 2015, www.timeout.com/music-arts-culture/50-best-music-festivals-in-the-world (accessed May 25, 2016).

123 Darryn King, "Top Ten US Classical Festivals," *Sinfini Music*, June 20, 2014, www.sinfinimusic.com/uk/features/whats-on/events/top-ten-us-classical-festivals (accessed May 25, 2016).

124 Currin, "Why the Summer Music Festival Bubble Is About to Burst."

125 Ben Sisario, "Governors Ball, Now in Its Fifth Season, Hits Its Stride," *New York Times*, June 4, 2015.

126 Knopper, "How Coachella, Bonnaroo and More."

127 Sisario, "Coachella Festival Fends off Rivals."

128 Jon Pareles, "Stepping Back to Allow Hopeful Artists to Step Up," *New York Times*, March 23, 2015.

129 Joe Coscarelli, "Paying a Price to Play at South by Southwest," *New York Times*, March 16, 2015.

130 Ibid.

131 Joe Coscarelli, "Paying Their Own Way to SXSW Worked Out," *New York Times*, March 26, 2015.

132 Jeff Gordinier, "Pork Belly, Lobster and, Yes, Music," *New York Times*, May 15, 2012.

133 Ibid.

134 Tristan Parker, "How Street Food Conquered Music Festivals," *Time Out*, April 29, 2015, www.timeout.com/london/music-festivals/how-street-food-conquered-music-festivals?package_page=48331 (accessed May 25, 2016).

135 Gordinier, "Pork Belly."

136 Ibid.

137 Sisario, "Live Nation Buys Controlling Stake."

138 Sisario, "Governors Ball."

139 Ben Sisario, "Pop Music Festival in Partnership Deal," *New York Times*, January 13, 2015.

140 Sisario, "Coachella Festival Fends off Rivals."

141 Sisario, "Live Nation Buys Controlling Stake."

142 Currin, "Why the Summer Music Festival Bubble Is About to Burst."

143 Ibid.

144 Sisario, "Coachella Festival Fends off Rivals."

145 Ibid.

146 Staples, "Keeping E.D.M. Festivals."

147 Ibid.

148 Currin, "Why the Summer Music Festival Bubble Is About to Burst."

149 Ibid.

150 Hugo De Greef, "Festival Production Management Training," *European Festival Association*, July 2015, http://vti.be/sites/default/files/Festival%20Production%20Management%20Training%20Call_FIN.pdf (accessed May 29, 2016).

151 Ibid.

152 Ibid.

153 Ibid.

154 Currin, "Why the Summer Music Festival Bubble Is About to Burst."

155 Ray Waddell, "Coachella Breaks Boxscore Record (Again)," *Billboard*, July 7, 2014, www.billboard.com/biz/articles/news/touring/6150327/coachella-breaks-boxscore-record-again (accessed May 25, 2016).

156 Currin, "Why the Summer Music Festival Bubble Is About to Burst."

157 Emma Webster, "Association of Independent Festivals Six-Year Report 2014," *Association of Independent Festivals*, http://aiforg.com/wp-content/uploads/AIF-Six-Year-Report-2014.pdf (accessed May 25, 2016).

158 Steve Knopper, "Why VIP Packages Are Ruining Rock Festivals," May 22, 2014, *Rolling Stone*, www.rollingstone.com/music/news/why-vip-packages-are-ruining-rock-festivals-20140522 (accessed May 25, 2016).

159 Ibid.

160 Ibid.

161 Ibid.

162 Ibid.

163 Currin, "Why the Summer Music Festival Bubble Is About to Burst."

164 Christopher Lawrence, "90,000 Attend Rock in Rio's Final Weekend," *Las Vegas Review-Journal*, May 17, 2015, www.reviewjournal.com/entertainment/the-reel/90000-attend-rock-rio-s-final-weekend (accessed May 25, 2016).

165 Ibid.

166 Ibid.

167 "Who We Are," *Nile Breweries Ltd*, www.nilebreweries.com/?page_id=4?age-verified=4ae18fc4b2 (accessed May 25, 2016).

168 Bamuturaki Musinguzi, "The Live Music Scene in Uganda," *Music in Africa*, April 1, 2015, http://musicinafrica.net/live-music-scene-uganda?section-context=overview-texts

169 Currin, "Why the Summer Music Festival Bubble Is About to Burst."

170 Ibid.

171 Locker, "From Coachella."

172 Ibid.

173 Ibid.

174 Ben Sisario, "Mercedes-Benz to Sponsor US Version of Rock in Rio," *New York Times*, March 9, 2015.

175 Ibid.

176 Knopper, "How Coachella, Bonnaroo and More."

177 Mount, "Music Festivals: From Peace and Free Love."

178 Currin, "Why the Summer Music Festival Bubble Is About to Burst."

179 Alex Young, Frank Mojica, and Dean Essner, " Festival Outlook: The OutKast Effect," *Consequence of Sound*, January 24, 2014, http://consequenceofsound.net/2014/01/festival-outlook-the-outkast-effect (accessed May 25, 2016).

180 Ibid.

181 "The Labyrinth 2013," *Time Out*, www.timeout.com/tokyo/clubs/the-labyrinth-2013 (accessed May 25, 2016).

182 Derek Staples, "Keeping E.D.M. Festivals Fresh in 2015: A Chat with the Top Curators," *Consequence of Sound*, March 4, 2015, http://consequenceofsound.net/2015/03/keeping-E.D.M.-festivals-fresh-in-2015 (accessed May 25, 2016).

183 Zack O'Malley Greenburg, "The World's Highest-Paid DJs: Electronic Cash Kings 2014," *Forbes*, August 19, 2014, www.forbes.com/sites/zackomalleygreenburg/2014/08/19/the-worlds-highest-paid-djs-electronic-cash-kings-2014 (accessed May 25, 2016).

184 Ibid.

185 Winston Ross, "Oregon's Pickathon Points the Way to Music Festivals Going Green," *Billboard*, August 1, 2014.

186 "Roskilde Festival Has Won Prestigious Green Award," *Roskilde Festival*, January 15, 2015, http://roskilde-festival.dk/news/2015/roskilde-festival-has-won-prestigious-green-award (accessed May 25, 2016).

187 Currin, "Why the Summer Music Festival Bubble Is About to Burst."

188 Ibid.

189 "2015 Tickets Sell out in 25 Minutes," *Glastonbury Festivals*, October 5, 2014, www.glastonburyfestivals.co.uk/2015-tickets-sell-out-in-25-minutes (accessed May 25, 2016).

190 Chris Riemenschneider, "Two Twin Cities Outdoor Music Festivals Are Canceled," *Star Tribune*, February 7, 2014, www.startribune.com/two-twin-cities-outdoor-music-festivals-are-canceled/247346591 (accessed May 25, 2016).

191 Owen R. Smith, "The Reasons behind Canceling July Sasquatch!" *Seattle Times*, March 28, 2014, www.seattletimes.com/entertainment/the-reasons-behind-canceling-july-sasquatch (accessed May 25, 2016).

192 "A Note to Our Friends, Fans and Patrons," *Mountain Oasis Festival*, www.mountainoasisfestival.com/note-friends-fans-patrons (accessed May 25, 2016).

193 Thomas H. Green, "Have We Finally Hit 'Peak Festival'?" *The Telegraph*, April 25, 2015, www.telegraph.co.uk/culture/music/music-festivals/11560934/Have-we-finally-hit-peak-festival.html (accessed May 25, 2016).

194 Knopper, "How Coachella, Bonnaroo and More."

195 Mount, "Music Festivals: From Peace and Free Love."

196 Green, "Have We Finally Hit 'Peak Festival'?"

197 Nina Ulloa, "Large Music Festivals Are OVER. Here's Why . . . " *Digital Music News*, June 11, 2015, www.digitalmusicnews.com/permalink/2015/06/11/large-music-festivals-are-over-heres-why, (accessed May 25, 2016).

198 Ibid.

199 Ibid.

200 Ibid.

CHAPTER 7

Revenue Streams: Music Publishing

CHAPTER OVERVIEW

Music publishing is a large and important area of the music industry, generating revenue through licensing agreements that exploit music copyrights. Royalty revenue comes through contractual relationships with songwriters, composers, and recording artists. Promoting songs, supervising the collection and payment of royalties, and placing songs in movie and TV soundtracks and commercials allows for the development of multiple and recurrent revenue streams. Kobalt Music, an innovative music publisher, is highlighted. The DIWO (Do It With Others) section offers practical advice to music professionals on how to collect all the royalties you are due.

Disclaimer: This chapter is intended to provide an introduction for non-specialists or newcomers to the subject of copyright and related rights. It explains in layperson's terms the fundamentals underpinning copyright law and practice. It describes the different types of rights which copyright and related-rights law protects, as well as the limitations on those rights. For specific answers to and detailed guidance on deeper aspects of global copyright law, please consult with legal counsel.

KEY TERMS

Monetization	The Black Box
Clearing a sample	Recoupable
Freemium model	Writer's draw
Infrastructure	Self-plagiarism
Record label audit	Royalty
Sub-publisher	

INTRODUCTION TO GLOBAL MUSIC PUBLISHING

Music publishers work for musicians, songwriters, and composers. They license the intellectual property of their clients for a variety of uses, collect royalties owed for those uses, and distribute a portion of the royalties collected to the client. Royalties are earned in various ways. Each time a song or composition is downloaded on iTunes, sold on an album, reproduced in a live concert, or played on the radio, a television show, in a movie, or through other media outlets, money is owed to the rights owner. Publishers' main products and services are mechanical royalties, performance royalties and synchronization (synch) royalties.[1]

The three traditional roles of a publisher are music acquisitions, creative development, and rights management. A music publisher's job is to find ways to use a writer's music, keep track of the revenue earned through the music's usage, and distribute a portion of the money to the writer. Publishers earn money from the licenses they grant to others for use of a writer's work. Common uses include songs in commercials and multimedia applications, films, video games, concerts, recordings, TV shows, and radio, in printed or digital form, throughout the world.

Underlying Composition

Music publishing is focused on the rights associated with the underlying composition—the music and lyrics. Songwriters and composers play a leading role in this sector of the music industry. In nearly every conceivable use of a song, the user is required by law to get a license and pay the rights owner of the underlying composition or song. Publishers acquire copyrights through the purchase of entire catalogs of music or of individual works.

The music publishing sector of the music industry is in transition. One of its primary sources of revenue has been licenses issued for use in recorded music. With the significant decline of physical album sales over the last decade, publishers are working to find new revenue sources such as mobile outlets, digital streaming services, and wireless music subscription services.

Historically, a handful of major record companies have dominated the music publishing sector. These major labels benefit from access to the majority of popular music and valuable catalogs of classic hits. Today there are three major record labels (Sony Music Entertainment, Universal Music Group, and Warner Music Group), each of which has a major publishing company: Sony/ATV Music Publishing, Universal Music Publishing Group, and Warner/Chappell Music, respectively.

Digital Delivery

Today, the shift in the delivery of music toward digital media and the ease and affordability of digital recording equipment has encouraged a surge in the number of small independent record labels, many of which are also publishing music independently.

In exchange for receiving a publisher's professional assistance, a songwriter/composer traditionally transferred ownership of the economic rights of her songs to the publisher. This meant that the publisher received the exclusive rights that reside with copyright ownership as granted by law. However, individual musicians today can easily enter the music publishing industry, since they instantly own the publishing rights to the music they write.

Some composers and songwriters want to retain control of their intellectual property and are comfortable trading the ease of online promotion and distribution of their music with signing over their copyrights to a publisher. Many composers choose to create their own publishing company and administer it themselves. Some writers prefer to get help from a smaller or alternative music publishing operation that they feel may deliver a more personalized service and exact fewer harsh demands than a large firm. Another option for a writer is to affiliate with a publishing operation that will perform only those specific services she needs, in exchange for a percentage of revenue generated, without relinquishing any rights ownership.

The growing independence of artist-entrepreneurs is another reason for the turmoil in the publishing sector. In a traditional contract, a writer would be required to relinquish her rights ownership to the publisher, who would oversee all aspects of the intellectual property's exploitation, in exchange for a split in royalties collected. With fewer writers signing traditional contracts, the publishers' revenue from royalty splits has declined.

Changes caused by consumers' eager embrace of the digital revolution also offer abundant opportunities for new uses of music. Video games, interactive media, webcasting, online social networking, and commercial branding are among the newer opportunities for music licensing. Add to that the more traditional sources of music licensing—films, documentaries, corporate videos, advertisements and commercials, toys, printed music, instructional music DVDs, recordings in all formats, ringtones, television, and live theater—and it becomes clear that, if it can overcome the challenges to monetizing digital content, music publishing could remain a large and prosperous sector of the music industry.[2]

Challenges to Overcome in Monetizing Digital Content

Here are a few of the obstacles that challenge the current music publishing sector:

- Pitching and licensing a song by traditional publishers faces a lot of competition from the widespread availability of music online—much of it free and readily available to advertisers without going through a publishing company.

- The music industry operates worldwide, so the lack of an international infrastructure governing digital intellectual property severely affects the growth potential for music publishers. This challenge was discussed in full in Chapter 5.

- Finally, illegal music downloading and copyright violations remain a persistent drain on revenue from legal music licensing.

THE MAJOR FUNCTIONS OF A MUSIC PUBLISHER

No two music publishers are identical, but there are some basic building blocks that define the traditional music publishing industry. Here is a general overview of their most common tasks:

Find and support up-and-coming songwriters. The industry is built upon the work of millions of composers and songwriters. Music publishers try to find and sign writers whose music will have wide appeal to potential licensors.

Verify copyright protection for the songs it owns. Publishers make sure that copyrights are properly registered and ownership of songs is correctly registered with all pertinent international royalty collection agencies.

Find revenue-generating uses for the songs it owns. While some songwriters' music is so popular that the publisher is swamped with requests to license their songs, other publishers must be proactive in finding placements for the music in its catalog. A publisher makes money only when the songs it owns are licensed and producing revenue. One of the valuable areas of expertise that a songwriter taps into when signed to a publisher is the publisher's large network of people who work in the fields that use music, such as film, television, record labels, and advertising agencies.

Negotiate licenses and fees for use of its songs. Publishers' creative staff spend a lot of time pitching songs to potential users and hammering out deals that will result in licenses and royalty payments.

Keep track of all monies owed from licensing the music in its catalog. This administrative function is important, complex, and time-consuming. It involves careful accounting and follow-up on all licenses issued by the publisher, plus royalty payments from collecting societies.

Some publishing companies, such as Kobalt Music Group, focus primarily on revenue collections. This business model has upended the formerly staid music publishing industry. Kobalt and others are using highly sophisticated digital tracking tools to locate nearly every possible place that a songwriter/composer's work has been used. While Kobalt does in fact sign and nurture a small group of writers, its main goal is to collect royalties for the use of a songwriter/composer's work around the globe.

Oversee printed music production and distribution. Printed and digital musical scores are an important but less profitable business area for publishers than they were in previous years. Printed music was a substantial part of a publisher's business in the early 20th century, but today it has shrunk in importance, accounting for less than 10 percent of most publishers' total annual revenue.[3] Most music publishers do not produce their own sheet music, but license print rights to third-party sheet music companies.[4]

Protect copyrights of songs against infringement through legal channels such as litigation or settlement of claims. When an unauthorized use of the publisher's music or lyrics occurs, such as uncleared samples in a recording or unlicensed lyrics on a website, the publisher may take legal action.

Industry Globalization

The music publishing industry has a high level of globalization, particularly among its largest players. The top three multi-national companies are publishing arms of the three major record labels, which compete on a global scale. All have major offices in the US as well as internationally. All music publishers are trying to tap into new, foreign markets to offset the decline revenue from sales of recorded music. One such area of expansion is the growing South American market.[5] As emerging countries get improved access to the internet, the opportunity to license music in these markets will increase.

The music publishing industry is a dense yet fragmented sector made up of companies ranging in size from the massive majors to small subsidiaries of the majors, as well as large and small independent publishers. Some of the largest independent music publishers are Imagem, Peermusic, Olé, and Rough Trade.

International Publishing Trade Associations

The International Confederation of Music Publishers (ICMP) is the world trade association representing the interests of the music publishing community internationally. Members of the ICMP include music publishers' associations from Europe, the Middle East, North and South America, Africa, and the Asia-Pacific region. The ICMP's mission is to increase copyright protection internationally and act as an industry forum for consolidating global positions.[6]

Here are the trade associations for the top ten global music markets:

US—NMPA (National Music Publishers Association) and MPA US (Music Publishers Association of the United States).

Japan—MPAJ (Music Publishers Association of Japan).

Germany—DMV (Deutscher Musikverleger-Verband).

UK—MPA UK (The Music Publishers Association Ltd.).

France—CSDEM (Chambre Syndicale De l'Edition Musicale) and CEMF (Chambre Syndicale des Editeurs de Musique de France).

Australia—AMPAL (Australasian Music Publishers Association).

Canada—CMPA (Canadian Music Publishers Association).

Republic of Korea—KMPA (Korea Music Publishers Association).

Italy—FEM (Federazione Editori Musicali).

Brazil—UBEM (União Brasileira de Editoras de Música).

Primary Sources of Revenue

Large Record Labels

Approximately 36 percent of publishing revenue derives from the leasing and licensing of intellectual property within and between the three major labels (Sony, Warner, and Universal) and their subsidiaries, according to Ibis World Reports, with rights frequently transferred from one to the other. While this revenue source has shown rapid and persistent decline over the last decade, increased publishing opportunities advertising, films, television, and radio have helped somewhat to offset the revenue losses from falling album sales.[7]

Advertisers

If an advertising firm wants to use music in ads to help its clients promote their brands and products, the firm will need to procure a license. For ads in which music or copyrighted sound recordings are used—such as TV, film, and sports events—a synchronization (synch) license is required. Music in ads is nothing new, as corporations understand the benefit of making an emotional connection with customers through music. What has changed in this market is the greater accessibility to music that was previously unknown or impossible to find. Now companies that want to use unique sounds or artists can simply search on the internet. Using music by unknown artists will most certainly be less expensive than licensing a song by someone well-known. And it may be possible to license directly with the artist, bypassing the need to work with a music publisher.

Film, Television, and Radio Producers

Broadcasting music in radio, TV, and film requires a license from the rights owner of the music. The types of licenses for broadcasting are performance, communication rights, and synch. Musicians who own their copyrights may be willing to license their music at a lower rate in order to receive the wide benefit of having it heard in the mass media. As you've seen, rights owners who license their own work will not have to go through a publisher, which in general will result in less revenue for music publishers.

Online Music Platforms

The marketplace with the largest growth potential for publishers—both individuals and corporations—is online music platforms. Even though the digital delivery of music makes it easier to download illegally, the proliferation of devices like iPods, tablets, and smartphones has driven global demand for online music via companies such as iTunes, Amazon, Spotify, Pandora, Deezer, YouTube, and Vevo. These online music platforms are required to have licenses for the music they play.

There are global issues with the amount of royalties paid by the different types of online music platforms. For example, there is a significant disparity between iTunes radio and the services of YouTube and Spotify; iTunes Radio is considered "non-interactive" in the US, while the other two are interactive streaming services. This matters because the two types of services make different kinds of payments. In general, non-interactive internet radio simulcasts and services like Pandora and iTunes Radio pay lower rates than interactive services like YouTube and Spotify. While this defies logic to most of us, it appears that the more choices that are given to a listener on a platform, the higher the per-stream payment.

Spotify Logo,
EMMANUEL DUNAND/AFP/Getty Images

Does Freemium Drive Paid Service?

The online music marketplace continues to debate whether giving listeners free access to music, usually burdened with ads, encourages them to convert to paid monthly subscribers for an ad-free service. Online music platforms need revenue from ads and subscriptions. Spotify is an enthusiastic supporter of this so-called freemium pricing model.

"Our free service drives our paid service," says Daniel Ek, Spotify's co-founder and chief executive.[8] But many artists, publishers, and record labels are pressuring Spotify—and free outlets like YouTube and SoundCloud—to generate more revenue for them. In 2014 industry superstar Taylor Swift removed her entire catalog from Spotify, apparently because the company would not restrict her music to its paying subscribers.

Pause and Reflect

Do you believe that the freemium model drives people to becoming a streaming subscriber? What was the point Taylor Swift made when she removed her music from Spotify's free service?

SoundCloud

Sound designer Alex Ljung and artist Eric Wahlforss created SoundCloud to address an unmet need in the music track-sharing community. "We both came from backgrounds connected to music," said Ljung. "And it was just really, really annoying for us to collaborate with people on music—I mean simple collaboration, just sending tracks to other people in a private setting, getting some feedback from them, and having a conversation about that piece of music."[9]

SoundCloud has matured into a full-fledged, user-friendly collaborative publishing tool for both indie artists and high-profile bands. Today the site often is the first choice of labels and artists when releasing brand-new music. But until quite recently, SoundCloud did not have any formal licensing deals, and therefore paid no royalties to artists and rights owners when their music played on its site. Under pressure from many outspoken players in the music industry, it struck a deal in 2015 covering approximately 20,000 independent record labels through Merlin, a European outfit that represents small companies in digital negotiations. The deal covers some of the biggest and most influential independents, like Beggars Group (home to Vampire Weekend and FKA Twigs), Secretly Group (Bon Iver), and the electronic label Warp.[10]

Other Markets

Video Games and Apps

Other markets for the industry include media formats such as computer and video games, which often use licensed music on their soundtracks. Video game developers, in particular, are a source of solid growth. Not only are there games dedicated to music that generate significant revenue, but developers of different video-game genres are willing to pay for appropriate songs to enhance their gaming experiences.[11] For example, sporting video games such as FIFA and Madden use licensed songs on their soundtracks.

Composer Steve Reich has influenced generations of pop, jazz, and classical musicians over the last half-century with his cultural curiosity for everything from African drumming to concept art.[12] Now there is an app from London Sinfonietta and Touchpress dedicated to Reich's "Clapping Music." Reich's original 1972 piece is an example of his elegantly simple minimalist musical principles: have two musicians clap a single, simple rhythm over a span of 12 eighth notes (quavers), and then have one of the players move the pattern one eighth note ahead after each set of repetitions until the patterns coincide again a few minutes later. The app turns the activity into a competition between the clapper and the software's perfect beat, making it easier (and less likely to collapse in laughter) than performing "Clapping Music" with a live person.[13]

Types of Royalties

Publishers and rights owners earn revenue from three main types of royalties: mechanical, performance, and synchronization.

Mechanical Royalties

Mechanical royalties are revenues that come from music used in recordings. This may include physical recordings (CDs, vinyl, and tapes), music videos, ringtones, digital songs, and music used in other recorded items. In the US, music publishers collect mechanical royalties directly from record companies or via the Harry Fox Agency, which was purchased by performing rights organization Sesac in 2015. In Europe, publishers and their writers receive performance royalties from the more than 20 collecting societies, such as SACEM, GEMA, and SGAE. Mechanical royalties are paid to the publisher either directly from record companies or from collection societies. The publisher then distributes a percentage of the money received from mechanical royalties to everyone who may have copyright ownership in the work, as well as to the writers and composers of the composition, even if they no longer have ownership.

Performance Royalties

Performance royalties continue to be a solid, even growing, revenue producer for the industry. The explosion in digital media distribution services, which require performance licenses, is a ray of hope for the music industry as it continues to search for a replacement to the sagging revenue from mechanical royalties. The growing number of music uses that require performance licenses—such as live music performances on stage, at music festivals, and broadcasts on TV and radio—form the bedrock of financial health in this segment.

A closer look shows that performance royalties come from hundreds of sources besides the obvious live performances of music in concert halls and theaters. Royalty revenue is derived whenever a licensed song is "performed" via broadcast on TV, radio, cable, and satellite, at sporting events, in restaurants or bars, online, and wireless streaming. Hit pop songs often propel substantial sales of albums or songs, which in turn increases the desirability of licensing the work for use in other media like radio, advertisements, live performances, or TV shows. Demand for specific songs is greater when music publicity is widespread, reviews are good, and if an artist or song has recently won a televised award such as a Grammy or the Eurovision Song Contest.

The US is the only developed country that does not require terrestrial TV and radio broadcasters to pay a performance royalty to the rights holder of sound recordings (usually record labels) and the recording artists who perform on sound recordings. For decades, US terrestrial broadcasters have successfully lobbied Congress to continue their exemption from compensating artists and labels for using their recordings on the air. This means that the rights holder of an *underlying composition* gets paid by the terrestrial broadcaster when her song airs, but the rights holder and recording artist of the song *recording* do not. This is not the case for music that is transmitted by other media, such as satellite and the internet.

Synchronization (Synch) Royalties

When previously recorded music is used in conjunction with a moving image, it requires permission from both the owner of the underlying composition and the owner of the recording if a master recording is used. The permission is granted in what is known as a synchronization (synch) license. Synch royalties result from music used in audiovisual productions such as films, television programs, and commercials, DVDs or video games—in other words, the use of the song in combination with visual images.

Significant licenses have been issued worldwide for a number of major advertising campaigns, TV programs, and video games as a way to bolster awareness for the artist and to boost demand for music sales. For example, if a film director wants to use Stevie Wonder's recording of "Superstition" from his

2002 album *The Definitive Collection* in a movie, the director must get permission in the form of a synch license from both the rights holder of the underlying composition and the rights holder of the recording. Rarely are these the same person or company. In nearly all cases, there will be a fee to license the music. The director and the rights holders will negotiate a rate for the ways in which the director wants to use the music. This could include how the song is used in the film, whether or not it is used in advertisements for the film, shown in movie theatres, on television, on the internet, in airplanes, or other uses. The duration of the license and the geographic territories the license covers are also negotiated.

It's possible that one or both of the rights holders will decline to grant the synch license, or that the fee to use Mr. Wonder's song is outside of the film director's budget. If money is the sticking point, the director could consider re-recording the song by a less expensive artist as long as the song is not a sound-alike recording. The director still needs a synch license from the publisher, but the price for using the recording may drop significantly.

> A synch license gives the film director the right to include a song in his film, but a synch license alone is not sufficient to show the film in public. In addition to a synch license, a TV station will need a performance license to show the film.

A Few More Ways for Publishers to License Their Music

Revenue from the following sources tends to flow irregularly and typically represents a small percentage of industry revenue:

- Publishing sheet music, folios (collections of songs), and books or films about the creators of music or the songs themselves.

- Creating libraries of pre-cleared music sounds, drum beats, loops, and music for use in film, television, advertising, recordings, and interactive media. This kind of music is also known as production or stock music. Many production music companies are owned by the major labels' publishing companies, such as Killer Tracks, which is owned by Universal.

- Compiling and marketing special collections, projects, and events that involve the songs in their catalog. Ideas might include a postage stamp series featuring specific composers, or a deluxe box record set with photos of manuscripts and songs from a specific time period in a songwriter's career.

- Granting licenses for derivative works to be made from the songs in the publisher's catalogue.

- Granting sampling licenses (for the underlying composition but not to the recording) to producers and other musicians who want to reuse parts of previously recorded, protected music in a new recording.

- Granting cover licenses to artists who wish to replicate an existing song for a performance or commercial use.[14] Live performances that are recorded require cover licenses.

- Licensing musical material for clothing and other merchandise.

"Thou Shalt Not Steal"

The US is the cradle of music sampling and, owing to its strict interpretation of copyright laws, a hotbed of sampling lawsuits. One of the earliest music sampling cases was *Grand Upright Music Ltd. v. Warner Bros. Records* in 1991. Rapper Biz Markie, signed to Warner Bros. Records, had sampled without permission Gilbert O'Sullivan's song "Alone Again (Naturally)" on a track of his album *I Need a Haircut*. In delivering his decision to Warner Bros. to cease distribution of Markie's album, Judge Kevin Thomas Duffy began with a biblical quote: "Thou shalt not steal." Judge Duffy's decision signaled the strict interpretation of sampling laws by US courts and changed the business structure of hip-hop music. From then on, labels insisted that their artists clear all samples before releasing the record.[15]

Biz Markie

Steve Pyke/Premium Archive/Getty Images

Pause and Reflect

What are your thoughts about the potential effect of sample clearing on an artist's creative expression? Look at this question from both the artist's and the rights owner to the music that is sampled.

Digital Sheet Music

With the closure of many traditional music stores, where can a classical musician find printed music? Sheet music is now easily accessible digitally through retail websites, apps, or free catalogs like the Internet Music Score Library Project (IMSLP) Petrucci Music Library.[16]

Tonara is an interactive sheet music app for iPads, headed by pianist Ron Regev. While some of the digital programs involve foot pedals for turning pages, Tonara can detect a performer's place on the page via the microphone on an iPad and flip the page automatically at the right moment.[17] In addition to these wonders, a touring musician's entire music library can fit onto a hard drive or be stored in the cloud, eliminating the need to lug around heavy suitcases full of printed scores.

However, traditional music publishers face illegal downloading concerns because of the ease of downloading and sharing digital sheet music among musicians. "Yes, there are a few publishers that understand the problem and are adjusting in the way that recording companies adjusted to the MP3 revolution," explains Regev. "The problem is that many of them are trying to cling to their old models as they see their income dwindling."[18]

Common Ways to License Music

SONG USE	TYPE OF LICENSE
First use of a song	First-use mechanical
Cover song on recording	Mechanical—compulsory
Film, video, documentary	Synchronization
Corporate training DVD	Synchronization
Terrestrial radio & TV (small performances)	Performance—blanket OR Direct license with rights holder
Ringtones, ringbacks	Mechanical
Mastertones	Mechanical
Electronic greeting cards	Mechanical
Non-interactive digital streaming radio	Performance
Interactive digital streaming radio	Mechanical
Download available for purchase on web	Mechanical
Printed music, folios, special collections	Print
Theatrical stage productions (grand rights)	Performance
Derivative work	Derivative
Lyrics licensed to print greeting cards, books, magazines	Lyric reprint
Music business services (Muzak, airlines)	Mechanical
Video games	Synchronization
Radio ads	Commercial sync license (and master rights if using existing recording)
Television ads	Synchronization

INSIDE A MUSIC PUBLISHING COMPANY

Large, full-service publishing companies can be a one-stop solution for a songwriter who wants her songs to produce revenue. Major publishers have the infrastructure (e.g., skilled employees, systems, and processes) to take care of all aspects of the complex legal and accounting paperwork associated with copyright ownership and exploitation.

A large music publishing company usually has a professional staff that can provide a wide range of services. Traditionally, a company is organized into departments with specific functions, such as creative, promotion, mechanical licensing, synch licensing, foreign, finance, business and legal affairs, copyright, royalty, and information technology. Music publishing staff are knowledgeable about the laws of copyright that pertain to music and licensing. They will have a large network of potential clients with whom they are in frequent communication, pitching songs in their catalog for placement in, for example, a film or TV show.

A publishing company's creative staff understands the needs of each potential music user and recommends music from the publishing company's catalog that makes sense for the user's project and budget. The creative staff are skilled negotiators who know the value of their catalog, the financial resources of the potential user, and the current industry rates for music usage. They must constantly be looking for new ways to use music in order to expand the revenue streams of the writers and their company.

Some of the work of publishers is administrative in nature. Paperwork may seem less exciting than pitching songs to a major movie producer. In fact, it's the attention to detail that forms the foundation of the publishing industry, ensuring that the correct amount of money is flowing to the creators. These can include such things as proper copyright registration; filing complete and correct information with collecting societies, PROs, and mechanical rights organizations; making sure royalty statements from record labels are accurate; auditing record labels (hiring an accountant to check the label's financial records) when errors are suspected or detected; tracking revenues that are due from music users; following up on every detail involved in negotiating a license; keeping up with the complex and changing copyright laws; and helping to develop and use new technologies to streamline administrative tasks.

Smaller, independent publishing companies generally have fewer resources and may offer only some of the services of a major. However, many writers feel that indie music publishers provide a higher level of support and personal attention than a large company of megastars could provide.

Spotlight on . . . Kobalt Music Publishing

Founded in 2000, the British firm Kobalt Music Group upended the music publishing industry by seizing an opportunity to streamline the lucrative but impenetrable world of international copyright collection societies—"the patchwork of organizations that, country by country, gathers money from radio, television and digital outlets and funnels it back to songwriters and publishers."[19] Music publishers partner with national collection societies, like Socan in Canada, Tono in Norway, and Acum in Israel, to collect royalties for their writers whose music is played outside their home country. This cumbersome system has been in place for decades and controls the flow of billions of dollars in royalties each year.

Kobalt's founder, Willard Ahdritz, says that when it comes to the digital market, the system is hobbled by inefficiencies, delays, and hidden costs. For example, Spotify can account for thousands of sources of income that are differentiated by country, account type, and other factors. There is no international database of songs; each country's collecting society controls its own author's works. With the language barriers, inevitable human error, and accounting delays, it is not uncommon for a writer to be paid two years after her music was used. Finally, as money passes from one society to another in its travel from user to rights owner, each society takes a cut off the top, whittling away at the payment the writer finally receives.[20]

An Opaque System

"It is very clear that the music industry was not in good shape pre-digital," Ahdritz said. "It was opaque, with old systems, a very territorial business. It needs a new structure to handle this new digital world."

Christina Perri (a Kobalt artist)

Jeff Golden/Getty Images Entertainment

In its early days, Kobalt was the upstart in the music publishing world with its radical business model that relied on a lean, technology-driven system. While most publishers take ownership of song copyrights and split income 50/50 with their writers, Kobalt lets its writers keep their copyrights, instead charging an administration fee of about 10 percent.[21] Kobalt's clients include Paul McCartney, Herbie Hancock, Bob Dylan, Skrillex, Kelly Clarkson, Trent Reznor, and Punch Brothers, among many others.[22]

Kobalt's focus is to collect every penny of royalties due for each song's use, whether it is a big hit or a small blip. This means looking into every nook and cranny of the sprawling world of digital music, tracking down song plays, and collecting the money that is owed to rights owner. For example, the songwriting royalties of a Kobalt client for a global hit song in 2013 totaled US$4.76 million. Kobalt found 900,000 sources of income for the song, including US$2,400 from a use in Norway that resulted in a payment of US$8 to Kobalt.[23] While this may sound like an extreme way to run a business, it reflects the reality of the fragmented world of earning royalties from streaming music: tiny payments for each use, but the potential for millions of uses.

700,000 Different Revenue Streams

Today, a typical hit song generates around 700,000 different revenue streams. Every month Kobalt finds money owed from music used in 1.5 billion video streams on YouTube alone in the US. "If we as an industry can get this right, we should be able to double the industry's total revenue from $15B to $30B," says Ahdretz. "We have seen in other industries that clear rules, robust technology and real transparency drive liquidity, which in turn drives growth. [Kobalt is] now putting [that] in place on a global scale. The potential for the music industry is enormous. And then once we get the money flowing again, we obviously have other topics to discuss: What is a fair rate? Why do master rights get 14 times more than the songwriter's rights?"[24]

Kobalt recently purchased its own collections group, AMRA, and uses the agency as a central clearinghouse for digital licensing around the world, a change that Ahdritz believes could double or triple the amount that songwriters receive from digital outlets like Spotify.[25] He credits Spotify for helping to significantly reduce the illegal global download market. "In Scandinavia in 2009 we had an 80 percent illegal market. Today it has shrunk to 4 percent . . . Spotify . . . single handedly took the region from a dark, illegal, non-monetized majority to a thriving, paying majority."[26]

A Lucrative Funding Round

"Someone needs to save the industry. Someone needs to be brave, don't you agree?" asks Ahdritz.[27] Clearly he feels that Kobalt is up to the task, and others agree with him.

Kobalt completed a US$60 million funding round in February 2015 to enhance its technology infrastructure and expand operations. Google Ventures lead the Series C funding round, which also included the private investment firm of Dell founder and CEO Michael S. Dell.[28]

Not everyone in the change-resistant music publishing world is a fan of Kobalt's business model. Kobalt has been called a company made up of efficient bean counters rather than music specialists. "I think music publishing is about more than collecting data," said Martin N. Bandier, chief executive of Sony/ATV, whose catalog includes Beatles and Motown hits. "I think it's about signing songwriters; working with those songwriters; maximizing, exploiting, creating opportunities for the songwriters; finding opportunities to create Broadway shows."[29]

Moby (a Kobalt artist)

Kevin Winter/Getty Images Entertainment

But Moby, a longtime Kobalt client, is more realistic: "Kobalt is more like a tech company than a music company. As a result, no one ever told them to steal from their artists."[30]

The Challenges of Big Data

Some countries' collecting societies have been unable to handle the vast amounts of music royalty data that has come flooding in from Kobalt and other new companies. As a result, there are entire regions of the world where little or no money finds its way back to composers. Ahdritz said Kobalt receives "almost nothing" from digital streams in places like Russia, the Middle East, Latin America, and Southeast Asia, where the sheer amount of big data has overwhelmed the collecting societies' outdated methods.[31]

Defenders of the existing (that is, pre-Kobalt) international collecting system argue that change would discredit the importance of the collecting societies' deep knowledge of their local territories. "The truth is that the strength of collective management has never been so robust and so necessary for creators than it is today," said Jean-Noël Tronc, chief executive of SACEM, the French agency.[32]

Speeding Up Payments to Artists

How long is too long to wait to be paid for your song's licensed use? "Imagine a songwriter had a million-streams-a-day hit during Christmas last year and receives a check in June this year which doesn't reflect the value, and then decides to criticize our model on blogs," said Will Page, Spotify's director of economics and a former chief economist at PRS for Music, the British collection society. "The reality is that we paid in for that hit a month after its exploitation, yet the songwriter may well get paid out a year later [from her collecting society]."[33]

Kobalt purchased AMRA to help solve this very problem. Major digital providers like Spotify and YouTube will be able to link their data collection information with just one collection service, instead of the current method of linking with dozens of societies around the world. This would mean royalties could be paid out weeks, not months or years, after the work was used.[34]

"Part of the problem is that the music industry has been focused on the music," Ahdritz said. "And that is what a lot of people in music have a passion for. But my point is that there is a day when you're not on tour, when you are off the hits, and it is then that you think, 'Where is the money?'"[35]

Pause and Reflect

Compare the traditional way that music publishers do business with the business model of Kobalt. Compare the comments of Ahdritz, Bandier, and Moby. Do you think Kobalt will succeed in convincing the staid music publishing business to change?

Red Bull Music Publishing

Red Bull Music Publishing is an example of a hybrid music publishing company that is not connected with a major label. The fact that Red Bull is an energy drink company may appear to be an unlikely position from which to challenge the music publishing industry, but the Red Bull Music Academy has been around since 1998.[36]

As part of Red Bull Media Company, Red Bull Publishing helps develop aspiring composers and songwriters by partnering them with established artists and brands. Red Bull Music Publishing's global administrative team takes care of any rights generated from its many music activities and makes those works available as pre-licensed material to its clients and Red Bull partners.[37]

In addition to music, the company's multi-platform products and services include print, TV, online, mobile, games, and cinema. Being an "umbrella brand" streamlines the process for Red Bull of fully integrating its array of professional services to best serve its clients and collaborators. For example, Red Bull commissions, produces, and curates soundtracks, scores, production music, and songs across every genre and musical style. Red Bull Music Publishing manages the rights, and the musical assets are made available through the Red Bull Content Pool Audio Library.[38]

INDUSTRY FORECAST

Ibis World forecasts that physical record sales will continue to decline over the next five years, but at a slower rate than in previous years due to the anticipated global economic improvement. Although there has been an appreciable consumer shift toward digital music, a certain level of demand for physical media is expected to remain. For example, niche products such as vinyl LPs and related equipment have proved to be surprisingly stable in popularity and growth.[39]

According to IBIS World, easier access to online music publishing services and royalties from streaming internet radio or webcasting will be the primary revenue drivers for the future. The challenge for music publishers will be to acquire enough intellectual property protection to ensure that streaming radio sites produce revenue for the songs they play.[40]

The biggest wildcard in projecting the future financial health of the publishing sector is the possibility of changes in rate regulations made by governments or other influential bodies, and the negotiation of rates for new services. The rate-setting process is vitally important to all music publishers and their songwriters. In the US, for example, the Copyright Royalty Board oversees the royalty rates for physical and digital products, including streaming subscription services.[41] Mechanical royalties are paid at a penny-rate-per-unit in the US and as a percentage of the wholesale price in other countries.

The proliferation and popularity of music-oriented games such as *Guitar Hero*, *Rock Band*, and *SingStar* has created a healthy and growing market for music rights. It is a lucrative market for artists, game developers, and music labels. Artists can gain much-needed mass exposure, developers can improve game sales, and labels can increase song sales.[42]

Multi-national professional services network PricewaterhouseCoopers (PwC) forecasts that the single biggest shift in total revenue for video games will come as emerging and densely populated countries see revenues from social/casual gaming overtake traditional gaming revenue. By 2019, social/casual gaming revenue is expected to exceed traditional console and PC gaming revenue in nine markets: South Africa (where social/casual gaming currently is 50 percent of revenue), the Philippines, India, Singapore, Chile, Argentina, Indonesia, Malaysia, and Nigeria (predicted to be 90 percent of revenue).[43]

TOOLS FOR THE DIWO (DO IT WITH OTHERS) ENTREPRENEUR: HOW TO MAKE MUSIC PUBLISHING WORK FOR YOU AS A REVENUE STREAM

The Short Version of How Music Royalties Work

As an artist-entrepreneur trying to make a living with your music, it's crucial that you put aside any reservations you may have about becoming involved in and understanding what kinds of royalty streams are available to you. As you will see, the music royalty landscape is quite complex, but rich with opportunity for artist- and music business-entrepreneurs who know when they are earning royalties and how they can get the money.

The first thing to know is that in music there are two copyrights to every piece of *recorded* music: the master rights and the publishing rights. The master rights refer to the sounds you hear when the recording is played. The publishing rights refer to the underlying musical composition—its notes, melodies, chords, rhythms, and lyrics. If you compose, record, and distribute a song to the public and retain your copyright ownership, you are entitled to earn royalties from both master- and publishing-related royalties. If you are a song's composer but are not involved in its recording, you are entitled to earn royalties from publishing-related royalties only.[44]

Here is an overview of how money will flow to you when your music is legally licensed for use (you will receive exactly nothing when your music is downloaded illegally).

Publishing-Generated Royalties

Performance Royalties

You are earning performance royalties when your songs are "performed" publicly, which includes a wide variety of opportunities:

- broadcast on terrestrial, online, or satellite radio;

- broadcast on terrestrial, online, or satellite TV;

- played on online streaming music services;

- used in live performances in public venues by you or anyone else;

- used as background music in businesses and retailers

How the Money Gets to You

Each major world territory has at least one performing rights or collection society.

Register your compositions with every collecting society in every territory where you think your music will be played. The collecting society will send you the money it collects on your behalf only if it knows the music is yours and it has your current contact information.

Mechanical Royalties

Mechanical royalties are per-unit payments made by a recording company to the music rights owner (traditionally a publisher) for the reproduction of copyrighted musical compositions appearing on CDs, cassette tapes, vinyl albums, and other manufactured formats. Each time a consumer purchases a sound recording (a "unit"), the record company makes the required royalty payment to the rights owners of the musical work which is then passed on to the songwriter. Download providers are also required to pay mechanical royalties for use of a work protected by copyright.[45]

If you use a worldwide digital music distributor such as TuneCore or SoundCloud and receive reports of sales and streams, you are earning mechanical royalties.

How the Money Gets to You

Affiliate with every mechanical collection agency in the territories where you think you will generate download sales and streams. For iTunes play in the US, the mechanical royalty share goes straight from iTunes to the label or its digital music distributor. In countries outside of the US, your mechanical royalty is picked up from iTunes.[46]

Print Royalties

Print royalties are earned when a work is transcribed onto paper, printed in songbooks, and published for personal use by music amateurs. There is very little royalty money to be earned through print except by massively popular songwriters, living or not, whose work appears in a songbook.

Master-Generated Royalties

Master-generated royalties come from download sales and streams of recorded music. Every time your master recording is downloaded or streamed, you are owed a royalty. Master rights holders are usually labels or artist-entrepreneurs who have their own label.[47]

How the Money Gets to You

A label or its representative collects royalties directly from stores and streaming sites and distributes the appropriate royalty to the artist. An unsigned artist-entrepreneur with her own label collects and keeps the recording royalties directly from the user.

YouTube Recording Royalties

YouTube is a massive player in the global music industry and is currently the most popular site for people to find music. Master rights holders (labels or performing artists themselves) earn royalties every time their recording is streamed in a YouTube video *if their video has an advertisement attached to it*. YouTube earns its revenue from advertising partnerships, then shares the earnings with musicians and music rights owners.

It's important to clarify that *publishing* rights owners (publishers and songwriters) also receive money from YouTube, but YouTube sends those royalty payments to PROs and collecting societies.[48]

Who Collects YouTube-Generated Recording Royalties?

YouTube collects royalties using technology called Content ID, which tracks each music play in a video using an audio fingerprint. As you can imagine, YouTube's database of fingerprinted music is enormous. You will become acquainted with Content ID if you upload a video to YouTube that includes unlicensed music. If you're a master rights holder (a label or performing artist on a recording) and your recordings are on YouTube, you have the ability to earn YouTube royalties via Content ID. The more views, the more revenue you generate.

How the Money Gets to You

Label master rights holders distribute royalties to their artists. Most unsigned artist-entrepreneurs use a third party to collect YouTube recording royalties.

Neighboring Rights Recording Royalties

Neighboring, or related, rights is a term in copyright law used to describe the rights of performers and master recording owners to publicly perform a sound recording. If you're a sound recording owner (record label or performing artist), you and the artists performing on those recordings will earn neighboring rights royalties when your master recordings are publicly performed or broadcast on:

- an internet or satellite radio platform;
- cable TV music channels;
- terrestrial radio outside of the US;
- background music services;
- public performance venues.

How the Money Gets to You

Neighboring rights collection societies, such as Symphonic Distribution's Neighboring Rights Administration Service,[49] will collect your neighboring rights royalties if you have registered your master recordings with each collection society in the territories in which you are getting or expect to get radio play. Keep in mind that you earn neighboring rights royalties when your master recordings are publicly performed or broadcast, not sold. If you notice a spike in sales in a specific market, ask your rights administrator to look into whether or not your song also is receiving radio play. If it is, you are earning neighboring rights royalties.

The neighboring rights collection societies distribute royalties to performers and master recording owners who are registered with that society. If you're a performing artist and know your recordings are getting radio airplay, talk to the record label that released your music. They may already be collecting these royalties on your behalf.[50]

International Royalty Collection

As you've already learned, international societies collect royalty revenues for songwriters, composers, and publishers; deduct a fee; pay out those royalties to a locally registered publisher; or send the money to the writers' and publishers' affiliated societies. It sounds pretty straightforward. In reality, however, songwriters, composers, and music publishers around the world lose tens of millions of dollars in unclaimed royalties each year.[51]

These unclaimed royalties accumulate in a Black Box until the writers and publishers who are owed royalties can be located. You read that correctly. The primary reason royalties go unclaimed is improper, or lack of, song registration with the international societies. Proper song registration is something that is totally within your control and must be meticulously kept up to date.[52]

Remember that royalty rates and the way royalty income is determined and processed are different for each country. With millions of copyrights to manage and track, it is impossible for these societies to be proactive in seeking international royalties for every single one of their members. This is a problem, but one that is out of your control. So focus your efforts on keeping your song registrations current and do your bit for royalty distribution.[53]

A peek inside the collecting society back office reveals that much of the data submitted to societies is still paper-based and must be manually entered into databases. Add to that astounding piece of information language differences, spelling errors, and unfamiliar writer names and you can understand why it's nothing short of a minor miracle that anyone other than Top 40 artists actually receive the money that is due to them. Most international territories pay broadcast mechanical royalties together with public performance royalties, but the US does not have a royalty society set up to receive mechanical royalties from abroad.[54]

Music Gaming

Simple downloadable, inexpensive, and free games available on social media sites, smartphones, and tablets represent intriguing opportunities for composers.[55] If your music is selected for use in a game, you most likely will be offered a license that provides for a one-time buy-out fee per composition, meaning that you will not receive any further payments no matter how big a blockbuster the game with your music becomes. The typical buyout ranges from US$2,500 to more than US$20,000, depending on the value of the music, the budget for game development, and the bargaining power of the two parties.[56]

Tips for Getting Your Music Placed in Games

- Stay in touch with the gaming marketplace by researching trends and forecasts.

- Find out the names and contact information of developers whose games would match well with your music.

- Approach the developers with a pitch that focuses on how you can help the developers solve their problems rather than why the developers should license your music.

- Be realistic. Go for the smaller developers until you've got a significant track record.

- Have a clean, easy-to-use website where developers can stream or download your music.

- Clear all music samples in your music and get the paperwork ready so you can send out a license within 24 hours.

- Stay humble. Remember that the primary connection here is between the game user and the art on the screen, not the music.

Music Sampling

Some bands don't bother to clear samples. They may not understand their legal obligation or they may think no one will discover it. But legally it's considered a copyright infringement of both the sound recording and the underlying composition if samples are used in a record without the copyright owners' permission. Copyright infringement lawsuits can be lengthy and expensive. It's not worth it—get the samples cleared or re-record the song without the sample. See the information earlier in this chapter on what type of license you need to sample previously recorded, copyright-protected music.

If You Are Thinking about Signing with a Music Publisher . . .[i]

Main Points to Be Considered in a Publishing Negotiation

The relationship. Before signing a contract, a songwriter and publisher will discuss the type of relationship that makes sense for both parties. The acquisition of rights to the songwriter's work and what services and revenue splits the songwriter may receive in return are key points in any agreement.

Contract duration. How long will the contract be in force? What is the process for and consequences of an early termination or a contract extension?

Rights transfer. When a copyright owner transfers her rights to a third party, such as a publisher, all the rights and privileges that pertain to copyright ownership transfer as well. (Reminder: we are talking about the rights to the underlying composition, not the recording of the song.) In a traditional publishing contract, the writer assigns (transfers) her copyright ownership to the publisher for the duration of the copyright period as defined by federal law.[ii]

---

i Find qualified, professional legal assistance before signing any legal document.
ii There are publishing deals, described later in this chapter, that do not include copyright ownership transfer.

Advances. An advance is money paid to the writer by the publisher. Issues to discuss in a negotiation include the size of the advance, the payment periods, and whether or not the advance is recoupable (will be deducted from the writer's future royalty earnings).

Co-writing. It is very common in today's music industry for songwriters to collaborate. While this may complicate the rights-ownership landscape, most publishers accept co-writing as a fact of life. For example, when a writer who has an exclusive agreement with a publisher works with a writer who self-publishes, the publisher will request its signed writer to make her best efforts to obtain the co-writer's share for the publisher rather than for the co-writer's own publishing company. As the frequency of collaborative writing increases, this clause becomes challenging for publishers to enforce.

First-use mechanical licenses. Copyright law gives the rights owner the exclusive right to decide who makes the first copy of her song. Thus, when a writer assigns her copyright to a publisher, the first-use right transfers to the publisher. First-use mechanical licenses are not subject to the statutory rates that guide the recording of cover songs *after* their first recording and publication. Publishers will negotiate first-use licenses on the open market, meaning that the cost to record the song for the first time will vary depending upon the reputation of the writer, her prior success, how strongly the potential song-user desires to use the song, and other factors.

Ownership and promotion of demo recordings. Usually publishers own everything created by their writers, even their demo recordings. While it is not common to release a demo as an actual finished recording, it can be an intriguing opportunity for a publisher to consider, particularly after a famous recording artist dies and there is high demand for her material, including previously unpublished songs or versions of songs.

Timeliness of royalty payments from the publisher. It is the industry standard for publishers to send royalty statements and payments to the writer twice a year. Publishers retain the money they collect on behalf of the writer for 45 days to three months *after* the closing of each six-month collection period. This means that a writer whose song was used in an advertising campaign that ran at the beginning of a six-month collection period might not receive payment for up to eight months after the commercials aired. It's clear why advances can be life-saving to writers. On the other hand, it can take three years or more for a publishing company to fully recoup the advances paid to a writer, even if money begins flowing in right after signing the writer.

Audits. An audit allows the writer to bring in an accountant to review the publisher's books. The writer may suspect that she has not received all the royalties owed to her and wants a third-party professional to examine the publisher's accounting records. An audit clause may also include the right of the publishing company to audit the writer/artist's record label, for the same reasons.

Making changes to a work. US copyright law gives the rights owner the exclusive right to make derivative works from a song. If a potential licensee wants to make substantial changes to a song's lyrics or music (beyond a key change or recording a pop song as a jazz arrangement, for example), the potential user will seek a license to make a derivative of the work. As stated earlier in the chapter, this is a negotiated license, meaning it is not governed by a statutory rate. If the desired terms are not met, the rights owner can refuse to grant a license to make the derivative work.

Major Copyright Lawsuits

The complexity of copyright issues in the US involving parody and fair use is reflected in the number of high-profile lawsuits in the music industry. Here are two cases that are worth exploring:

Campbell v. Acuff-Rose Music, 510 US 569 (1994). The rap group 2 Live Crew borrowed the opening musical tag and the words (but not the melody) from the first line of the song "Pretty Woman" ("Oh, pretty woman, walking down the street").[57]

Fisher v. Dees, 794 F.2d 432 (9th Cir. 1986). The composers of the song "When Sunny Gets Blue" (Marvin Fisher and Jack Segal) claimed that their song was infringed by Rick Dees' "When Sonny Sniffs Glue," a 29-second parody that altered the original lyric line and borrowed six bars of the song.[58]

Luke Skyywalker of 2 Live Crew

Michael Ochs Archives/Getty Images

Take Note . . .

As in any negotiation, the final contract reflects the relative strengths of the parties at the bargaining table. A new but promising songwriter will have less bargaining power than a well-established writer whose works have been popular for years and have produced significant amounts of revenue. Skilled legal counsel is an essential part of the writer's negotiating team and will work on her behalf to get the best deal possible.

Six Different Types of Publishing Contracts

If talks go well, the publishing company will issue a contract to the songwriter. While each publishing company has its own contract language, drawn up by its legal counsel and based on years of experience with their writers, there are six general types of agreements or relationships that the songwriter may consider, depending upon her stature and a proven track record of writing songs that are commercially viable.

The first two types of contracts listed below are generally offered to writers who have come to a publisher's attention but have not yet reached their full potential. Experienced and successful songwriters more commonly seek and/or are offered the third, fourth, and fifth contracts listed. The sixth type of contract is a hybrid. It's called a development deal and pairs an experienced writer (who is often a producer and recording artist as well) with a new writer:

- Exclusive agreement.
- Individual song agreement.
- Administration agreement.

- Co-publishing agreement.

- Joint venture/co-venture agreement.

- Development deal.

Exclusive Agreement

In an exclusive writer–publisher contract, the writer agrees to allow only one publisher to exploit the work she creates during a specified period of time (usually no fewer than five years) and transfers 100 percent of the copyright to the publisher. There is often a minimum song commitment involved or certain measurable goals set, such as income generated by songs. The term continues until the minimum song commitment or income goal is met and perhaps longer if the commitment or goal is met prior to the specified length of time.[59]

In exchange, the writer will receive regular (often monthly) payments, called a "writer's draw," against future earnings from the exploitation of the songs during the period of exclusivity. These regular payments can be an enormous help to songwriters, reducing the anxiety of waiting for royalties to be paid by copyright users such as record labels and PROs. The writer's draw is almost like a salary, except that all monies paid will be deducted from future revenue that the writer earns. This means when the publisher receives payment from a copyright user, the money goes into the writer's account to recoup, or pay back, the draws that have been paid to the writer.[60]

Typically songs created during the term of the agreement are assigned to the publisher for the life of copyright. The agreement itself (i.e., the length of time the songwriter is signed exclusively to the publisher) is for a certain number of years. Once the draw has been recouped, the publisher pays the writer her contractual percentage of royalty earned. In effect, the publisher is taking a calculated risk that it will be successful in licensing the writer's work. The publisher must bring in enough money to cover the draws it is paying the writer, as well as make a profit, in order for the publisher to stay in business.

There are many benefits for a developing writer in signing an exclusive agreement. Having a steady income for the period of the agreement allows the writer to focus on her songwriting without worrying how she'll pay her rent and bills. In addition, the publisher will often provide access to recording studios where the writer can work with other writers, create new work, and record demos.

Individual Song Agreement

In this agreement, a songwriter transfers to a publisher 100 percent of the copyright for a specific song or songs in exchange for a nominal advance and a split of the future revenues from licensing the song. The writer is exclusively bound only to that publisher for those specific songs. She may work with any number of publishers on a per-song basis. Why would a songwriter do this? She may feel a particular publisher will be better qualified and more eager to promote certain of her songs. Similarly, some publishers may be interested in only specific types of songs from a writer because that is their area of expertise. Again, the business-savvy songwriter will do extensive research into each publisher to be certain she is placing her songs in the right hands. The duration of the licensing period is a factor to be discussed in the contract.

Administration Agreement

In this type of contract, a songwriter will retain the rights to her songs and pay a percentage of her earned income to a publisher in exchange for the publisher performing any number of the common administrative functions inherent in music publishing. This type of agreement may suit the needs of writers who record their own works as artists, or writers whose style of music is not conducive to being covered on albums or licensed in commercials, film, or TV. An administration agreement may be appealing to songwriters whose works are in high demand and who have little need for the A&R function of a publisher. The major difference—and it's a very big deal—between an administration agreement and other types of publishing contracts is that the writer does not have to give up any of her copyright in an administrative agreement.

As in other contractual arrangements, an administration agreement can be tailored to meet the needs, expertise, and financial requirements of the two parties involved (publisher and writer). The most common duties found in administration agreements include filing copyright registrations, updating information with mechanical and collecting societies, and registering songs with the collecting societies.

For these types of services, the administering publisher would receive approximately 7–10 percent on all income collected. If the writer is looking for additional help from the publisher, the fee could increase to 20 percent and may even involve partial ownership of specific songs. Depending on the administering publisher's areas of strength, the duration of the agreement, and the level of enthusiasm for the writer's songs, an administration agreement could even include song promotion, securing new uses for the songs, demo recording, license negotiation, contract drafting, and connections to and advice about foreign territory licensing.

At this point you may be wondering why a publisher would enter into an administration agreement with a writer, as it appears that the publisher is doing the same kind of work as an exclusive or co-publishing contract, but without the major benefit of owning the copyright. For some publishers, the chance to work with a very well-known catalog of music will allow them to burnish their reputation, which in turn may attract more high-profile writers. There are publishers who accept an administration agreement in order to strengthen their connections in a specific musical genre. Still other publishers may find that administrating a catalog from, say, a well-known recording artist or popular television series will be so lucrative that it is a good strategic move, even if they cannot own the copyrights.

The common elements in an administration agreement, no matter how much or how little the writer wants from the publisher, include the following:

- Term of the agreement—How long will it last, how can it be renewed or terminated?

- Scope of work—What services will the publisher provide to the songwriter? How will that affect the administration fee charged by the publisher?

- Physical territory covered by the agreement—In what countries or areas of the world will the administering publisher work for the writer? Will there be an additional fee for working outside the writer's home country?

- Royalty payments—Will they include gross income for each song, or more detailed information about how the income for each song has been distributed?

- Royalty statements—What information will be included in the statements? How often will statements be sent?

For the additional services required of the publisher—particularly song promotion that results in new uses and cover records—the writer will expect to pay an additional percentage to the publisher. The writer may decide to create incentives for the publisher to actively seek new uses of her music by building into the contract additional percentages for specific deals. For example, the contract could state that the publisher will receive an additional 5 percent on revenues generated by a song if the administering publisher secures a cover deal of the song with a high-selling recording artist. Another type of incentive for the publisher to be proactive in finding new uses for a writer's music is for the writer to offer a percentage of the copyright if certain specific goals are achieved.

As you can see, an administration agreement can cover many types of services. The writer–publisher relationship can range from the complex but straightforward task of collecting monies and sending out royalty statements and payments to being proactive about finding and securing new opportunities in which to license the writer's music, thus bringing more revenue to both the administrative publisher and the writer.

Co-publishing Agreement

A co-publishing agreement is offered primarily to well-established or highly desirable writers. In such an agreement, the songwriter does *not* transfer 100 percent of the copyright to the publisher in exchange for receiving the contractual percentage of the revenue earned, as in the exclusive and individual song agreements. In a co-publishing arrangement, the songwriter usually receives some type of recoupable advance and retains a portion of her copyright in her own publishing company, where she will earn publishing royalties, *plus* her writer's share. In effect, the writer is receiving a portion of the money that would have gone to the publisher. Typically, a co-publishing deal will stipulate the right of the publisher to administer the writer's retained publishing interest.

Why would a publisher enter into an agreement with these terms? When a writer has a proven track record of creating hits and/or easily licensed music, the publisher is taking a calculated risk that the amount of money it can earn from exploiting the music will be very substantial and could more than make up for "losing" part of its traditional copyright ownership.

Joint Venture/Co-venture Agreements

Another creative partnership that publishers can enter into is called a joint or co-venture agreement. In this relationship, a publishing company and a successful, well-known songwriter (or a small indie record label) find mutual benefit in working together to discover and help develop new talent. In a joint or co-venture, a publisher will gain access to new talent that is identified by the songwriter or indie label, thus adding more A&R capabilities to the creative services offered by the publisher. The songwriter (who also may be a recording artist and producer) identifies the up-and-coming writer, and is able to attract and nurture her with financial and other support from the publishing company. The writer and the publishing company co-own the rights to the music created by the up-and-coming writer. In addition, the publisher usually receives the right to administer the new compositions worldwide.

In a joint venture/co-venture agreement, all parties benefit. The up-and-coming writer is mentored by a successful writer/artist/producer and is signed to the publishing company. The publishing company supports emerging talent and enlarges its catalog of new songs that can be promoted globally. If the new songwriter becomes successful, both the publisher and the writer who signed her will benefit financially, as they co-own the rights to her songs. Depending on the nature of the contract that the new writer signs with the publisher, she also may receive a percentage of royalties earned by her songs.

Other issues to be considered when negotiating a joint venture/co-venture agreement are:

Duration of the Agreement. What happens to song ownership when the contract period ends? Can the agreement be extended or suspended?

Advances. New writers may receive advances that are either paid entirely by the publisher or paid as a split by the co-venture partners (the experienced writer and the publisher). In addition, the experienced writer may also receive advances from the publishing company as a co-venture partner. In most cases, all advances are recoupable and are applied against earnings as they are received.

Development Deals

A development deal is another way for publishers to find new talent, nurture, and develop it in exchange for ownership of the copyright. The main goal of a traditional development deal is to have the songwriter recognized as a recording artist in her own right and offered a record deal by an independent or major label.

When a publishing company's A&R staff finds a songwriter who they feel could also be a successful performing artist, the company may make the strategic move of entering into a development deal with the songwriter. There are many contractual issues to be considered, but the primary goal is for the publisher to get the writer/artist signed to a label in the time specified in the contract. The strategic thinking on the publisher's side is that it would then be in a position to benefit from *two* royalty streams from its writer: revenue from exploiting the underlying compositions in any of the ways described earlier in the chapter *plus* royalty points from sales of the album or singles. (These royalty points will be part of the writer/artist's recording contract.) Even though recorded music sales have declined significantly over the past decade, people all over the world still purchase music. And the publisher would receive a percentage (points) of each sale under the terms of a development agreement.

In any contract, and particularly in a development deal, the writer and her attorney will attempt to push for specific, measurable, and quantifiable terms. These could include:

- duration of the contract;
- the type and size of the label to which the artist wants to be signed;
- a guarantee of a specific dollar amount of support from the publisher to make professional, studio-quality demos (or even full albums in some cases);
- a set timeframe in which the recording session of the demo will take place;
- advances to the writer/artist and clear language as to what financial assistance from the publisher is recoupable from future writer/artist earnings;
- funds for purchasing equipment that will help the writer/artist compose and record a great demo.

The publisher will want similar reassurances that the artist/writer will fulfill her part of the bargain, and could include in the contract:

- the specific number, nature, and quality of songs to be written and recorded in the contract period;

- the ownership of copyright to all songs produced during the contract;

- the right to negotiate and commit the artist/writer to a record deal;

- the percentage split of all monies from the recording deal;

- options for ending or extending the development deal;

- the option to convert the development deal into another type of songwriter/publisher contract, such as a co-publishing agreement.

We've only touched on the most salient points to be discussed and agreed upon in a negotiation between a writer and a publishing company. As you can see, contracts are complex, requiring comprehensive review and discussion with qualified legal counsel. Contracts may require many weeks or even months to come to closure. If both parties are confident that they want to work together, they may sign a deal memo before the contract is fully drawn up.

The *deal memo* is much shorter than a full contract. It outlines the most important points that have been agreed upon and allows the parties to get to work while the legal teams from both sides complete the negotiations and prepare the full contract for review and signature. After signing a deal memo, the writer may be able to receive advances that allow her to focus on writing songs and recording demos. The publishing company can begin to work on organizing a strategy for promoting and exploiting the writer's compositions.

> *Opportunities Ahead*
>
> Notice how many licenses require negotiations to determine a fee. Experienced publishers are skilled negotiators. How could an artist who is self-publishing learn how to negotiate effectively?

CONCLUSION

Music publishers play a major role in discovering and nurturing new songwriters. Publishers earn money for their writers and their company by placing songs in film and video, TV, record labels, advertising, games, internet applications, greeting cards, mobile phone applications, and all types of interactive entertainment. Publishers also have the infrastructure to take care of the legal and accounting paperwork associated with licensing songs and paying their songwriters.

There are plusses and minuses for songwriters who self-publish. It may be relatively simple and inexpensive for an artist-entrepreneur to become a DIWO music publisher, but the downside is that she will have to do most of the tasks herself. Anyone working in music publishing must understand complex music copyright laws, have a wide network of contacts in many areas of the music and entertainment industry, and know how to market, sell, and keep careful accounting and licensing records.

No matter which direction a songwriter chooses to go—sign with a publisher or become one—she'll need legal advice. Publishing contracts are complex and require expert analysis by legal counsel who specialize in the music industry. Legal advice when starting a publishing company or signing a contract is invaluable, and helps avoid costly errors and future legal problems.

Talking Back: Class Discussion

Most young writers would jump at the chance to be signed by a reputable music publisher. How can a writer perform her due diligence (deep research) on a potential publisher?

NOTES

1 James Crompton, "Music Publishing in the US," IBIS World Industry Report 51223, December 2014.
2 Ibid.
3 Kathleen Ripley, "Music Publishing in the US," IBIS World Industry Report 51223, July 2011.
4 Conversation with Heather Trussell, Vice President, Memory Lane Music Group, February 13, 2012.
5 Crompton, "Music Publishing."
6 Home, ICMP, http://icmp-ciem.org (accessed May 19, 2016).
7 Crompton, "Music Publishing in the US."
8 Ibid.
9 Eliot van Buskirk, "SoundCloud Threatens MySpace as Music Destination for Twitter Era," *Wired*, July 6, 2009, www.wired.com/epicenter/2009/07/soundcloud-threatens-myspace-as-music-destination-for-twitter-era/ (accessed May 19, 2016).
10 Ibid.
11 Crompton, "Music Publishing."
12 Tom Service, "A Guide to Steve Reich's Music," *The Guardian*, October 22, 2012, www.theguardian.com/music/tomserviceblog/2012/oct/22/steve-reich-contemporary-music-guide (accessed May 19, 2016).
13 Tom Service, "Steve Reich's Clapping Music App: In Pursuit of Rhythmic Perfection," *The Guardian*, July 13, 2015, www.theguardian.com/music/tomserviceblog/2015/jul/13/clapping-music-app-steve-reich-touch press-london-sinfonietta (accessed May 19, 2016).
14 Spencer Little, " Music Publishing in Australia," IBIS World Industry Report J5521, April 2015.
15 "Is Sampling Always Copyright Infringement?" *WIPO Magazine*, www.wipo.int/wipo_magazine/en/2009/06/article_0007.html (accessed May 19, 2016).
16 Home, *IMSLP Petrucci Music Library*, www.imslp.org (accessed May 19, 2016).
17 Naomi Lewin with WQXR Host Brian Wise, "Sheet Music: In with the Tablet, Out with the Page?" *WQXR Radio*, March 11, 2015, www.wqxr.org/#!/story/sheet-music-tablet-page (accessed May 19, 2016).
18 Ibid.
19 Ben Sisario, "Going to the Ends of the Earth to Get the Most Out of Music," *New York Times*, June 8, 2015.
20 Ibid.
21 Ibid.
22 "Roster-Featured," *Kobalt Music*, www.kobaltmusic.com/page-roster-featured.php (accessed May 19, 2016).
23 Ibid.
24 Richard Smirke, "Exclusive Q&A: Kobalt's Willard Ahdritz Is Demanding a Better Music Industry," *Billboard*, April 29, 2015, www.billboard.com/articles/business/6546323/kobalt-willard-ahdritz-interview (accessed May 19, 2016).
25 Sisario, "Going to the Ends of the Earth."
26 Smirke, "Exclusive Q&A."
27 Ibid.

28 Richard Smirke, "Kobalt Secures $60 Million Funding Round, Led by Google, to Scale Up Operations," *Billboard*, February 27, 2015, www.billboard.com/articles/business/6487355/kobalt-60-million-funding (accessed May 19, 2016).

29 Sisario, "Going to the Ends of the Earth."

30 Ibid.

31 Ibid.

32 Ibid.

33 Ibid.

34 Ibid.

35 Ibid.

36 "The Academy," *Red Bull Music Academy*, www.redbullmusicacademy.com (accessed May 19, 2016).

37 "Products," *Red Bull Media House*, www.redbullmediahouse.com/products/music/red-bull-music-publishing. html#c191 (accessed May 19, 2016).

38 Ibid.

39 Andrew Johnson, "Sound Recording & Music Publishing in the UK," IBISWorld Industry Report J59.200, December 2014.

40 Ibid.

41 Ibid.

42 Crompton, "Music Publishing."

43 "Video Games: Key Insights at a Glance," *PwC Network*, www.pwc.com/gx/en/global-entertainment-media-outlook/assets/2015/video-games-key-insights-4-social-gaming.pdf (accessed May 19, 2016).

44 Kaitlyn Raterman, "Music Royalties 101: What They Are and How to Collect," *SonicBids*, August 27, 2014, http://blog.sonicbids.com/music-royalties-101-what-they-are-and-how-to-collect (accessed May 19, 2016).

45 "Understanding Mechanical Royalties," *BMI*, www.bmi.com/news/entry/Understanding_Mechanical_ Royalties (accessed May 19, 2016).

46 Ibid.

47 Ibid.

48 Ibid.

49 "Neighboring Rights," *Symphonic Distribution*, www.symphonicdistribution.com/neighboring-rights/ (accessed May 19, 2016).

50 Ibid.

51 Keatly Haldeman, "Five Ways to Collect More International Royalties," *Royalty Insider*, www.royaltyinsider. com/collect-international-royalties-improve-royalty-collection (accessed May 19, 2016).

52 Ibid.

53 Ibid.

54 Ibid.

55 Hiroko Tabuchi, "With Sales Plummeting, Nintendo Pares Outlook and Cuts a Retail Price," *New York Times*, July 29, 2011.

56 The American Society Of Composers, Authors And Publishers (ASCAP), "Licensing Songs for Video Games," www.ascap.com/music-career/articles-advice/ascapcorner/corner16.aspx (accessed May 19, 2016).

57 "Campbell v. Acuff-Rose Music, Inc., 510 US 569 - Supreme Court 1994," scholar.google.com/scholar_case? case=16686162998040575773&q=Campbell+v.+Acuff-Rose+Music,+510+US+569+ percent281994&hl=en& as_sdt=2,39&as_vis=1 (accessed May 19, 2016).

58 "Fisher v. Dees 794 F.2d 432 (9th Cir. 1986), *Music Copyright Infringement Resource*, http://mcir.usc.edu/ cases/1980-1989/Pages/fisherdees.html (accessed May 19, 2016).

59 Conversation with Heather Trussell.

60 Ibid.

CHAPTER 8

Revenue Streams: Broadcasting and Digital Media

CHAPTER OVERVIEW

Digital media and broadcasting offer many revenue-producing opportunities for artist- and music business-entrepreneurs. Mastering the user experience is the main focus for entrepreneurs in digital media and broadcasting, where dramatic changes have occurred in a relatively short span of time. Television now has serious competition from Google and other online content providers. The advertising industry is seeing revenues migrate from traditional broadcasting to online broadcasting. Podcasting may be the future of radio. We spotlight two indie filmmakers whose story has lessons for music entrepreneurs. The chapter concludes with advice for DIWO (Do It With Others) musicians who want to get music synched with film, video, video games, and commercials.

KEY TERMS

OTT	Public broadcasting
Convergence	Programmatic buying
Interactive webcasts	ISP
Geo-Fencing	Network neutrality
Podcasting	Music supervisor
Long-form radio journalism	Library music
Curated	

MASTERING THE USER EXPERIENCE

It has become abundantly clear over the past technology-driven decade that the entertainment industry is struggling to keep pace with consumer preferences and expectations. We have learned—sometimes quite painfully—that in the eyes of our customers, there is no meaningful difference between digital and traditional media. Consumers see their world as fluid and multi-faceted, where digital offerings are delivered across platforms to create a robust content universe.[1]

As the industry thrashes about trying to figure out how to monetize its intellectual property, the message from consumers can be heard loudly and clearly: we will consume content when, where and how we choose to, and we want it delivered with an intuitive interface that can be personalized and accessed across devices. We can be certain that customers will seek out those offerings that combine an outstanding user experience with on-demand content, and is available on mobile devices.[2]

For artist- and music business-entrepreneurs, what matters now is the ability to combine content with a user experience that is differentiated and compelling on the consumer's platform of choice.

The industry is entering an age of "contextual awareness" as a result of unrestricted access to copious amounts of consumer data, including location and behavioral information. The traditional boundary between advertising and content has blurred. Audience metrics can accurately measure depth of engagement. The rise of over-the-top[3] (OTT) entertainment and media offerings further expand consumer choice.[4]

Put simply, entrepreneurial opportunity awaits those who embrace the fact that mastering the user experience is critical to success and to sustaining future growth in the entertainment and media marketplace.[5]

CONVERGENCE: THE MEDIA BUZZWORD

Our digital life has been emancipated from devices and moved into the cloud. Remote storage has changed the way entertainment products are delivered and consumed, freeing up space on personal gadgets so we can stream music and video without worrying if we'll have enough capacity.

The convergence of media services has blurred the distinction between them, giving customers multiple entry points to information, entertainment, music, lifestyle, news, and social sharing.

Almost every day, another new and exciting tech gadget or service hits the market. The breathtaking pace of newer, faster, sleeker devices, game-changing technologies, and the fleeting popularity of digital media startups only add to the chaos.

Traditional media may still control a lot of the money, but today true innovation is occurring in the digital media space. A roiling mash-up of creativity, culture, and technology is driving this area, and music plays an important role in this. Creating content for cross-platform media is a large global industry and a huge opportunity for entrepreneurs.

The Economics of Digital Music

The public's transition to digital music services represents the ongoing move from music ownership to music access. The economic impact is significant. *Purchases* (ownership) return a small but noticeable chunk of money. *Streams* (access) result in much less money, with revenues measured in parts of pennies.

Billboard's Glenn Peoples sums up the new economics of the digital music era this way: "We're increasingly living in a streaming world but we want download royalties. When the download market was growing, people wanted to return to the boom years of the CD. But in ten years, streaming revenues will be the norm. Just as today's young musicians grew up without CD revenues, musicians of the future will know little else than streaming royalty rates."[6]

The lesson here? Music professionals make more money selling their music than streaming it, but fans often choose streaming over ownership.

Advertising dollars account for roughly 90 percent of the budgets of streaming radio, podcasts, and portable music players. Digital media are competing with traditional broadcasters for advertisers, whose fortunes are tied to the general health of the economy and fluctuate accordingly. Satellite radio companies have dual revenue streams of subscription fees and advertising on non-music channels.[7]

In its traditional format, radio stations attract advertisers by playing music that appeals to the specific segments of the population the advertisers are trying to reach. Radio personalities, including well-known DJs, and the level of interaction with listeners also play a large role in keeping people tuned in to a specific station over time.[8]

Interactive "on demand" webcasts allow listeners to choose the actual songs they hear and require a negotiated license agreement with the rights holders. Webcasts that don't allow individual song choice are known as non-interactive or passive listening experiences.

Pressure is growing on music subscription services to limit free access to music. Global digital music streaming revenue grew by 31.2 percent in 2014. Despite the fact that music subscription service leaders claim that free tiers are essential to pull in new users and give a taste of what subscription services offer, major record companies have started to question whether the amount of music available on advertising-supported tiers is too high.[9]

Introducing more paid-for tiers to drive consumer spending on subscriptions could be a good middle ground between the two sides. Despite the increasing number of consumers taking up music subscription services, the range of paid-for tier options is currently limited. In a number of Northern European countries, streaming already accounts for the majority of spending on recorded music.[10]

Musical Selfies

"Musical selfies" is how classical pianist-turned-software-entrepreneur Robert Taub describes his new app, Hook'd. Unlike sing-along apps that play renditions of hit songs re-recorded by studio musicians (covers), Hook'd features original tracks straight from the record labels and BadAss Studio Effects—with the vocal track removed.[11]

Singers of any technical prowess can choose a song, record a video, enhance the vocals (if needed), and drop that Hook to a friend . . . or the world. Hook'd for Messenger enables users to message personalized, micro music video performances via the Facebook Messenger Platform.[12]

Are We Suffering from Digital Media Overload?

Some weeks it seems as if a new digital media service is launched every day. While it's exciting to be among the first to try out a new app or online product, the sheer volume of these

Social Media coming out of head wearing glasses
VLADGRIN/Shutterstock.com

businesses can be overwhelming. Has the digital music media sector reached a saturation point, with too many choices for the plugged-in? Is the relentless pressure to be active on the newest networks causing social media burnout?

As many as 95 percent of new products introduced each year fail, according to Cincinnati research agency AcuPoll. That's true even when these new products or services are rolled out by big, deep-pocketed companies and attached to well-known brands.[13]

Why do they fail? Some products are fussy or complicated to use. Many are too similar to others in the marketplace. Often it's bad timing of the new product launch, or the product doesn't live up to the marketing hype. Some new companies run out of money trying to compete with category leaders.

The Digital Media Hotness Rating Scale

Find a new digital entertainment product that has launched recently. Spend three minutes answering these eight questions to decide if the product has merit and utility:

1. Can you describe the business in ten words or fewer?
2. What need is it addressing, what problem is it solving, and for whom?
3. Who is the target customer?
4. What is innovative about the product and the user experience?
5. How will it make money?
6. What opportunities does it open up for partnerships with other companies, media, or markets?
7. Is mobile and/or video at the center of this new product?
8. Do you think it's going to become a must-have product or service? Why or why not?

Putting on the Digital Brakes

The downside of a 24-7-365 mindset is getting a good deal of attention from physicians and academics. Dr. Genevieve Bell is an Australian anthropologist consulting with the corporate tech giant Intel to anticipate consumer trends. She was assigned to figure out what the "other" wanted in terms of the digital landscape— "other" being everyone non-American. Bell's research revealed that leading corporate thinkers are worried about the negative effect on creativity caused by always-on cell phones and long hours at the office.[14]

In Europe, the issue of tech distraction has caught the attention of the highest levels of government. French labor unions and corporate officials have reached an agreement that obliges workers to "disconnect from remote communications tools" for 11 consecutive hours each day. Companies can decide which window of time to shut down email servers.[15] For example, Volkswagen shuts down its server after hours, with a complete lock out from 5PM on Friday to Monday morning.[16] Every building on the General Mills campus in Minneapolis (US) contains a meditation room. And the US Army is teaching soldiers meditation techniques to cope with combat-related stress.[17]

Another aspect of our digital abundance is that it encourages multi-tasking, which can negatively affect the quality and efficiency of cognitive work. There is peer and work pressure to stay connected 24-7, contributing to a nagging feeling that we may be sacrificing wellbeing for constant access. Researchers at Bowling Green State University (US) have found that the inability to distance oneself from work prevents the brain from recharging for the next day.[18] Most of us are tethered to technology more than we'd care to admit. The tech gadgets we may be "addicted to" make it hard to find a healthy balance between the real and virtual worlds.[19]

Radio

Broadcast radio has been a powerful music partner for decades. Major labels still use it to great effect to break artists and promote new releases. Many people in the industry believe that success on radio is necessary for an artist to achieve global recognition.

Traditionally, listeners selected a terrestrial radio station whose music they liked and whose broadcast strength allowed them to hear it clearly. If they moved too far out of the station's signal, they would lose it. DJs or station managers chose the music. Advertisers used jingles to sell their products and services to anyone who tuned into that station. Since advertising paid the bills, stations worked hard to keep listeners from changing to another station. "Don't touch that dial!" became the DJ's mantra.

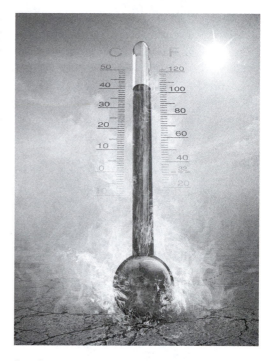

hot day

adlike/Shutterstock.com

iRadioPhilly

The 21st century version of old-fashioned radio can be found at iRadioPhilly in Philadelphia (US). iRadioPhilly is a local streaming web radio service with 23 curated music stations playing around the clock. DJs go out into the community to webcast local concerts and shows, and name their stations after some of Philadelphia's iconic music institutions (such as American Bandstand). The free service is similar in style to satellite-delivered Sirius XM subscription radio.[20]

iRadio Philly turned a profit after only four years of operation. Besides the web, it is available on smartphone menus and streaming audio players from Sonos and Bose. The Philadelphia team owns the iRadio domain name in New York, San Francisco, Los Angeles, and other cities.[21]

Wildfire Radio, a streaming internet radio service operating in Collingswood, New Jersey, "is solvent, [we] pay all our licensing fees, and still generate revenue," says Wildfire's owner Marcus Darpino. Revenue sources include ads, studio rental, and network subleasing, a term meaning that it builds and runs stations for other entities which provide their own content.[22]

In some ways web radio is ahead of the curve. Both iRadio Philly and Wildfile Radio can laser-focus ads to specific listeners using a tool called "Geo-Fencing." Ad loads are no more than four 30-second spots per hour, compared to 16 minutes on some commercial stations.[23]

Pandora

Pandora is a dominant player in internet radio, with more than 81 million people streaming about 1.7 billion hours of music every month. In January 2015, Pandora delivered more audio to mobile devices in the US than YouTube did video, according to comScore. But Pandora and the music industry have a rocky relationship due to its attempt to reduce the royalties it must pay for using copyright protected music. It is trying to stay competitive with the giant US terrestrial radio broadcasters that, unlike webcasters, do not have to pay record companies or performing artists for music they use.[24]

Podcast icon

ValentinT/Shutterstock.com

Podcasting

Podcasting is finally having a moment. Podcasting—delivering radio-like programs directly to a cell phone or computer—has been around for more than 15 years. Depending on who you ask, podcasting is either the new savior of the radio industry or an intriguing but ultimately doomed technology experiment.[25]

Podcasting owes its current "media darling" status to a true-crime investigation show, called "Serial," from the National Public Radio (US) network. "Serial" caught the attention of listeners and mainstream media in a big way.

Perhaps radio's awkward little cousin is simply one of those rare digital media that grows slowly and steadily. Edison Research reports only a 3 percent increase in the number of Americans who have listened to podcasts between 2013 and 2015.[26]

Yet some of the largest podcasting companies have loyal listeners and solid advertising revenue. An example is Gimlet Media. Founded by entrepreneurs Alex Blumberg and Matthew Lieber, the Brooklyn, NY-based start-up raised nearly US$1.5 million, employs 18 people, and broadcasts three podcasts, called narratives. Audio critics praise the Gimlet podcasts for their professional sound quality and production-heavy journalism.[27]

Podcasters and advertisers are encouraged by the slow but steady growth in listenership, but agree there is still much to be worked out, such as creating standards for podcast audience measurement. The Interactive Advertising Bureau (IAB) hosted its first podcasting upfronts in New York City in the fall of 2015. An upfront is an opportunity for advertising executives to get a private advance look at new content developments in order to plan their media buys. NPR and WNYC participated at the upfronts, along with Panoply, Podtrac, AdLarge, and Midroll—all companies that aggregate podcast ad space for multiple media outlets.[28]

Podcast Entrepreneurs in Israel

On a 13,000-mile road trip around the US a few years ago, Mishy Harman got hooked on podcasts of "This American Life," the wildly popular, 60-minute public radio show created by Ira Glass, known for its homespun stories and fact-finding reporting.[29]

Midway through his cross-country trip, Harman decided he had to replicate the show in Israel, his home country. He talked three of his childhood friends into contributing money for equipment. Eager to get started, the men were undaunted by the fact that none had any experience whatsoever in creating a radio program. "We had no idea what we were doing," Harman said. "But there was a feeling that this was something we could teach ourselves."[30]

Long-Form Radio Journalism

Harman contacted "This American Life" producer Nancy Updike for advice, who introduced the men to Ira Glass, the public radio master of long-form journalism. Glass gave the team the OK to replicate his show's style and format after they met in New York for a crash course on how to make a radio documentary.[31]

Back home in Israel, Harman and his friends created and launched their show in a trial run of four episodes. Buoyed by the attention and positive reviews of the show, with more than 200,000 listeners for each episode, the show received the green light to create a full season. After five years, "Israel Story," the name of Harman's Hebrew-language radio documentary, has now spun off an English-language online version on the weekly podcast of the Jewish news magazine *Tablet*.[32]

Harman and his co-founders turned their broadcasting inexperience into an opportunity to challenge the status quo. "Israeli media is owned almost exclusively by graduates of [the popular army radio station] Galei Zahal, and they have a set format to how they do their storytelling," Harman said. "We're this tiny country, but there's a space for another kind of Israeli news, news that isn't the regular kind."[33]

Public Radio

Like other traditional media, public broadcasters struggle to find stable funding and loyal listeners. Yet public broadcasting's image as a stodgy public service vehicle created by governments to inform and educate the people is hindering its efforts at attracting younger listeners and advertisers.[34] The Mapping Digital Media research, coordinated by the Program on Independent Journalism of the Open Society Foundations, found that share and reach of state and public service broadcasters fell in most of the 56 countries it studied between 2005 and 2010.[35]

Some public service national broadcasters, such as the UK's BBC, are revered for the quality of their productions and the impartiality of their reporting. Research cited in a 2012 report by the British Academy showed that exposure to BBC news increased political knowledge among all sections of the population, even those with low levels of interest in politics. Other well-run, trusted public service broadcasters can be found in Canada, Japan, the US, and Sweden.[36]

In the US, National Public Radio (NPR) is struggling to erase a multimillion-dollar deficit while expanding its digital presence across multiple platforms. NPR's "One" app became the first news provider on iTunes. Podcasts are a big area for growth at NPR in both listenership and revenue. Even so, the network's listening audience for its well-known NPR-branded programs and newscasts fell by nearly 4 percent in 2014.[37]

Cross-Border Circulation of European Music Repertoire in the EU

The European Music Office, with the Dutch conference and festival Eurosonic Noordeslag, released the results of a 2012 study that monitored the cross-border movement of European music repertoire within the EU. The survey participants represented a sample of large and small countries from different parts of the EU. The participants were France, Germany, the Netherlands, Poland, Spain, and Sweden.[38]

The following are excerpts from the major points of the study:

- Europe may be a single *market* for English-language repertoire, but Europe as a single music scene does not exist.

- Europeans remain strongly attached to their own national musical cultures.

- There is a solid local market for domestic artists who sing in the language of their country. However, these artists' opportunities will likely be limited to their own country, regardless of the musical genre.

For cultural, historical, and sociological reasons, Europeans do not embrace their neighbors' cultures when they are expressed in their national languages. This factor directly impacts the tendency of radio broadcasters to favor an Anglo-American repertoire, especially the US music that arrives in Europe with impressive, already-tested marketing and creative clout. As a result, Europe as a music market is a one-language region (English) plus local languages.[39]

The survey demonstrated that the only real pan-European successes are imports from the US, with the relatively recent exception of Adele. The airplay charts for the period covered by the survey (2010–11) were dominated by Jennifer Lopez, Rihanna, Bruno Mars, Lady GaGa, and the Black Eyed Peas, among others. These are the only artists whose songs crossed European borders.[40]

Adele is one of the rare examples of a European artist who appeals to all European audiences. The survey showed that fellow Brits Taio Cruz and Tinie Tempah were building a pan-European following. French superstar DJ David Guetta is now in the same league as US artists, with global releases and sales in the millions.[41]

But for most European artists, even the ones singing in English, building a pan-European career is often a one-market-at-a-time effort. A few examples include Caro Emerald, whose popularity expanded beyond the Netherlands to neighboring countries and eventually the UK. Belgium's Selah Sue has used France as the launchpad for her international career after winning the European Border Breakers Award (EBBA) in 2012 for Belgium. In France, ZaZ and Ben L'Oncle Soul, also past winners of the EBBA, have become two of the hottest Gallic exports despite the fact that both sing in French.[42]

The study revealed that the UK provides the overwhelming majority of artists crossing EU borders. In general, the UK is the biggest supplier of acts and covers music genres from mainstream pop to R&B, alternative, and E.D.M. Poland has the highest diversity of countries represented on radio, with 25 different countries supplying repertoire. Sweden achieved pan-European success with Swedish House Mafia, Tim Berg and Mohombi. The Netherlands has DJs Tiesto and Armin Van Buuren, as well as metal band Within Temptation, who continue to have success throughout Europe.

The survey concluded that what unites Emerald, Sue, ZaZ, and L'Oncle Soul is not that they had instant hit singles, but rather that they built up their popularity from the buzz around them, reaching out directly to their audiences through live appearances as often as possible. Radio stations may be the gateway to the European mass market, but live music and the new digital media services are the key to reaching new audiences.[43]

Pause and Reflect

Theoretically, web radio has limitless capacity and reach. With the possibility of having millions of stations broadcasting worldwide, each radio station has the potential to reach billions of people. Imagine what you could accomplish with a strong brand and compelling content for a worldwide audience.[44]

Curated Playlists

"Playlists are the new radio," declares Jay Frank, an independent record company executive and consultant with analytics firm DigMark. Digital music services are proliferating and, in order to provide unique value to their listeners, are featuring the individualistic, curated playlists created by their DJs. The thinking goes that if you like the personality of the DJ, you will tune in and stay on her "station," a key goal of traditional radio.[45]

"Into the unknown we go," said DJ Zane Lowe in June 2015 as he launched Beats 1, Apple Music's live internet radio station. Lowe is full of personality. Sporting a charming New Zealand accent, he had been a top announcer on the BBC station Radio 1. His DJ style includes many of the cozy features of traditional radio, including promotional recordings, hints about upcoming new songs, and reminders to "tune in the next day" for an unnamed "something special." However, his eclectic playlist shows the distinctly different approach to music between internet and commercial radio. Traditional radio aims for the middle of the road, whereas Lowe and his internet radio colleagues are free to take risks by playing obscure songs and unknown artists in order to reveal their unique taste in music.[46]

Fail Quickly So You Can Fail Often

Digital radio is a crowded and risky marketplace for entrepreneurs because of the challenge in agreeing on licensing rates from the music rights owners. New ventures can encounter "performance issues," known as music licensing regulations, whose requirements and costs vary considerably. This has contributed to the demise of some online music services. Here's how Evolver.fm sums up the licensing challenges for start-ups using music:

> For . . . music technologies, the usual progression goes something like this:
>
> Big splash ▶ Performance issues ▶ Get sued ▶ Go under/get bought ▶Be lame[47]

That prediction describes the fate of Turntable.fm, a DJ service which made its big splash in the summer of 2011 and went under in March 2014.

When Turntable.fm launched in 2011, adding 140,000 users in its first month, investors were waiting in line to give entrepreneur Billy Chasen their money. "It was exciting, and odd, and a little scary," he recalls. Barely two years and millions of songs later, Chasen closed down operations, bringing an end to "one of the most compelling experiments in music discovery in web history."[48]

Chasen says trying to play by the rules contributed to the demise of Turntable.fm. "We wanted to do it all the right way, nothing shady, always working with the labels." Legally he had to pay a royalty every time a song was streamed, whereas some services dabble in the legally gray area of piggybacking on copyrighted music hosted by sites like YouTube or SoundCloud that might have been uploaded illegally. He didn't have licensing deals in certain international territories, which meant Turntable.fm couldn't legally operate there, significantly curtailing its growth. With all these challenges, Chasen tried transitioning Turntable.fm from a DJ service to a live-performance experience, but ended up shutting down the service three months later.[49]

Some point to the Turntable.fm tale as an example of how the music industry's current system of licensing and royalty fees is crippling American startups. Companies like Rhapsody have struggled, Spotify has raised millions but still can't turn a profit, and Pandora has had to raise prices for all its subscription customers.[50]

TELEVISION

Global TV and video consumption patterns are changing. All traditional television institutions are grappling with the challenge of new modes of viewing. To satisfy the growing social habit of "binge viewing," consumers want high-quality original programming delivered on-demand across many different devices. OTT services offer the best way to satisfy this consumer desire.[51] Younger viewers move easily among a variety of platforms such as smartphone apps, YouTube windows, cable boxes, bootleg streaming portals, Netflix accounts, and Amazon interfaces.[52]

Nielsen, the international firm that measures viewership, has been criticized for not having an appropriate way to measure the number of viewers who are watching a show on a platform other than traditional broadcast. The industry has yet to adopt a measurement standard for multi-platform viewing, which is critical because viewership is closely tied to how much stations can charge for ads during their programming day. And that leads to the big question of how to price ads on the various platforms. Erik Flannigan, a Viacom executive, feels that a viewer who watches a show via a digital stream will be more engaged with the program (and its ads). "Millions turn on 'The Today Show' out of pure habit and let it play for three hours in the background," he says. "Are they watching every ad? Are they engaged? No . . . passive viewing isn't [what] most young people . . . do anymore—they have a queue of shows they want to watch."[53]

Public Television

The economic crisis in Europe has created financial hardships for many public TV broadcasters, who have seen their budgets slashed due to a weak advertising market and reduced levels of funding from their national governments.[54]

Growing numbers of public service broadcasters outside the EU are experiencing political obstruction and intrusion as well as financial, technical, and political challenges. In 2009 the European Broadcasting Union (EBU) launched a Special Assistance Project to provide case-by-case support to its members in need. So far, broadcasters in Albania, Bulgaria, Croatia, Georgia, Hungary, Kosovo, Macedonia, Malta, Moldova, Montenegro, and Romania have received assistance.[55]

According to the EBU, there are some general trends in the television market affecting both public service and commercial broadcasters, including:

- growing consumption and multi-platform distribution of on-demand TV content/services;

- growing consumption and availability of HDTV content/services;

- growing penetration of internet-enabled TV sets and the continued development and launch of hybrid broadband broadcast platforms;

- rapidly increasing consumption of TV content on mobile devices such as laptops, tablets, and smartphones;

- continued convergence between television and the internet, with greater focus on socialization and personalization.[56]

Upending the TV Business

Netflix and other streaming services have upended the economics of the TV business. There is a pronounced decline in watching television with ads in favor of streaming services like Netflix that do not have ads.[57] As a result, TV advertising growth has slowed across the industry. In 2015 traditional television's share of the total ad market fell for the first time. Netflix plays a dual role in the industry: it is both a formidable competitor in terms of capturing viewership and a valuable partner to the TV industry. Even though it does not compete with traditional television for advertising dollars, it does provide a valuable new revenue source for licensing content from traditional TV.[58]

Amazon is another streaming service that is both a partner and competitor in the TV business. With its original series, *Mozart in the Jungle*, Amazon gave viewers a look into the inner workings of a fictitious major New York symphony. The program used humor to show the real pressures on orchestra administrators to raise money and maintain artistic standards while adapting their institutions for the future.[59]

Mozart in the Jungle

Brian Ach/Getty Images Entertainment

Is This Market Oversaturated?

Music-based television shows dominated the ratings on US television for more than a decade. It is rumored that *American Idol*, one of the most popular shows of all time, generated close to US$3 billion in profit for its network over its 13-year history.[60] But recent ratings have fallen so steeply that many wonder if audiences are weary of the format.

"They flooded the market," said Simon Cowell, the British entrepreneur who is an expert in turning amateur singers into superstars with shows like *American Idol*, *The X Factor*, and *America's Got Talent*. "Something has simply gone awry."[61]

Cowell said the business model for music-based TV shows changed its focus from finding hit singers to getting top ratings. He said he only got into television as a way to find performers who would sell records and concert tickets for his label.[62] "Who does better? The 'Voice' judges or the 'Voice' contestants?" he asked. "It's quite obvious the judges have sold a ton more records."[63]

Tyanna Jones, American Idol

Stephen J. Cohen/Getty Images Entertainment

International Content Distribution

Television content, once a product of the traditional top-down broadcasting model, with its rigidly scheduled programming for passive consumption, is being transformed. Responding to consumer demand, there are now opportunities for viewers to become involved in the content itself through posting online, Tweeting, and reacting to content on other digital platforms. This has had a significant effect on the international distribution of television-type content, which is expected to continue its shift toward an interactive, experiential, and on-demand audiovisual environment.[64]

In linear television, as the traditional format is known, international distribution has taken place in a predictable fashion. Companies called distributors have content to license, either original or from other sources. Buyers need licensed content to fill their schedules and product lines. In addition to traditional broadcasters, buyers also include cable and satellite networks, DVD companies, product licensees, and now online players such as iTunes and Netflix.[65]

During the 1980s and 1990s, a combination of deregulation and satellite television created a massive global expansion of television channels. Taking advantage of this opportunity, some countries (primarily the US) made internationally attractive television content that sold well. For those with the right content, it was a lucrative business.[66]

Now, in the 2000s, the television market is undergoing a radical change due to the creation of new digital channels and internet on-demand services. The latest development is OTT video delivery directly to television sets via the internet. Once again, the major players are US companies, including Apple, Netflix, Google, and Amazon.[67]

Pause and Reflect

There are hints that linear TV will disappear in the face of multiple multimedia platforms and that on-demand content might eventually replace scheduled programming. Do you agree or disagree with this forecast, and why?

Small Screen Is Big Player at Sundance

The independent film world is trying to come to terms with the recent inroads made by television as a creative and financial force. In the last few years television has usurped some of the indie film world's prestige. Analysts estimate that digital and video-on-demand services are replacing art houses as the primary outlet for more than 90 percent of independent films. As if to publicly reveal its struggle to accept this innovative and energetic art form, some Sundance festival staff refer to it as "episodic storytelling," not "television."[68]

"Now the dream is to write and direct an indie film, get into Sundance and then use that to become a big-time TV series creator, like Lena Dunham, or a show runner or a TV director," said Reed Martin, author of *The Reel Truth*, a guide to making an independent film. "TV is where all the money is, and where a lot of the creative risk-taking is celebrated these days."[69]

ADVERTISING

Advertising is the economic engine of broadcasting. Both traditional and digital broadcasting receive approximately 90 percent of their revenue from advertising. Advertisers want viewers to watch or listen to their ads, and broadcasters want to offer free (or "feels like free") programming to meet customers' demands.[70]

In their quest to find new ways to reach consumers, who are constantly bombarded by content on multiple devices, advertising campaigns have moved heavily into multiple media platforms. Advertisers now demand tools to measure audience behavior in digital ads in order to determine the effectiveness of an ad campaign.[71]

"Programmatic buying"—digital advertising technologies that rely on data and algorithms to buy and sell ads—is affecting how advertisers allocate their money. Companies are able to look at data in real time and make decisions about ad spends, thanks to the enormous amounts of digital data available. Programmatic digital spending is predicted to nearly triple worldwide by 2018, according to a study from Magna Global, the research and ad-buying unit of the Interpublic Group.[72]

The sheer penetration of traditional television still has enormous appeal to advertisers. Television dominates the US market, which received US$68.5 billion of ad spending last year. But the amount advertisers will spend on digital video ads in the US is forecast to grow to US$12.8 billion by 2018, according to the research firm eMarketer.[73]

FILM AND VIDEO

The following interview between Fractured Atlas and filmmakers Brenna Sanchez and Tom Putnam is compelling for its candid tone and enthusiastic assessment of the independent film and video marketplace. Music entrepreneurs will find practical advice from these two

Egyptian man watching TV in café
© Ingetje Tadros/Getty Images

film entrepreneurs, as there is much overlapping of the issues in the industries.

Spotlight on . . . Entrepreneurs Tom Putnam and Brenna Sanchez of TBVE Films

Fractured Atlas is a nonprofit technology company that provides business tools for artists. Each year it awards arts entrepreneurs whose stories and ventures embody the spirit of entrepreneurship in the creative economy. Entrepreneurs Tom Putnam and Brenna Sanchez, veteran filmmakers based in Los Angeles (US), were honorees of the 2015 Arts Entrepreneurship Awards for the work they have done with their production company, TBVE Films, notably a documentary entitled *BURN*, which explores the themes of human struggles, hope, and personal courage in the face of overwhelming odds. In making the film, Putnam and Sanchez followed a group of Detroit firefighters for more than a year and captured the world, both emotionally and literally, of men who have the thankless task of saving a city many have written off as dead.

The following is excerpted from Fractured Atlas journalist Jason Tseng's February 2015 interview with Putnam and Sanchez.[74]

Tseng: How did you fund the film?

Putnam: *BURN* may be one of the largest films funded entirely by charitable donations—no investors. We raised $1.1M through fiscal sponsorships, corporate donations, in-kind donations, and Kickstarter. We define crowdfunding as a "portfolio," using all of these resources together . . . Many filmmakers approach crowdfunding by telling their potential audience what *they* need to complete their film. That seems backwards to us.

We crafted our messaging to what we thought our *audience* wanted—"Did you like that video we posted? Great! Donate now and we'll be able to give you more of it!" We mined our donor lists into [our] Mailchimp database, and create[d] segments from our donor lists, ticket sales, webstore sales, incoming communications, etc. We currently have about 38,000 email addresses in our database.[75]

Tom Putnam and Brenna Sanchez with film BURN

Scott Legato/Getty Images Entertainment

Tseng: How did you build a fanbase for your film?

Putnam and Sanchez: *BURN* exists because of social media. It's how we built our fan base, raised money for the film, and how we distributed the movie . . . Facebook has consistently been our strongest platform. At the end of the day, Facebook works if you post frequently and develop a strong voice and connection with your audience. "Hey guys" posts aren't going to cut it . . . You have to really work to know your audience. The more we post, the better we do. [But] the more you post about the same thing, the more fans you'll lose.[76]

Tseng: . . . you self-distributed your film. Can you talk about how you decided to take on all of that?

Putnam and Sanchez: . . . Because we were in the red, hadn't paid ourselves, and were committed to giving back significantly to our Detroit firefighters, we were very profit-minded. It is a business, after all. That level of desperation drove us to push harder than we knew was possible, and to turn down low-ball offers without losing any sleep. With no offers in hand, we were essentially forced to self-distribute BURN theatrically, as well as on DVD and Blu-Ray.[77]

Here are the lessons learned that Putnam and Sanchez share with artists and filmmakers:

- Plan ahead to self-distribute.

- Build strong partnerships.

- Give your audience a call to action.

- Follow the laws of supply and demand.

- If you're going to call your art your business, you'd better start making money from it.[78]

Pause and Reflect

What lessons did Putnam and Sanchez learn that you can benefit from in your creative endeavors? Describe the team's relationship with their fans, their sponsors, and the people they filmed in *BURN*. What can you take away from their experience and apply it to your work?

Global Internet Service Providers (ISPs)

Ibis World forecasts that the developed markets of Europe, North America, and North Asia will continue to dominate the global ISP industry. Due to the rapid growth of Chinese broadband subscribers, these markets account for more than 80 percent of global connections and roughly 82 percent of revenue in the ISP industry. Broadband penetration in the emerging markets of South America, Southeast Asia, India, and Central Asia has increased considerably over the past five years. Notably, the wired ISP market in many of these emerging regions is much less competitive than similar services offered by wireless providers. Revenue from internet subscriptions is forecast to increase at an annualized rate of 10.6 percent per year, to reach $782.6 billion in 2019.[79]

Over the next five years, as subscriptions to high-speed services expand, the industry will experience increased competition, which puts downward pressure on prices and profitability. This is good news for subscribers, but could be challenging for internet services. Ibis World anticipates that there will be more mergers and acquisitions in the industry in order to keep costs down and boost revenue. Additionally, the industry will see a push by major telecommunications services to become fully integrated (offering all forms of communication services including wired and wireless internet, telephony, and TV). This will enable companies to bundle services at a lower collective rate than offering each service individually, which appeals to subscribers from both a financial and convenience point of view.[80]

Access Technology

Ibis World forecasts that the predominant internet access technology is likely to change in the next five years to fiber internet services, which are more advanced services now available in Japan and South Korea. Fiber-to-the-home (FTTH) and fiber-to-the-node (FTTN) require public sector investment, as is occurring in Australia and the US. In time, FTTN will become widespread in most developed countries. As average network speeds increase, opportunities for new, previously unimagined businesses and services will develop.[81]

Mobile Coverage

In many emerging markets with low internet penetration, some wireless carriers are expected to skip over 3G and jump straight to fourth generation (4G) in the next few years, which will provide download rates in excess of 100 megabits per second. As a result, mobile operators will be in a good position to capture a greater proportion of available internet connections.[82]

Network Neutrality

Network neutrality is the principle that all content on the internet should be equally accessible to all users and that internet companies cannot discriminate or block one set of content in favor of another. The US recently joined Chile and the Netherlands in adopting legislation that requires all internet traffic to be treated equally by ISPs. Current EU rules allow ISPs to offer different services to different customer groups, but forbid discrimination in an anti-competitive manner. In Germany, T-Mobile has blocked voice-over-internet-protocol (VoIP) provider Skype. Spanish telecommunications carrier Telefonica will levy a fee on Google and other search engines for use of its network and will push its own content aggressively. Russian ISPs have long been shaping traffic by treating peer-to-peer protocols like BitTorrent and Skype as lower-priority traffic. In South Korea, VoIP is blocked on high-speed FTTH networks except where the network operator is the service provider.[83]

Content and Copyright

There is growing pressure from copyright authorities around the world for ISPs to regulate the activities of subscribers on their internet services. The central issue is whether or not, and in what circumstances, an ISP should bear legal liability for the infringing acts of subscribers and others who use their services. The music industry has been advocating for increased ISP content liability for more than a decade.[84]

Internet Privacy Issues and Opportunities

Entrepreneurs James Kinsella and Robert McNeal recently launched a cloud computing service, Zettabox, that will take on Google, Dropbox, Microsoft, and other established companies. The founders believe that the start-up's unique value proposition—storing people's data within Europe, where privacy laws are more stringent than those in the US—will be a big attraction for Europeans.

To compete with its much larger rivals, Zettabox, with 25 employees divided between London and Prague, is emphasizing its European roots and people's growing appetite for greater online privacy. It will also allow individuals and companies to retain information in data centers in specific European countries, so that they can comply with domestic rules that often restrict what type of data can be stored internationally.

"Europe needs a European service," Kinsella said. "Europeans have no say over where their data is held by American companies. We're offering an alternative to that."

TOOLS FOR THE DIWO (DO IT WITH OTHERS) ENTREPRENEUR: GET YOUR MUSIC PLACED BY MUSIC SUPERVISORS

One popular revenue stream for both artist-entrepreneurs and music business-entrepreneurs is licensing music for use on TV shows, films, video games, movie trailers, and commercials. Music supervisors are the people who find that music, pitch it to a producer or director, and then negotiate a synch license with the song's rights owner.

"For a placement to be effective, the vibe of the song has to fit perfectly with the action and emotion of the scene, and it has to be available within the project budget," says music supervisor Lindsay Wolfington, who places music for the shows *The Royals*, *Shadowhunters*, *The Night Shift*, and *The Bold and the Beautiful*. Wolfington explained that some video TV episodes may have only US$10,000 for the entire music budget. She pays US$1,000–3,000 for each placement in her current shows. Other projects can pay up to US$20,000 for a network TV spot and US$80,000 for a movie trailer placement.[85]

Wolfington spoke at a recent music supervisor pitching session hosted by the National Association of Record Industry Professionals (NARIP) and offered these suggestions for artist- and music business-entrepreneurs: "Find a licensing company or 'song plugger' who has good relationships with music supervisors and is excited about your music." She recommended a few third-party song-plugger/licensing companies, including Secret Road, All Media, Cellar Music, The Music Playground, Razor and Tie, Big Yellow Dog, and Words and Music.[86] "Pitch songs for which you own 200 percent of the song. That means you own 100 percent of the master and 100 percent of the publishing. Most music supervisors do not want to spend time to track down multiple owners of a song to get their permission for a license."[87]

The following are features of the type of email Wolfington prefers to receive from a pitch person: be polite and charming; don't be cocky; don't assume anything; don't pretend to know me when you don't. The best email to send goes like this:

Subject line: Sounds like (popular artist), for (TV show currently working on)

Body: I've been watching your show and I saw you do _____. My music sounds like _____ (this type of music and maybe these bands). I own 200 percent of these songs.

Then include links to box.com of the mp3s. [Wolfington prefers box.com because she can stream and/or download the song.][88]

"Only pitch music when you have something that works for a supervisor's current projects and never pitch a fee. The supervisor will come back with a fee range if she's interested in your song. Follow up no more often than every two months, but do not ask if she's listened to your song. If you're going to follow up, email new music in a new email. If a music supervisor doesn't use your song or reply to you, it may only mean that it doesn't work for the projects she is currently working on."[89]

"Most music supervisors rely on the metadata that you've imbedded in your music. When they add songs to folders, they don't add in contact info. So when they're going through their folders and find a song to use, they need to know whom to contact. Some music supervisors no longer accept unsolicited music. If that's the case, try to become acquainted with the supervisor's assistant or coordinator. They will most likely become a supervisor themselves one day and it's good to have that relationship."[90]

A word of caution: A music licensing company is not the same thing as a pre-cleared music library. Wolfington recommended that songwriters find a licensing company with song-pluggers who will be energetic in pitching your music to people like her. On the other hand, music library companies collect music from thousands of indie artists, set a standard (low) rate for its use, and pre-license it so that indie filmmakers can get inexpensive music with a few keyboard strokes. Music library companies organize their songs with mood-describing tags such as moody, anthemic, and agitated. While these companies offer a valuable service, be cautious about getting branded as a "library artist" as opposed to one who writes original music.[91]

Opportunities Ahead—Thinking Like an Entrepreneur

Think back to the music industry problems you identified in Chapter 2. Combine two or three in a sort of "opportunity mash-up" exercise. Use your creative problem-solving skills to imagine a single digital media solution to the combined problems. Answer the following questions about your new venture concept:

- Who are your customers?
- What problem(s) are your solving for them with your new venture?
- Do you think they'll be willing to pay for your service or product?
- If not, how will you make money?
- How can you give your venture a brand identity to distinguish it from the competition?
- Rate your venture on the Digital Media Hotness scale. What are your chances of making it to your second year?

CONCLUSION

Cloud storage, advances in digital technology, and communications convergence have encouraged an outpouring of entrepreneurial products and services in the music industry. These new media entrepreneurs are challenging the traditional ways in which we discover, enjoy, and share music today. Have we reached the social media saturation point or is this the landscape of the future?

 Talking Back: Class Discussion

Choose an area—radio, television, film, video, advertising—and identify two or three features that you believe will still be around ten years from now. Then look at all the remaining features. If you were an entrepreneur in that area, how would you pivot (adjust) your business model to thrive in the next 12 months?

NOTES

1 "Beyond Digital: Empowered Consumers Seek Out Tailored, Inspiring Content Experiences That Transcend Platforms and Can Be Shared," *PwC Global Entertainment Media Outlook, 2015–2019*, www.pwc.com/gx/en/global-entertainment-media-outlook/key-industry-themes.jhtml (accessed May 20, 2016).

2 Ibid.

3 OTT refers to video, television, and other services provided over the internet rather than via a service provider's own dedicated, managed IPTV network.

4 Ibid.

5 Ibid.

6 Glen Peoples, "Business Matters: Did You Know 48 Streams Equals One Download?" *Billboard*, July 19, 2011.

7 Ibid.

8 Ibid.

9 "Music: Key Insights," *PwC, 2015–2019*, www.pwc.com/gx/en/global-entertainment-media-outlook/assets/2015/music-key-insights-4-music-subscription.pdf (accessed May 20, 2016).

10 Ibid.

11 James Barron, "From a Classical Pianist, an App Lets You Graft Your Voice onto Actual Hit Songs," *New York Times*, July 21, 2014.

12 "Who We Are," *MuseAmi*, www.museami.com/who-we-are (accessed May 20, 2016).

13 Forbes.com on MSNBC.com, "New, Improved . . . and Failed," www.msnbc.msn.com/id/36005036/ns/business-forbes_com/t/new-improved-failed (accessed May 20, 2016).

14 Simon Cronshaw and Peter Tullin, "Intelligent Naivety," *Remix Publications*, www.remixsummits.com/books (accessed May 20, 2016).

15 "Addicted to Technology? Good Reasons to Take a Tech Break," *Forbes*, February 16, 2015, www.forbes.com/sites/northwesternmutual/2015/02/16/addicted-to-technology-good-reasons-to-take-a-tech-break (accessed May 20, 2016).

16 Cronshaw and Tullin, "Intelligent Naivety."

17 "Addicted to Technology?"

18 Y. Park C. Fritz, and S.M. Jex, "Relationships between Work-Home Segmentation and Psychological Detachment from Work: The Role of Communication Technology Use at Home," Department of Psychology, Bowling Green University, Ohio, October 16, 2011, https://www.ncbi.nlm.nih.gov/pubmed/21728434 (accessed May 20, 2016).

19 "Addicted to Technology?"

20 Jonathan Takiff, "Tuned-in Web: Local Streaming Radio Services Growing in Popularity," *Philadelphia Inquirer*, May 17, 2015.

21 Ibid.

22 Ibid.

23 Ibid.

24 Ben Sisario, "Pandora Making Bid to Unruffle Music World," *New York Times*, February 23, 2015.

25 Farhad Manjoo, "Podcasting Is Blossoming, But in Slow Motion," *New York Times*, June 18, 2015.

26 "Podcast Consumption," *Edison Research*, www.edisonresearch.com/category/podcast-research (accessed May 20, 2016).

27 Manjoo, "Podcasting Is Blossoming."

28 Mike Shields, "Podcasts Aim to Lock in Advertising Revenue with Upfront Event in September," August 12, 2015, http://blogs.wsj.com/cmo/2015/08/12/podcasts-aim-to-lock-in-advertising-revenue-with-upfront-event-in-september (accessed May 20, 2016).

29 Debra Kamin, "If That NPR Guy Moved to Israel and Knew Hebrew . . . " New York Times, August 15, 2014.

30 Ibid.

31 Ibid.

32 Ibid.

33 Ibid.

34 Marius Dragomir and Mark Thompson, "Public Broadcasting Services Can Deliver Democratic Values. Few Do," *Open Society Foundations*, October 28, 2014, https://www.opensocietyfoundations.org/voices/public-broadcasting-services-can-deliver-democratic-values-few-do (accessed May 20, 2016).

35 "Public Media and Digitization: Seven Theses—Mapping Digital Media Global Findings," *Scribd*, www.scribd.com/doc/240547273/Public-Media-and-Digitization-Seven-Theses-Mapping-Digital-Media-Global-Findings (accessed May 20, 2016).

36 Chris Hanretty, "Public Service Broadcasting's Continued Rude Health," *British Academy for the Humanities and Social Sciences*, April 25, 2012, www.britac.ac.uk/policy/Public-service-broadcasting.cfm (accessed May 20, 2016).

37 Nancy Vogt and Katerina Eva Matsa, "Public Broadcasting: Fact Sheet," Pew Research Center, April 29, 2015, www.journalism.org/2015/04/29/public-broadcasting-fact-sheet (accessed May 20, 2016).

38 Emmanuel Legrand, "Music Crossing Borders—Monitoring the Cross-Border Circulation of European Music Repertoire within the European Union," *European Music Service*, January 2012.

39 Ibid.

40 Ibid.

41 Ibid.

42 Ibid.

43 Ibid.

44 Thomas Giger, "The Future of Radio as Social Audio Network," *Radio: I Love It*, June 2012, www.radioiloveit.com/radio-future-radio-trends/the-future-of-radio-as-the-worlds-social-audio-network (accessed May 20, 2016).

45 Ben Sisario, "Spotify Is Expanding to Include Video and Predictive Playlists," *New York Times*, May 21, 2015.

46 Ben Sisario, "Apple Music Makes Debut with D.J. Carrying the Flag," *New York Times*, June 30, 2015.

47 "Invite-Only Turntable.fm Takes 'Social Music' Beyond the Buzzword," *Evolver*, http://evolver.fm/2011/05/24/invite-only-turntable-fm-takes-social-music-beyond-the-buzzword/ (accessed May 20, 2016).

48 Ben Popper, "Turntable.fm Shuts Down for Good as Founder Launches New Social App," *The Verge*, March 19, 2014, www.theverge.com/2014/3/19/5526484/turntable-fm-founder-shuts-down-his-music-startup-and-launches-new (accessed May 20, 2016).

49 Ibid.

50 Ibid.

51 "Key Insights: TV Subscriptions and License Fees," *PwC, 2015–2019*, www.pwc.com/gx/en/global-entertainment-media-outlook/assets/2015/tv-subscriptions-and-licence-fees-key-insights-5-tv-and-video-consumption.pdf (accessed May 20, 2016).

52 Jonah Weiner, "The Laugh Factory," *New York Times Magazine*, June 21, 2015, 40.

53 Ibid.

54 David Lewis, "The Situation of Public Broadcasting in Europe," *European Broadcasting Union*, January 20, 2012, www.ebu.ch/files/live/sites/ebu/files/Publications/Speeches/2012.01.20-DL-Vilnius.pdf (accessed May 20, 2016).

55 Ibid.

56 Ibid.

57 Emily Steel, "Research Confirms the Crowd: Netflix and Others Are Upending the TV Business," *New York Times*, December 8, 2014.

58 Ibid.

59 Ibid.

60 Emily Steele and Ben Sisario, "'Empire May Provide Fox the Big Hit It Needs," *New York Times*, January 27, 2015.

61 Bill Carter, "Overextended, Music TV Shows Fade," *New York Times*, May 11, 2014.

62 Steele and Sisario, "Empire."

63 Ibid.

64 Jeanette Steemers, "Selling Television: Addressing Transformations in the International Distribution of Television Content," *Media Industries Journal*, 1(1) (2014), www.mediaindustriesjournal.org/index.php/mij/article/view/16 (accessed May 20, 2016).

65 Ibid.

66 Ibid.

67 Ibid.

68 Brooks Barnesian, "Television Becomes a Force at Sundance Film Festival," *New York Times*, January 22, 2015.

69 Ibid.

70 Agata Kaczanowska, "Television Broadcasting in the US," Ibis World Industry Report 51312, April 2011.

71 Sydney Ember, "An Increasingly Packed Field Stokes Media Competition for Digital Advertising Dollars," *New York Times*, April 27, 2015.

72 Ibid.

73 Ibid.

74 Jason Tseng, "Up Close with Arts Entrepreneurs: TBVE Films," *Fractured Atlas*, February 27, 2015, https://www.fracturedatlas.org/site/blog/2015/02/27/up-close-with-arts-entrepreneurs-tbve-films (accessed May 20, 2016).

75 Ibid.

76 Ibid.

77 Ibid.

78 Ibid.

79 Jeremy Edwards, "Global Internet Service Providers," Ibis World Industry Report l5121-GL, December 2014.

80 Ibid.

81 Ibid.

82 Ibid.

83 Ibid.

84 Ibid.

85 Ari Herstand, "The Only Way to Guarantee Your Music Is Heard by a Film/TV Music Supervisor," *Digital Music News*, June 15, 2015, www.digitalmusicnews.com/permalink/2015/06/15/the-only-way-to-guarantee-your-music-is-heard-by-a-filmtv-music-supervisor (accessed May 20, 2016).

86 Ibid.

87 Ibid.

88 Ibid.

89 Ibid.

90 Ibid.

91 Ibid.

CHAPTER 9

Revenue Streams: Recorded Music

CHAPTER OVERVIEW

In this chapter you will learn about the revenue-generating opportunities for artist- and music business-entrepreneurs in the area of recorded music. You will see that illegal downloading and copyright infringement remain a major impediment to the recording industry's revenue stream. The importance of record producers is explored. CD Baby, the online distributer, is profiled. DIWO (Do It With Others) artists will find many practical suggestions for earning revenue in the recorded music sector.

KEY TERMS

A&R	Pre-production
IFPI	US Termination Rights
Infringement	Royalty artist
Baidu	Recoupable
Niche label	Broader Rights

CURRENT PERFORMANCE

For the past 15 years, the global recorded music industry has wrestled with a steep and seemingly relentless decline in sales of physical music. The huge and powerful record labels failed to anticipate the massive changes that the disruptive technology of the internet would have on its business model. Once music could be digitized and transmitted through a relatively small digital MP3 file, it didn't take long for consumers to embrace the concept that they could access music on their computers without having to purchase it.

Rampant file-sharing and illegal downloading presented an enormous challenge to the record labels, which were completely unprepared for this challenge. Enjoying the huge profits from its strongest product—physical albums in the form of CDs—the recording industry had grown complacent and inattentive to changes in the technology marketplace. Now caught in a defensive posture, the labels tried to regain their accustomed control over the music industry. But their efforts were clumsy and ineffective, and included suing their customers and planting malware in their CDs. The damage to the recording industry's reputation was severe. Few customers were sympathetic to the efforts of labels and artists to point out that file-sharing is copyright infringement, and results in loss of revenue to all parties involved.

Artists themselves realized that there was an alternative to getting their music into the hands of their fans without the interference of major labels. Many technology-based entrepreneurs entered the scene to provide file-sharing access—much of it without benefit of copyright clearances—such as Napster, My.MP3.com, Kazaa, Grokster, eDonkey, and Gnutella. This nightmare for the record labels began to subside with the launch of Apple's iTunes Music store in May 2003, which promoted sales of individual tracks to be played on Apple's profitable iPod, and introduced the term "digital rights management" into the conversation.

Soon it seemed that music was everywhere, easily accessible, and, for the most part, free. Music consumers were discovering indie artists from all corners of the world. Advertisers tapped into this edgy and cheap way of finding music to connect products with young, hip customers. Eventually, lawsuits were filed and many of the illegal downloading services were closed down. Over time, the public has come to understand the harmful aspects of illegal downloading, but it still goes on today. The result of all this tumult is that many feel that music has lost value in the eyes of the public. Recorded music has become a commodity, a basic good that is easy to find, inexpensive or free, with artists easily interchanged as "products."

To give you a sense of the scope of this persistent sales decline, at its peak in 1999, the global market for recorded music was valued at US$26.6 billion. In 2010 the figure was US$15.9 billion. The global market for recorded music appears to have bottomed out between US$15 billion and US$16 billion, where it has remained for the past few years.[1]

The major record labels own the major publishing companies, with each holding the rights to millions of songs. Music publishing revenues have traditionally been strong and steady and, in the years of declining recorded music sales, the publishing side of the music production and distribution industry has helped prop up the recording side of the business.[2]

Streaming sites like Spotify and Deezer are a relatively new revenue source for the recording industry's music publishing sector. As the public continues to show its preference for music access over music ownership, streaming sites have become popular in both their free and paid services. Music publishers license their songwriters' works to each streaming site, as well as to other users of copyrighted material such as TV, radio, film, videos, advertising agencies, and other record labels. The use of songs in advertising has become an important source of revenue for labels' publishing divisions. The brand, the label, and the publisher all benefit from a song's exposure in a well-funded ad campaign or popular film.[3]

Music purchased online was equal to sales of physical music formats for the first time in 2015. CD sales remain robust primarily in parts of the world that do not have a strong technological infrastructure, even as this once-popular format becomes obsolete in more developed nations. However, in two of the world's major markets—Germany and Japan—the vast majority of recorded music revenue still comes from sales of physical formats like CDs: Germany at 70 percent and Japan at 78 percent.[4]

A closer look at the breakdown of recorded music revenue reveals that income from music sales in all formats is inversely proportional to the increase in revenue generated by music streaming sites. Again, the consumer's preference for access (streams) versus ownership (downloads) is hobbling overall revenue growth for this beleaguered industry sector.[5]

The 2015 International Federation of the Phonographic Industry (IFPI) report showed how various global markets were adjusting to a streaming world. For example, Sweden's recording revenue derives almost entirely from streaming (92 percent of digital revenue). In Canada, where Spotify was not available until 2014, streaming revenue comprises only 8 percent of digital revenue.[6]

Addressing the Value Gap

There is a significant imbalance or "value gap" between the amount of revenue extracted by certain digital online music platforms and the amount of revenue returned to rights owners of the music. This gap is due to the differences in the way legislation in many countries affects digitally transmitted music. The value gap is one of three main reasons why the recorded music industry continues to struggle for sustainable annual revenue growth. The second reason is that, despite the wide variety and ease of legally obtaining music, customers persist in illegal downloading and companies continue to advertise on illegal music sites. Third, revenue from legal online sales has not made up for the significant decrease in physical media sales.[7]

Outdated copyright law and government regulations account for the fact that, according to the US National Music Publishers' Association, at least as much money is lost every year as is generated.[8]

A Young Person's Market

Online music retailing appeals strongly to consumers in the 15–34 age bracket, who have enthusiastically endorsed all things digital. The younger generation is uniformly comfortable with listening to and purchasing music online, whereas older generations may still be uncertain about how to discover and consume music online.[9]

Because of this, brand marketers and artist development staff (known as Artist and Repertoire, or A&R) target two primary age groups: consumers aged 10–19 and those aged 20–29. The 10–19 age group has proven to be insatiable music consumers, with parents supplementing their children's relatively small disposable income levels. Consumers aged 20–29 are less likely to depend on their parents because they have moved into the workforce and now have their own discretionary income. These consumers grew up using the internet and may be influencers on social networks.[10] Marketers have long pursued these young consumers who still have a strong interest in music. Together, the 10–19 and 20–29 age groups account for nearly 31 percent of global industry revenue.[11]

The subset of consumers aged 20–24 has more fully embraced online digital downloads—legal or illegal—than older consumers. Those living in countries with a growing or well-developed middle class may be attending undergraduate or graduate school, or another type of specialized training. This could result in financial constraints and a willingness to use illegal free music sites rather than purchase music on legitimate sites.[12]

The market share of 25–29-year-olds has seen solid growth, perhaps owing to an expanding middle class and higher education levels in countries outside North America and Europe. This group was among the earliest to adopt peer-to-peer file-sharing and may be the age group most comfortable with the online purchasing of music.

Global Release Day

In the spring of 2015, the music industry's worldwide trade group, the IFPI, announced that all new albums would be released on Fridays everywhere. Despite some industry grumbling, the IFPI moved ahead with its decision and the plan was put into place in July, 2015.

"Music fans live in the digital world of today," states IFPI CEO Frances Moore. "Their love for new music doesn't recognize national borders. They want music when it's available on the Internet—not when it's ready to be released in their country. An aligned global release day puts an end to the frustration of not being able to access releases in their country when the music is available in another country."[13]

In the days of brick-and-mortar retail, when consumers waited in line at their local record store for the new release of their favorite artist, the day of the week release didn't matter very much. For example, Britain released on Mondays, the US on Tuesdays, and Japan released on Wednesdays, and those music lovers adjusted their schedules accordingly. However, the growing influence of digital purchases has made the first week of sales of a new release crucially important. The IFPI acknowledges this and has pledged to help each country adjust its sales period so that it can enjoy a full, first-week sales opportunity.[14]

The IFPI claims that the move to a single global release day will help deter online leaks of new albums. Additionally, this could make it easier for labels to plan their marketing campaigns more effectively, while engendering "excitement and a sense of occasion around the release of new music."[15]

Pause and Reflect

Does it matter to you on which day of the week new releases occur? How do you feel about the effect on the charts this change may have?

Industry Profitability

Over the past 15 years, high profit margins earned by the industry's *publishing* segment have been the recording industry's saving grace. In the absence of steady profitability from the production segment of the industry, many companies continue to struggle to maintain a stable bottom line. Profit levels during the industry's peak in the mid-1990s were as high as 13.0–15.0 percent of revenue, compared with roughly 5.8 percent in 2015.[16]

Recording companies maintain that they must continue to spend millions of dollars on marketing and product development of their artists in order to remain globally competitive. In regions such as North America and Europe, where consumers embrace digital music sales, labels have enjoyed stronger profitability. The much lower costs of digital production and distribution, compared with costs of physical product, helps to increase profitability.[17]

A 2015 report about streaming music services, issued by credit rating agency Moody's, stated that the marketplace was "overly crowded," but responded favorably to the benefits of the technological competition. Even though streaming services must pay significant licensing fees to copyright owners in order to use their music, the abundant financial resources of the technology companies that own the streaming services allows rights owners to bid up the price of their catalogues as streaming services compete with each other for more paying customers.[18]

Industry profitability has been severely damaged by the significant level of illegally downloaded music in Asia, most notably in China. Ibis World estimates that music production and publishing revenue from China is only US$82.6 million, yet it is the world's second-largest economy. The vast difference between China's population and growing middle class and its very small contribution to music *sales* leads to the assumption that illegal downloading may be to blame. On a positive note, this discrepancy indicates that there is still a lot of potential to increase music sales in China.[19]

Seeking revenue wherever it can be found, record companies are now positioning themselves as participants in revenue streams from every area of an artist's career. Multiple rights deals, also known as 360-deals, include touring, publishing, endorsements, and sale of merchandise, in addition to the majority of the record sale income that labels have always enjoyed. Many labels also demand a percentage of revenue from other areas of an artist's work such as films, retail product lines, books, and artists' fan clubs.[20]

Performers and recording artists now have the opportunity to forge a career without waiting to be signed to a label. Musicians can control when and how their music is released to the public, which is now a global audience. Increased exposure from recorded music can lead to larger crowds and ticket sales at the artists' live shows. Merchandise sales—at shows and online—also add to the artists' bottom line. While many independent artists still long for the support of a label, entrepreneurial musicians can take action and make decisions about their careers that make it possible to have a satisfying and sustainable life in music.[21]

The recording industry grows or contracts at various rates around the world. There are three tiers or groups of countries that demonstrate the challenges. First, the music production sector faces the largest challenges and the weakest revenue performance in nations such as Japan, the US, and much of Europe. This sector accounts for approximately 70 percent of the total global industry revenue. However, the changing technological constraints experienced in these countries present a daunting challenge to future revenue stabilization.[22]

The second tier of industry growth and contraction comprises so-called developing nations where revenues are severely affected by rampant illegal downloading. The industry in these countries or regions—China, Brazil, Mexico, and Indonesia—have experienced steeply declining sales of physical media due to the proliferation of free (but illegal) product. The countries in this tier have lower per-capita internet penetration than Japan, the US, and Europe, which hinders the growth of legitimate online music sales.[23]

Developed nations with emerging economies—such as South Korea, South Africa, and Russia—comprise the third tier. Industry growth in these areas has occurred through stronger and more stable currencies that, in turn, fuel more vibrant economies. The result is consumers with more disposable income who represent an opportunity for music industry sales, even if historically these countries have not accounted for a significant share of overall global industry revenue.[24]

Industry Outlook

The recording industry's greatest challenge moving forward is the consumer perception that music has been devalued and should be available at little or no cost.[25] The ease of music access, first through file-sharing and now by free all-you-can-eat online subscription music services, is responsible for this irrevocable change in consumer behavior. Sales of digital music may continue to increase incrementally, but nearly everyone in the industry has given up hope that digital sales will make up for the financial shortfall caused by the decline in sales of physical media.

Illegal Access Remains a Problem

As reflected in its 2015 report, the IFPI maintains that illegal music consumption is an ongoing and pervasive challenge that negatively affects sustainable growth. Copyright laws that have not kept pace with technological changes are one contributing factor. Another is the apparent lack of cooperation from advertisers, ISPs, and payment providers in stemming this pernicious problem.[26]

Neilsen and comScore have provided data to the IFPI which shows that approximately 20 percent of non-mobile internet users routinely access music services that are infringing copyright. Illegal digital access comes in many forms and changes quickly. Tumblr, Twitter, BitTorrent file-sharing, and unlicensed cyberlockers are just a few currently in vogue. BitTorrent is especially active, with an estimated four billion music downloads in 2014, most of which were illegal. Linking sites and social networks are major contributors to this problem.[27]

Thanks to years of educational efforts on behalf of the music industry, a majority of consumers acknowledge that illegally accessing music hurts artists and others. The global market research company, Ipsos, studied consumer attitudes across 13 countries concerning illegal music access and reported their findings to IFPI: 52 percent of respondents agreed (either strongly or a little) that downloading or streaming without the copyright owner's permission was theft. Additionally, 53 percent of respondents felt that licensed services should appear above illegal access sites in search engine results. Fifty-two percent agreed that companies should not advertise on illegal sites. Overall, survey respondents believe that ISPs should make stronger efforts to curb advertisements on and access to sites that distribute music illegally. Even those respondents who regularly use illegal sites believe that action should be taken by governments and ISPs to reduce access to or block the sites.[28] Apparently, it is too difficult for individuals to stop using these sites even knowing that their actions infringe on copyright and harm artists and other individuals in the music industry.

To date, ISPs in 19 countries have agreed or been ordered to block access to approximately 480 copyright infringing music sites. Even this relatively modest accomplishment, which has taken years of legal wrangling and persuasion, is encouraging. It may signal that the technology industry is willing to work in a serious way with the music industry and governments in trying to eradicate the copyright infringement websites.[29]

Search Engines

Consumers routinely use internet search engines to discover music. Search rankings (the order in which they appear on the page) are very influential and can, knowingly or not, drive consumers to websites with unlicensed music. Researchers involved in a 2014 Carnegie Mellon University study, *Do Search Engines Influence Media Piracy?*, stated: "Our results suggest that reducing the prominence of pirated links can be a viable policy option in the fight against intellectual property theft."[30] This conclusion resulted from data showing that when internet users were presented with the choice of purchasing a film from a list of sites consisting primarily of licensed content providers, 94 percent of them purchased from a licensed site. Fifty-seven percent of internet users purchased a film when the majority of sites listed from their search linked primarily to infringing sources.[31] One interpretation of the study is that consumers recognize the difference when presented with a search engine list of choices between infringing and non-infringing sites. The question remains, then: what will it take to convince search engines to stop listing infringing sites since consumers may not have the willpower to choose the non-infringing choices?

Advertising and Payment Providers

Effective action is slow in coming from the advertising industry to stop companies from placing ads on infringing sites. Surprisingly, many of these ads are placed by well-known, "blue chip" brands with legal departments that surely must know that this action encourages copyright infringing activity. Spain, France, the UK, the US, and other countries have taken the lead in bringing this pressing issue to the fore.

Perhaps like consumers, brands ignore the ethical implications of participating in infringing activities because the benefits to them are so large. MediaLink conducted research for the Digital Citizens Alliance in 2014, which revealed that 596 infringing sites generated US$227 million annually in advertising revenue. Ads placed on such sites generate wide and valuable exposure for the brand. The ad agencies that place these ads are paid to do so by the brands. And the infringing sites receive payment from the brands via the ad agency for posting these ads.

Another contributor to the ease of accessing unlicensed music is the payment providers who enable the transaction between consumer and website. While many of these payment facilitator companies are themselves reputable, they are contributing to the global problem of copyright infringement by helping consumers have access to unlicensed music and other intellectual property. A 2014 report from the Digital Citizens Alliance and NetNames revealed that 30 unlicensed download and streaming cyberlockers generate approximately US$100 million each year by making possible consumer purchases of unlicensed material.[32]

It is clear who benefits financially from these infringing activities. Yet those who create and own the music—performers, songwriters, labels—are the losers. They receive no revenue from transactions on infringing sites.[33]

Apps for Mobile Devices

Millions of consumers worldwide use mobile apps to download music. The growing popularity and availability of content on smartphones and other devices has the unfortunate side-effect of opening yet another avenue for infringing activity. Downloading, internet searches, streaming, and stream ripping are some of the ways that mobile device owners can easily find unlicensed music. Google and Apple, two of the largest companies in app development, have responded to some of the industry's requests to remove apps that facilitate access to unlicensed music. However, app development moves at such a rapid pace that much more stringent policies will need to be in place to significantly reduce infringing activity via apps.[34]

The protection of music that is leaked before its release date is a major priority for the IFPI's Anti-Piracy Unit (APU). Each new album has a protection plan, designed by the APU, that focuses on the likely channels that will be used for illegal distribution. Links to unlicensed rock repertoire are usually found on dedicated internet forums, while unlicensed pop music most often appears via distribution links on social networks.[35]

When pop artist Taylor Swift's album *1989* began to show up illegally in social media, the APU had to move quickly to remove the infringing links on Twitter and other networks. In just half an hour, a single link to infringing music can be Retweeted more than 27,000 times.[36]

Since the availability of digital music, leaks of music have plagued artists and labels. Icelandic artist Bjork's entire album, *Vulnicura*, was leaked two full months before its intended release in 2015. The artist and her label, One Little Indian Records, decided to release the full album digitally within a few days. Derek Birkett, the label's founder, candidly reveals the confusion and anxiety that prevailed in those 48 hours. "Basically what happened is I panicked and gave [the album] to iTunes because I told them, 'All these deals are going down and we're losing a lot of money,' I told them to put it on the cover and we'd give them the exclusive. Then I realized the political implications of giving iTunes the exclusive." Some of Bjork's longstanding physical retailers were angered by the digital exclusive, fearing that physical sales would be adversely affected. "We had to switch some of our partners for other partners. It had a massive, massive impact on us," Birkett said.[37]

In early January 2015, as she was preparing for the unannounced release of her album *Rebel Heart*, Madonna experienced the leak of nearly 30 songs, including unfinished demos. The veteran artist called the leaks "a form of terrorism" and compared the theft to "artistic rape." Many of the songs were "stolen long ago and not ready to be presented to the world," Madonna claimed in public statements."[38] Moving quickly and purposefully, she and her team completed and officially released six songs from *Rebel Heart* in less than a week. The songs were available for purchase on iTunes and Amazon, with the remainder of the album's songs promised in eight weeks.[39]

Madonna @ Costume Institute Benefit Gala "Rebel Heart" cloak

Andrew H. Walker/Getty Images Entertainment

Madonna and her team took an entrepreneurial approach in addressing the problem of leaked *Rebel Heart* songs by *selling* the six hastily completed tracks. Many artists who find themselves victims of advance leaks are resigned to giving away the music. Madonna took a bold stand in showing that her music has monetary value, even if it is leaked before completion.[40]

Pause and Reflect

Is illegal downloading a common activity for you and your friends? Did reading the above information about the millions of dollars lost to artists each year from advertising, payment providers, and cyberlockers have an impact on your thinking?

Physical Formats Still Sell

The IFPI's 2015 Digital Music Report shows that, despite anecdotal claims to the contrary, consumers continue to purchase music in physical formats. The report noted that Argentina had a trend-busting 17 percent growth in physical sales. Sales of vinyl product increased 55 percent from 2014 and now represent 2 percent of total global revenues.

The following shows the percentage that physical product sales represent of total global recorded music sales for each country:

- US—26 percent (US$1.3 billion).

- Japan—78 percent (US$2 billion).

- Germany—70 percent (US$2 billion).

- Poland—71 percent.

- Austria—65 percent.

- France—57 percent.

- South Africa—62 percent.

Digital Downloads Decline

Global downloads (sales), the once-hoped-for savior of the music industry, declined 8 percent in 2014, according to the IFPI. Downloads of both albums and individual songs dropped in nearly all major markets except Japan, where album sales grew by 20 percent. Yet digital downloads make up slightly more than 50 percent of total global revenue in the digital marketplace. Emerging economies that are experiencing growth in internet penetration showed an increase in digital sales. These countries include South Africa, Poland, Slovakia, Turkey, and China, among others. Altogether, the countries where digital downloads held steady or grew helped in part to stem the global decline in this format.[41]

Bright News in Emerging Markets

For more than five years, Latin America has been the bright spot in terms of the growth of music sales. The region now accounts for 4 percent of worldwide revenue. Brazil is Latin America's largest and most established market. The IFPI report shows a remarkable increase of 32 percent overall from digital revenues in Latin America. Countries with stand-out growth are Venezuela (up 272.8 percent), Peru (96.5 percent), Colombia (94.9 percent), Paraguay (69.1 percent), and Argentina (up 67.7 percent).[42]

Mini-Case Study: Lucas Lucco, Brazil

Brazilian singer-songwriter Lucas Lucco was born in the small town of Patrocinio. He began writing music at age 11, later joining a band called Skypiras. He began posting his music to YouTube in 2011 and soon had more than 50 million views of his songs "Princesinha" and "Pra Te Fazer Lembrar." Sony Music Entertainment Brazil got word of his spreading popularity and signed him to the label in late 2013. States Alexandre Schiavo, Sony Brazil's president: "Lucas [is] a bright young talent, with a strong view of how he [wants] to present himself and his music. He came to prominence through online videos and he continues to be highly engaged with this medium, writing all the storylines for his videos himself."[43]

Continuing to climb in public awareness, Lucco's debut DVD album, *Tá Diferente,* was released in late 2013 and featured Colombian reggae superstar Maluma. This was quickly followed by the popular singles "Vidas," "Destino," and "Vai Vendo" in 2014.[44]

Under the label's guidance, Lucco's single, "Mozão," attracted more than 55 million YouTube views thanks to a marketing campaign that included social media, digital, and broadcast outlets. "Mozão" quickly became Brazil's most-watched YouTube video and the country's bestselling ringback tone in 2014.[45]

Lucco's digital fame propelled him into a busy touring career. He performs approximately 20 shows per month in Brazil. His expanded rights deal with Sony allows the label to share in his live performance revenue.[46]

Performance Rights Revenues Are Strong

Performance rights are paid to record companies from third-party businesses such as radio stations, bars, and restaurants. According to the IFPI, improved efficiencies in collection and increased demand for music from third-party sources helped push performance rights income to US$948 million in 2014. The sector now accounts for 6 percent of total industry revenues, with Latin America (+12.6 percent), Europe (+7.5 percent), and Asia (+0.7 percent) all reporting a rise in income.[47]

The Potential of China

With 650 million online users and a number of licensed digital providers, China is an alluring growth area for music. In order to realize the potential, however, two cultural issues must be resolved. One is the ingrained habit of not paying for music. The other is a long history of illegal music consumption.[48]

Up until 2011, ringtones were the only meaningful source of licensed digital income for music rights owners. This was due to the fact that most services in the digital marketplace offered unlicensed music. In an effort to develop the Chinese market, the major recording companies worked with subsidiary One-Stop-China to license the music services provided by Baidu, China's largest search engine. This was accomplished in 2011. The year 2014 was the third consecutive year of growth, which suggests that licensing music on Baidu has had a positive impact. Streaming revenues account for most of the 5.6 percent increase in value in the China market. While remaining optimistic, music labels and services have a lot of work ahead of them in realizing China's full potential as a major music revenue generator.[49]

Mini-Case Study: Wakin Chau, Taiwan

Veteran singer-songwriter Wakin Chau has been signed to Taiwanese indie label Rock Records for more than 20 years. In addition to solid album sales and hit singles, he has an active regional and international touring career.[50]

In the last few years Rock Records has invested heavily in expanding its digital presence and efforts on behalf of its artists. One of Wakin's early excursions into the power of social media and fan interaction was at his 2014 Taipei concert, appropriately titled "What Do We Sing Today?" Fans responded to Rock Records' Facebook and Spotify promotional campaign for the show by choosing songs from Wakin's vast recorded repertoire of more than 40 albums. The fans' choices became part of the concert's set list. Those who participated in the social media selection won prizes, including merchandise signed by Wakin.[51]

The online campaign was supported by Wakin's promotional work with Rock Records' YouTube channel. It is one of the most-watched channels in Taiwan, with more than a million subscribers. Despite this impressive figure, Danny Tuan, head of Rock Records' new media affairs department, acknowledges that the karaoke audience is still the primary market for music videos in the territory.[52]

Rock Records and other Taiwanese labels routinely tap into international social networks like Facebook as effective channels for their artists' exposure and increased fanbase. Tuan explains that many performers also use WeChat, Sina Weibo, and Xiami to connect with their fans in mainland China. With its newly opened licensed services, China has become an important market for the label. Rock Records has made significant deals there that open up new opportunities to promote the label's artists. "Consumers across Asia can engage with our artists instantly on platforms such as Facebook, YouTube, iTunes, Spotify, and KKBOX," Tuan explains. "There's no time lag anymore as new music goes out across the region on these platforms at the same time."[53]

MAJOR GLOBAL MARKETS

Here is a list of the top global music territories in 2015, according to the IFPI:

US (US$4.9 billion)

Japan (US$2.6 billion)

Germany (US$1.4 billion)

UK (US$1.3 billion)

France (US$843 million)

Australia (US$376 million)

Canada (US$342 million)

South Korea (US$266 million)

Brazil (US$247million)[54]

The US is by far the largest single global music market. The strength and size of the US market comes from several sources. The first is the US advertising industry. Valued at 35 percent of the worldwide total advertising revenue, the US leads the world in licensing music as a marketing tool. Music that is used in commercial advertisements on TV, radio, websites, and other outlets must be licensed. This in turn produces revenue for the rights owners, such as labels, publishers and songwriters. Additionally, music used in film and television is a significant revenue generator, much of it coming from Hollywood (California).[55]

By contrast, in other global markets the concept of licensing music for use in advertising, television, and films is still in its early stages. According to Ibis World, European countries comprise 12 of the top 20 music markets, yet publishing revenue from this region is far below that of the US. As we've learned in other chapters, developing countries and regions present an opportunity for growth, this time in the area of commercial music licensing. India is one such country that has great potential.[56]

Competition from Smaller Labels

Universal Music Group, Warner Music Group, and Sony Entertainment are the top three global music production and distribution companies. Together they generate approximately 75 percent of worldwide music revenue and have enormous influence on every aspect of the industry. But that influence is waning due to the opportunities created by powerful digital technologies.[57]

Responding to the ease of digital music delivery, as well as the lower costs of digital (rather than analog) recording equipment, a significant number of small record labels have entered the industry.

These labels are gaining traction through entrepreneurial business models that identify and exploit an industry niche. An area where small labels are finding success is in focusing on one genre or related genres.[58]

Easy Star Records is one such independent label, with more than 13 active artists who champion reggae and dub. Founded in New York City almost 20 years ago, Easy Star's accolades include three of the top-selling reggae albums ever: the Easy Star All-Stars' *Dub Side of the Moon*, *Radiodread* and *Easy Star's Lonely Hearts Dub Band*.[59]

The UK's Toolroom Records is another indie label that focuses on one niche genre: dance or house music. Founded by DJ/producer Mark Knight, the label features more than 40 dance music artists including Juliet Fox, Adrian Hour, Ramiro Lopez and Mihalis Safras.[60]

Major labels, which feature many different genres—from classical to rock and country—face the task of marketing each genre to its specific demographic. Each consumer market has its own nuances of music discovery, and it is up to the large labels to deliver their sales and promotional messages appropriately. To do this successfully, the large labels must have employees with wide and deep knowledge of all types of genres, marketing and advertising techniques, and industry connections.[61]

In this area, smaller labels have an advantage over major labels. With only one primary genre on which to focus, the message delivery can be more easily targeted than for the multi-genre major labels. The small labels work to build a compelling brand by featuring artists from a single genre that appeal to a cohesive audience.[62] Cross-promoting their artists in concerts, on social media, and through street teams becomes a much more focused and targeted effort. Many indie labels—with limited funds and smaller numbers of employees—are taking the lead in using social media to promote their artists, which streamlines the marketing process and costs.

Indie labels are adept at using their artists' music to promote consumer products and services, as opposed to the major labels' tradition of selling music as a stand-alone product.[63] This shift underscores the profound change in the industry brought about by digital music delivery. Small labels can move nimbly to adjust to changes in consumer behavior, whereas major labels have had to spend years divesting of large recording studios, expensive equipment, manufacturing plants, and physical distribution platforms, all relics of the time when consumer purchases of music in physical format ruled the day.

Brands are eager to find the indie labels' up-and-coming artists, who lend cachet and a coolness factor to their products or services—and whose services are undoubtedly less expensive than a world-renowned artist on a major label.

Small labels are not exempt from the struggle to make a profit, but they are staying in business as lean and creative entrepreneurial ventures. Their single-genre focus allows them to create cost-effective marketing plans for a demographic that can be smaller, regional, and less expensive than the major labels. In this way, indie labels are profiting from the sliding fortunes of the major music companies.[64]

Major Labels Prevail

The sheer size and power of the major labels—even after downsizing—guarantees that they will remain viable for the foreseeable future. Major labels are profit-driven corporations, sign hundreds of artists representing all types of genres, and must market to diverse geographic regions and age groups. The majors have lost some of their marketplace dominance and appeal to smaller labels, which can offer more personal service to artists. Once the gatekeepers of the recording industry, major labels are no longer the only option for artists who want to have a solid career.

Internet technology and a profusion of online marketing tools allow many musicians to start their careers on their own. Consumers today have many more ways to discover new artists than in the pre-digital years when major labels had absolute control over who got signed, recorded, and promoted in the marketplace.

However, there is no doubt that major labels have the financial resources and marketing savvy to move a mid-career artist into the stratosphere. Despite the many drawbacks of worldwide fame and control by a corporate record label, a surprisingly large number of artists claim that getting signed to a big label is still their goal.[65]

As demonstrated in artist stories throughout this chapter, major labels have a commanding presence in traditional media marketing and in building an international audience for their artists. With the additional and lucrative benefits of having large music publishing and licensing departments, major labels are able to sustain losses when an artist or ensemble is unprofitable, or at least shift the loss to another artist or group that is profitable. The changes in consumer behavior regarding music access vs. ownership plus the rising competition from tech-savvy independent labels have shifted the major labels' artistic focus to proven and profitable hit-makers. For some artists, the allure of becoming a global artist will be a reality only through an association with a major label, no matter what the risk.

INDUSTRY GLOBALIZATION

During the period of global expansion by major labels in the 1990s, most artistic talent came from the US, the UK, Australia, and Canada. More recently, artists from all over the world have come to the public's attention via the internet. Northern Europe and the Scandinavian countries have seen solid market growth. To a lesser extent, South Africa and South America are two areas where there is potential for continuing growth. The popularity of Latin music in the US contributes to South America's growing global exposure.[66]

Most recently the BRICS nations—Brazil, Russia, India, China, and South Africa—along with Japan have joined the European and American music markets as major players. Other countries and regions, such as France and Africa, struggle to maintain a foothold in the charts due to a variety of issues, including political instability and language barriers. Despite its global reach, the worldwide music marketplace remains predominantly an English-speaking world.[67]

PRODUCERS

Many of pop music's biggest stars are producers. Rick Rubin, Dr. Dre, Phil Spector, Pharrell Williams, and Teo Macero are only a handful of producers who have worked their musical magic for artists including Metallica, Snoop Dogg, the Righteous Brothers, Britney Spears, No Doubt, Mariah Carey, Miles Davis, and Dave Brubeck.

What exactly does a producer do? They're the people who make the artist's idea come alive.[68]

Recording producers guide an artist's project from inception to completion. Some producers have technical expertise in engineering, while others may be trusted friends who can give the artist honest advice. Usually an artist is too close to the recording situation to be able to step back and listen objectively. The most effective producers have deep musical knowledge and can communicate effectively with everyone involved in the recording. These might include the studio engineer, arrangers, back-up musicians, vocal coach, the artist's manager, and perhaps even any of the artist's friends and family who are present.[69]

A recording artist can expect to begin working with her producer well before she enters the studio. This period is known as pre-production. The artist relies on her producer to guide her in song selection and arrangement. The overall artistic message and sound of the recording is discussed. The recording studio is selected and scheduled. Back-up musicians and guest singers are planned, selected, contracted, and scheduled. The more details that can be worked out before entering the studio, the fewer cost overruns there may be for the recording project. Artists and ensembles that use home recording studios may have the luxury of spending extended periods of time writing and rehearsing in the studio without worrying about costs, as it is far less expensive to record outside of a commercial studio.

Once in the studio, the producer keeps the process running as efficiently as possible while encouraging the very best possible artistic efforts from everyone involved. A sound engineer is a critical partner in the instrumental recording and arrangement phase. In pop music the back-up musicians are typically in a different room from the lead vocalist, who often is in a small sound booth wearing headphones in order to hear the other musicians. The engineer will set up microphones in the studio in order to capture each instrument or group of the same instruments (guitar, violins, bass, drums, piano) separately from the others. This will produce a multi-track recording that allows the engineer, in consultation with the producer or artist, to make adjustments and corrections to individual tracks later on.

Working with the lead vocalist is one of the producer's most important roles. It is nearly impossible for the vocalist to have a sense of how the entire song sounds while it is being recorded. The producer does have this perspective, however, and can guide and counsel the vocalist in deciding whether or not they've captured the best possible performance or need to do another take. This can be an exhausting and frustrating phase of the recording process, particularly if the artist is working with more than one producer—a process that has become rather common. You can see why it is crucial for the producer–vocal soloist relationship to be built on mutual trust and respect.[70]

What makes a recording a success? So many factors go into the complex process of creating a recording that it is impossible to know precisely. Was there a good working relationship between the producer and the artist? Did the recording studio have the proper vibe for the project? How closely did the finished product meet the artist's expectations from both an artistic and engineering perspective? The artist's recording label will measure success in sales and licenses. The artist's fans may be disappointed or delighted with the final product. Radio stations will be happy if there are radio-friendly hits on the recording and may become good partners in promoting the music.

In short, no matter how hands-off or involved the producer was in the project, if everyone involved feels they made the best music possible, the recording was a success.

Best Producers Ever

The *New Musical Express* (*NME*), a British music journalism magazine that covers rock, alternative, and indie music, recently named its "50 Greatest Producers Ever."[71] While I say "hats off" to *NME* for the effort, I did notice one glaring omission: where are all the women?

A bit of research revealed that the dearth of female producers is getting some attention in the press. While there are powerful women in high positions at record companies, few can be found on the other side of the sound desk. According to the BBC, there have been only three women nominated for Best Producer at the Brits or the Grammys. To date, no female producer has ever won.[72]

So, to balance out the story, here are some female producers who deserve our attention.

Patrice Rushen

Trisha Leeper/WireImage/Getty Images

Sylvia Massy, producer

Earl Gibson III/WireImage/Getty Images

Trina Shoemaker won a Grammy for her work as a sound engineer on Sheryl Crow's *Globe Sessions* album. After high school, Shoemaker worked low-level jobs around recording studios in Los Angeles, eventually becoming an apprentice to Daniel Lanois, who helped shape the sound of U2 and Brian Eno.[73]

Alicia Keys has successfully blended her classical piano training with R&B and hip-hop. She arranged, composed and produced her debut album, *Songs in A-Minor* (2001), and her four releases that followed. Outside of music, she has written a book, *Tears for Water: Songbook of Poems and Lyrics*, has starred in two films, and has co-produced and composed music for the short-lived Broadway play *Stick Fly* in 2011.[74]

"Missy" Elliott is an American producer, singer, rapper, and songwriter. She has worked with Beyoncé, Janet Jackson, Mariah Carey, Keyshia Cole, Ciara, and Whitney Houston.[75]

Grammy-nominated Patrice Rushen is a classically trained pianist who plays the flute, clarinet, and percussion. Mentored by Quincy Jones, she was the first woman to be musical director for the Grammys. She also directed the Emmys, the NAACP Awards and Janet Jackson's *Janet* world tour. She has written and produced for a long list of stars, including Stevie Wonder, Chaka Khan, and Prince.[76]

Sylvia Massy produced Tool's 1993 multi-platinum LP, *Undertow*, which put her on the map as a top producer, working primarily in the realm of alternative rock. Her sound engineering credits include tracks on albums by Sevendust, System of a Down, Red Hot Chili Peppers, Johnny Cash, and Powerman 5000. As to the question of why there are so few female music producers, Massy explains: "A career in music production means a lot of 14 hour days in a dark studio with little outside contact. Women can find it hard to meet new people in that type of environment, and most eventually gravitate into fields that allow them to grow socially."[77]

Sonia Pottinger, who passed away in 2010, is best known for her wide-reaching work in the Jamaican music scene in the 1960s and 1970s. During the heyday of reggae, she produced albums for bands like The Ethiopians, Delano Stewart, The Melodians, Alton Ellis, and Toots & the Maytals. *Harder Than the Rest,* the iconic 1978 LP by roots reggae group Culture, is one of her best-known works.[78]

Janelle Monáe has brought funk, rock, soul, and theatrical performance together to create her own musical niche. She served as arranger on her debut album, *The ArchAndroid* (2010), and was executive producer, songwriter and engineer on her follow-up, *The Electric Lady* (2013).[79] She launched Wondaland Records, a venture with Sony Music Entertainment's Epic Records, in 2015 "after seeing there was a big absence of female entrepreneurs in the music industry who understand how to develop and market innovative artists."[80] She cites Madonna and her label, Maverick Records, as a source of inspiration for Wondaland. Additionally, veteran music businesswomen Julie Greenwald and Sylvia Rhone are role models for Monáe as she finds her footing as a music entrepreneur.[81]

Kara DioGuardi is one of the most respected songwriters in pop music, with more than 50 charting singles for artists including Christina Aguilera, Natasha Bedingfield, Avril Lavigne, Darius Rucker, and Pink, among many others.[82] She has co-production credits

Janelle Monáe performs on NBC Today Show

Al Pereira/Wirelmage/Getty Images

on Kelly Clarkson's "Walk Away" and Britney Spears' *Blackout,* and shares an executive producer credit with Lindsay Lohan on *A Little More Personal (Raw).* She published a memoir in 2011, *A Helluva High Note: Surviving Life, Love, and American Idol*, and served as a judge for two seasons on the hit TV show *American Idol*.[83]

Without a doubt, sexism in the studio is a factor, but it may not be the biggest issue. "The bottom line is, women aren't interested," says Susan Rogers, former studio engineer for Prince and now an associate professor at the Berklee College of Music in Boston (US). She says that in her production and engineering courses, only one out of every ten students is a young woman.[84]

Rogers stresses that there "are no social barriers to a woman becoming a record producer."[85] A closer look reveals that the problem of under-representation of women sound engineers extends to other areas of the arts, including radio, film, TV, and theater. The nonprofit organization Women's Audio Mission, based in San Francisco (US), was created to provide opportunities for women "in direct response to the economic and social inequity that women face in music production and the recording arts."[86] The organization offers mentoring, internships, workshops, and events, as well as an online curriculum called Sound Channel that has helped train more than 6,500 students from 127 countries.[87]

In a 2013 "Women in Music: Roundtable Discussion" in *M-Magazine*, produced by PRS for Music (UK), only 13 percent of its more than 100,000 songwriter, composer and publisher members were female.[88] The British Academy of Songwriters, Composers and Authors (BASCA) membership is only 20 percent female. And in the Music Producers Guild (MPG), a UK support organization for producers and engineers, women comprise only 4 percent of members.[89]

Rogers says that the real barriers to a woman becoming a record producer are biological. "The typical lifestyle of a record producer is very intensive, very competitive, all-consuming. In order to be able to maintain that level of focus and attention and dedication to your craft, it has to come at the expense of reproduction."[90] Rogers chose career over marriage and family.

Shoemaker shares her experience of balancing motherhood and studio production. "Having a baby was a big deal, a game changer," she says. "I was 39 when I got pregnant, so I was already well established, but it did change everything. It took me out of the running for a lot of jobs."[91]

For the record, *NME*'s top ten producers ever were Dr. Dre, Butch Vig, Brian Wilson, Brian Eno, Rick Rubin, Phil Spector, Nile Rodgers, Quincy Jones, Sir George Martin, and Joe Meek.[92]

Producer Collaboration

It has become quite common for multiple collaborators to work and rework songs for maximum effect and hit potential. For her album *Rated R*, Rihanna worked with producers and writers including Ne-Yo, Ester Dean, Makeba Riddick, Rob Swire, and the two-man Norwegian team Stargate.[93]

For her latest album, *Rebel Heart*, music industry veteran Madonna took the advice of her manager, Guy Oseary, and collaborated with Swedish DJ and producer Avicii. Before the album was finished, rapper Kanye West and American producer and songwriter Toby Gad had also worked with Madonna on many songs. This was a major departure from her previous hit albums, where she worked primarily with a single producer for each—William Orbit (*Ray of Light*), Nile Rodgers (*Like a Virgin*), and Patrick Leonard (*Like a Prayer*).[94]

"I didn't know exactly what I signed on for, so a simple process became a very complex process," Madonna said about the collaborations.[95] The new artistic model of working on a track and then handing it off for reworking by others didn't appeal to her, and she insisted on completing her songs in person. "I never leave the room," she said. "Sometimes I think that makes them mad."[96]

Madonna and Avicii

Tim Mosenfelder/Getty Images Entertainment

Madonna explains that everyone she worked with was, without a doubt, tremendously talented: "It's just that everybody I worked with has also agreed to work with 5,000 other people. I just had to get in where I could fit in."[97]

British singer-songwriter James Arthur claims that working with multiple producers on his debut studio album, *James Arthur*, was not conducive to being creative. "It takes a couple of days to build up a rapport with a producer and then after that you're on to the next one," explained the 2012 *X Factor* winner and 2013 NRJ "International Breakthrough of the Year" winner.[98] His album included the following "Producer" credits: Salaam Remi, Richard Adlam, Biffco, Tiago Carvalho, Matt

Furmidge, Bradford Ellis, Ash Howes, Da Internz, Naughty Boy, Hal Ritson, Gustave Rudman, Graham Stack, Richard "Biff" Stannard, TMS, and Steve Robson.[99]

Spotlight on . . . CD Baby, the Anti-label

Derek Sivers followed a well-traveled entrepreneurial path when he founded CD Baby in 1997. He started the business in order to solve a problem (selling his own recordings online) and, in the early years, operated the company out of his home. Along the way to selling the company in 2008 for US$22 million, he built an enterprise that today serves a vital niche in the music industry: independent recording artists who do not have or want to be affiliated with a major label or publishing company.[100]

CD Baby's original "niche" was independent artists who wanted help selling their physical CDs. The company's business model has grown to include digital downloads, apps, streaming, and user-generated video content. However, sales of CDs—a medium which many believe is practically extinct—remains a large part of its business. CD Baby's unassuming Portland, Oregon, headquarters includes a warehouse containing more than two million CDs. CD Baby distributes physical product— including the resurgent vinyl record—to stores as well as directly to consumers.[101]

Willis Earl Beal, Australia

Mark Metcalfe/Getty Images Entertainment

But this isn't a story about a quaint, technology-averse music business. Working with hundreds of thousands of recording artists in today's world must include many other services besides sales of physical product to help fans discover artists, while also aiding artists in remaining financially afloat. Though increasingly focused on the web,[102] in fact, CD Baby is a vital lifeline for its more than 325,000 artists who need help with digital music distribution. The company has placed approximately one of every six songs that appear in the iTunes catalog and actively works with more than 60 other downloading sites to place its artists' music.[103]

From a business perspective, CD Baby can serve as the back office for musicians who want to remain independent of major labels and publishers. Tracking, collecting, and distributing royalties has become a big part of the bundle of services the company provides. CD Baby helps artists keep track of their music used in streaming sites and user-generated online video, two growth areas of revenue for musicians. More than two million of its artists' tracks have been uploaded to YouTube alone.[104]

Artists who use CD Baby's services represent a wide range of musical styles and levels of career development. Some clients have never had a record label contract and are eager to explore other options that will give them more control over their careers. Others have had a rocky experience with a label and have decided never to look back.[105]

"We're the anti-label in a lot of respects," said Tracy Maddux, the company's chief executive. "We've been doing this longer than anyone else, and with five million tracks in our catalog, we're a lot bigger than anyone else [in the same niche]."[106]

Typing "independent music distribution" into a Google search box led to singer-songwriter Willis Earl Beal's discovery of CD Baby. Beal's first two albums were released on a conventional label, but he was writing so much more music than the label wanted to release that he struck out on his own. "For a middle-ground indie artist like myself, CD Baby is perfect," he explained. "It might not be ideal for somebody like Bruno Mars, but I [know] what I want to do and you get to control everything, which is cool."[107]

Some well-known artists, including Bon Iver, the National, Jack Johnson, Sara Bareilles, the Antlers, and Macklemore, have used CD Baby as a jumping-off point. They utilized CD Baby to distribute their recordings in their early years. Then, as their careers built to a point where they were attracting large audiences and selling thousands of records, they moved on to more traditional record label management and distribution.[108]

"We build the highway," said Phil Bauer, the former rapper who is CD Baby's director of distribution. "The musicians drive the car." CD Baby's business model is straightforward: it has specific and consistent price points for handling a single work or an album-length work. Artists are free to choose their CD's sales price. CD Baby takes a specific dollar amount for the sale of each physical recording and charges a percentage commission on digital sales.[109]

CD Baby is not without its musician critics who complain about its size ("it's hard to get noticed") and rather high commission (9 percent at the time of writing). Some artists take their business to CD Baby's competitors, which include TuneCore, Ditto, Reverbnation, and Mondotunes. However, long-standing CD Baby clients claim that, despite the fees, they have found value in certain features, such as weekly royalty payments and instant access to sales data, which are compelling enough for them to remain with the company.[110]

Indie singer-songwriter Ingrid Michaelson has released all of her CDs through CD Baby. Receiving sales figures in a timely way helps her see in what parts of the world her music is selling strongly as she plans a tour. She explained: "Sometimes you see that a song you're trying to push as a single is not selling more than the other ones, and that can make you re-evaluate your choices. So it's a great tool to have."[111]

Ingrid Michaelson
NBC Universal/Getty Images

From a business model perspective, CD Baby may stand to benefit from "termination rights," a provision of US copyright law which allows artists to take back ownership of their recordings from labels after 35 years. Some musicians may choose to sever ties to the labels that originally had distribution rights to their music and take on distribution of their recordings through CD Baby or one of its competitors.[112]

Another area of potential growth for CD Baby is collecting a share of the licensing fees and ad revenues generated by its artists' music that is used on YouTube and in apps. The upswing in this area may help offset the stalling out of anticipated growth from digital sales (downloads).[113]

Overall, CD Baby's longevity and success may be attributed to its understanding of the roiling music marketplace and its ability to work with musicians in exploiting the ever-changing streams of revenue than can flow to its artists. "I never set out saying 'I don't want to sign to a label,'" Michaelson said. "But why change from something that's working?"[114]

> ### *Pause and Reflect*
>
> Do you or any of your friends use an online indie distributor to sell your music? Explore the sales data that is available to artist-entrepreneurs on any of the distribution websites and see if you can understand why it is so valuable to them.

A PROFOUND SHIFT IN A VENERABLE INDUSTRY

Eric Garland, founder of Competitive Futures, a forecasting and trend analysis firm, describes the recording industry's future this way: "Nothing is everything. There is no ONE thing that is everything. That is a really profound shift in a long and established history for the recorded music industry. Everything has always been about one thing. We all bought vinyl. Then we all bought cassettes, then CDs. There was always one monolithic product or experience that defined the business both culturally and financially. What the last [15] years are . . . remind[ing] us is that there will not be one thing. There will be many things, and perhaps all together those streams will resemble something that is a sustainable business."[115]

The traditional role of record labels was A&R (finding new artists and music for labels to record), selling records, and licensing recordings for other uses. Over the years, the industry moved from a collection of small independent labels started by entrepreneurs to an industry dominated by large, corporate-owned companies. Indie labels often served as a kind of farm league, where the entrepreneurs did the heavy lifting involved in discovering and nurturing new artists. After reaching a certain level of success with the indie label—measured in record sales or radio airplay—many of the artists moved on to the bigger machine of the majors.

Sometimes major labels bought entire indie labels or merged with other companies and acquired former indies. As the record business consolidated, lawyers and businesspeople replaced the entrepreneurs who had founded smaller labels.

The majors controlled nearly all the aspects of their business. They owned recording studios, publishing companies, employed their own A&R people and producers, manufactured the records, distributed them to retail outlets, and marketed their artists through retail and other commercial partnerships. Labels had a cozy relationship with radio stations. (Remember payola? These were illegal financial incentives paid to radio stations to place certain songs in on-air rotation to saturate the market and boost ratings.) As long as people bought records, listened to music on the radio, and waited patiently for record labels to find and introduce new artists and songwriters, everything was great—for the recording industry anyway.

The labels owned the rights to nearly all of their artists' master recordings. From a business perspective, this made sense. Labels invested time and money into developing artists and getting their music reproduced and distributed without knowing for certain that they would be able to sell their only product: recordings. But from an artistic perspective, some artists and fans chafed at the restrictions labels placed on their music. Labels controlled nearly everything about the artist's records, including what songs would go on it, who would produce it, how the record would be marketed, and where it would be sold. In exchange for label support, artists signed multi-year contracts committing to a specific number of new album releases.

The labels also controlled how, when and if a new album was released. It often took years for artists and labels to complete a recording. Sometimes the artist's main supporter at the label quit or was fired before completing the album, leaving the artist and her project on the shelf, unreleased. Occasionally the public's tastes in music changed over the time period it took to complete the recording, so the label cut its losses and didn't release the album at all.

The top performers, known as royalty artists, were paid a percentage of the money (a royalty) that the labels received from selling the CD. Labels acted like a combination parent and loan officer, bankrolling the costs of recording, marketing, distributing, and tour support. The artist paid back the label not with real cash, but from future sales of her records.

Few people outside the recording sector knew that artists received royalty checks only if they'd sold enough albums to cover (recoup) the label's investment costs. When an album didn't sell well, the debts from the first release would be added to the cost of the next album release. This is known as cross-collateralization. An artist could be in debt to her record label for years, or even forever, if her records didn't sell enough to cover the label's financial investment. On the other hand, artists were not legally bound to make up their unrecouped accounts when they left the label.

Labels used their massive marketing muscle to push artists into the mainstream media. Many of those artists became superstars. Labels were very successful at "turning spins into purchases," meaning that the more airplay a song received, the more copies of the record were sold. It was not widely known that these very successful artists, selling millions of records, made up for the nine out of ten artists on the label whose record sales never covered the label's investment costs.

In the past there was a clear distinction between the independent labels and the major labels. The biggest differences were money (majors have more), size (majors are multi-national conglomerates), marketing and distribution power (majors spend more), artistic freedom for recording artists (indies give more), and time spent to develop careers (indies win hands down).

Today the bright line between indies and majors has disappeared. In the late 1990s, major labels began investing in and doing joint ventures with indies that created cost- and profit-sharing deals. Now the three majors own independent distribution networks including the Alternative Distribution Alliance (Warner Music Group), RED (Sony Music Entertainment), and Fontana (Universal Music Group). Indie labels, many of them owned by these very companies, use independent distribution networks to get their records into the physical retail marketplace.

Recording Industry Trade Associations

The recording industry has strong trade organizations that support and promote the creative and financial health of the major music companies. Nearly every country has its own recording industry organization and most are members of the International Federation of the Phonographic Industry (IFPI).

The *IFPI* is chaired by the legendary opera singer Plácido Domingo. Representing the global recording industry, it has a membership comprising approximately 1,300 record companies in 66 countries, and affiliated associations in 55 countries. Its mission is to promote the value of recorded music, campaign for record producer rights, and expand the commercial uses of recorded music in all of its member markets.[116]

A few other organizations of interest are noted below.

The Recording Industry Association of America (*RIAA*) is the trade organization that collects and compiles information on both shipment and purchasing trends of recorded music in the US. It supports and promotes the creative and financial wellbeing of the major music companies in the US. It is the organization responsible for certifying record sales as Gold®, Platinum®, Multi-Platinum™, and Diamond. Its Los Premios De Oro y Platino™ is an award given to acknowledge and celebrate Latin music sales.[117]

Independent labels join forces for more clout in the marketplace under the umbrella of several organizations:

Plácido Domingo

Gisela Schober/German Select/Getty Images

WIN, the acronym for the Worldwide Independent Music Industry Network, is a global forum for independent music companies and their national trade associations. Since 2006, WIN has served its members as an "advocate, instigator and facilitator . . . in response to business, creative and market-access issues faced by the independent sector everywhere."[118]

The Independent Music Companies Association (*Impala*) is a Brussels-based nonprofit organization dedicated to small and medium-sized cultural enterprises (SMEs), which contribute significantly to growth and jobs in Europe. It now serves more than 4,000 members, which include prominent independent labels and national trade associations.[119]

Merlin, the "global digital rights agency for the world's independent label sector," was launched at the 2007 MIDEM international music exhibition, conference, and festival. Today Merlin has more than 650 members, representing 20,000+ labels and distributors across 40 countries. For digital music services, it can streamline licensing by allowing music users to globally license the music of their members via a single deal rather than hundreds of individual local deals.[120]

The American Association of Independent Music (*A2IM*) is a nonprofit trade organization that represents more than 350 independently owned American record labels. Its mission is to "help independent labels improve business by promoting access and parity through advocacy, education and connection-building with one another and affiliated businesses."[121]

Regulation and Policy

The recording industry is heavily regulated by widely divergent national laws which govern the usage and rights related to intellectual property and copyright. Most countries in the developed world have laws related to the need to compensate rights owners in the form of licensing fees if the property—in this case, music—is reproduced in any format.[122]

However, the value of intellectual property—most notably music—is threatened by the ease of downloading digital files, where it is easy to bypass intellectual property rights. The problem is confounded by the legal inability of governments to act, rather than their reluctance to do so. The unanswered question is "whose responsibility is it to enforce any new laws?" The music industry suggests that ISPs should be responsible for policing and removing file-sharing sites. ISPs claim that they are under no obligation to do so and that music companies should be responsible for protecting their own intellectual property.[123]

In the early days of illegal downloading, music companies were highly litigious in pursuing individuals and companies that provided access to illegal music. Organizations such as CISAC and the IFPI contend that these legal actions have had an impact in lessening the amount of music that is illegally traded in developed nations. The challenge facing the industry now is in developing nations, where growing populations of internet users are expected to begin downloading large amounts of music and other data. In general, developing countries do not have strong legislative frameworks in place that prevent the unauthorized trading of intellectual property. As a result, the regulatory climate around music and music rights will continue to be a major source of concern for the foreseeable future.[124]

HOW LABELS INVEST IN THEIR ARTISTS

When an artist signs a traditional deal with a label, there is an understanding that the label will support the artist's development in many ways. While each deal is different, the most common forms of support are the payment of an advance, the funding of a recording, music video production, tour support, and promotional costs. According to the IFPI, it can cost between US$500,000 and US$2 million to break an artist in a major recorded music market.[125]

Typical Investment by a Major Record Company in a Newly Signed Artist

Advance	US$50,000–350,000
Recording	$150,000–500,000
Video production	$50,000–300,000
Tour Support	$50,000–150,000
Marketing and Promotion	$200,000–700,000
Total	$500,000–2 million

(Source: IFPI member record companies)

Advances

Record company advances enable artists to give up their day jobs in order to focus on writing new music, rehearsing, recording, and performing. Artists usually must repay advances by foregoing future royalties earned from sales and streaming. This common method of repayment is known as "recouping" an advance. In other words, artists' advances will be repaid not in cash by the artist (as in a bank loan). Instead, the label will withhold any royalty payment to the artist from future music sales until the advance is repaid. If the artist's future sales are insufficient for the label to recover its advance, it is considered an unrecouped advance. As you can see, the record label is bearing the risk of its investment in the artist in what is clearly a highly competitive and uncertain marketplace.[126]

Prior to the advent of digital music, labels could count on recouping their investment from album sales, both physical and online. This usually took 18 months to two years for a Top 40 artist. Now, with streaming music services becoming ever more popular with consumers, it takes a longer period of time to recoup an advance. For artists, the label's upfront financial investment has become even more important.[127]

A new pop artist or ensemble that is signed to a major record label in one of the major markets (US, Europe, Canada) often receives an advance somewhere between US$50,000 and US$350,000. If there is a bidding war for an artist amongst labels, the advance amount could go even higher. Most artists and ensembles receive far lower, if any, advances if they are unproven and/or signed to a small label. In such cases the label may offer artists a revenue-sharing deal that supports the artist as soon as money from sales and other sources begins to flow.[128]

Recording Costs

With recording costs significantly lessened due to digital equipment and the industry's awareness of the need to manage their budgets more efficiently, the amount a label is willing to spend varies widely between individual projects. Well-known recording artists whose music sells are good investments for labels. These artists may receive well over a million (US) dollars for their recording project. Many of these artists work with one or more superstar producers on an album whose fees, combined with those of top-ranked session musicians, studio engineers and others, add significantly to the cost of a project. An emerging pop act in a major market may receive somewhere between US$150,000 and $500,000 for her recording budget.[129] Both artist and label work hard to sell the recording through social media, touring, and personal appearances. If sales are good, the artist may receive a bigger recording budget for her next project, and the label will have made a solid investment.

Video Production

As with recording costs, producing a video in conjunction with the project varies widely depending upon the artist's style, her fans, and how the video will be used. YouTube and Vevo are two music companies that are widely used for artist discovery. A typical video production budget for an emerging pop act in a major market ranges from US$50,000 to $300,000 for three videos. (It is common to produce more than one video per recording project.) Superstar artists' videos can cost more than US$500,000. Some of the most innovative and creative videos produced today are very cost-effective, with some costing as little as US$10,000.[130] A label's investment in video production will help drive demand for the artist and her recording.

Tour Support

Touring is expensive for all artists, particularly for musicians who have an international fanbase. Upfront money for a tour is crucial, as many big expenses are incurred before the first concert ticket is sold. Increasingly, labels have moved into multiple rights or 360-deals with artists that give the labels a cut of touring revenue in exchange for financial tour support.

An emerging pop artist whose recording company wants them to tour internationally can expect between US$50,000 and $150,000 in support. Large ensembles and soloists who travel with many support musicians will require even higher levels of support to match the corresponding increase in costs.[131] As we have seen, the level of financial support for touring depends on many variables, including the financial resources of the label, its willingness to invest in a new pop or rock artist, and the types of venues that the artist or ensemble will need for its live shows.

Is It Luck or Skill?

Major labels may be willing to provide a high level of support to an artist they believe could be the next Beyoncé or Kanye West. They'll spend close to US$2 million developing their product (an album) before it even goes on sale.

To put this into perspective, if the artist turns out to be a mega pop-star hit, the label will recoup its investment and the artist will see a profit. But the numbers are tough—most new acts don't come anywhere near the wattage of Beyoncé. It's a guessing game as to what will catch on. The A&R process—finding and signing new artists—is probably more luck than skill.

Even Lady Gaga wasn't an overnight sensation. American radio stations resisted her European-influenced, four-on-the-floor beat. Jimmy Iovine, the former chairman of Gaga's label Interscope, said it took six months to get her first single, "Just Dance," on the air. It rose quickly to the top of the charts. "The masses will accept something new," Iovine said. "It's the people in between who will fight you."[132]

Recognizing that an artist's fans receive information about the artist from many sources, recording companies use sophisticated marketing approaches to target specific groups of consumers. Digital media is a crucial arena for labels in reaching an artist's fans. This is the newest area for marketing dollars and, even though digital media can be highly effective, it has by no means eliminated the need to continue to advertise across traditional media, such as television, radio, billboards, and print. Recording companies have deep knowledge of how to use traditional media to market their artists.[133]

The use of "data mining"—gathering statistical information about customers from their use of media and electronic devices—has become a rich area of information in the music industry. Data collection, along with focus groups and consumer research, round out the labels' ability to predict the most cost-effective ways to connect their artists to their fans. For recording companies that want their artists' music to reach a mass audience, exposing performers to fans in different markets using many types of marketing tools is crucial to the label's investment.[134]

Pause and Reflect

How good are you at predicting which indie artists will become global artists? Can you tell which new artists are being supported by a record label? If so, what are the clues?

Broader Rights Deals

The nature of the partnership between labels and artists has evolved in recent years. With the stark decline in consumer purchases of music—for decades, its major revenue source—labels have sought to become more involved in all aspects of an artist's career and revenue streams. Virtually all recording contracts today are what is known as broader or multiple rights deals. When an artist enters into this type of agreement, she is agreeing to share revenue she earns from areas such as touring, merchandise sales, sponsorships, book deals, and even public appearances with her record label. In the past, artists' managers primarily arranged and shared in the income from these revenue streams.

In order to provide value to the artist in exchange for a larger slice of her revenue pie, some record labels offer one-stop shopping by running in-house music merchandising firms, booking agencies, and, of course, publishing companies—all with the express intent of servicing the artists' recording projects. The percentage of revenue the artist agrees to give to her label for these additional services varies, depending upon how actively the label will be involved in each area. Broader rights contracts where the recording company is primarily an investor, as opposed to an active participant, are known as passive deals.[135]

'Stache media is an example of an in-house firm that services broader rights deals. Owned by Sony Music Entertainment as part of the RED distribution family, 'Stache is a marketing agency that specializes in "advertising, lifestyle marketing, digital and influencer marketing, publicity, brand and strategic marketing, licensing, retail marketing, art direction and design and consumer insights for the music industry."[136] It serves more than 60 indie record labels, as well as artists from Sony-owned labels and Sony joint ventures with Descendant Records, Ultra Records, Red Bow Records, and RED Associated Labels.[137]

THE CHALLENGES: TURNING PROBLEMS INTO OPPORTUNITIES

Three of the key challenges facing the recording industry are mentioned below. As you read these, look for ways to turn the negatives into positives. Find opportunities in each of the problems and come up with creative solutions or even potential new revenue streams for recording artists.

Ownership vs. Access

With the convenience and affordability of cloud storage and legal streaming options, millions of customers are migrating to services that provide access to music as they move away from owning music. This leaves the recording industry struggling to figure out how to monetize a significant consumer behavioral change of preferring access over ownership.

It's a Singles Business

When people *do* buy music, they prefer to purchase single tracks and build playlists instead of albums. Sites such as iTunes encourage consumers to purchase songs on an individual basis, which has reduced the economies of scale[138] that the sale of albums achieved.

Record labels make more money selling albums, so this change in consumer behavior is a major factor in their revenue slide. It has even impacted the traditional way of counting and charting sales. Nielsen created the Track Equivalent Albums (TEA) category to tabulate the number of digital tracks sold by a given artist. TEA is computed by dividing the total number of tracks sold by ten, which approximates the average number of tracks on a full-length album.

Termination Rights

There is a provision in the revised US Copyright Act of 1976 that gives creators of works of art the right to reclaim ownership of their work after 35 years if they have assigned it to a third party and meet certain conditions. This "termination right" affects recordings from 1978 and later, and could be a major revenue loss for labels. Loretta Lynn, Tom Waits, Bob Dylan, and Charlie Daniels are among the well-known artists who have filed to regain control of their work from the labels that own the master recording.

Mini-Case Study: New Jazz Label Takes a Calculated Risk

Sometimes an entrepreneur will start a new venture that, at first glance, seems counter-intuitive in a specific marketplace. Wynton Marsalis, the renowned jazz musician and educator, has taken just such a step in launching a new record label devoted to the decidedly traditional genre of jazz.[139]

Blue Engine Records, Marsalis' venture, is the private label for Jazz at Lincoln Center (JALC). With some heavy lifting from its partner, Sony Music Entertainment, Blue Engine will showcase the best live concert recordings from the hundreds of archived shows JALC has presented since its founding in 1987. New studio and live shows will also be part of the mix. "The identity of our institution has not been available—unless we're live," states Marsalis, JALC Managing and Artistic Director. Blue Engine has an exclusive agreement with RED Distribution, a division of Sony Music, for global distribution.[140]

Blue Engine does have competition in this small market. Other jazz labels based out of clubs include Smalls Jazz Club (in Greenwich Village, New York City), Ronnie Scott's Jazz House (in London, England), and Discos Pendiente (in Santiago, Chile).

Marsalis has good advice for entrepreneurs: "You start small—you figure out how to serve the audience and [your] mission." Given that Blue Engine albums will be released over a 15-year period, Marsalis' additional caveat, "We wouldn't want to rush things," shows that he takes his own advice.[141]

TOOLS FOR THE DIWO (DO IT WITH OTHERS) ENTREPRENEUR: DIGITAL MUSIC SERVICES

Streaming and Download Services to Help You Attract Fans

Fool's Gold, Jagjaguwar, and Secretly Canadian are three labels that hope their partnership with Drip.fm, a subscription streaming and download service, will help them attract fans with exclusive music, a sense of community, and an intimate connection with bands and artists. Sub Pop records, an indie label that introduced the artists Nirvana and the Shins, has partnered with Drip.fm. Fans who sign up for the Sub Pop feed on Drip.fm will pay US$10 per month in exchange for albums, singles, and special exclusives from the label. Sub Pop's new idea may help bring back the days when fans had intense brand loyalty to labels.[142]

Indie Artists Curate Their Own Streaming Services

Some indie musicians are creating their own streaming services to appeal directly to their fans. Two such artists are Nicolas Jaar and Ryan Hemsworth, who founded Other People and Secret Songs, respectively.

The economics of streaming has been tough on indie artists, given the large number of streams needed to produce even a small amount of revenue. Jaar explained that his music doesn't appeal to the masses, so he needs to find a way to cultivate a small yet loyal following. His 2011 debut album got him off to a solid start.[143]

Jarr started Other People by offering his subscribers a weekly mix of songs which they could download for a US$5 monthly fee. Within six months, he says that Other People began to be profitable. "The truth is that touring can be really bad for making music, bad for the creative process," he explains. "When I started Other People I was really trying to find a way to have a self-sustainable label so I don't have to be touring all the time."[144]

"Ignore the Labels if You Want to Get Signed"

Technology, the internet, and changing consumer behavior have taken a serious financial toll on the traditional recording industry. Yet many young artists still cling to the myth of being "discovered" and then getting signed to a label. If you recognize yourself in the previous sentence, artist manager Ethan Schiff of Hypebot has advice for you:

> I often hear artists declare from day one that their goal is to get signed to a label. The problem with this line of thinking is that it distracts you from the unbelievably difficult task of building a fan base and developing outstanding material. You might argue that you can do both and that, in fact, the goal of signing to a label will only motivate you further and drive you to put more effort into your work. But I wouldn't believe you.

> I believe starting a project with the goal of making the most deliberate music possible, coupled with an absolutely relentless focus on turning your supporters into a true community, is a much better use of brainspace than having phrases like "would a label want this?" in the back of your head every step of the way.[145]

Schiff believes that artists who already have traction and their fans' attention will be the only musicians of interest to a label. Artists must be confident of their own value and demonstrate that to labels through an unwavering dedication to their music, work ethic, live shows, emails to fans, and social media posts. Schiff further encourages every serious musician who wants the support of a label to "start your own movement and truly create something that spreads . . . [and] labels will come to you. If you begin by hoping to be validated by someone else, you've missed the point completely."[146]

For DJs Who Think They Want to Get Signed to a Label

Blaise DeAngelo, General Manager of indie label OWSLA (co-founded by Skrillex, Tim Smith, Kathryn Frazier, and Clayton Blaha), says having great ideas and confidence in your own artistic direction are the two most important things for an E.D.M. artist who is interested in working with a label: "Producers [who] have good technical skills and can make a song if you give them the idea are a dime a dozen, right? We're interested in people [who] have those ideas. You can teach an artist how to mix better, how to make better sounds, how to work with the technical side of the audio engineering. But what you can't teach is that confidence in being able to generate and harvest ideas, and to pursue those ideas confidently, unwaveringly, without trying to follow trends."[147]

> *Opportunities Ahead*
>
> Sketch out a business model for a recording company that you would like to launch. Where are the opportunities and the potential pitfalls? How would you position your company for success in this fractured and crowded marketplace?

CONCLUSION

The recording industry faces many challenges due to changes in technology, consumer habits, and regulatory issues. Major labels' revenue has fallen to half its peak 1999 value. Illegal downloads and other copyright infringements are a major reason why record labels continue to lose money. Producers play an important role in this industry. CD Baby is one of many online tools for DIWO artist-entrepreneurs. There are abundant opportunities to create revenue streams in recorded music for music entrepreneurs.

Talking Back: Class Discussion

What are the best routes for an unsigned band or ensemble that has a loyal local following to attract the attention of a label? It may help to select an actual band or ensemble to answer these questions: what are their goals in making a recording? Do they have sufficient repertoire, performing experience, energy, and commitment to support a new recording with a tour?

NOTES

1 Ben Sisario, "Online Music Sales Eclipse CDs and LPs," *New York Times*, April 15, 2015.
2 James Crompton, "Global Music Production and Distribution," IBIS World Industry Report Q8712-GL, January 2015.
3 Ibid.
4 Ibid.
5 Ibid.
6 Ibid.
7 Crompton, "Global Music Production."
8 Ben Sisario, "New Venture Seeks Higher Royalties for Songwriters," *New York Times*, October 29, 2014.
9 Crompton, "Global Music Production."
10 Sydney Ember, "Marketers Vie for Eyes Typically Trained on Phones," *New York Times*, September 28, 2015.
11 Crompton, "Global Music Production."
12 Ibid.
13 Kory Grow, "Music Industry Sets Friday as New Global Release Day," *Rolling Stone*, February 26, 2015, www.rollingstone.com/music/news/music-industry-sets-friday-as-new-global-release-day-20150226 (accessed May 22, 2016).
14 Ben Sisario, "Global Deal to Release New Albums on Fridays," *New York Times*, February 27, 2015.
15 Grow, "Music Industry Sets Friday."
16 Crompton, "Global Music Production."
17 Ibid.
18 Ben Sisario, "Music Sales Drop 5 Percent as Habits Shift Online," *New York Times,* September 26, 2014.

19 Crompton, "Global Music Production."

20 Bob Donnelly, Esq., "Buyer Beware: Why Artists Should 'Do a 180' on '360 Deals,'" *Billboard*, March 27, 2010, www.billboard.com/biz/articles/news/1209534/buyer-beware-why-artists-should-do-a-180-on-360-deals (accessed May 22, 2016).

21 Ibid.

22 "2015 Report," International Federation for the Phonographic Industry (IFPI), 38.

23 Ibid.

24 Ibid.

25 "2015 Report," 7.

26 "2015 Report," 38.

27 Ibid.

28 "2015 Report," 7, 39.

29 "2015 Report," 40.

30 Liron Sivan, Michael D. Smith, and Rahul Telang, "Do Search Engines Influence Media Piracy?" Carnegie Mellon University, Heinz College Research, September 2014, http://papers.ssrn.com/sol3/papers.cfm?abstract_id=2495591 (accessed May 22, 2016).

31 Ibid.

32 Ibid.

33 "2015 Report," 40.

34 Ibid.

35 Ibid.

36 Ibid.

37 Nadia Khomami, "Björk's Record Label Discuss 'Nightmare' Leak That Led to Early Release of 'Vulnicura,'" *NME*, January 23, 2015, www.nme.com/news/bjork/82411#h2bQrkGFeCzQkeRF.99 (accessed May 22, 2016).

38 Joe Coscarelli, "When Digital Thieves Strike, Artists Act Quickly to Seize Opportunity," *New York Times*, January 22, 2015.

39 Ibid.

40 Ibid.

41 Ibid.

42 Ibid.

43 Ibid.

44 Ibid.

45 Ibid.

46 Ibid.

47 Ibid.

48 "2015 Report," 29.

49 Ibid.

50 Ibid, 37.

51 Ibid.

52 Ibid.

53 Ibid.

54 Richard Smirke, "Seven Takeaways from IFPI's Study of the Global Music Market Last Year," *Billboard*, April 20, 2015, www.billboard.com/articles/business/6538815/seven-takeaways-from-ifpi-recording-industry-in-numbers (accessed May 22, 2016).

55 Crompton, "Global Music Production."

56 Ibid.

57 Ben Sisario, "EMI Is Sold for $4.1 Billion in Combined Deals, Consolidating the Music Industry," *New York Times*, November 11, 2011, www.nytimes.com/2011/11/12/business/media/emi-is-sold-for-4-1-billion-consolidating-the-music-industry.html?_r=2 (accessed May 22, 2016).

58 Crompton, "Global Music Production."

59 "About," *Easy Star Records*, www.easystar.com/about (accessed May 22, 2016).

60 "About," *Toolroom Records*, www.toolroomrecords.com/about (accessed May 22, 2016).

61 Crompton, "Global Music Production."

62 Ibid.

63 Ibid.

64 Ibid.

65 Ibid.

66 Ibid.

67 Ibid.

68 Cliff Goldmacher, "Producers: What They Do and Why You Should Consider Using One," *BMI*, October 29, 2009, www.bmi.com/news/entry/Producers_What_They_Do_Why_You_Should_Consider_Using_One (accessed May 22, 2016).

69 Ibid.

70 Ibid.

71 Tim Chester, "50 of The Greatest Producers Ever," *NME*, www.nme.com/list/the-50-greatest-producers-ever/262849/page/1#SUlkfRdAbqvuyXik.99 (accessed May 22, 2016)

72 Mark Savage, "Why Are Female Record Producers So Rare?" *BBC News*, August 29, 2012, http://ww.bbc.com/news/entertainment-arts-19284058 (accessed May 22, 2016)

73 Ibid.

74 "Topics: Alicia Keys," *BET*, www.bet.com/topics/a/alicia-keys.html (accessed May 22, 2016)

75 Nate Patrin, "The 10 Best Missy Elliott Songs," *Stereogum*, March 3, 2015, www.stereogum.com/1783705/the-10-best-missy-elliott-songs/franchises/10-best-songs (accessed May 22, 2016).

76 Natelege Whaley, "Unsung Hitmakers: Female Music Producers," *BET*, www.bet.com/music/photos/2014/07/female-music-producers.html#!062014-Music-Female-Music-Producers-Elliott-Alicia-Keys-Erykah-Badu (accessed May 22, 2016).

77 Katie Bain, "Where Are All the Women Producers? Here Are 5 Famous Ones," *LA Weekly*, January 20, 2014, www.laweekly.com/music/where-are-all-the-women-producers-here-are-5-famous-ones-4320912 (accessed May 22, 2016).

78 Ibid.

79 Whaley, "Unsung Hitmakers."

80 Tony Case, "Janelle Monáe Is Building a Music Empire That Will Spark a Revolution in Your Head," *AdWeek*, March 15, 2015, www.adweek.com/news/advertising-branding/janelle-mon-e-building-music-empire-will-spark-revolution-your-head-163457 (accessed May 22, 2016).

81 Ibid.

82 "Bio," *Kara DioGuardi*, www.karadioguardi.com/#bio (accessed May 22, 2016).

83 Bain, "Where Are All the Women."

84 Savage, "Why Are Female Record Producers So Rare?"

85 Ibid.

86 "About," Women's Audio Mission, womensaudiomission.org/about (accessed May 22, 2016).

87 Ibid.

88 "About Us," *PRS for Music*, www.m-magazine.co.uk/about/ (accessed May 22, 2016).

89 Ibid.

90 Savage, "Why Are Female Record Producers So Rare?"

91 Ibid.

92 Chester, "50 of the Greatest."

93 Larry Getlen, "Every Song You Love Was Written by the Same Two Guys," *New York Post*, October 4, 2015, www.nypost.com/2015/10/04/your-favorite-song-on-the-radio-was-probably-written-by-these-two/ (accessed May 22, 2016).

94 Jon Pareles, "Get Back Up and Dance," *New York Times*, March 6, 2015.

95 Ibid.

96 Ibid.

97 Ibid.

98 Alistair McGeorge, "James Arthur Says Working with Multiple Producers 'F**** Up' Creativity," *The Mirror* (UK), November 6, 2013, www.mirror.co.uk/3am/celebrity-news/james-arthur-says-working-multiple-2681818 (accessed May 22, 2016).

99 "James Arthur," All Music, www.allmusic.com/album/james-arthur-mw0002586669/credits (accessed May 22, 2016).

100 Larry Rohter, "CD Baby, a Company for the Niche Musician," *New York Times*, August 12, 2014.

101 Ibid.

102 Ibid.

103 Ibid.

104 Ibid.

105 Ibid.

106 Ibid.

107 Ibid.

108 Ibid.

109 Ibid.

110 Ibid.

111 Ibid.

112 Ibid.

113 Ibid.

114 Ibid.

115 David M. Ross, "Facing Forward with Scott Borchetta, Jay Frank, and Eric Garland . . . ", *Music Row*, February/March 2011, 15.

116 "About," IFPI, http://ifpi.org/about.php (accessed May 22, 2016).

117 "About Us," *RIAA*, www.riaa.com/aboutus.php?content_selector=about-who-we-are-riaa (accessed May 22, 2016).

118 "Welcome," *Worldwide Independent Network (WIN)*, http://winformusic.org (accessed May 22, 2016).

119 "Impala's Mission," *Impala Music*, http://impalamusic.org/node/4 (accessed May 22, 2016).

120 "What We Do," *Merlin*, http://merlinnetwork.org/what-we-do (accessed May 22, 2016).

121 Home, *A2IM*, http://a2im.org (accessed May 22, 2016).

122 Crompton, "Global Music Production"

123 Ibid.

124 Ibid.

125 IFPI, "How Record Labels Invest," http://ifpi.org/how-record-labels-invest.php (accessed May 22, 2016).

126 Ibid.

127 Ibid.

128 Ibid.

129 Ibid.

130 Ibid.

131 Ibid.

132 Jon Pareles, "Even Offstage, Lady Gaga's Ready for the Stage," *New York Times*, May 18, 2011.

133 IFPI, "How Record Labels Invest."

134 Ibid.

135 Ibid.

136 "Services," *Stache Media*, http://stachemedia.com/services (accessed May 22, 2016).

137 Robin Pogrebin, "Jazz Archive Jump-Starts a Record Label," *New York Times*, June 30, 2015.

138 Economies of scale are proportionate savings in costs gained by an increased level of production.

139 Ibid.

140 Ibid.

141 Ibid.

142 Jonah Bromwich, "Independent Music Labels and Young Artists Offer Streaming, on Their Terms," *New York Times*, July 6, 2014.

143 Ibid.

144 Ibid.

145 Ethan Schiff, "Ignore the Labels if You Want to Get Signed," *Hypebot*, www.hypebot.com/hypebot/2013/05/ignore-the-labels-if-you-want-to-get-signed.html (accessed May 22, 2016).

146 Ibid.

147 Nina Ulloa, "The OWSLA Guide to Getting Signed by a Record Label," *Digital Music News*, June 14, 2015, www.digitalmusicnews.com/permalink/2015/06/14/owsla-spills-the-secret-to-getting-signed-by-a-record-label (accessed May 22, 2016).

PART 4

You as Entrepreneur

CHAPTER 10

Hands on: Start Something That Matters

CHAPTER OVERVIEW

All the work you have done so far has prepared you well for this final task: starting something that matters. In this chapter you will be guided through the process of selecting one of your ideas for a new music venture and preparing to write a business plan to shop it. Making meaning in the world is the single most important aspect of launching a new venture. Problem-solving exercises will help you find the right entrepreneurial venture for your life's goals. The guidelines presented here are applicable to ventures where you and your music are the product or service, as well as to ventures that are not quite as personal. All other aspects of developing your venture are presented here, with a section on legal and tax issues for businesses launched in the US.

KEY TERMS

Risk vs. reward	Profit/loss forecast
Value proposition	Cash-flow projection
Business model	Gross profit percentage
Market research	Positioning your offering
Prototype	Debt and equity financing
Assumptions	Capital for nonprofits
Basic formula for making financial projections	Grant funding
	Venture capital funding
Variable and fixed costs	Elements of a business plan
Break-even point	

MAKE MEANING

There are as many types of entrepreneur as there are people in the world. Some have a business with only one employee: themselves. Others want to achieve rapid growth and profitability in a few years and then sell their business. Between these two extremes one can find the majority of music entrepreneurs. In fact, some musicians are accidental entrepreneurs; they own a business, but they don't even realize it.

Rather than focus on hypothetical questions about your ability to work for yourself to earn a living, it is more productive to concentrate on only one essential question:

How will I make meaning with my new business?[1]

Every business that's worth starting will make the world a better place. Channel your energies and resources into doing something worthwhile. You may make lots of money or you may fail, but the goal is to improve and repair the world, even if your company is for-profit.

Think about existing businesses that improve your life. Look carefully at their products and services. Examine their business model. Who are their customers? With whom do they compete? What are they doing better than their competitors?

Now think about businesses that you feel are making a real difference in peoples' lives anywhere in the world. How do they measure success? How do they earn money?

All of these businesses have at least this in common: they started small, they found a solution to an urgent need or problem, and they press on day after day making the world a better place through the work they do. The entrepreneur who started the company probably had a million questions and was nervous about the possibility of failing, but she put all that aside in pursuit of the guiding star: my business will make the world a better place, even if I start out serving only a few people.

Gather your confidence and creativity, as you are poised to figure out what business you'll create that will make meaning in the marketplace. Remember the definition of music entrepreneur from Chapter 2:

> A music entrepreneur is someone who sees opportunity
>
> where others see only problems, and creatively channels
>
> his or her passion for music into a new business that challenges
>
> the status quo and has value in the public marketplace.

You may decide to start your venture on the side while you're working at a traditional job. Perhaps you are a one-person entity and want to create a business around your music. No matter where you end up along the entrepreneurial spectrum—for-profit, not-for-profit, social endeavors—the information that follows will help.

If you're not quite sure where your passion lies, begin by answering these questions:

1. How would I spend my time if I did not have to worry about making money?

2. If I could do any kind of work, what would it be?

3. To what type of cause do I say "yes" when I'm asked to volunteer?

Take some time to think about the questions before you answer. When you finish, you'll be a long way toward understanding what motivates you to work hard at something.

Test Your Ideas

It is time to brainstorm to find an entrepreneurial opportunity that's right for *you*. First, think about things in your musical experience that are annoying, don't work well, don't exist, or are real problems for you or your friends. Take your time. Jot down everything that you notice, no matter how small or large.

Sit down with a friend and look over your list. Being able to articulate your ideas is important. You're looking for problems that can be turned into opportunities for a new venture. Can you demonstrate that the problem affects someone besides you? If not, the marketplace may be too small to support your venture. On the other hand, if you've identified a new product or service that people don't yet know they want or need, then you may have something to build on.

Go through all the ideas from your brainstorming. A few ideas will naturally rise to the top of the list because they seem more viable and exciting. Put the other ideas in a box for later exploration. For now we'll focus on the ideas at the top of your list to determine if they can become entrepreneurial opportunities.

Using the structured problem-solving steps you learned in Chapter 2, put each of your ideas through the test to see if they might be opportunities:

- How can you solve the problem you've identified? What would Oprah do? This is a "blue sky" way of seeing if there actually are any solutions to the problem, even if you take money out of the equation.

- Use the 99% solution to see how you can get most of the benefits for a fraction of the cost. Now you're looking for realistic solutions to your problem that acknowledge the limited resources most people have.

Your Personal Mission Statement

This section is for anyone who didn't complete the Personal Mission Statement exercise in Chapter 2. If you have your Personal Mission Statement done, skip to the section entitled "Finding the Right Entrepreneurial Opportunity . . . for You."

A personal mission is a short statement outlining what makes life meaningful for you and how you will focus your energy on it to create a sustainable life. How can you discover your mission? Start by noticing the things that are important to you *beyond* music. The goal is to look at yourself as a whole person, not just your musical self. Your list might include teaching, a spiritual path, family, your health, and community activism. Whatever is important to you beyond music will allow you to fulfill your mission, even when you aren't making music. When you lead with your mission, you will be acting in the world as your authentic self. This will make you more powerful and more fulfilled.[2]

The following step-by-step guide from Think Simple Now, an online personal development community, will help you get started in crafting your mission statement. While you're working on this, please keep in mind author Stephen Covey's observation:

> Writing or reviewing a [personal] mission statement changes you because it forces you to think through your priorities deeply, carefully, and to align your behavior with your beliefs.[3]

A personal mission consists of three parts:

What do I want to do?

Who do I want to help?

What is the result? What value will I create?

Steps to Creating Your Personal Mission Statement

Step I: The Nine Questions Exercise

Find a place where you will not be interrupted. Turn off your phone. Write down your answers to each question below, quickly and without editing:

1. What activities make you lose track of time?

2. What makes you feel great about yourself?

3. What qualities do you admire most in someone who inspires you?

4. What do people typically ask you for help in?

5. What would you regret not fully doing, being, or having in your life?

6. What were some challenges, difficulties, and hardships you've overcome or are in the process of overcoming? How did you do it?

7. What social or political causes do you strongly believe in or connect with?

8. How could you use your passions and values to serve and contribute to that cause?

9. What are your highest values? Select five from the list below and prioritize the words in order of importance.[4]

Achievement	Fitness	Passion
Adventure	Friendship	Performance
Beauty	Giving service	Play
Challenge	Health	Productivity
Comfort	Honesty	Primary relationship
Creativity	Independence	Respect
Curiosity	Intimacy	Security
Education	Joy	Spirituality
Empowerment	Leadership	Success
Environment	Learning	Time freedom
Family	Love	Variety
Financial freedom	Motivation	*Other:*

Step 2

List action words that are meaningful to you. Examples include: accomplish, empower, encourage, improve, help, give, guide, inspire, integrate, master, motivate, nurture, organize, produce, promote, travel, spread, share, satisfy, understand, teach, write, etc.

Step 3

Based on your answers to the nine questions above, list everything and everyone that you believe you can help.

Step 4

Identify your end goal. How will the "who or what" from Step 3 benefit from what you can do for them?

Step 5

Combine Steps 1–4 into two to three sentences. This is the first draft of your Personal Mission Statement.

Finding the Right Entrepreneurial Opportunity . . . for You

Once you've written a solid first draft of your Personal Mission Statement, continue on by answering the following questions:

- Identify the area(s) in the music industry in which you are intensely interested in working.

- Identify problems in those areas.

- Use the four creative problem-solving methods to evaluate potential solutions to the problems.

- Then, identify and write down one or two problems or potential solutions that may become your new business. Answer these questions:

    ○ Does the potential business align with my Personal Mission Statement? If not, explore why. If so, state how it does align.

    ○ Could this potential business idea move me closer to achieving my life's goals? How?

    ○ Will the opportunity open or close any doors, now or in the foreseeable future? Describe.

Consider the following issues when reviewing your answers above:

Capabilities

- What's my actual role in this new opportunity?

- Do I have the skills I need and/or can I get them quickly?

Lifestyle

- Will I be in control of my life to the extent that I want to be?

- What is the impact of this opportunity on my social life, where I live, how much and where I travel, and the time commitment?

- What is the impact on my personal finances, both now and in the foreseeable future?

Relationships

- What impact could this new opportunity have on my relationship with friends, family, or a significant other?

- Am I comfortable with that impact? Are my friends, family, and significant other comfortable with it?

A Hypothetical New Venture

Sketch out a hypothetical new entrepreneurial venture in an area of the music industry that interests you. At this point, keep it simple. You won't have all the information you need, so just take a deep breath and plunge in.

As you work, review your answers in the "Finding the Right Entrepreneurial Opportunity . . . for You" section. Use your Personal Mission Statement as a guide. Write down one or two sentences that fully describe (as best as you can) how each criterion will need to play out in order for your hypothetical new venture to be in alignment with your Personal Mission Statement. You may find that you need to refine or change the wording in your personal mission statement as you apply it to a business setting. This is all part of the process.

Congratulations! You've now completed a first draft of your Personal Mission Statement and have a hypothetical new venture (or two) in mind that aligns with your mission. Put your work aside for now and turn your attention to other facets of becoming an entrepreneur.

Understanding and Evaluating Risk

Entrepreneurs take calculated risks after carefully evaluating the pros and cons of a situation or decision. Risk is defined as the combination of:

- the likelihood that loss will occur as a result of an action; and

- the possible magnitude of the loss.

Making a distinction between the probability of an event occurring and the magnitude of the resulting loss is fundamental to assessing a situation where risk is involved.[5]

Each of us evaluates situations involving risk and reward every day, even if we're not aware of it. For example, we want to decide whether or not to carry an umbrella when rain is forecast. Rain is an occurrence that can cause loss for urban dwellers (getting wet, ruining your shoes). We combine that with the likely size of the loss that it may cause (the loss will be small if I'm wearing a rain jacket, but could be large if I've got on a very expensive pair of shoes). So now we've made a distinction between the likelihood of an event occurring (rain is forecast) and the size of the potential loss (feeling damp and ruining your shoes).

Reducing Risk

Reducing risk means taking actions that either: (1) reduce the probability of the harmful event occurring in the first place; (2) reduce the probable severity of the loss if it does occur; or (3) a combination of these two. The general rule of thumb is to minimize risks while maximizing the rewards you will experience from exposure to those risks, and considering the costs incurred in doing so. Common examples of risk reduction in driving are:

- servicing your car regularly and properly, particularly in relation to safety items such as tires, brakes, lights, and steering;

- replacing your old car with one that has modern safety features and high safety ratings in crash tests;

- not texting while you drive.[6]

Transferring Risk

Transferring risk means giving it over to another person or organization, partially or completely, along with the potential losses and potential rewards that go with it. Risk can be transferred to a party that is in business for that very purpose, such as an insurance company, or to any other party legally capable of assuming risk. For example, whenever you sign a contract to rent an apartment, a car, or a boat, apply for a credit card, or rent a power tool, risk is transferred from the other party to you.[7]

If you take the time to read the small print that often comes with online purchases, apps, or access to certain websites, you may be shocked at the extent to which risk can be transferred from the company to you. Most of us just click "I agree" and don't give it another thought.

Use the exercise below to practice evaluating risk and reward. Write your answers in each box.

Risks of Not Buying Apartment Insurance	Rewards of Not Buying Apartment Insurance
Risks of Buying Apartment Insurance	**Rewards of Buying Apartment Insurance**

Big Achievers Share the Greatest Risks They Ever Took

Tim Westergren, Founder of Pandora Radio

In the winter of 2001, Pandora was out of money. We had a choice: cut our losses and throw in the towel or find a way to keep going. We decided to keep the company alive and start deferring salaries. Ultimately, over 50 people deferred almost $1.5M over the course of two years (a practice that is illegal in California). When we were finally rescued by an investment in 2004, I had maxed out 11 credit cards.[8]

Kai and Charles Huang, Co-founders of RedOctane, Creator of the Guitar Hero Videogame

Kai: The launch of "Guitar Hero" meant the survival of the company. We had been in business for six years by that time. We saved the company from bankruptcy twice; this was a third time. The biggest kick in the gut was knowing that if we couldn't raise the money, "Guitar Hero" wouldn't launch and we didn't know what we were going to do. We finally borrowed US$500,000 in the eleventh hour from a family friend. We were US$2 million in debt when we launched the product."

Charles: A couple years later, somebody said to me, "Wow, I can't believe you took all your money and bet it on a plastic guitar." (Happy ending: Video-game publisher Activision later bought RedOctane for US$100 million.)[9]

Time Management

How often do you reach the end of a day or a week and wonder "Where did all that time go? Why didn't I accomplish even half the things I set out to do?" You may feel overwhelmed or out of control in some areas of your life. As an entrepreneur you may feel stuck, worried that you are unable to see clearly how to keep your business growing.

Despite the fact that there are many things in life that are out of our personal control, it is quite possible to learn how best to organize your time in order to achieve a healthy work/life balance.

People playing Guitar Hero *video game*
FRANCK FIFE/AFP/Getty Images

The first step is to recognize that you want to make a change in how you organize your time. Be ready to make this a priority and be willing to do the necessary work.

The second step is to make a commitment to finding ways to make changes in how you manage your time.

And, finally, you must have someone who agrees to help, inspire, and hold you accountable to your plan. Without an accountability coach to keep you on track, it is easy to become distracted and make excuses for not doing the work you set out to do. You will be speaking with your coach at least once a week. Set up a schedule for that now.

With these first three things in place, it's time to begin.

Even though there are many of us who will help you along the way, time management is a process that *you* will guide and define for yourself. Once you get going, you will discover how your ideas are working for you. If something needs to be adjusted, make the change. Don't be afraid to jump in no matter how uncertain you are of the outcome. This is your plan, your life. You're in charge.

Days 1 and 2

The best way to start is to make an inventory of how you currently spend your time. Begin with yesterday. What did you do? Be honest about how you spent your day and do not judge yourself. Write this down either as an hour-by-hour reckoning or a morning/mid-day/evening overview. Or use some other method that makes more sense to you. Do you recall what you hoped to achieve by day's end? Did you meet that goal? If not, what got in the way?

If yesterday is a blur, don't worry. Begin with today. What's on your to-do list for today? Is anything scheduled for a fixed time, such as a doctor's appointment or dinner with friends, or is the day yours to define? What do you hope to accomplish by the end of today? How do you think you will fill your time so that you can meet that goal? What might get in the way of your plans? Think it through and make notes of your answers.

Days 3, 4, and Perhaps 5

Write down in one place all the things that are currently on your to-do list, whether your to-do list is in your mind, on a calendar, in sticky notes all over your laptop, on your phone, or all of the above. Include your obligations as well as personal, professional, planning, and thinking time, ongoing regular meetings, grant or other deadlines in the future, sleeping, and exercise. Write down everything that is nagging at your mind, causing you anxiety, keeping you up at night with worry, and things you feel (or someone said) you "should" be doing.

This is the messy part of the process. Just embrace it. Use a stream-of-consciousness approach—write it all down, in no particular order and without editing or judging. You may need several days to complete this. That's fine, don't rush it. If you feel stuck or discouraged while you're putting this together, take a break and return to your work when your head has cleared.

Days 6 and 7

In your mind, create an image of how you *want* to see yourself in three months' time. Then answer these questions and make notes of your answers. How are you filling the hours in your day three months from now? At the end of most days, do you feel you have a healthy balance between your work, personal time, and professional opportunities? In this image, what specific things have you accomplished or are close to accomplishing? How are you handling things that come up unexpectedly, both in your work and private life? What are the activities or distractions that keep you from following your daily plans?

Day 8

Take out your notes from your "three months from now" exercise. Compare that to how you spent the past two days. What will it take to get you from where you are today in managing your time to where you see yourself in three months? Work with your accountability coach to identify the specific issues that are preventing you from managing your time well. List each distraction and note exactly how you will resist it the next time it pops up. Then go about your days using these new coping skills. If one doesn't work, find a new way. It takes a long time to change our habits, so reward yourself when you've achieved a goal.

Three Months from Day 1

Take out the notes you wrote on days 6 and 7 of your time management plan. Compare your past few days with the image you created of how you saw yourself in three months. Congratulate yourself on your accomplishments. Redouble your efforts in the areas where you missed the mark. Managing your time well is a habit that will serve you well for your entire life.

Pause and Reflect

By now you've dug deeply into understanding what motivates you to work hard. You've identified some problems in the music industry and thought creatively about realistic solutions. Your "problem and solutions" list has probably gotten shorter than when you began this process. What remains are ideas that may have the potential to become entrepreneurial opportunities that will make meaning in the world.

The Value Proposition

There's still more refinement to do before you select the one opportunity you will pursue as a new venture. For each of your remaining ideas, you will now try to determine what value your business will deliver to your potential customers. This is called creating a Value Proposition. Each of your ideas solves a problem or satisfies a need for your potential customers, and it has value to them. Creating a Value Proposition is simply articulating the benefits your business will confer on its customers.

Do you want to sell products or services to your customers? This decision dictates the kind of personnel, premises, and marketing you need. Each type of offering requires different approaches and skills, and each has different challenges and rewards. Take your time in making your choice and refer to the notes you made while creating your Personal Mission Statement.

Pros and Cons of a Product Business

Products offer a consistent solution to customers' problems. If you sell products, you sell identical versions to numerous customers. You may offer advanced or improved versions of products, but even those remain very similar to each other. Your prospective customers can evaluate features before they buy, and if you do not sell to one prospect, you can try to sell the same item to another prospect. When you sell a *product*, you can focus more on selling than on customizing the product.[10]

When you sell products, you'll need to store inventory. Whether you manufacture goods or purchase them for resale, you must constantly re-evaluate your sales projections so that you know how much inventory to have on hand to meet demand. This means you spend money on products before you make any income from them. You will have storage and personnel costs for inventory, along with potential losses due to damage or theft.[11]

Pros and Cons of a Service Business

When you sell a service, you sell something that is intangible. You can adjust the features of a service to meet the needs of each client or customer. You can offer a trial period for using your services and, if the customer does not continue the service, you do not have to deal with disposing used goods.

You may find it difficult to describe your service to prospects. In fact, people you pitch to may not be able to visualize what you do. You can counter this by focusing on how your service benefits customers. Customers may express more reluctance when buying a service because, unlike a product, they can't evaluate it before they use it or return it if they aren't satisfied.

Understanding Your Business Model

Just as an architect prepares blueprints to guide the construction of a building, an entrepreneur designs a business model to guide the creation of an enterprise. Every organization—whether for-profit, nonprofit, government, NGO, or otherwise—has a business model, because every organization needs money to carry out its work.[12]

The following is a clever way of looking at the building blocks of a business. This model has been designed by 328 "work-life wizards" from 43 countries and made into a book entitled *Business Model You*. I highly recommend reading the book if you are a one-person business. For those of you whose ventures are larger, I recommend the companion book, *Business Model Generation*. Read through the nine building blocks of a business model in *Business Model You* terminology and think about how they might apply to your new venture:[13]

- *Customers*—they are the reason you are in business. Serving one's customers is the reason for an organization's existence.

- *Value provided*—the unique benefits you provide customers. These are customer benefits created by "bundles" of services or products. The ability to provide exceptional value is the key reason why customers select one organization over another.

- *Channels*—how you market, sell and deliver value to customers.

- *Customer relationships*—how you and your customers communicate with each other.

- *Revenue*—how the money flows into your business.

- *Key resources*—the human, physical, intellectual, and financial help your business requires.

- *Key activities*—the most important things you must do to make your business model work.

- *Key partners*—the supporting network that makes your business model effective in the areas of collaboration, resource-sharing, or financial backing.

- *Costs*—the expenses you will incur to create and deliver value, maintain good customer relations, and generate revenue.

To use visual tools to help you see your venture's business model, download a PDF of the personal Business Model Canvas at BusinessModelYou.com.[14]

Get to Know Your Customers

After you have decided whether your venture will be a product or a service business, write out each of your potential venture ideas on a separate page and answer these questions as best you can:

- Who will my customers be? It helps to visualize them.

- Where do they live (i.e., urban/rural/suburban; region/country/continent)?

- How old are they?

- What is their income range?

Thinking of your customers in groups with similar traits, such as the examples above, is known as a demographic analysis. The goal is to learn as much as you can about your customers so that you can tailor your marketing plans as precisely as possible.

Next, try to put your customers into smaller groupings by estimating the likelihood of their buying your product or service. This is called customer or market segmentation in business terms, but all it means is looking at slices of the population in priority order, starting with those most likely to want or need your product. The top priority slice is called your primary target market. From there it goes to a secondary and perhaps even to a tertiary target market. Most of your research and energy will be spent on the primary target market for your product or service.

An entrepreneur's main role is helping her customers solve their problems. For each group of potential customers you have identified, list the *specific* problem (or set of problems) your product or service will help the customer solve. If you think you've got a great problem-solving product or service, do some market research and ask people in your community if they agree with you. Just because *you* think it's a problem doesn't mean it actually is for anyone else.

Test your assumptions at every point along the way. Don't take anything for granted. And truly hear what your potential customers are saying. Their comments may mean that you need to revise some aspect of your venture or maybe even start over with a new idea. But without customers to buy your product or service, you do not have a business.

Channels

The next area to consider is how you will get your service or product to your customers. Consider all angles, including physical delivery, online delivery, inventory and fulfillment requirements, and all associated costs.

Finally, decide what are the best ways of letting your customer know about your product or service. Before you begin, review the Branding and Marketing chapter and build those concepts into your marketing plan.

Competition

Every business has competition. Once you have a clear idea of your product or service and your customers, it's time to see what competition already exists in the marketplace.

The easiest way to research this is do an online search using key words that define your product and see what comes up. Be as open-minded as you possibly can be during this process. Many entrepreneurs have fallen in love with their idea by this point and are outraged when they discover someone else has beaten them to the market. If that is the case for you, it does not necessarily mean you have to abandon your idea. You will simply have to prove how your product or service is unique in some way(s) for solving the customer's problem.

Now answer these questions about your competitors. What will your competitors do better than you, and why? What will you do better than your competitors, and why? How do your specific competitors market their products/services? How will you market yours?

At this point you've developed a Personal Mission Statement, have ideas for one or two hypothetical ventures, decided whether they will be product- or service-based companies, and have researched your customers and your competitors. Put your work aside for now and turn your attention to the following exercise in order to refine your ideas even further.

Exercise

Describe your product or service in one paragraph. Include the following information:

- What your product or service does. Consider using the KISS method,[15] which means comparing your offering to something people already use or know about, i.e., "My website is a Facebook for pet owners."

- A specific description of your intended customer.

- The specific and expressed problem or unmet need it will solve for the customer.

- Existing products or services in the marketplace that are similar to yours.

- Why those products or services don't meet the customer's needs.

- Details about how your customers will find and purchase your product.

Describe your competition in one paragraph. Include the following information:

- The names of at least three competitors.

- What the companies do and why you consider them competition.

- A comparison of the one key characteristic that differentiates your product or service from those of your competitors.

You now have enough information to write your Value Proposition. Keep reworking it until it is one sentence long. Remember, each of your ideas solves a problem or satisfies a need for your potential customers, and it has value to them. The Value Proposition simply describes the benefits that your offering will provide.

Market Research

Ultimately, confidence is a major ingredient of decision-making. Market research as much as you like, but you've got to make some decisions at the end of the day, and have the guts to do it.[16]

Andrew Simonet, author of *Making Your Life as an Artist*

There are entire industries devoted to providing precisely the type of data and statistical information you will need to further evaluate your potential venture. The business libraries of colleges and universities are among the best places to begin your search, since they subscribe to publications that can be very costly for individuals. Seek out the business librarian for guidance.

While each country will have its own data resources and journals, here is a general source list to get you started:

For general music industry information: Discogs, *Pollstar*, *Celebrity Access*, *Digital Music News*, *Musical America*, *RIAA*, *IFPI*, one or more *Giga OM Newsletters* (e.g., Cloud, Media, Mobile), *paidContent Daily Newsletter*, *Canadian Media Wire*, *Consequence of Sound*, *ArtsJournal Newsletter*, *Billboard*, PollstarPro, *Opera News*, *Symphony (League of American Orchestras)*, Next Big Sound, major newspapers such as the *New York Times*, reputable blogs and columns.

Sources for analyzing trends: Alexa, Compete, comScore, Google Analytics, SoundScan, Mediabase, *Billboard* charts.

Business databases that may be found in a college or university business library.

For company information:

Hoover's (company and industry search)

ReferenceUSA (use custom search to input your own criteria)

D&B Million Dollar Directory

Industry Information

IbisWorld

First Research

For marketing information:

Global Market Information Database (GMID)

Mintel

eMarketer—digital commerce

Demographics

SRDS-Local Market Audience

Census.gov (American Factfinder)

Marketresearch.com

For statistical information:

Statistical Insights

Tablebase

Journal/newspaper articles

Ebsco Business Source Premier

Proquest

Business Full Text

Factiva

VidStatsX (for YouTube statistics)

Prototypes

If possible, make a prototype of your product (and even your service) in order to test it in the marketplace before you launch. People will understand what you're offering much more quickly if they can see or hear it in action. Many entrepreneurs skip this step because they don't understand how to build something tangible from an idea. Consider using 3D printers, asking a designer for help, or creating a visual such as an infographic or hand-drawn animation explaining your concept. Short videos also may be effective as prototypes.

Making Financial Projections for Your Offering

Many entrepreneurs wonder why they need to understand accounting concepts and processes if they're just going to hire a professional to take care of their finances. Here are a few good reasons why you need to be informed:

- To improve your chances of making a profit.

- To understand what your numbers mean and how to use them to answer specific financial questions.

- To price your goods and services more competitively.

- To trim costs strategically.

- To pace your growth more effectively.

- To be sure you are paying the correct amount of tax.

- To avoid tax penalties.

- To have well-organized financial information to file tax returns and tax registration papers.

- To guard your business against unethical activities by the person you hired to take care of your finances.

- To allow you to make assumptions (educated guesses) about how much money your venture will spend and how much it will take in. Assumptions are used to calculate whether your business will be sufficiently profitable.

- Profitability is important to attract investors, demonstrate that your idea will have a chance of succeeding, help you plan, manage cash-flow, and grow your business.

The basic formula for making financial projections is:

Sales revenue

– costs of sale (variable costs)

Gross profit

– overhead (fixed costs)

= Net Profit

– taxes

= After Tax Profits

In the following pages you will learn many different ways of looking at your business using financial calculations in order to see if your venture idea could work.

Budget Overview

A budget is an essential tool for planning a new project, making a funding application, or drawing up a business plan. It's a practical plan that estimates the costs of a specific project or venture and predicts the amount of money it will generate, plus any extra funds that may be needed to ensure success.[17]

Budgets show estimated income and expenditure over a specific period of time, and whether you are projecting a deficit, break-even, or surplus.

Most organizations work with an annual budget that covers all aspects of the business. This helps you analyze expected costs and benefits of different activities before you begin, and provides an opportunity for making changes.[18]

Key Terms and Definitions

Project budgets look at income and expenses relating to that project over the period of time the project runs.[19]

Company budgets cover a 12-month period and include projects and other activities taking place during that time, as well as the income and expenses involved in running the company itself. Income for an arts organization may include:

- grants, donations, and sponsorship (including sponsorship in-kind);
- fees for running workshops, teaching, consulting, project management, and exhibiting;
- royalties and license fees;
- ticket sales, bar sales, and box office commission for events;
- sale of work (via galleries or agents);
- bank interest;
- owner's contribution, such as savings.[20]

Variable costs (also called product costs, costs of goods sold, costs of sale, or direct costs) are expenditures that are directly associated with the production of your product or service. These costs go up or down (vary) based on the volume of goods or services you produce. For service businesses, one of the biggest variable costs is wages paid to the provider of the services. Variable costs for an arts organization might include:

- materials used to create, package, and ship work that is for sale;

- equipment and facilities rented for specific events, rehearsals, productions, or workshops;

- catering, ticket printing, posters, and publicity for specific events;

- staffing costs for those who are hired only to work on specific projects (wages, fees, insurance).[21]

Fixed costs (also called overheads) include all regularly repeating expenses that are not tied specifically to the production of your product or service. Fixed costs for an arts organization might include:

- staffing costs for people needed regardless of specific projects or activities, such as the general manager, administrator, or technical manager. Costs will include wages, benefits, and staff development and training;

- rent, insurance, utilities, cable and internet, and loan payments.[22]

Contingency is an expense amount (usually 5–10 percent of the entire project cost) that is put into a budget in case of unexpected costs.

In-kind gifts are services or materials (but not money) given to an organization to help it conduct its day-to-day activities. For an arts organization, in-kind gifts might include office equipment, practice or studio space, instruments, and volunteer labor. There are guidelines to help determine the market value of in-kind gifts so that they are accurately recorded as a form of income.

Matching funds are revenues that your organization must contribute in order to receive monetary distributions from the grant.

The break-even point is the moment at which a company's sales exactly cover its expenses. In other words, the company sells enough units of its product to cover its expenses without making a profit or taking a loss. If it sells more, it makes a profit. If it sells less, it takes a loss. The formula for determining the break-even point is: Fixed Costs – Variable Costs = Break-even Point. Use income and expense estimates for a year or more to see, in theory, whether your business will turn a profit.

A one-year profit/loss (P&L) forecast is a formal, month-by-month projection of your venture's net profit (profit after expenses are deducted) for the first year of operations. Explanations for how you arrived at each projected revenue or expense item are listed at the bottom of the forecast under "Assumptions."

Start-up costs include everything that needs to be in place in order for you to make your first sale. You will have to pay for these items before you bring in any money from sales of your product or service. Keep start-up costs as low as possible. Start-up costs will appear only in your first year's P&L statement and cash-flow forecast.

Cash-flow projection is a monthly picture of your cash position. It is a snapshot of all your sources of income and expenses, including loans, transfers of personal money into the business, start-up costs (which occur only in your first year of operation), and all other types of cash inflows and outflows. A cash-flow projection shows if you will have enough cash on hand for key dates such as payroll, loan payment, rent, or inventory purchase. It does not show you if your business operations are generating enough income to cover expenses. Cash-flow projections are crucial in running a business. If you are short of cash, you must act to cover your obligations, such as getting a bank line of credit or a cash infusion. Preparing a one-year cash-flow projection, and monitoring it closely, will help you plan ahead for such situations.

The *difference between the break-even point and the P&L forecast* has to do with timing. The break-even analysis looks at profit and loss on an annual basis. A P&L forecast calculates monthly net profit. A P&L forecast is only concerned with money earned from normal business operations, not loans or investment income. It will show you whether your business operations are generating enough income to cover your expenses. It does not show if you will have ready cash to meet specific payouts such as rent and payroll.

Assumptions are educated guesses about how much you will sell and how much it will cost to make your product. Every document you create must show what assumptions you made about a cost or expense. Add your assumptions at the bottom of every page of the document, in a font that is slightly smaller than the narrative font.

Gross profit percentage is the numerical representation of money you've made from selling a good or service after you subtract the cost of producing it. Gross profit percentage shows how efficient your business is as it produces your goods or services. The higher your gross profit percentage, the healthier your business and the more profit you will make. Most entrepreneurs want to see average gross profit expressed as both dollars and percentages for the year.

To calculate gross profit percentage:

- Add up the costs of goods or services sold over a specific period of time.

- Calculate gross profit dollars (total revenue – cost of goods or services sold).

- Convert gross profit dollars to percentage (gross profit/total revenue × 100).

Pricing Your Product or Service

What price will the end user be charged for each product or service? There are two ways to approach this important question. One way is to look at the competition in the marketplace and see what it charges for similar products. Another method is to use a formula to determine an hourly rate for you or your employees if you have a service-based venture. No matter what approach you take, remember that the business must generate more income than expenses in order to remain viable and grow.

Nonprofit businesses also must generate more income than expenses. Even though many charities offer free or very low-cost services, revenue must come from somewhere in order to cover costs of doing business. For these ventures, revenue may come in the form of grants from foundations, governments, or individuals.

If you are a *service business*, use the spreadsheet on this book's companion website entitled "Billable Rate" to determine your hourly rate. Under the heading "Assumptions," give a detailed explanation as to how you determined the price point(s) for each of your services. Include an explanation of how the price point(s) is sensitive to your customers' buying habits and how it compares to your competitors' pricing strategy.

If your business *sells products*, determine the price point for each product. Next, under the heading "Assumptions," give a detailed explanation as to how you determined the price point(s) for each of your products. Include an explanation of how the price point(s) is sensitive to your customers' buying habits and how it compares to your competitors' pricing strategy. Ventures that sell products, as opposed to services, do not use an hourly rate computation.

Estimating Income and Expenses

- Categorize each expense as either a fixed or a variable cost.

- Estimate sales revenue using "bottom-up" forecasting.[23] This means using real scenarios to estimate potential revenue. For example, to conservatively estimate how much revenue your sales team can bring in during their six-month period of subscription sales calls to your single-ticket customers, you would use this type of calculation: each salesperson can actually speak to eight customers in a day of calls; there are 240 working days per year; 25 percent of the single-ticket customers will become subscribers; the average subscription purchase will bring in US$200; your sales team consists of five people; so your "bottom-up" computation forecasts US$240,000 in subscription purchases for the six-month period of calls. A much less realistic way to estimate sales revenue is a 'top-down" forecast, which typically starts with a large number and works down to extrapolate projected sales figures. A top-down forecast for your subscription sales campaign could look like this: there are 900,000 people in this city. If only 2 percent of them purchase a subscription at an average price of $200, we will earn US$3.6 million! Top-down forecasting can lead to grossly exaggerated revenue projections, as you can see from the example.

- Calculate the average gross profit percentage by product or service category.

- Determine the average gross profit for your business as a whole.

Adding It All Up

At this point you have done a lot of thinking and planning in order to determine your best assumptions for the first year or two of your new venture. It's now time to pull together all the various ways of looking at your numbers by using the following steps:

- Estimate annual sales revenue for each main category of products or services.

- Calculate your average gross profit percentage (how much of each sales dollar will be left over after paying for the products or services themselves).

- Calculate the gross profit for each main category of services and products (*calculate*: total revenue minus cost of goods or services sold).

- Calculate the average selling price for your business as a whole (*calculate*: the selling price for each main category divided by the number of categories).

- Determine an *average* gross profit for your business as a whole (*calculate*: the gross profit for each main category divided by the number of categories).

- Determine an average gross profit percentage by dividing your average gross profit by your average selling price.

- Estimate your fixed costs. Don't forget to pay yourself.

- Calculate your break-even point (*calculate*: annual fixed expenses divided by average gross profit percentage). Express the break-even point in both dollars and units sold. Does this number look reasonable and doable? If not, go back and review your costs and sales estimates. If you can't make the numbers work realistically, you may need to abandon this idea or change it substantially.

- Prepare a P&L forecast (*calculate*: use your estimates for annual sales revenue and variable costs). Break them down by month to calculate your gross profit. Then subtract your fixed expenses from gross profit to arrive at net profit.

- Prepare a cash-flow forecast (*calculate*: monthly cash inflow from sales and other liquid sources[24] minus cash outflow for purchases, fixed costs and tax obligations). This shows your estimated net cash-flow for each month.

Pause and Reflect

Look carefully at the numbers your calculations have produced. Does your venture look possible from a cost analysis? If not, make reasonable changes using the website spreadsheets. However, resist the urge to over-estimate revenue and under-estimate expenses in order to make the numbers work. It is much better to know *now* that the venture in its current iteration is not feasible rather than find this out five months after launching and you've run out of cash. Even if you decide to scrap the venture, take what knowledge you gleaned from exploring this hypothetical venture and find another idea or approach to serve your customers.

Positioning Your Offering

You will be talking to people all the time about your new start-up, whether it's a pitch for funding or trying to make a strategic hire. It's important to have a strong Positioning Statement, which is simply answering the question: "What do you do?" Effectively answering this question means understanding precisely how your company differs from the competition and explaining it in a brief yet powerful statement that focuses on the benefits to the customer. Here is an outline to help you create your Positioning Statement (this is not the same thing as your Value Proposition).[25]

Give Your Venture a Name

- Review Chapter 4.

- If you are starting your business in the US, read the section in this chapter entitled "United States Legal and Tax Issues for New Ventures."

- Choose a name that is short, easy to say, and has the potential to become a verb, as in "fedex this birthday gift to my sister" instead of saying "send this birthday gift to my sister using a reliable package delivery service."

- Avoid numbers in your name.

- Choose a name that doesn't sound like an existing product or service.

- Avoid trendy words so your name won't become something passé.[26]

Create a One- or Two-Sentence Positioning Statement (Reminder: A Positioning Statement is Not the Same Thing as a Value Proposition)

- Grab the attention of potential customers with a pitch that is meaningful to *them*.

- Include facts or statistics in your pitch to support your claims.

- Avoid negative or off-color language, don't bash your competitors, and stay away from "fluff" words such as unique, invaluable, and amazing.

- State clearly how your company makes meaning.[27]

Funding Your Offering

The following entrepreneurial funding overview is based on a June 2015 Educational Policy Brief from the Ewing Marion Kauffman Foundation, based in Kansas City, Missouri (US), that aims to foster economic independence by advancing educational achievement and entrepreneurial success.[28]

How Entrepreneurs Access Capital and Get Funded

Most entrepreneurs rely on private external financing in two forms: debt and equity.

Debt financing from banks is the dominant form of financing new ventures, providing roughly 40 percent of the initial start-up capital in a new business.[29]

Equity financing is less common, but the stories of 30-year-old billionaires in Silicon Valley show how impactful equity financing can be. Angel investors and venture capitalists are the main sources of equity funding, providing less than 3 percent and 1 percent of start-up capital, respectively. Despite their relatively small numbers, active equity investors can be very helpful to new ventures through their expertise, networks, and guidance.[30]

Aside from these forms of finance, young firms are frequently turning to non-traditional channels to raise capital. Crowdfunding and online loan platforms are growing at an astronomical rate. In the first half of 2014, more than 20 percent of start-ups that applied for loans did so through an online lender. Other sources, like accelerators, government prizes, and grants, round out the funding mix.[31]

Crowdfunding

The four main types of crowdfunding are: donation-based (e.g., Kiva), reward-based (e.g., Kickstarter), debt-based (e.g., Prosper, Lending Club), and equity-based.[32] Here are a few platforms that are especially popular with the arts community:

- Kickstarter funds creative projects that range from films and concert tours to art and technology. Since its launch in 2009, more than 9.3 million people have pledged more than US$1.9 billion to successfully fund 90,803 creative projects. (Kickstarter updates its funding statistics daily.) Every project has its own funding goal and deadline, following the principle of all-or-nothing: either the project reaches its funding goal or it doesn't receive any money at all. To date, 37.2 percent of projects have reached their funding goals.[33]

- In 2008, newly launched Indiegogo focused only on the indie film industry. Today it is a leading international crowdfunding platform, having raised millions of dollars for thousands of campaigns worldwide. It charges a 9 percent fee on the funding campaigns. If the funding goal is reached, 5 percent is paid back to the campaign.[34]

Kickstarter Homepage

Gil C/Shutterstock.com

- Founded in 2011, Crowdfunder's mission is to "democratize access to opportunity and capital for entrepreneurs, and empower everyday citizens to invest in the next big thing." For entrepreneurs, it provides a guided process, a collaborative online environment, and an investor network to help them raise investment capital. For investors, it provides the opportunity to "get in on the ground floor of exciting companies that were previously exclusive investment offerings only available to top Silicon Valley venture capitalists or industry insiders."[35]

- CrowdRise is a blend of crowdfunding and social networking. It provides opportunities to raise money for alternative causes, such as animal welfare, arts and culture, civil rights, disease and disorder, education, the environment, and poverty.

- Peerbackers is focused on funding entrepreneurs and innovators. The platform has hosted thousands of creative, civic, and entrepreneurial projects from around the world.

- Patreon, founded in 2013, is a community of creators and patrons. Creators can seek funding for their ongoing, everyday work such as songwriting or blogging. Patrons sign up to support their favorite creators by giving them a "tip" for each new creation. Patrons set a monthly maximum tip amount and can view and post in the artist's stream.

Debt and Equity Funding

Loyalty Capital

ZipCap is a start-up lender that makes loans to merchants based on "loyalty capital." The aim is to offer small merchants (like restaurants, boutiques, and service providers) access to low-interest loans financed by investors who want to support their local economy.[36]

ZipCap's merchants start by recruiting an "inner circle" of customers who pledge to spend a specific amount of money in a fixed period of time. ZipCap then allows businesses to borrow against a portion of the pledges. At the heart of ZipCap's system is the idea that successful merchants have a network of repeat customers with strong connections to their favorite neighborhood businesses.[37]

Online Lenders

Even though a small business may be established and profitable, obtaining a bank loan or credit line can still be an arduous task. The paperwork takes days to prepare, approval decisions can drag on for weeks or months, and the process "involves selling your soul and begging on your knees," says Yaniv Liron, founder of Lumina, an 11-year-old web design and development business.[38]

Liron turned instead to Fundbox, an online company that gives business owners cash advances against their outstanding invoices. Fundbox, like other non-traditional lenders, specializes in loans too small or too risky to interest banks and traditional lenders. It also offers credit lines up to US$25,000.[39]

Online lenders say they have two advantages over banks: algorithms and lending models that allow them to operate profitably in traditionally risky market, and fewer regulatory constraints. Online firms largely work outside the banking system in a new marketplace that currently "falls between the cracks" for federal regulators.[40]

Fundbox's online lending competitors include:

- BlueVine—advances funds against invoices.

- Kabbage and OnDeck—small-term lenders.

- Funding Circle, Lending Club, Prosper—peer-to-peer lenders.

- PayPal and Square—payment processors, which offer loans to some of their merchants.

Grant Funding

Nonprofit organizations often turn to granting organizations, such as foundations, corporations, and governments, for help in closing the gap between their earned revenue (money that comes in from sales of its product or service) and their actual expenses. Writing successful grant proposals requires research and experience. It can be a difficult and frustrating process, particularly for newcomers to the nonprofit world.[41]

Here are some important factors to consider if you think grants may be a good source of funding for your venture:

- Avoid relying on a single major donor or granting source to fund more than 20 percent of your revenue.

- Commit in advance to finding enough time and resources to research foundations and grant writing opportunities for your venture.

- Commit yourself to applying for a grant *only* if:

  o you match all the foundation's qualifications;

  o you're willing to find an experienced grant writer to prepare tailored applications for each foundation;

o   you understand that it's rare to be accepted for a grant without an existing relationship with the foundation and, like all rejections, "no" might mean "no for *now*";

o   you accept that grant writing is for those who are patient and willing to play the long game.[42]

The Nonprofit Finance Fund and the Foundation Center are two excellent resources for information about funding for nonprofits.

Capital for Nonprofits

The term "capital" in the cultural nonprofit world refers to the funding and financing available for an organization to achieve its mission over the long term. Capital is generated through budget surpluses, special fundraising, or borrowing. For nonprofits, revenue covers business-as-usual expenses, while capital supports extraordinary, time-limited investments that contribute to an organization's liquidity, adaptability, and durability. There are different types of nonprofit capital, including working capital, change/growth capital, risk and opportunity capital, facilities capital, and endowments.[43]

Most nonprofit arts organizations are in a constant financial struggle. The Nonprofit Finance Fund (NFF) believes that a major contributing factor is that the vast majority of them are "mis-capitalized"—meaning financially structured in ways that do not appropriately reflect the organization's goals and mission. NFF contends that cultural nonprofits can improve their long-term financial health by adopting business models that remedy mis-capitalization.[44]

One suggestion is for nonprofits to report capital separately from revenue in financial statements. Conventional nonprofit accounting and reporting allows for the treatment of revenue and capital as the same. The problem is that when capital and revenue are conflated, an organization's reports show an overly optimistic picture of operating health. By segregating revenue and capital, an organization's leadership will see when their original plan is veering off course and will be able to make course corrections based on real data about operational health before the problem becomes a crisis.[45]

Trends in Venture Capital Funding

For Tech Entrepreneurs: More Female Venture Capitalists
Venture capitalists (VCs) are, in a way, the gatekeepers to Silicon Valley for tech entrepreneurs. If VCs are a group of white men who studied at places like Stanford, it is no wonder that most of the entrepreneurs fit the same mold.[46] But as more women start investment firms, those demographics have begun to change.

Cowboy Angels, Illuminate Ventures, Forerunner Ventures, and Aligned Partners are some of the new firms started by experienced, financially successful women, just as men with last names like Kleiner and Draper did in the past. In addition to having significant investing or operations experience, the women offer a broader and more diverse network for recruiting and finding new start-ups, as well as a deeper understanding of female consumers, who are often the dominant users of new products.[47]

For Tech Entrepreneurs: A New VC Strategy
The recent buying sprees by Facebook, Google, and other internet giants rushing to become conglomerates are making fortunes for the venture capital industry. Facebook acquired the social media companies WhatsApp (US$16 billion) and Instagram (US$1 billion). Google acquired Nest (US$3.24 billion) and Waze (US$1 billion). Apple bought the music brand Beats Electronics (US$3 billion).[48]

This has revolutionized the traditional VC strategy. The goal for tech entrepreneurs is no longer building a business; rather, tech entrepreneurs want to develop a product in a hot market, like social media, that the web conglomerates will buy at very high prices. Conglomerates are spending billions on acquisitions of start-ups in order to avoid becoming obsolete because they didn't get in early on a new disruptive technology.[49]

Making Money and Making a Difference

Consumer companies like TOMS shoes and Warby Parker eyewear have demonstrated that altruism can also be good for business. DBL Investors is one of a growing number of VC firms that invest in companies with a social mission.[50]

DBL is named after the characteristic that defines social entrepreneurship ventures: emphasis on the double bottom line (DBL), or the notion that a company can make money (the first bottom line) and make a difference (the second bottom line). With social ventures, the second bottom line needs to be central to how the company is doing business. But if a company is not successful at meeting the first bottom line, there can be no social impact.[51]

Known as "impact investors," VC firms such as DBL do not demand a quick return, as do most traditional VCs. Rather, they view early-stage investing as an opportunity to make socially responsible practices a standard part of corporate culture.[52]

DBL Investors backed Pandora Media, the internet radio company, in 2006, when it had 50 full-time equivalent employees working in Oakland, CA. Pandora had a strong commitment to stay in the city, which was an asset to DBL. "One of the pillars of social impact is job creation, especially in places that need jobs," says Nancy Pfund, founder of DBL. "It can have a huge multiplier effect . . . such as bringing in restaurants, gyms, services, and other employers to the area." Pandora got involved in teaching music in local schools and Pfund's team facilitated that. The program is still ongoing.[53]

More Active Role for Angels

Traditional angel investors are people who believe in an entrepreneur's dream and invest early, usually keeping a low profile and asking only for periodic updates. But tech entrepreneur Joshua Reeves has found a way to benefit from his 56 angels' innate talents, almost all of whom run their own companies. Each month he sends his investors requests for things he wants them to work on for him, such as thoughts on new types of software. He says his angels think of themselves as company-builders and are eager to attack problems.[54]

Elements of a Business Plan

The traditional communication tool that entrepreneurs use when seeking funds is a business plan. For our purposes here, we will look only at the main *elements* found in most business plans, not how to write the plan itself. You have worked on all the elements listed below in the previous pages of this chapter:

- The problem you have identified.
  - Demonstrate that this problem affects someone besides you.
- The solution you propose.
  - Use the 99% solution from Chapter 2 (think of ways to get 99 percent of the benefits for only 1 percent of the cost) and define your product or service.

- Your business model.
  - Positioning Statement plus elements from Business Model Canvas.
- The underlying magic.
  - What makes your idea so special, and why will it work?
- Marketing and sales information.
  - Who are your customers?
  - How will you reach them?
  - How will you make them passionate about your product or service?
- Your competition.
  - Specific companies, their market share, what they do better than you do.
  - How you will overcome the competitive challenges they pose?
- Your management team.
  - Who does what—top team members only—and why they're the best.
- Financial projections and key metrics.
  - "Bottom-up" sales projections.
  - Price points of product or service.
  - Break-even point (in dollars *and* units).
  - Start-up costs.
  - P&L statement for one or two years.
  - Cash-flow projection for one year.
- Current status, accomplishments to date, timeline, and use of funds.
  - What have you done so far?
  - Benchmarks for short-term and middle-term.
  - Source and use of cash—now and in future.

Seek the help of an experienced writer of business plans if this is your first formal plan.

US LEGAL AND TAX ISSUES FOR NEW VENTURES

Every country has its own legal and tax structures that affect new ventures. The information provided here only applies to the US. To find information for other countries, look at Startup Nations, a global network that promotes knowledge sharing and collaboration for new ventures, including a guide to start-up capital.[55] For information about starting a nonprofit venture, look at the International Center of Not-for-Profit Law.[56]

Choosing a Business Entity

(This information applies *only* to the US.)

The key issues to consider when choosing the type of legal entity that is best for you and your start-up are liability, taxation, costs, and complexity. As you read through the following information, think about the pros and cons of each entity for your venture.

A *Sole Proprietorship* is a business owned by an individual. For US Internal Revenue Service (IRS) purposes, the owner (sole proprietor) and the business are one and the same, meaning that business profits are reported and taxed on the owner's personal income tax return, which is relatively straightforward to complete. The main downside of a sole proprietorship is that its owner is personally liable for all business debts.[57]

A *Partnership* refers to a legal structure for a business of two or more individuals. Each partner is personally liable for all debts of the business, and each partner claims a share of the business' income or losses on the partner's individual tax return (this is known as "pass-through taxation").[58]

A *Limited Partnership* is a business structure that allows one or more owners to enjoy limited personal liability for partnership debts while another partner or partners (called general partners) have unlimited personal liability. General partners run the business and limited partners (who are usually passive investors) are not allowed to make day-to-day business decisions.[59]

A *Limited Liability Partnership* (LLP) is a type of partnership recognized in a majority of states that protects a partner from personal liability for negligent acts committed by other partners or by employees not under her direct control. Some states restrict LLPs to professionals such as lawyers, accountants, architects, and health-care providers.[60]

A *Limited Liability Company* (LLC) is a business ownership structure that shields its owners' personal assets through the doctrine of limited liability (like a corporation), but has pass-through taxation (like a partnership), where profits (or losses) are passed through to the owners and taxed on their personal income tax returns.[61]

A *Corporation* is a legal structure authorized by state law that allows a business to organize itself as a separate legal entity from its owners. One advantage of incorporating is that a corporation's owners (shareholders) are shielded from personal liability for the corporation's liabilities and debts. A corporation's so-called "double taxation" occurs because the *entity* is taxed, and the *dividends* paid to non-employees cannot be deducted as business expenses (salaries and bonuses can be deducted as business expenses).[62]

A *B Corporation*, or Benefit Corporation, is a type of for-profit corporate entity, legislated in 28 US states, that includes positive impact on society and the environment in addition to profit as its legally defined goals.[63]

A *"C Corp"* is common business slang to distinguish a regular corporation, whose profits are taxed separately from its owners under subchapter C of the Internal Revenue Code, from an S Corporation. An S Corporation's profits are passed through to the shareholders and taxed on their personal income tax returns under subchapter S of the Internal Revenue Code.[64]

A *Low-Profit Limited Liability Company* (L3C) is a company organized to perform services or engage in activities that benefit the public. Unlike a nonprofit, an L3C is operated like a regular profit-making business and is allowed to make a profit as a secondary goal. Illinois, Michigan, Utah, Vermont, and Wyoming are among the small but growing number of states that have passed legislation allowing L3Cs.[65]

An S Corporation is the term that describes a profit-making corporation whose shareholders have applied for and received subchapter S Corporation status from the IRS. Electing to do business as an S Corporation lets shareholders enjoy limited liability status, but be taxed as a pass-through tax entity, where income taxes are reported and paid by the owners, like a partnership or sole proprietor. (A regular, or C, Corporation is taxed as a separate entity from its owners.) To qualify as an S Corporation, a number of IRS rules must be met, such as a limit of 100 shareholders and US citizenship for all shareholders.[66]

501(c) status refers to a section of the IRS Revenue Code that highlights the 26 types of nonprofit organizations that are exempt from some federal income taxes. The 501(c)(3) code relates to religious, educational, charitable, scientific, literary, and other types of businesses. 501(c)(3) is the nonprofit code commonly associated with arts organizations, although others could apply.[67]

Choosing a Cash or Accrual Accounting Method

- Check the IRS rules before making a decision. In general, if you have inventory, use the accrual method unless your annual sales are less than US$1 million. If they are, either cash or accrual will work.

- The following industries may *not* use the cash method of accounting: sound recording, publishing, mining, wholesaling, manufacturing, and retailing.

- Choose either cash or accrual based upon which method will give you the most control over your finances.

Key Terms for Naming a Business

Legal Name is the official name of the entity that owns a business.

Sole Proprietorship is the full name of the owner, i.e. Harry Potter.

General Partnership is the last names of all the owners, or a new name created and defined in a written partnership agreement.

Corporations, LLCs, and Limited Partnerships must register their names with a state filing office.

Trade Name is the name that a business uses with the public. It may or may not be the same as the name of the business owner or the legal name of business.

Fictitious Business Name is the term used when a trade name is different from the legal name. For example, if Harry Potter names his sole proprietorship Quiddich Consulting, "Quiddich Consulting" is a fictitious business name because it does not contain Harry's last name. Fictitious business names are also called DBA (doing business as) or PKA (professionally known as). An example is Madonna Ciccone, PKA Madonna.

Trademark is a word, phrase, design, or symbol used to market a product. Technically, a mark used to market a service is called a service mark. Slogans, logos, and packaging designs can be protected by trademark.

Trademark Infringement occurs only when the use of a mark by two different businesses is likely to cause customer confusion.

The Dilution Exception covers the following scenario: even when customer confusion is unlikely, courts will stop a business from using a trademark that's the same or similar to another mark if the use could diminish ("dilute") its distinctiveness. For example, a euphonium duo calling itself Eu Two could be required to change its name because it sounds like the name of the famous Irish band U2.

Business Name and Domain Name Research

Ideally your business name will be same as your domain name. Contact your state corporate filing office to learn the exact procedure. Here are common sources:

- Internet—huge, fast, and free.

- Trade publications.

- State trademark registry—limited only to that state.

- County fictitious business name database—limited only to that county.

- Federal Trademark Database—the Trademark Electronic Business Center in the US Patent and Trademark Office (USPTO).

- University or public library.

- Internic.com for list of domain name *registrars* online.

Register your trademark to strengthen your rights to it. Register with your state, with the federal government if you are engaged in national, international, or territorial commerce, and with the Supplemental Register in the USPTO.

Domain Name Conflicts and Cybersquatting

The International Corporation for Assigned Names and Numbers (Icann) is the international group in charge of internet domain name policy. Icann has procedures for resolving cybersquatting disputes that can be less expensive and faster than a lawsuit.

US Federal, State, and Local Start-Up Requirements

- For corporations, LLCs, and limited partnerships only: file organizational documents with your Secretary of State or its filing office.

- Obtain a federal employer ID number (FEIN), even if you don't have any employees.

- Register your fictitious business name with your county or state.

- Obtain a local tax registration certificate.

- Obtain a permit to sell retail goods and collect state tax (if applicable).

- Obtain specialized vocation-related licenses or environmental permits (if applicable).

"Why Am I Filling out All These Forms?"

The seemingly endless pile of forms that need to be completed and submitted are important to the legal system in order to identify you, protect the public, and keep track of your finances for tax purposes.

Paying Taxes

The agencies behind the taxes are (at the least) federal, state, county and possibly city. Due to the complexity of the US tax laws, it is highly recommended that you hire a small-business attorney and tax advisor before you launch your company.

Are you running a hobby or a business? The government defines a hobby as an activity where the owner has other means of support to allow her micro business to exist.

You may deduct the losses from your hobby business to partially offset your personal income tax obligation. However, not every hobby counts as a business for tax purposes. To prove your hobby is a business, you will need to pass the IRS "3-of-5" test: if your business makes a profit in three out of five consecutive years, it is legally presumed to have a profit motive, not just a hobby motive.

Choosing a Business Location

The following are issues to take into account if you are working from home:

- Home business tax deduction.
- Zoning laws, condo and apartment regulations.
- Noise, parking, pollution, foot traffic in building, disturbing neighbors.

The following are issues pertaining to commercial leases:

- Rent: gross lease (includes insurance, property taxes, and maintenance costs) or net lease (you'll be charged separately for the above items).
- "Location, location, location" is a key consideration if you are selling to the public.

CONCLUSION

Making meaning is the single most important reason for an entrepreneur to start a new venture. It is wise to be clear about your own personal mission before deciding upon the type and scope of a new business. Understanding risk and managing your time well are ongoing challenges for an entrepreneur. When shaping a new business, there are many decisions and assumptions to make in order to determine whether or not it is financially feasible. Finally, you must understand and abide by the legal requirements for creating and doing business in a particular country or countries.

NOTES

1 Guy Kawasaki, *The Art of the Start* (New York: Penguin, 2004), 5.
2 Ibid.

3 Tina Su, "Life on Purpose: 15 Questions to Discover Your Personal Mission," *Think Simple Now*, http://think simplenow.com/happiness/life-on-purpose-15-questions-to-discover-your-personal-mission (accessed May 23, 2016).

4 http://thinksimplenow.com (accessed May 23, 2016).

5 "Risk Management," *General Auto Insurance*, www.generalautoinsurance.com/coverage/risk-management (accessed May 23, 2016).

6 Ibid.

7 Ibid.

8 Jane Lee, "Gallery: Big Achievers Share the Greatest Risks They Ever Took," *Forbes*, March 7, 2011, www.forbes.com/2011/03/07/greatest-risk-they-ever-took-2011-entrepreneurs_slide_14.html (accessed May 23, 2016).

9 Ibid.

10 Kevin Johnston, "Small Business: Selling a Product vs. Selling a Service," *Houston Chronicle*, http://small business.chron.com/selling-product-vs-selling-service-55446.html (accessed May 23, 2016).

11 Ibid.

12 Tim Clark, Alexander Osterwalder, and Yves Pigneur, *Business Model You* (Hoboken, NJ: Wiley, 2012), 26–9.

13 Ibid, 35–47.

14 Ibid, 31.

15 KISS is an acronym for "Keep It *Similar*, Stupid."

16 Andrew Simonet, *Making Your Life As An Artist* (Manitoba, Canada: Artists U, 2014) static1.squarespace.com/static/53767189e4b07d0c6bf4b775/t/54183ec9e4b01d2bfeb25c3c/1410875081691/Making+Your+Life+as+an+Artist+by+Andrew+Simonet.pdf (accessed May 28, 2015).

17 "Budgets," *Cultural Enterprise Office*, 2014, www.culturalenterpriseoffice.co.uk (accessed May 23, 2016).

18 Ibid.

19 Ibid.

20 Ibid.

21 Ibid.

22 Ibid.

23 Kawasaki, *The Art of the Start*, 81.

24 A liquid asset is one that is easily converted to cash.

25 Kawasaki, *The Art of the Start*, 3.

26 Ibid, 35–6.

27 Ibid, 40.

28 "How Entrepreneurs Access Capital and Get Funded," *Ewing Marion Kauffman Foundation*, June 2, 2015, www.kauffman.org/~/media/kauffman_org/resources/2015/entrepreneurship%20policy%20digest/june%202015/how_entrepreneurs_access_capital_and_get_funded.pdf (accessed May 23, 2016).

29 Ibid.

30 Ibid.

31 Ibid.

32 Ibid.

33 Mariia Siniagina, "Major Crowdfunding Platforms Overview," *StartUp Nations*, March 30, 2104, www.startupnations.org/major-crowdfunding-platforms-overview (accessed August 16, 2015).

34 Ibid.

35 Ibid.

36 Stacy Cowley, "A Start-Up That Makes Loans Based on Loyalty When Banks Will Not," *New York Times*, May 21, 2015.

37 Ibid.

38 Stacy Cowley, "Online Lenders Offer a Faster Cash Lifeline for Small Businesses," *New York Times*, April 9, 2015.

39 Ibid.

40 Ibid.

41 Marc Koenig, "Don't Start Your Nonprofit Grant Writing Until You Read This," *Nonprofit Hub*, http://non profithub.org/grant-writing/when-to-start-nonprofit-grant-writing (accessed May 23, 2016).

42 Ibid.

43 "Glossary of Financial Terms," *Nonprofit Finance Fund*, www.nonprofitfinancefund.org/financial-terms/C?title= (accessed May 23, 2016).

44 "Change Capital Arts," *Non-profit Finance Fund*, www.nonprofitfinancefund.org/case-change-capital-arts (accessed May 23, 2016).

45 Ibid.

45 Claire Cain Miller, "Female-Run Venture Funds Alter the Status Quo," *New York Times*, April 2, 2015.

47 Ibid.

48 Steen Davidoff Solomon, "New Strategy as Tech Giants Transform into Conglomerates," *New York Times*, August 6, 2014.

49 Ibid.

50 Sarah Max, "A Focus on Making Money and Making a Difference," *New York Times*, October 28, 2014.

51 Ibid.

52 Ibid.

53 Ibid.

54 Quentin Hardy, "Angel Investors Lend Expertise as Well as Cash," *New York Times*, March 31, 2015.

55 *Start Up Nations*, www.startupnations.org (accessed August 16, 2015).

56 *International Center for Not-for-Profit Law*, http://icnl.org (accessed May 23, 2016).

57 "Small Business," *Nolo Legal Encyclopedia*, www.nolo.com/legal-encyclopedia/small-business (accessed May 23, 2016).

58 Ibid.

59 Ibid.

60 Ibid.

61 Ibid.

62 Ibid.

63 Ibid.

64 Ibid.

65 Ibid.

66 Ibid.

67 Ibid.

INDEX